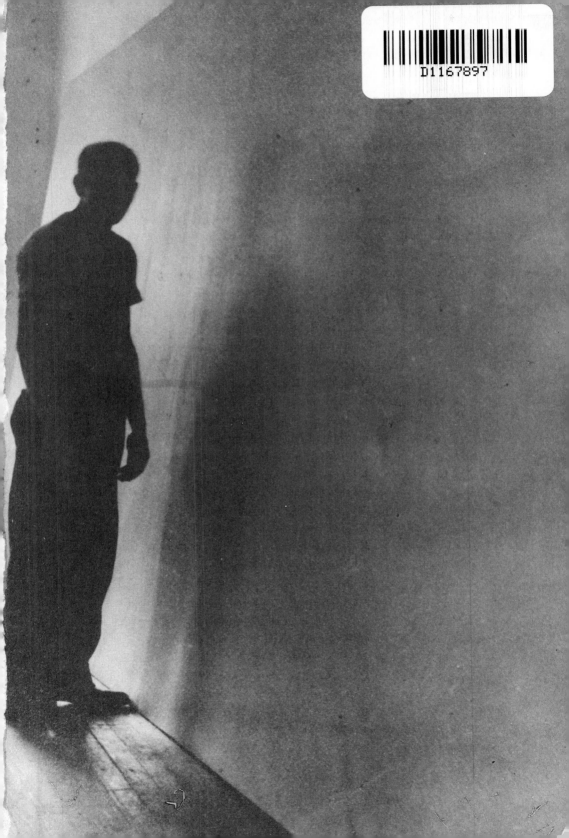

SUCH
DESPERATE
JOY

Imagining Jackson Pollock

EDITED BY
HELEN HARRISON

THUNDER'S MOUTH PRESS
NEW YORK

Published by
Thunder's Mouth Press/Nation Books
841 Broadway, Fourth Floor
New York NY 10003

Copyright © 2000 Helen A. Harrison

Library of Congress Catalog-in-Publication Data

Such desperate joy: imagining Jackson Pollock / edited by Helen A. Harrison.
    p. cm.
  ISBN 1-56025-284-7
  1. Pollock, Jackson, 1912-1956. 2. Pollock, Jackson, 1912-1956—Influence.
 I. Harrison, Helen A.

N6537.P57S832000
759.13—dc21   00-044299

Distributed by Publishers Group West.

Designed by Pauline Neuwirth, Neuwirth & Associates, Inc.

Manufactured in the United States of America.

To Roy

CONTENTS

PERSONAL RESPONSES: THE ART

X

xi

EDITOR'S NOTES
AND ACKNOWLEDGMENTS

THIS anthology is a survey of responses to Jackson Pollock and his art, supplemented by documents that relate to his life and career. Chronologically, it spans the complete range of material on Pollock, from his birth in 1912 to the present, but it is not intended to be comprehensive. In selecting the contents, I favored creative endeavors, original or previously unpublished contributions, and published pieces that have not been collected or reprinted. Most of the Pollock biographies and monographs are still in print. Many important essays on Pollock's work, and all of his own statements about it, are available in Pepe Karmel's excellent collection, *Jackson Pollock: Interviews, Articles, and Reviews*, published earlier this year by the Museum of Modern Art. Very little of that material—two of Pollock's statements, and one of Krasner's—is also included here. The rest, from an obscure memoir of Pollock that appeared in a now-defunct magazine to a greeting card that humorously posits a childhood incident as the source of his abstract imagery, is brought together for the first time in this volume.

The editorial focus is on subjectivity, emphasizing interpretation over analysis. Individual attitudes, conjectures, speculations, and suppositions take pride of place, and the contributors's opinions are their own. I did, however, correct inadvertent mistakes and inaccuracies, some of which have been perpetuated from one source to the next. An outstanding example is Pollock's own misrepresentation of the year he came to New York City, which he consistently gave as 1929. Actually he arrived in 1930. This and other corrections throughout the text are enclosed in {ogee} brackets.

My search for material was greatly simplified by my access to the research collections of the Pollock–Krasner House and Study Center. As the Study Center's Director, I am responsible for maintaining and developing these holdings, including an extensive Pollock bibliography, a large oral history collection, documentary archives (including those of both the Pollock and Krasner catalogues raisonné) and files on Pollock–related creations. They have been my primary source, and I am grateful to the State University of New York at Stony Brook, which owns and operates the Study Center through its non-profit affiliate, the Stony Brook Foundation, for authorizing me to use them freely for this project.

Among the Study Center's most valuable holdings are the audiotaped interviews made by Jeffrey Potter for his fascinating 1984 book, *To a Violent Grave: An Oral Biography of Jackson Pollock*. Several of those tapes, as well as other audio and video recordings from the Study Center's oral history collection, provided material for the book. Jeffrey Potter, B. H. Friedman, author of the outstanding 1972 biography, *Jackson Pollock: Energy Made Visible*, and Francis V. O'Connor, whose pioneering Pollock research set the high standard for subsequent studies, were extremely helpful, both as contributors and as liberal sources of information. Chris Busa, the founder and editorial director of *Provincetown Arts*, also played a dual role, by writing a remarkable essay and by recommending me to Thunder's Mouth Press. His editorial acumen and graceful prose are superior models for my own efforts.

I am indebted to the artists who provided evidence of their creative vision, the authors and publishers who granted permission to reprint copyrighted pieces, and the people who wrote original material—in particular Ed Harris, who graciously took the time during post-production work on his feature film, *Pollock*, to share his unique insights into the character. Peter Namuth, representing the Estate of Hans Namuth, and Charles C. Bergman, who chairs the board of The Pollock–Krasner Foundation, Incorporation were generous and supportive, as always. Without such enthusiastic cooperation, this collection would be less diverse, less intriguing, and less of a testament to Pollock's significance.

It has been a pleasure to work with Neil Ortenberg and Daniel O'Connor at Thunder's Mouth Press. Their concept for the book, initiated by Pollock's inclusion in a similarly eclectic anthology, *The Outlaw Bible of American Poetry*, established its flexible structure, panoramic content, and quirky point of view. That's also the way Jeff Gordon's mind operates, and I thank him for being the catalyst.

Helen A. Harrison
SAG HARBOR, NEW YORK
JUNE 2000

ON PLAYING POLLOCK

As an individual who found his calling in the arts, I was drawn to Pollock as an artist who achieved a mode of expression, a form of creativity, that was not derivative of the art of his own time, or of any other time. Yes, it was "derived," in that it came out of his understanding of its precedents. But the actual art, the paint on the canvas, was truly original. Pollock's desire to arrive at his own originality, the need, the courage to open himself up and surrender to that openness—and his unrestrained commitment to take it to its limit—drew me to him.

A desperate need for approval usually forces one into doing what is recognizable, something similar to what has already gained acceptance. Pollock's need for approval bordered on the psychopathic, but he had an even deeper need to create art that had no hint of the lie about it. That impulse drove him to make art that was neither recognizable nor accepted, and certainly was fair game for ridicule and abuse. But Pollock was his own toughest critic, and he knew that only he could judge what was pure and true and real as far as his work was concerned. He fought fiercely to be true to himself. He did not separate himself from his art. That aspect of his being—desperately needing approval, yet offering only his own truth, on his own terms—also drew me to him.

His fears. The fear of intimacy, of revealing himself. His inability to feel secure in the world, his paralyzing fear of opening himself to others and the responsibility that entails, not to mention the possibility of rejection. Particularly with women. The pain of loneliness he must have felt at times. And, despite all this fear, the ultimate self-confidence, the belief that he could be accepted. I think he mistook approval for love. I also believe that, despite his realization that life is a great mystery, and his deep appreciation of the natural world and its beauty, he never got close to understanding his personal mystery. I don't think he wanted to. Hence, the drinking.

Getting drunk is the best way to not answer questions, to be intimate without responsibility, to remove the pain of loneliness, to ignore all the confusion about being alive that wells up inside us. And yet, by all accounts, Pollock painted sober. He faced his fears and his pain and his confusion on a blank canvas. Though masked, some would say, in complete abstraction, he revealed himself. He stripped himself naked and said, "Here I am," and put it out for the world to see and judge. And on top of it all, what he painted is beautiful, is aesthetically coherent, has power and rhythm and passion and color and harmony. And truth.

I approached the role of Pollock intuitively. It was not what I would call an intellectual pursuit. Writing the script and editing what we shot was a process of distillation. The years I spent reading and thinking and feeling about Pollock, the time I spent "painting" and trying to understand emotionally what it is to be a painter—I had to trust that time, and trust that something had seeped into my bones that would allow me to portray Pollock honestly. I had no difficulty in choosing an interpretation because it all has been very personal. From everything I read and heard, I had to go with what touched my soul and what made sense to me, both intellectually and emotionally.

I've never been interested in exploiting Pollock. In fact, there was a period of time when I felt I really should leave the whole project alone, and let Jackson rest in peace. But then I realized that was only a desire to leave myself in peace. It's tricky, but I never wanted to pretend to be Pollock. I wanted to be Ed Harris, using all his tools as an actor and as a person to allow Pollock's experience on this earth to touch me, inspire me, lead me to an honest, true performance. I think the film is much more revealing of Ed Harris than it is of Jackson Pollock. I don't see how it could be any other way. I guess I used Jackson for a personal journey. The only reason I think he wouldn't mind is because the film is not a lie.

It was difficult to balance what I perceive as Pollock's innocence with what I see as his calculated ability to get what he wanted. I needed to reveal his gentleness and also his meanness, his confidence and his deep insecurity, his fear and his courage, his manners and his sometimes aggressive incivility, his love for people and his selfishness, his competitiveness and his search for purity. The biggest challenge, in acting terms, was to find a "voice" for him. By that, I don't mean a speaking voice, but the voice of a soul, of a complex human being who didn't leave a legacy of intimate revelation—except in his paintings. That's a lot. What they mean to me is something I don't want to try to put into words, and probably couldn't. That's not a cop-out. The film is, I hope, a reflection of what I feel about his work.

In addition to dealing with Pollock the man, I had to interpret Pollock as a painter. It's preposterous to think I could ever paint as he did, and yet I had to paint in the film. The most challenging part of all that was gaining enough confidence to paint *as* myself, *for* myself, but in his manner—to be committed first to myself as a painter, keeping my focus on creating my own art, not recreating someone else's.

One thing I learned about Pollock's art is that he fully believed—and lived by—his famous statement, "I don't use the accident, because I deny the accident." Art students probably realize this, but it was a revelation for me. One cannot even approximate Pollock's approach to painting unless every stroke, every drip, every pour, every slap, every fling, every shake, every splash, every spatter, and every flick has a specific intention.

And then there's Lee . . .

Ed Harris
April 2000

Ed Harris (Jackson Pollock) and Norbert Weisser (Hans Namuth) during the production of *Pollack*, May 1999, re-enacting Namuth's filming of Pollock at work on the concrete pad behind the Pollock-Krasner House.
Photos: Helen A. Harrison.

Herbert Matter. POLLOCK-KRASNER STUDY CENTER, JEFFREY POTTER COLLECTION.

To tell about a man's life by anecdote is swinish—yet history is now beginning to file away those peculiar sentiments that make glamour out of unhappiness, and unhappiness out of art.

With Pollock, we have a double tragedy—both death and a life in art, came too soon. Perhaps what I really mean is that life in the art *world* came too soon.

Jackson, oh Jackson—we did not know you. Why do we feel that it is our fault. Why is it that we make this terrible separation from what a man does and what he is, from what a man should do, and from what a man can't do. And how we watched you, El Matador, waiting for the slaughter or the glory.

—MORTON FELDMAN

INHABITING POLLOCK

I'M sitting at the kitchen table in the Pollock–Krasner House and Study Center, and outside the window I spot a couple of men walking across the yard. One of them is carrying a camera. That is not at all unusual. Every year, thousands of visitors arrive with cameras. This is where Jackson Pollock lived with his wife, Lee Krasner, from late 1945 until his death in August 1956, and where he created the poured paintings that established him as one of the most celebrated and controversial twentieth-century artists. The property, a National Historic Landmark, is open to the public. People come from all over the world to see it. I go out to greet the new arrivals and asked if they want a guided tour.

That's not what these particular visitors are here for. The fellow with the camera asks if they can just walk around the grounds, and I say sure, enjoy yourselves. But their visit is far from casual. The silent man, dressed in jeans and a denim jacket, has a curious gait, slightly stooped and shambling. When he turns I can see that his brow is furrowed and he's smoking a cigarette. Every so often he pauses, and the cameraman gets a shot of him next to the studio or against the backdrop of Accabonac Creek, which runs behind the property. Much time is spent on and around the concrete pad behind the house, where Hans Namuth filmed Pollock painting in 1950. Oh yes, I say to myself, we have another Pollock impersonator on our hands.

This is by no means the first I've encountered. Not all of them work in costume. One used to call the house from overseas, late at night, and leave heartfelt messages for Jackson on the answering machine. One wrote from prison to declare that he was Jackson's soulmate: they were both trapped, and found psychic release in art. One even proposed to recreate the fatal car crash as, I suppose, the ultimate act of bonding. A mother, who was evidently grooming her young son for a life of undisciplined self-indulgence, proudly announced that she wanted the boy to grow up to be just like Jackson.

The first Pollock impersonator on record is none other than Hans Namuth, the photographer and film maker whose still and moving images of Pollock at work established and perpetuated his "action painter" persona. When structuring his eleven-minute Pollock film, Namuth and his editor, Paul Falkenberg, decided they needed some transitional footage between the first outdoor sequence—showing Pollock painting a canvas spread out on the concrete pad—and an interior scene at the Betty Parsons Gallery in Manhattan, where a selection of finished canvases is on display. With a cigarette between his lips and a can and stick in his hands, Namuth pretended to fling paint at a nonexistent canvas. The shadow of this dramatic gesturing was projected on a blank wall and filmed, as if Pollock's disembodied aura had been captured by the camera. I don't know whether Namuth filmed this himself, using an automatic setting, or whether it was shot by Falkenberg. But it is certainly Namuth, for in the outtakes, he steps far enough into the frame to be clearly identifiable.

Why didn't Pollock himself perform the shadow dance? Maybe he was asked and refused, although that seems unlikely, as he complied with all the film maker's other demands, including a narration, even though he disliked the sound of his own voice. Or maybe Namuth rehearsed the idea and liked his own performance—which in retrospect he described as "not convincing." Years later, he said that he came to regret his impersonation. At the time, however, when he was so intimately involved with intensive observation of Pollock's astonishing creativity, was it just too tempting to play the role, even uncredited? Perhaps.

A decade later, another cinematic impersonation parodied Namuth's film and debunked what by then had become the Pollock stereotype. In "Day of the Painter," a fourteen-minute film that went on to win the 1960 Academy Award for a short subject, Ezra Reuben Baker plays an artist who sloshes, scrapes, and even shoots liquid paint from what looks like a flare gun onto a large sheet of plywood laid out on a tidal mud flat. The painter works from a catwalk several feet above, while a few locals and various water fowl critique the proceedings. Robert Prunier Davis, who wrote, directed and shot "Day of the Painter," deliberately mimics Namuth's film, including closeups of the artist's paint-spattered boots, his hands mixing house paints, and his concentrated expression. When the painting is finished, our hero cuts it into several segments, seemingly at random. His art dealer then arrives in a sea plane, pulls up to the dock and selects one small piece, after which the rest are dumped into the water.

Like the Namuth film, for which the young avant-garde composer Morton Feldman provided an original score, "Day of the Painter" features music composed especially to complement the action. But in this case, the score, complete with quacking-duck effects, is silly rather than serious, heightening the film's satiric intention. In truth, Baker's performance is less impersonation than caricature. His action painter is a cool careerist, whose breezy paint-splashing and blasé junking of unmarketable work is the opposite of Pollock's earnest, sincere intensity.

There are men who identify with Pollock as a kindred spirit, those of both sexes who believe that cloaking themselves in his mantle will enhance their own creative powers: people who think of smoking unfiltered Camels or drinking Pollock's favorite brand of whiskey or beer as a communion ritual, admirers who buy into the tortured-genius stereotype. But that kind of imitation is superficial. There are other, more productive means of appropriating and adapting the Pollock persona, as evidenced by the visual and performing artists who use him as raw material. For them, impersonation is creative role-playing, a metaphoric springboard for their own art. Simultaneously respectful and irreverent, arrogant and humble, they glory in the paradox of deconstructing Pollock and fashioning a new character made of truth, fiction, and supposition, to serve their own ends. It is a gesture directed, like the looping lines of Pollock's imagery, both toward and away from him. This is how the process of "imagining Pollock" is most fruitfully realized.

It's easy to reduce Pollock to a romantic cliché: the virtuoso whose creativity burned so hot it consumed him, its brilliance dimmed by alcohol and finally extinguished in a mad rush to oblivion. It's also tempting to see similarities between Pollock and other doomed American icons. Like Elvis Presley, he lost control of himself and dissipated his talent. Like Marilyn Monroe, he was insecure and couldn't handle fame. Like James Dean, his end came violently in an automobile wreck. And, like them, he died young.

Unlike them, however, Pollock was not a star. His celebrity never achieved the magnitude of an entertainer's, nor was his art popular. That is as true today as it was in 1949, when *Life* magazine's headline asked, "Is he the greatest living painter in the United States," and the vast majority of readers answered "no." More than half a century later—after three retrospective exhibitions, numerous major museum and gallery shows, various television documentaries, four biographies, magazine and newspaper articles galore, monographs in several languages, and work in museums and private collections around the world—Pollock's art remains incomprehensible and unappealing to many people, including those who admire and appreciate other innovations, like Impressionism and Cubism, that were once considered inept, grotesque, or subversive.

3

What is it, then, that makes some people such passionate Pollock fans? After more than a decade as the steward of his property, I've come to believe that one key factor is the open-ended nature of his legacy. Instead of describing, explaining, or answering questions, his art invites speculation and encourages flights of fancy. You never know where a Pollock is going to take you. As far as his personality is concerned, the myth is reductive, while the realities—and I use the plural deliberately—are complex, sometimes contradictory. That's why they're so intriguing. For example, several of his intimates describe him as a tall man, although he was actually an inch shy of six feet, and had such bad posture that his height at ease must have been rather less. He was famously taciturn, but there are also accounts of long conversations and deep discussions, and Krasner said he was sometimes "hideously verbal." Some who knew him recall his good humor, kindness, and sweet nature, while others remember him as sad, thoughtless, and rude. How can you impersonate someone you can't even describe? That he was far from simple and straightforward is beyond doubt. Were there, in fact, as many Pollocks, hidden and exposed, as there are mysteries and revelations in his violent/peaceful, chaotic/ordered, profound/meaningless, lyrical/apocalyptic paintings?

The Pollock we have today is cobbled together from information and deduction, fact and conjecture, analysis and inference. As imagined Pollocks proliferate, the search for a definitive Pollock gives way to the quest for a personal one. The simplistic stereotype comes closest to a standard model, but the customized, deeply subjective version is far superior, because it is the most adaptable to each individual's psychic needs.

Helen A. Harrison

THE LIFE
AND THE
DEATH

Form V. S.
No. 11

WYOMING STATE BOARD OF HEALTH
BUREAU OF VITAL STATISTICS
Capitol Building   Cheyenne, Wyoming

CERTIFICATE OF BIRTH

Registration District No. ____

	Do not write in this space
	File No. 1912
	Registered No. 2656

PLACE OF BIRTH

1. County of __Park__
   Town or City of __Cody__ St.
   No. ____ If birth occurred in hospital or institution give name of same.

2. FULL NAME OF CHILD __Paul Jackson Pollock__
   (If child is not yet named, make supplemental report, as directed.)

3. Sex __Male__   If plural births __   4. Twin, triplet, or other ____   6. Premature ____ Full term ____   7. Legitimate? __X__

5. Number, in order of birth ____

8. Date of birth __Jan.28,__ 19 __12__ (Month, day, year)

FATHER

9. Full name __Le Roy Pollock__

11. Color or race __White__   12. Age at last birthday __36__ (years)

13. Birthplace (city or place) __Pruggold County__ __Iowa__ (State or Country)

OCCUPATION

14. Trade, profession, or particular kind of work done, as spinner, lawyer, bookkeeper, etc. __Stone Mason and Cement Work__

15. Industry or business in which work is done, as silk mill, sawmill, bank, etc.

16. Date (month and year) last engaged in this work. __January__ 19 __12__   17. Total time (years) spent in this work __10__

MOTHER

18. Full maiden name __Stella May McClure__

19. Residence (usual place of abode) (If non-resident, give place and State)

20. Color or race __White__   21. Age at last birthday __37__ (years)

22. Birthplace (city or place) __Pruggold County__ __Iowa__ (State or Country)

OCCUPATION

23. Trade, profession, or particular kind of work done, as housekeeper, typist, nurse, clerk, etc __Housewife__

24. Industry or business in which work is done, as own home, lawyer's office, silk mill, etc. __Own Home__

25. Date (month and year) last engaged in this work. __January__ 19 __12__   26. Total time (years) spent in this work ____

27. Number of children of this mother (At time of this birth and including this child) ____ (a) Born alive and now living __5__ (b) Born alive but now dead ____ (c) Stillborn ____

28. If stillborn, period of gestation ____ months or weeks

29. What prophylactic was used to prevent ophthalmia neonatorum?

CERTIFICATE OF ATTENDING PHYSICIAN OR MIDWIFE

I hereby certify that I attended the birth of this child, who was ....m. on the date above stated
(Born alive or stillborn)

When there was no attending physician or midwife, then the father, householder, etc., should make this return.

Give name added from a supplemental report. _____ (Date of)

(Signed) __Stella May Pollock (Mother)__ __M.D.__ Midwife
or ____

Address __1352 Montecito Circle, Los Angeles, Cal.__

Filed __5/31__ 19 __38__ __C. M. Anderson, M.D.__ County Registrar
State ? Registrar

County Registrar

N. B.—In case of more than one child at birth, a SEPARATE RETURN must be made for each and the number of each, in order of birth, stated.

WRITE PLAINLY WITH UNFADING INK—THIS IS A PERMANENT RECORD—PREFERABLY PRINT SURNAME

Jackson Pollock's birth certificate, 1912.

Dear Charles and Frank:

   I am sorry for having been so slow with my correspondence to
you. I have been very busy getting adjusted in school, but
another climax has arisen. I have been ousted from school again.
The head of the Physical Ed. Dept. and I came to blows the other
day. We saw the principal about it but he was too thick to see
my side. He told me to get out and find another school. I have a
number of teachers backing me so there is some possibility of my
getting back. If I can not get back I am not sure what I will
do. I have thought of going to Mexico city if there is any means
of making a livelihood there.
   Another fellow and I are in some more very serious trouble. We
loaned two girls some money to run a way. We were ignorant of
the law at the time. We did it merely through friend ship. But
now they have us, I am not sure what the outcome will be. The
penalty is from six to twelve months in jail. We are both minors
so it would probably be some kind of a reform school. They found
the girls today in Phoenix and are bringing them back.
   If I get back in school I will have to be very careful about
my actions. The whole outfit think I am a rotten rebel from Rus-
sia. I will have to go about very quietly for a long period
until I win a good reputation. I find it useless to try and fight
an army with a spit ball.
   I have read and re-read your letter with clearer understanding
each time. Altho I am some better this year I am far from knowing the meaning of real work. I have subscribed for the "Creative Art", and "The Arts". From the Creative Art I am able to
under stand you better and it gives me a new outlook on life.
   I have dropped religion for the present. Should I follow the
Occult Mysticism it wouldn't be for commercial purposes. I am
doubtful of any talent, so what even I choose to be, will be
accomplished only by long study and work. I fear it will be
forced and mechanical. Architecture interests me but not in the
sense painting and sculptoring does. I became acquainted with
Rivera's work through a number of Communist meetings I attended
after being ousted from school last year. He has a painting in
the museum now. Perhaps you have seen it, Dia de Flores. I found

the Creative Art January 1929 on Rivera. I certainly admire his work. The other magizines I could not find.

As to what I would like to be. It is difficult to say. An Artist of some kind. If nothing else I shall always study the Arts. People have always frightened and bored me consequently I have been within my own shell and have not accomplished anything materially. In fact to talk in a group I was so frightened that I could not think logically. I am gradually overcoming it now. I am taking American Literature, Contemporary Literature, Clay Modeling and the life class. We are very fortunate in that this is the only school in the city that have models. Altho it is difficult to have a nude and get by the board Schwankavsky is brave enough to have them.

Frank I am sorry I have not sent you the typwriter sooner I got a box for it but it is too small. I will get another and send it immediately. How is school going? Are you in any activity? Is Mart still in the city? We have not heard for a long time in fact the letters have slacked from all of you.

Sande [Sanford, another brother] is doing quite well now. He has an office and handles all the advertising. He continues to make his weekend trip to Riverside.

Affectionately
Jacks

dear charles

   i am continually having new experience and am going through a
wavering evolution which leave my mind in an unsettled state.
too i am a bit lazy and careless with my correspondence i am
sorry i seem so uninterested in your helping me but from now on
there will be more interest and a hastier reply to your letters.
my letters are undoubtedly egotistical but it is myself that i
am interested in now. i suppose mother keeps you posted on family matter.
   school is still boresome but i have settled myself to its
rules and the ringing bells so i have not been in trouble
lately. this term i am going to go but one half day the rest i
will spend reading and working here at home. i am quite sure i
will be able to accomplish a lot more. in school i will take
life drawing and clay modeling. i have started doing some thing
with clay and have found a bit of encouragement from my teacher.
my drawing i will tell you frankly is rotten it seems to lack
freedom and rhythm it is cold and lifeless. it isn't worth the
postage to sent it. i think there should be a advancement soon
if it is ever to come and then i will send you some drawings.
the truth of it is i have never really got down to real work and
finish a piece i usually get disgusted with it and lose interest.
water color i like but have never worked with it much. altho i
feel i will make an artist of some kind i have nver proven to
myself nor any body else that i have it in me.
   this so called happy part of one's life youth to me is a bit
of damnable hell if i could come to some conclusion about myself
and life perhaps there i could see something to work for. my
mind blazes up with some illusion for a couple of weeks the it
smoalters down to a bit of nothing the more i read and the more
i think i am thinking the darker things become. i am still
interested in theosophy and am studing a book light on the path
every thing it has to say seems to be contrary to the essence of
modern life but after it is under stood and lived up to i think
it is a very helpful guide. i wish you would get one and tell me
what you think of it. they only cost thirty cents if you can not
find one i will send you one.

we have gotten up a group and have arranged for a furnace
where we can have our stuff fired. we will give the owner a commission for the firing and glazing. there is chance of my making
a little book money.

   i am hoping you will flow freely with criticism and advice and
book lists i no longer dream as i used to perhaps i can derive
some good from it.

   i met geritz at a lecture on wood block cutting he asked about
you and sends his regards the fellow mentioned of coming here
has not arrived

you
jack

Jackson, Sanford, Betty Nelson (a friend) and Frank Pollock,
Riverside, California, 1928.
POLLOCK-KRASNER STUDY CENTER, JEFFREY POTTER COLLECTION.

Jackson Pollock, Riverside, California, 1927.
ARCHIVES OF AMERICAN ART, SMITHSONIAN INSTITUTION

Jackson, Charles and Manuel Tolegian, a fellow art student, New York, ca. 1930.
POLLOCK-KRASNER STUDY CENTER, JEFFREY POTTER COLLECTION.

February 1932
winter

Dear Dad,

I have waited so damned long to write to you, Dad, I guess there is no need of making excuses.

Guess it's pretty lonesome being in camp all alone and not working, well if i were there, we could try our hand at check-ers, or talk about the ideal life and civilization. Suppose you still get the *Nation* there, I thought the article by Ernest was very good, the best of the bunch "If I Were A Constitutional Dictator". The one by Chase was good I think. It's looking as though we're going to be enlisting for the capitalists govern-ment. The Manchurian business is beginning to be involved.

Things are about the same here. I'm going to school every morning (Art Students League of New York) and have learned what is worth learning in the realm of art. It is just a matter of time and work now for me to have that knowledge a part of me. A good seventy years more and I'll make a good artist. Being an artist is life itself—living it I mean. And when I say artist I don't mean it in the narrow sense of the word, but the man who is building things, creating, molding the earth, whether it be in the plains of the West or in the iron ore of Pennsylvania. It's all a big game of construction; some with a brush; some with a shovel; some choose a pen. Benton (Thomas Hart Benton) is just getting another big mural job; for the Whitney Museum of American Art. Mural painting is forging to the front and by the time I get up there there will be plenty of it. Sculpturing I think is my medium. I'll never be satisfied until I'm able to mould a mountain of stone, with the aid of a jack-hammer, to fit my will. There are to be some mural jobs for the new Radio City which is under construction. That's the new artists' job—to construct with the carpenter, the mason. The art of life is construction—the planning—the fitting in of masses—activities.

Well Dad, I've started so many letters and then let them lay in the desk that I think I'll really get myself together and send this one which started some weeks ago.

It is very cold here now. Seems to me the coldest yet this winter. Certainly tough on the poor old fellows in the bread lines, and no place to flop.

Benton is ill with the grip or typhoid fever. Hard luck to get sick just as he gets a job, hope he is better soon.

It's getting round about the time when we all wonder what we are going to do this summer. None of us, I think, has more than a vague notion of what we would like to do. It looks as though we will just have to wait and see what turns up. Chas will come out West if he is fortunate enough in getting the scholarship, otherwise it is very doubtful. Frank I think is still coming. He is still at the library at night and peeling spuds. He had a cold last week but is well now. I certainly would like to get out there too, but I've got to think of my next year here. I would like to get work in a rock quarry or stone factory where I could make a little money and at the same time learn something about stone and the cutting of it. I'm about as helpless as a

LeRoy McCoy Pollock, ca. 1929-31. PHOTO: WALTER FISS. POLLOCK-KRASNER STUDY CENTER, JEFFREY POTTER COLLECTION.

Jackson and his father, Grand Canyon, AZ, 1927. ARCHIVES OF AMERICAN ART, SMITHSONIAN INSTITUTION.

kitten when it comes to getting my way with jobs and things. There seems to be nothing definite as to what we each will do. If I am unable to make it out there I will try and get a lot of drawing done on my way West. I suppose a little later we will have more of a notion of what we can do.

I don't suppose Jay is having too cozy a time of it this winter. Do you hear from him? Got a very interesting letter from Mort. Glad he is finding himself—will write to him. Didn't get Sande's letter yet. This is bird of a funny family you've got Dad. Every so often one of us has a revolution all his own. Kind of interesting to see what we'll all settle down to in the end. I've got a long way to go yet toward my development—much that needs working on—doing everything with a definite purpose. Without purpose with each move then chaos.

I still tamper with the mouth harp. Can't play a darn thing. But it kind of puts me to sleep at night and I get a kick out of it.

Well Dad I took time out to eat about two pounds of fresh cooked spinach. I will close for this time and will write more often. I'm usually in such a turmoil that I haven't anything to write about and when I do after I've written it it looks like all bunk. Got Mother's letter some time ago with the token. I shouldn't allow it I guess.

Love
Jackson

49 East 10th Street
New York City

Dear Dad,

Friday evening, have just finished a big wash of about seven sheets and a few towels and ends. Life here differs little from what we had up in Santa Yuez valley. The same old house-keeping (sic) with a pot belly stove the only difference is that New York is about ten times dirtier. But I like the life, it's hard on the bums' existence and after all they are the well-to-do of this day, they didn't have as far to fall.

Benton has a huge job out in Indianapolis for one of the state office buildings. Two hundred running feet, twelve feet high and the panels are to be exhibited at the Chicago World's Fair when they are finished in May. After a lifetime struggle with the elements of everyday experience he is beginning to be recognized as the foremost American painter today. He has lifted art from the stuffy studios into the world of happenings about him which has more meaning to the masses.

Of course Benton had to give up his class, we have a substitute whom I think little of and probably won't stay with him long. Manuel Tolegian is studying with John Stuart Curry. I have joined a class in stone carving in the mornings. I think I'll like it. So far I have done nothing but try to flatten a round rock, but it's great fun and damned hard work. If I am able to learn anything about it I'll take it for a full day and stick with it for three or four years—then the rest of my life.

Frank has a very uninteresting job but seems to manage to keep up with it. He is gone all day and half the night with it. I think he intends to try to go West this summer again. Chas of course wants to get out if he can raise the money. For myself I'll probably try to stick it through. Think it will do me a lot of good and possibly give me a better footing for the following year. Chas is working along and improving doing some lithographs too.

Well Dad by god it certainly is tough getting laid up. I hope you are better now. It was a long stretch too, you had better take it easy for some time and for heck sake don't worry about money—no one has it. This system is on the rocks so no need to pay rent and all the rest of the hokum that goes with the price system. Curious enough the artists are having it better now than before. They are

14

getting more aid. The fat-bellied financiers are turning to art as an escape from the somewhat forceful reality of today. Fat women, lean women, short and tall come with their dogs to lose themselves in the emotional junk of the artist. Unfortunately that's the kind of stuff they want, they don't have to think when they look at it. Stuff that has significance is too near reality, it bothers them, tells them something. Possibly it's just a matter of time when there maybe will be a demand for the real stuff after all. That isn't my worry—mine is to produce it.

Writing a letter is a hell of a job for me. Suppose I should make more of an effort. Well here is a try at one.

We have had extremely fine weather as a matter of fact for the most part it has been like spring—a bit chilly at times, but just enough to put some pep in a fellow.

It's past my bedtime so my love to all.

Jack

1100 Valentine Road
Kansas City, MO.

Oct. 3d-38

Dear Jack-

I saw your stuff in N.Y. and later a picture that my brother has. I am very strongly for you as an artist. You're a damn fool of you don't cut out the monkey business and get to work.

Tom.

Dear Jack

I was worried about you for 4 months, and can't tell you how relieved I was to hear from you.

We all hope and pray that you settle down & work–& we mean work hard paint hard–So few have the ability to say something interesting in their work–you have–Tom & I & many others believe in you

Tom gave up drinking last July and this summer he had a most productive one and greatly improved.

When we got to Springfield we found Nat & Alma on the wagon too.

Do let us hear from you. Remember our house is always open for you.

With love as always–

Rita

Thomas Hart Benton, *Portrait of Jackson Pollock as a young man*, 1934. Pencil on paper, 14 x 10 5/8 inches.
UNIVERSITY OF KANSAS ART MUSEUM, GIFT OF THOMAS HART BENTON.
PHOTO: POLLOCK-KRASNER STUDY CENTER, B.H. FRIEDMAN COLLECTION.

Portrait of Jack Pollock, a young man

Berlin

Copy

3rd.May, 1941

The Examining Medical Officer
Selective Service System
Local Board No 17
412 Sixth Avenue
N.Y.City

Dear Sir,

Mr Jackson Pollock has been referred to me by Dr. J.L.
Henderson. Pollock has been coming to me for a number of
psychoanalytical interviews during the past 6 months in connection
with his difficulties of adaptation to social environment. I have
found him to be a shut-in and inarticulate personality of good
intellegence, but with a great deal of emotional instability, who
finds it difficult to form or maintain any kind of relationship.
I would say that the problem is fairly deep-seated and not due to
any superficial tendencies towards evasion, or to immaturity of
outlook.

Altough he has not during these months shown any manifest
symptoms of schozophrenia, yet in the course of the interviews,
it has become evident that there is a certain schizoid disposition
underlying the instability. It is for this reason that I venture
to suggest that Pollock be referred for a psychiatric examination.

Very truly yours,

(Mrs. V. de Laszlo, M.D.,
Zurich, Switzerland)

Letter to the Examining Medical Officer, Selective Service System, 1941.
ARCHIVES OF AMERICAN ART, SMITHSONIAN INSTITUTION.

26th May, 1941

Order No.
867

The Examining Medical Officer
Selective Service System
Local Board No. 17
412 Sixth Avenue
New York City.

Dear Sir,

[F]urther to my letter to you with reference to Jackson Pollock, Order No. 867, Pollock has reported to me that he has
undergone a special psychiatric interview at Beth Israel Hospital on May 22nd.

On that occasion he was told to obtain from me a statement to
the effect that he has been admitted to the Westchester Division
of the New York Hospital on June 11th, 1938. I have had occasion
to see a letter from the then attending M.O., Dr. Wall, in which
it was stated that Pollock would be dismissed in September of
that same year.

I can therefore testify that Jackson Pollock has been a resident free patient at the Westchester Division of the N.Y. Hospital during four months in 1838. As far as I am aware he was
admitted under the diagnosis of acute alcoholism.

Very truly yours
(V. de Laszlo,
M.D., Zurich, Switzerland)

19

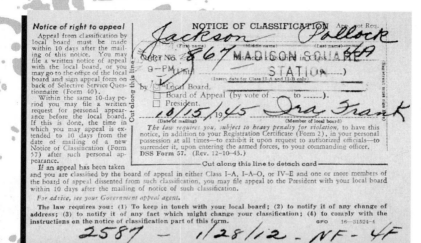

NOTICE OF CLASSIFICATION App. not Req.

Jackson *Pollock*
(First name)   (Middle name)   (Last name)

Order No. 867 MADISON SQUARE in Class ____

9-PM Unit   STATION   )
(Insert date for Class II-A and II-B only.)

by ☑ Local Board.
☐ Board of Appeal (by vote of ____ to ____).
☐ President.

10/15/1945   *Ira Frank*
(Date of mailing)   (Member of local board)

2587 — 1/28/12 — NF - 4F

Jackson Pollock's Selective Service (draft) card, 1945.

Jackson Pollock's Social Security card, undated.

FRAGMENT OF A POEM,
on a torn sheet with a drawing.

JACKSON POLLOCK

CA. 1942

Fragmentary poem on a sheet of paper
with a drawing, ca. 1942
PHOTO: POLLOCK-KRASNER STUDY CENTER, JACK-
SON POLLOCK CATALOGUE RAISONNÉ ARCHIVES.

The rock the fish

was winged

and split of

Two—so one could

grow to be and

was the sun

[The word "sun" is a correction of "son"]

21

ARTICLES OF AGREEMENT, MADE AND ENTERED INTO ON FEBRUARY,_1946, BETWEEN JACKSON POLLOCK AND ART OF THIS CENTURY, WITNESSETH,

1. Between March 15, 1946 and March 15, 1948, Art Of This Century will have the sole and exclusive right to buy, exhibit, sell, and distribute all works of art by Jackson Pollock, in consideration whereof Art Of This Century agrees to pay Jackson Pollock the sum of $300.00 each month of the aforementioned period.

2. Art Of This Century further agrees to loan to Jackson Pollock, on or before March 15, 1946, the sum of [insert in Lee's handwriting, "around"] $2000.00, [insert in Lee's handwriting, "maximum"] to be repaid by Jackson Pollock at the rate of $50.00 per month. Art Of This Century shall have the right to deduct the sum of $50.00 from each monthly payment of $300.00 to Jackson Pollock until such time when the loan of $2000.00 shall be fully repaid.

It [insert: is] further agreed that the pictures of Jackson Pollock now in possession of Art Of This Century and acquired prior to this contract by Art Of This Century as agent of Jackson Pollock, will remain in the possession of Art Of This Century agent for Jackson Pollock, When sold, two thirds of the sales price of each of these pictures shall be applied to payment of the aforementioned loan, and one third of the sales price shall be retained as commission by Art Of This Century.

3. Jackson Pollock shall have the right to retain for his own possession one picture each year during the period of this contract. All other works of art by Jackson Pollock shall become the property of Art Of This Century, consideration for which is described above in these articles of agreement.

4. It is further agreed that Jackson Pollock shall accept no other remunerative employment during the period of this contract and that Art Of This Century will have the sole and exclusive right to renew this contract with Jackson Pollock, providing terms are satisfactory for both parties to this agreement.

[signed]
Jackson Pollock

Draft of *POSSIBILITIES I* statement

JACKSON POLLOCK

C. 1947.

I work on unstretched canvas taked [sic] to the wall or floor. I need the resistance of a hard surface & on the floor I can literally work from the four sides use heavy empasto [sic] or a fluid running paint & —with foregn [sic] matter added such as gravel sand, broken glass. I seldom use painter tools, such as brushes, easel etc. The source of my painting is the unconscious. I approach painting the same way I approach drawing, that is direct—with no prelimary [sic] studies. The drawings I do are relative to my painting but not for it. When I am painting I am not much aware of what is taking place—it is only after that I see what I have done.

Techine is the result of a need. —

New needs demand new Technics ———

Total control — demands of the accident ———

States of order —

Organic intensity ———

energy and motion made visble ———

memories arrested in Space,

human needs and motives ———

acceptance——— —

Jackson Pollock

Handwritten notes, 1950.

23

AN INTERVIEW with Jackson Pollock

TAPED BY WILLIAM WRIGHT
in the fall of 1950 for presentation on WERI Radio, Westerly. RI.

FALL 1950

Mr. Pollock, in your opinion, what is the meaning of modern art?

Modern art to me is nothing more than the expression of contemporary aims of the age that we're living in.

Did the classical artists have any means of expressing their age?

Yes, they did it very well. All cultures have had means and techniques of expressing their immediate aims—the Chinese, the Renaissance, all cultures. The thing that interests me is that today painters do not have to go to a subject matter outside of themselves. Most modern painters work from a different source. They work from within.

Would you say that the modern artist has more or less isolated the quality which made the classical works of art valuable, that he's isolated it and uses it in a purer form?

Ah—the good ones have, yes.

Mr. Pollock, there's been a good deal of controversy and a great many comments have been made regarding your method of painting. Is there something you'd like to tell us about that?

My opinion is that new needs need new techniques. And the modern artists have found new ways and new means of making their statements. It seems to me that the modern painter cannot express this age, the airplane, the atom bomb, the radio, in the old forms of the Renaissance or of any other past culture. Each age finds its own technique.

Which would also mean that the layman and the critic would have to develop their ability to interpret the new techniques.

Yes—that always somehow follows. I mean, the strangeness will wear off and I think we will discover the deeper meanings in modern art.

I suppose every time you are approached by a layman they ask you how they should look at a Pollock paining, or any other modern painting—what they look for—how do they learn to appreciate modern art?

I think they should not look for, but look passively—and try to receive what the painting has to offer and not bring a subject matter or preconceived idea of what they are to be looking for.

Would it be true to say that the artist is painting from the unconscious, and the—canvas must act as the unconscious of the person who views it?

The unconscious is a very important side of modern art and I think the unconscious drives do mean a lot in looking at paintings.

Then deliberately looking for any known meaning or object in an abstract painting would distract you immediately from ever appreciating it as you should?

I think it should be enjoyed just as music is enjoyed—after a while you may like it or you may not. But—it doesn't seem to be too serious. I like some flowers and others, other flowers I don't like. I think at least it gives—I think at least give it a chance.

Well, I think you have to give anything that sort of chance. A person isn't born to like good music, they have to listen to it and gradually develop an understanding of it or liking for it. If modern painting works the same way—a person would have to subject himself to it over a period of time in order to be able to appreciate it.

I think that might help, certainly.

Mr. Pollock, the classical artists had a world to express and they did go so by representing the objects in that world. Why doesn't the modern artist do the same thing?

H'm—the modern artist is living in a mechanical age and we have a mechanical means of representing objects in nature such as the camera and photograph. The modern artist, it seems to me, is working and expressing an inner world—in other words—expressing the energy, the motion, and other inner forces.

Would it be possible to say that the classical artist expressed his world by representing the objects, whereas the modern artist expresses his world by representing the effects the objects have upon him?

Yes, the modern artist is working with space and time, and expressing his feelings rather than illustrating.

Well, Mr. Pollock, can you tell us how modern art came into being?

It didn't drop out of the blue; it's a part of a long tradition dating back with Cézanne, up through the cubists, the post-cubists, to the painting being done today.

Then, it's definitely a product of evolution?

Yes.

William Wright, Springs, 1947. Photo: Courtesy of Lois Wright.

Shall we go back to this method question that so many people today think is important? Can you tell us how you developed your method of painting, and why you paint as you do?

Well, method is, it seems to me, a natural growth out of a need, and from a need the modern artist has found new ways of expressing the world about him. I happen to find ways that are different from the usual techniques of painting, which seems a little strange at the moment, but I don't think there's anything very different about it. I paint on the floor and this isn't unusual—the Orientals did that.

How do you go about getting the paint on the canvas? I understand you don't use brushes or anything of that sort, do you?

Most of the paint I use is a liquid, flowing kind of paint. The brushes I use are used more as sticks rather than brushes—the brush doesn't touch the surface of the canvas, it's just above.

Would it be possible for you to explain the advantage of using a stick with paint—liquid paint rather than a brush on canvas?

Well, I'm able to be more free and to have greater freedom and move about the canvas, with greater ease.

Well, isn't it more difficult to control than a brush? I mean, isn't there more a possibility of getting too much paint or splattering or any number of things? Using a brush, you put the paint right where you want it and you know exactly what it's going to look like.

No, I don't think so. I don't—ah—with experience—it seems to be possible to control the flow of the paint, to a great extent, and I don't use—I don't use the accident—'cause I deny the accident.

I believe it was Freud who said there's no such thing as an accident. Is that what you mean?

I suppose that's generally what I mean.

Then, you don't actually have a preconceived image of a canvas in your mind?

Well, not exactly—no—because it hasn't been created, you see. Something new—it's quite different from working, say, from a still life where you set up objects and work directly from them. I do have a general notion of what I'm about and what the results will be.

That does away, entirely, with all preliminary sketches?

Yes, I approach painting in the same sense as one approaches drawing; that is, it's direct. I don't work from drawings, I don't make sketches and drawings and color sketches into a final painting. Painting, I think, today—the more immediate, the more direct—the greater the possibilities of making a direct—of making a statement.

Well, actually every one of your paintings, your finished canvases, is an absolute original.

Well—yes—they're all direct painting. There is only one.

Well, now, Mr. Pollock, would you care to comment on modern painting as a whole? What is your feeling about your contemporaries?

Well, painting today certainly seems very vibrant, very alive, very exciting. Five or six of my contemporaries around New York are doing very vital work, and the direction that painting seems to be taking here— is—away from the easel—into some sort, some kind of wall—wall painting.

I believe some of your canvases are of very unusual dimensions, isn't that true?

Well, yes, they're an impractical size—9 × 18 feet. But I enjoy working big and—whenever I have a chance, I do it whether it's practical or not.

Can you explain why you enjoy working on a large canvas more than on a small one?

Well, not really. I'm just more at ease in a big area than I am on something 2 × 2; I feel more at home in a big area.

You say "in a big area." Are you actually on the canvas while you're painting?

Very little. I do step into the canvas occasionally—that is, working from the four sides I don't have to get into the canvas too much.

I notice over in the corner you have something done on plate glass. Can you tell us something about that?

Well, that's something new for me. That's the first thing I've done on glass and I find it very exciting. I think the possibilities of using painting on glass in modern architecture—in modern construction—terrific.

Well, does the one on glass differ in any other way from your usual technique?

It's pretty generally the same. In this particular piece I've used colored glass sheets and plaster slabs and beach stones and odds and ends of that sort. Generally it's pretty much the same as all of my paintings.

Well, in the event that you do more of these for modern buildings, would you continue to use various objects?

I think so, yes. The possibilities, it seems to me are endless, what one can do with glass. It seems to me a medium that's very much related to contemporary painting.

Mr. Pollock, isn't it true that your method of painting, your technique, is important and interesting only because of what you accomplish by it?

I hope so. Naturally, the result is the thing—and—it doesn't make much difference how the paint is put on as long as something has been said. Technique is just a means of arriving at a statement.

Pollock's "PROTEEN" diet

GRANT MARK

FALL 1951

During the fall of 1951, in an effort to solve his drinking problem, Pollock sought treatment from Grant Mark, a biochemist who owned a firm called Psychological-Chemistry, Inc., with offices on Park Avenue in Manhattan. Mark saw Pollock regularly for about two years. His treatment involved a regimen of weekly mineral injections, regular salt-water baths to draw the poisons out of Pollock's body, and daily doses of a soy-milk emulsion he called "Proteen," which was the basis of a highly restricted vegetarian diet. Apparently, although the diet specifically excludes alcohol, Pollock thought of Proteen as an antidote rather then a substitute. As he rationalized it to Jeffrey Potter, "With me it's some kind of chemical derangement. Once my chemistry is figured out, alcohol will find its own level." Several of Pollock's friends considered Mark to be a charlatan and his treatment worthless. A Springs neighbor, Dr. Raphael Gribitz, described Mark and his staff, some of whom were medical doctors, as "a group of people who were exploiting [Pollock] to an excessive degree. Jackson had a deep-rooted problem and I wanted to know at least he had no chance at all." (*To a Violent Grave*, pp. 145–146)

While this Emulsion is a complete food
it is primarily a protein concentrate
with an unusually high amino-acid count.
It is therefore a substitute for poultry,
fish, meat, egg white and dairy products,
such as milk, cheese and etc. It is also
a substitute for sugar and starches.

It may be taken at room temperature or
warmed in a double boiler. Once warmed
it cannot bechilled again.

It generates ferment rapidly after the
vacuum has been broken or if it is allowed to get warm. It should be constantly
stored in a refrigerator not less than
45 degrees.

Before using, invert bottle if sealed, stir
if open, to insure even distribution. Unless
specified one waterglassful (8 ozs.) with
salads at lunch and dinner. If found difficult
at start add 1/4 light cream.

CAUTION: No aluminum or metal dishes should
be cooked in unless heavily enameled. Vegetables uneatable raw should be cooked in a
pressure cooker. All other cooking should
be done in stainless steel, glass or heavy
enamel. Blenders should have glass containers
with surgical steel knives. Vegetable juice
extractors should be of stainless steel or
enamel wherever juices come in contact with
the machine.

"Proteen" soy emulsion diet, 1951.

BREAKFAST

Fruit should be used for breakfast—one kind only, vary each day. (If unsatisfied, follow with w.g., cream and approved honey or raisins)

LUNCH

To be confined to Raw Vegetable Salad—as liberal an amount as can be consumed.

Basic ingredients at all times:

Shredded cabbage 8 ozs. (water glass)
Shredded carrots 4 ozs
Shredded beets 2 ozs
This should be garnished with at least five other items which can be eaten raw—such as:

celery	scallions	radishes
tomatoes	cucumbers*	peppers
endive	watercress	cauliflower
onions	parsley	avocado*

*Avocado and cucumber should not be used in the same salad. Cucumber should always be used with the rind.

PLUS eight ounces of Emulsion.

Note: Lettuce, romaine, and chicory are permitted but will not supply substantial nourishment and must not be substituted for the cabbage.

Sufficient amount of salad should be eaten to satisfy until dinnertime.

Fruit may be used during afternoon (2 hrs. after lunch if desired.)

DINNER

Repeat raw salad plus two or three cooked vegetables (those not eatable raw) such as:

Artichokes	Pumpkin	Mushrooms
Parsnips	Broccoli	Turnips
Asparagus	Squash	

PLUS eight ounces of Emulsion:

DRESSINGS

Raisins (manukka) can be added to salad, especially good with shredded carrots.

French dressing of soy oil—fresh lemon juice—mayonnaise. (Instructions will be given if requested.)

Other suggestions: Coconut well filled with liquid—to open push two eyes with ice pick—pour liquid in glass, drink immediately. Break shell, remove white meat and shred over salad or use in any manner desired, over desserts and etc.

Knox's pure gelatin can be used in many ways—with vegetables, fruits and such as flavoring and coloring with pineapple juice—placing pineapple wedges in the gelatin. (Unsweetened grape juice and almonds may also be used after citrus fruit.)

MALIC

FRUITS
Grapes
Apples
Apricots—fresh, or dried without sulphur
Blackberries
Boysenberries
Cherries—not Maraschino
Currants—red or black
Gooseberries
Loganberries
Melons—cantaloupe, casaba, honeydew, persian, watermelon (not to
    be eaten with other foods.)
Nectarines
Peaches
Pears—Anjou, Bartlett, Bosc, Comise, Seckle
Pineapple—unsweetened
Raisins—Manukka preferred
Raspberries—not frozen
Strawberries—not frozen
Canned fruits packed in own juice without added sugar: "S and W".

CITRUS
Limes
Lemons
Grapefruit
Tangerines

SWEET
Dried Dates
Dried Figs
Bananas

NO prunes—except large Santa Clara
NO rhubarb
NO plums
NO Cranberries

NUTS—UNSALTED, UNTOASTED & UNBLANCHED.
Almonds
Brazil
Cashews
Filberts
Pecans
Pistachios—white & fresh
Walnuts

Nuts can be used at any meal—all in limited amounts except almonds—use as many as desire. Nuts must be masticated thoroughly.

NO CHESTNUTS.

NO PEANUTS.

SEASONING THAT CAN BE USED:
Light herbs   Cinnamon
Rosemary   Nutmeg
Basil   Vanilla

No synthetic products should be used such as Saccharin or synthetic flavoring.

Tupelo Honey may be used.

NOT ALLOWED
Heavy condiments—salt, pepper, mustard, vinegar.

NO sugar—this includes nothing with sugar in it—such as canned fruits etc.

33

NO cereals—no foods made of wheat, barley, rye, or rice.

NO meat, fish, poultry.

NO egg white.

NO dairy products including milk, cheese and etc. with the exception of butter and cream—which are always allowed except in extreme reducing diets.

NO legumes such as dried beans, kidney or lima, lentils, peas, peanuts, and etc.

NO Jerusalem artichokes.

NO Potatoes (except skins)

NO spinach.

VEGETABLES

Artichokes, French

Artichokes—hearts

Asparagus

Avocado pears (Alligator pears)

Beans—baby lima, Fordhook, lima, soya, string, or wax.

Beets

Beet greens

Broccoli

Brussel sprouts (not frozen)

Cabbage—green, red, white, Chinese, or Savoy.

Carrots—California preferred

Cauliflower—not frozen

Cauliflower Greens

Chardon

Chicory

Corn—tiny, milky, fresh garden

Cucumber—with rind

Celery—Pascal or white

Celery knobs

Dandelion greens

Egg plant

Endive

Escarolle

Fennel (Finnochio)

Kale

Kohlrabi

Leeks

Lettuce

Mushrooms

Mustard greens
Okra
Onion—Bermuda, Spanish, red, silver, or Yellow.
Palm

VEGETABLES
Parsnips
Peppers—green or red
Potato skins—sweet or white
Pumpkin
Romaine
Rutabaga
Salsify (oyster plant)
Scallions
Squash—acorn, Hubbard, summer, white, Des Moines, Yellow.
Dorrel
Swiss Chard
Tomatoes—no starch added.
Turnip
Turnip greens
Watercress
Zuccini (vegetable marrow)
The desirable amount of vegetables to be consumed in relation to all other intake is 75 percent and 25 percent in fruits and all other foods.

BEVERAGES
NO coffee, tea, or alcohol

NO commercial drinks containing sugar or vegetable poisons such as colas.

ALLOWED
Peppermint tea—with honey or plain.
Hot water with honey and cream.
Black strap Molasses—1 tablespoonful to 8 ozs. of boiling water—only if approved with low blood sugars.
All unsweetened fruit juices, fresh if possible

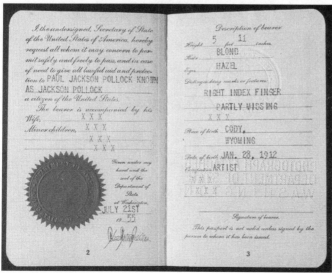

Jackson Pollock's passport, 1955.

"TOLL OF TEN LIVES In Motor Crashes Saturday in S'ampton, E. Hampton"

THE EAST HAMPTON STAR, THURSDAY, AUGUST 19, 1956, PAGE 1

- Factual corrections are in {ogee} brackets.

SUNDAY morning's radio announced that eight people were dead in three Saturday Automobile accidents—one accident in East Hampton Township, one in Southampton. A ninth victim died Monday morning, and a tenth on Tuesday. Dead in the East Hampton accident is Jackson Pollock, 44, internationally known artist who made his home at The Springs, and Miss Edith Metzger, 23, of 2086 Anthony Ave., The Bronx, New York City, assistant manager of a beauty salon, who was one of the two young women riding with the artist. The other girl, Miss Ruth Kligman, a model who lived at 103 Chancellor Ave., Newark, N. J., was taken to the Southampton Hospital with possible fractures.

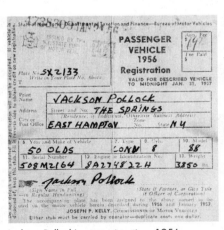

Jackson Pollock's car registration, 1956.

The police said that Mr. Pollock was at the wheel of the 1950 Oldsmobile convertible coupe when it turned over within 300 yards of his home, and driving at a high rate of speed. Traveling north on the Springs–Fireplace Highway, the car first ran off the east side of the road at a slight curve, then swerved and plowed 175 feet through underbrush on the west side to collide with four white oaks, pivoted, and turning [sic] end over end. The driver and Miss Kligman were thrown out.

37

Miss Metzger was pinned under the car and died of a fractured neck and chest injuries. The accident occurred at about 10:15.

Dr. Marshall J. Hamby of Richmond Hill, L. I., who was passing by, and Dr. William Abel of East Hampton attended the injured girl. Patrolman Earl Finch of the East Hampton Town Police arrived on the scene shortly after the accident, to find the green car lying on its back about three feet off the road.

Jackson Pollock, a Springs year-round resident for the past {10½} years, has provoked much discussion since he introduced his unorthodox painting techniques in 194{7}. His works have been displayed in the best museums and galleries here and abroad. In this vicinity they have been shown at Guild Hall, in the East Hampton Sag Harbor School of Fine Arts, and in private homes.

Mrs. Pollock, who was in Paris, returned here on Monday.

Mr. Pollock was born in Cody, Wyoming, Jan. 28, 1912, the son of LeRoy and Stella May {McClure} Pollock. He studied at the Art Students League in New York with Thomas Benton, a famous realist. He did not

Jackson Pollock's body at the accident scene, Fireplace Road, Springs, 11 August 1956.
PHOTO: DAVE EDWARDES. POLLOCK-KRASNER STUDY CENTER, JEFFREY POTTER COLLECTION.

become well known until he broke away from tradition and developed his "drip method" of painting which consisted of spreading a canvas on the floor and dripping on it paint, cement, sand, broken glass, and other materials. His style was widely copied.

He is survived by his wife, the former Lenore Krassner, by his mother, and {four} brothers. The funeral service was held yesterday afternoon at 4:30 in the Springs Chapel, the Rev. George Nicholson officiating. Burial was in Green River Cemetery.

A Verified Transcript from the Register of Deaths

Date of Death August 11, 1956   Registered No. 27

Place of Death Springs Road, The Springs

Name of Deceased Jackson Pollock

Age, 44 Years, 6 Months, 13 Days

Sex Male   Color or Race

Single, Married, Widowed or Divorced Married

Full Name of Husband or Wife Lenore Pollock

Date of Birth 1/28/12   Birthplace Wyoming

Citizen of what Country

How Long a Resident Here

In U. S. if foreign

Occupation Artist   S. S. No.

Father's Name Lee Roy Pollock

Mother's Maiden Name Stella May McClore

If Veteran, Name of War Unknown

Cause of Death Immediate Cause Compound fracture of skull. Laceration of brain, laceration both lungs. Due to: Hemothorax - shock

Time Dr. in Attendance till Death

Medical Attendant or other Attestant John H. Nugent, Coroner

Place of Burial Green River Cemetery, Springs

Undertaker Frederick S. Williams

I Hereby Solemnly Attest, That this is a true Transcript from the Public Register of Death as kept in the Town Clerk's Office

County of Suffolk , State of New York

Dated at East Hampton ,N. Y.

the 24th day of June 19 70

(Signed)

Official Title Registrar of Vital Statistics

Jackson Pollock's death certificate, 1956.

JACKSON POLLOCK 1912–56

THOMAS B. HESS

SEPTEMBER, 1956

JACKSON Pollock died in an automobile accident on August 11. He was driving back to his house in Springs, Long Island, going fast over a bumpy stretch of road that he knew by heart.

Pollock was the most famous of the artists who have come into prominence since 1940. His death is tragic not only because his career is cut short but because it is logical. Death is doubly tragic when it is logical: Similar logic seems to hint that it need not have happened. Pollock's was the tragic, logical death of a man whose greatness and strength are precisely the qualities that led him to a death that could have been avoided if he had not been so strong, or had been willing to compromise, or step backwards, or hold some strength in reserve—in other words, if he had not been Jackson Pollock.

The enormous extent of his influence on other painters is not a measure of his stature as an artist. Literally thousands of painters—more in Europe, by now, than in America—have adapted, in some way or other, the superficialities of the look of freedom which he was able to give to paint on canvas. They use his necessities as if they were tricks of commercial art or ways of jazzing-up academic compositions or devices to produce safe-and-sane spectacular abstractions. Because Pollock was contemptuous of all uncommitted efforts, he thought that this was absurd and funny. But it must have been depressing and in a way infuriating to see yourself as a boom when you are gambling everything on your own human, intellectual uniqueness.

Pollock's true influence was felt elsewhere; it was profoundly important and, I think, he was proud of it.

He was the first successfully to liberate painting from the dominant conventions of the School-of-Paris *cuisine*. When the interior evolution of his style led him to work with the canvas lying on the floor and, later, to toss and splash pigment on the picture—to throw the picture on the floor and attack it in a violent dance—to use the intellectual, critical faculties of the artist in such a way as to permit and sustain the moment of creativity and violence—and when he emerged from wrestling with the angel bringing with him paintings that kept intact the action of the fighting—at that point in time a new approach was opened to painters and a new appearance was made possible for pictures. It is fair to say, I believe, that the paintings of Willem de Kooning, Franz Kline, Mark Rothko, Clyfford Still, Hans Hofmann, Adolph Gottlieb, Robert Motherwell, Barnett Newman, Richard Pousette-Dart, Ad Reinhardt, Jack Tworkov, Esteban Vicente, and others who have made modern American painting the most vital movement at mid-century, were, in one way or another, given fresh impetus by the pictures Jackson Pollock exhibited in 1943–48.

Artists recognized in his pictures a new kind of fusion of paint and auto-biography, art and life becoming expressed in painting more intensely, and thus with greater accuracy, because they were indistinguishably together. After this contact with Pollock's art, the painters went their own ways. In some cases there was no apparent change in their pictures, in other cases the transformation was drastic, but this is not important. The decisive importance of Pollock's gesture was its signal for a general change of esthetic attitude in American painting.

In order to paint the way he did, Pollock had to commit himself totally to his art and to the gestures of faith he made in painting. In order to make this kind of commitment to art you must sacrifice other things. In certain periods, the pictures themselves are sacrificed for in Pollock's life the only way to criticize your pictures is to stop painting—which is a tremendous sacrifice. The ultimate sacrifice is of life itself, and in our terror which comes in the confrontation with this logic lies the tragedy of his death.

Pollock's career was brief. Like Rimbaud's, it involved an excess of violence which always was colored by tough laughter and never was tainted by sentimentality; like Caravaggio's or van Gogh's, it was filled with moments of stupendous creative activity, as if the artist knew how little time he had to paint in. That Saturday evening he drove from Springs to go to a concert at his friend Alfonso Ossorio's house. Part way there he decided he felt too tired, to go on. They stopped for some coffee and a rest; then decided to go back. Pollock was a heavy drinker, but he was sober on that drive.* The car skidded off a sandy shoulder of the road, veered to the

*This information is contradicted by eye witnesses.

41

other side at full speed into a clump of five trees. There were two friends with him in the car: Edith Metzger died, Ruth Kligman survived. Pollock was thrown clear, but died instantly, apparently from a concussion. On August 16 he was buried in Springs. He was forty-four: the same age as the late Arshile Gorky.

T. B. H.

In Memoriam:
THE ECSTASY AND TRAGEDY OF JACKSON POLLOCK, ARTIST

IVAN C. KARP

SEPTEMBER 26, 1956

To those who knew him, or only saw him during the months before his death, Jackson Pollock seemed like a formidable and defiant fortress that was being shattered by some dreadful calamity within.

Pollock, who generally drank a great deal, was sober, though fatigued, on the night of his violent death.* The road he traveled when his automobile crashed was the one most familiar to him the road to his home near East Hampton, Long Island.

We can only speculate whether the pain in him had come to the point where, driving at terrific speed, he had conceived a permanent release from the unrelenting pressure of his art. His last conversations, however, do not support this suggestion. They were, for Pollock, optimistic. He had expressed enthusiasm for his coming retrospective at the Museum of Modern Art. He was speaking of plans for an immediate course of work.

JACKSON POLLOCK was born in Cody, Wyoming, in 1912. He studied painting with Thomas Benton at the Art Students' League in {1930–32} but was, for the most part, self-taught. He is best known for works executed after the war, though his earlier paintings, which bear the influence of Picasso and of recent Mexican art, project the later directions by the concord of their excited surfaces with the calmer evolution of their forms. This agreement is apparent in *The Flame* (1937) and *Magic Mirror* (1941).

*contradicted by eye witnesses

43

The strangely mystical phenomenon of paint spilled and spattered by casual occurrence, so familiar to every artist's eye, was insistent in its call to Pollock. He had already harvested a lifetime of those mysterious and intriguing rhythms when, around 1943, once they had mellowed within him, he began to feed them to his canvases, directly out of the bucket.

NOTHING IN RESERVE

Pollock held nothing in reserve. In a sustained paroxysm of passion he poured his vision out of him, freeing a captive army of painters in the first attack and leaving behind on the now so celebrated battlefield his testimony to anti-painting, to originality in American art, and to the renunciation of aesthetic "hive life" by the artist.

The majority of the enlightened public quickly expressed, not shock, but an oddly disproportionate indignation. It might have disapproved or merely looked aside; instead, it was infuriated. Not because someone had finally tilted the paint can—this must have been anticipated—but because a painter had dared to shout, to bellow with all his resources, and from the summit of Art History, that what he had created, the subject matter itself, was the dynamics of the Mystery of Art.

ONE NOTABLE EXCEPTION

With the notable exception of Clement Greenberg, who was unswerving in praise and jubilation, critics and museum directors for years refused to grant Pollock his place, since in no comprehensible way did his astonishing canvases, which smiled on easel painting as we sometimes smile on antiques, merge with the acknowledged evolution of forms, with objects or landscape, with Cubism, Dadaism, or Mondrian. It seemed impossible for them to locate a basis for the usual historical allusions and tying-up of evidence. They failed utterly to recall Di Cosimo's fire or Da Vinci's *Deluge*, Turner's sunsets or the Catherine-Wheel convolutions of a Van Gogh sun or star. What appeared on those wide, unquiet spaces, bearing such titles as *Eyes in the Heat* and *Out of the Web* was Pollock's personal galaxy, the "spiral nebulae" of his own body, feelings, and sensibility, the ultimately unharassed confrontation of the painter and his material.

In the late '40s following the first assault, Pollock set off a series of small, sharp explosions, canvases in black and white describing animals, heads, and female forms, classical in their peculiar stateliness but never for a moment at rest. Then, in such works as *Convergence* and *Moon Vibrations*, color flowed again, impelled, as in a fit, by brush and palette knife, enfolding all that had previously passed in summary embrace. The American museums, critics, and public were, by that time, glowing and swelling with pride. Then Pollock stopped.

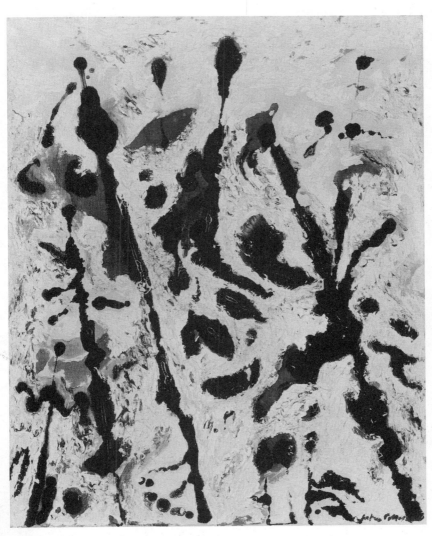

Jackson Pollock, *Moon Vibrations*, ca. 1953-55. Oil on canvas. 43 x 34 inches.
PRIVATE COLLECTION. PHOTO: POLLOCK-KRASNER STUDY CENTER,
JACKSON POLLOCK CATALOGUE RAISONNÉ ARCHIVES.

HE WAITED for a long time, but nothing happened. For two years he beckoned to the canvas, receiving only a meager response. He might have rested with his title secure, for it was enough to have severed the strangling grip of Europe and liberated the artists of an entire nation; it was enough to have made the younger painters of Europe turn, then seek, for the first time in history, across the Atlantic for direction and inspiration.

But Pollock's art, like all Expressionism, was essentially tragic. He continued the struggle, not to sustain his gesture of total commitment, but to surpass it, to put the very secret of his being on canvas, imploring us—and this is the meaning of the need to communicate in art—to join him in his ecstasy.

Turner had attempted this; so had Monet, Van Gogh. Ryder—Ryder who had said, for all of them, for Pollock too: "I am trying to find something out there beyond the place on which I have a footing."

JACKSON POLLOCK

B. H. FRIEDMAN

ORIGINALLY PUBLISHED IN *GUTAI #6*, 1
APRIL 1957 (JAPAN)

ALREADY the image of Jackson Pollock, the man, is fading. "The facts" are being distorted—equally by the sentimentality of friends and the viciousness of enemies. The apocryphists and mythologists are busy.

An honest biography of Jackson Pollock could be written in words—he wrote one of himself in paint. It reads like an existential parable ("existence precedes essence," "reality except in action," "total involvement"). And it is as painful to read as (for different reasons) Horton's life of Hart Crane. But the important thing is to go to his work.

Pollock's paintings are a visual record of acts, in a language more open, more frank, less tricked-up than that of any artist prior to his time. It is therefore all the more amazing that he (equals his work) should have been accused of painting deliberately difficult pictures. The real difficulty is that most of his detractors cannot face the honesty of the work, the inevitable, inseparable connection between his form and content. One need only look at last year's "15 Years" show at the Janis Gallery, or at the coming retrospective exhibition at the Museum of Modern Art, to be convinced that the techniques which Pollock invented represent neither originality for its own sake nor difficulty for its own sake, but rather originality, developed slowly and painfully, as the only means by which the artist could say what he had to say, as the only means by which he could make action and energy visible. Pollock's "abstractions" are "abstractions" of the creative act itself, of his own being. In this sense they are far less abstract than most representational pictures. Remember Blake's "If the doors of perception were cleansed, everything would appear to man as it is, infinite."

But the boys and girls with the slick magazines didn't want to look. They glanced. They weren't interested in freedom and self-determination, and they certainly weren't willing to accept the responsibility that goes with them. They were interested in the phenomena of the passing parade, the march of time. Pollock's painting was too big a pill for them to swallow. It didn't deaden the senses, like aspirin and Miltown. They choked on it. They just weren't used to a content that was basically democratic. How hard to think and feel as free people, when one's business is to condition thinking with slick formulas. And when you're dealing with the techniques of photographic illusion, when the angle of every shot is edited, it's also hard to accept an art in which there can be no tricks, in which every act is visible.

So they looked the other way (as they have with work which has similar implications—that of Clyfford Still, Willem de Kooning, Franz Kline, Mark Rothko). Or, if such painting did "reach" them, they saw its free, democratic, anti-totalitarian, anti-conformist implications, and that seemed as subversive as a red flannel suit.

Yes, Jackson Pollock was subversive as man-artist. It's half-true that he was violent and destructive, and that in the end he destroyed himself. The other half is in his tenderness and creativity. The ambivalence of his love, his passion, his being is clear enough *in his paintings*. In each of them, a balance is achieved between sudden violence or explosiveness and the delicate caressing web. The subconscious and the conscious connect, fuse—as they must in all great art, expressive of heightened awareness—as they do, for example, in Goya's *Capricios*, and in Picasso's *Guernica*. (Picasso assimilated the history of art—intellectually, programmatically. Pollock swallowed Picasso. And in Pollock's case it was that physical, that active, and in his most mature work it became that much his own.)

It is futile now to discuss what Jackson Pollock might have done if he had lived longer—as futile as the same kind of discussions about Shelley or Keats or Van Gogh or Seurat or Dylan Thomas. The important thing, as with those other artists who died young, is that he did what he did, that his concepts were given permanence and palpability, that to an unusual degree his being remains on canvas. The important thing is that when Jackson Pollock's body was buried one sad, sunny afternoon in Springs, Long Island, none of his paintings were buried with him.

JACKSON POLLOCK

SELDEN RODMAN

1957

"Painting is a state of being. . . ."

I ran into Jackson Pollock[1] less than a week after returning to New York from Taliesin West. There had been a party for Willem de Kooning, following the opening of his show at the Sidney Janis Gallery. The party was in a dive on 10th Street. By the time I arrived de Kooning had moved on, but among the stragglers I found Larry Rivers, Franz Kline, and Pollock. Kline said: "Everybody's gone to the Cedar Bar. Let's go." But Pollock wasn't going any-place. At least not yet. He was dancing. He had a battered brown fedora clamped over one eye, and his face was swollen and badly scratched.

I hadn't seen Pollock since a visit to his home in Springs, Long Island, about four years back, save for a brief encounter at the opening of Matta's show two years ago. On that occasion I had heard him mutter "Techni-color . . ." in his beard as he went out the door, leaving the thrill of redis-covery to Bernard Perlin and to me. I had heard rumors of the difficulties Pollock was having even four years ago, and they had been confirmed on my first visit to Springs. He had been trying to freshen or diversify his style by reintroducing figures, or at least figurative patterns, in the maze of paint. It was about the time de Kooning's "Woman" was attracting a lot of attention, de Kooning himself having momentarily abandoned the nonobjective for some pretty savage shafts directed at the feminine sex.

[1]This interview took place eight weeks before Pollock's tragic death in August 1956. I have not altered a word of it, believing that as it stands it would please him. I should also remind the reader that all allusions to Pollock by other artists in other sections of this book were made before Pollock's death.

Whether de Kooning diverged first, I don't know. It really doesn't Matta, as Ad Reinhardt, the abstract expressionist wit, would say. Pollock's trouble was stemming from the fact that the critics, having caught up with his weblike style after ten years of protest—at least having got used to it—resented the change. "At least Pollock was unique," they were saying in effect, "but now he begins to look like a hundred other abstractionists who can't make up their minds whether images are taboo or not."

Instead of taking this lag on the part of the critics in stride, Pollock is said to have brooded over it. Of course he had painted recognizable images before. When I first met him in the early thirties, he was a star pupil of the American regionalist Thomas Hart Benton, and could paint a thunderhead building up over a hayrick, or an ornery mule, with as realistic a flair as the crotchety Missourian. Then there was a period, just before the war, when Pollock had been on his own for the first time, but he had continued to paint from nature, only occasionally moving away from plant or animal forms to seek the complex attenuations he was later to popularize through abstraction, in some Bushmanlike hunter or pre-Columbian totem.

But the net result of his effort to reintroduce the figure four years ago is Pollock's present impasse. Talked out of his effort to move forward, he had too much integrity to move backward—or coast. For the decade between 1942 and 1952 he had been stupendously productive. The now-familiar patterns of streaked and dripped paint had become so sought after that he could have gone on producing and selling them indefinitely. But he refused to. For two years now he hasn't painted a picture.

Catching my eye at the 10th Street party, Pollock disengaged himself from his partner and came up to me. I had already been warned that my *Eye of Man*, with its strictures on contemporary formalism, might make me *persona non grata* at this affair. "Of course the painters won't have read it," my informant said, "but they'll all have read what Rosenberg and Hess have said about you in *Art News*."

"You—an art critic?" Pollock asked belligerently.

"Hell no," I said, "I'm just an 'aging anthologist'!"

He laughed and went back to his partner. "We'll talk about it later."

With David Smith I walked over to the Cedar Bar. De Kooning was there and ordered drinks for us. He insisted on paying for them, but Smith wouldn't let him. "Wait till you sell a painting, Bill." Smith hadn't been to the opening or heard that de Kooning's show was a complete sell-out. He himself had had a show of his sculpture recently at the Willard Gallery, the net result of which had been one piece *stolen*, and he was inveighing in his usual gruff, extremist but good-natured way against galleries, museums and collectors alike. I had heard that he had priced the sculptures himself, when Marion Willard was away—all of them high, and some over $5,000.

"According to Mrs. Willard, David," I said, "that was the only reason they hadn't been bought."

"According to me," he growled, "that was what they were worth, just figuring my time at a standard welder's-union hourly rate."

He was going to remove his things from the gallery tomorrow, he added. "No more galleries—ever! I'll sell them myself—or keep them. It doesn't matter which."

De Kooning looked sympathetic and ordered another round of drinks on the strength of that remark, but shook his head a little doubtfully. Half an hour later I started walking back home alone along 10th Street.

Just short of Astor Place I ran into Pollock, also alone, weaving his way toward the Cedar Bar. I was weaving by that time myself. He stopped me and asked where I'd been. To California and back, I told him.

"What did you see that was worth seeing?" he asked dubiously.

"On the last lap, the Pennsylvania barns," I replied.

He grunted. "Better than the houses, 'cause it was the livestock that really mattered." He reached out suddenly and grabbed a runt of a tree that was growing out of the sidewalk, pitiably supported by wire and bits of tire attached to stakes around it.

"What's the use of going further than this?" he muttered. "This tree's got everythin'. Leave it alone and it'll grow and grow an' be beautiful . . . No need to leave New York at all. . . . Thish tree's got everythin' . . . beautiful . . . beautiful!" And he drifted off into the moonlit fog of dawn, dropping a package of matches. I stooped over and picked it up. The words printed on it said: "There are good jobs for everyone in the telephone business."

About a month after this party, I called Pollock from Sag Harbor. Since he doesn't answer letters, I had no way of knowing whether he could be induced to talk for the record. He agreed; but a little while later I was out when his wife, Lee Krasner, called back and left a message for me: Jackson was not in a mood to see anyone; in his present frame of mind it wouldn't be good for him; call in the morning, but even then the chances will be poor. I decided to drive out next morning without further phone calls. When I arrived, Mrs. Pollock greeted me as though the phone talk had never taken place; Jackson was still in bed but she'd get him up. Meanwhile we had a second breakfast.

Lee Krasner is an abstract painter herself. I admired a mosaic table on the back porch and she told me it was her design. In the living room hung a very long panel by Pollock: a loosely composed but expressive head next to a dense tangle of black squiggles—impressive, like all Pollock's work, in a violent, compulsive way. The house is spacious inside, undistinguished from the exterior except for the back view of lovely meadows which roll

Jackson Pollock, *Portrait and a Dream*, 1953. Oil and enamel on canvas, 58 1/8 x 134 1/2 inches. DALLAS MUSEUM OF ART, GIFT OF MR. AND MRS. ALGUR H. MEADOWS AND MEADOWS FOUNDATION. PHOTO: HANS NAMUTH © ESTATE OF HANS NAMUTH.

away to a distant pond. Finally Pollock emerged, in nondescript blue slacks and a T-shirt, bearded and bleary-eyed, like a bear.

This simile, coming to my mind along with the memory of photographs of Dostoevsky and Rasputin, made me ask him, after our initial greeting, whether he was of Russian ancestry. He said no; he was Irish and Scotch–Irish, via Wyoming, on both sides. "I'm a Russian," his wife said; "at least, my parents were Russian Jews." But *she* looks strictly New England, like a character in Hawthorne or Edith Wharton. She told me that they had come to Springs originally for a brief visit in 1943, "when Hayter and the Surrealists were summering here," and that when they returned to their flat in the Village she had suggested renting or buying a house in Springs. "At first Jackson reacted against it violently—all his reactions are violent—but later the idea struck him (and with equal violence) as a good one. So we moved out that winter and bought the house and have been here ever since."

She had already told me that she and her husband were spending three days a week in New York with an analyst. "For me," she had said, "it's been extremely helpful, but Jackson is still resisting it—violently. This didn't cause the break in his tremendous productivity, though," she added. "That began two years ago." I was a little surprised when Pollock told me almost immediately of his forthcoming one-man show at the Museum of Modern Art; he seemed very pleased that they were doing it. "The idea scares me a little, though," he said.

He talks with difficulty, searching painfully, almost agonizingly, for the right word, with constant apologies "for not being verbal." The sincerity of the man is overwhelmingly apparent. He is uncouth and inarticulate and arrogant and very sure of his place in art and of the importance of the movement with which he is associated, but there is not a trace of showmanship or phoniness in his make-up. He is friendly and warm-hearted—though he resists showing it, and no doubt would like to be thought ruthless and without sentiment. In respect to his art, of course, he is; and this may be the tragic conflict that both makes his painting what it is and accounts for his inability to carry it further.

Having noticed Julian Levi's mailbox on one side of his house and Corrado Marca-Relli's on the other, I asked him whether he saw much of these artists. Levi might be called a neoromantic but Marca-Relli is an abstract expressionist, a painter of suggestive swirling figures reminiscent (but only in the fluidity of their forms) of de Kooning. Marca-Relli was a close friend, Pollock said. "Shall we walk over and see him?" We walked along the highway, a somewhat hazardous route, since he became involved in trying to tell me why none of the conventional labels fitted his own painting, and as he did so wandered off toward the center of the road—down which Sunday drivers were hitting 60—gesticulating and paying no attention to them at all except now and then to grab me by the elbow and say, "Look out! This road is dangerous!"

Marca-Relli, who was building an addition to his house, came to the door, and provided us immediately with cans of beer. His beard is black, and perhaps because it is much more luxuriant and curly than Pollock's brown one, gives him a more benevolent appearance. I told them that they reminded me of the Smith Brothers and that I'd like to photograph them together on the sofa, which was just big enough for two. I asked Pollock, meanwhile, to elaborate on this business of labels.

"I don't care for 'abstract expressionism,'" he said, "and it's certainly not 'nonobjective,' and not 'nonrepresentational' either. I'm very representational some of the time, and a little all of the time. But when you're painting out of your unconscious, figures are bound to emerge. We're all of us influenced by Freud, I guess. I've been a Jungian for a long time."

"When you start a picture," I asked him, "do you have any preconceived visual image in mind, or is the result wholly spontaneous, something that happens in the process of painting?"

When Pollock prepares to answer, he squints, screws up his face, tilts it to one side. "How do I know? I have and I haven't. Something in me knows where I'm going, and—well, painting is a state of being."

"You mean 'being' and 'becoming' are one?"

"Exactly—I guess."

"I don't blame you for guessing," I laughed. "I'm not sure what I mean myself."

53

Jackson Pollock and Conrad (Corrado) Marca-Relli, Springs, 1956.
PHOTOGRAPHER UNKNOWN. POLLOCK-KRASNER STUDY CENTER, JEFFREY POTTER COLLECTION.

"No. This is what I'm trying to get at. Painting is self-discovery. Every good artist paints what he is."

"I'm painting figures—human relations, if you like," Marca-Relli said, "in most of my pictures."

"But you're not communicating anything about specific people, are you?" I said, "—or their relation to the world?"

"Not in the sense Shahn and Levine are," he said, "if that's what you mean. But I hope I am communicating my emotion and my feeling about the world, both of which involve people."

"Whereas they—?"

"Are illustrators. Shahn is a great illustrator, at least he was in such work as the Sacco–Vanzetti series, which I admire very much. But it isn't painting. Painting, even in times when the artist was preoccupied with reproducing aspects of the visual world accurately, was something else again. Take Uccello's battle pieces. What makes them great painting is not what Uccello has to say about any specific battle or personages involved in them, but the excitement of what goes on in the picture in terms of images and their juxtapositions and *paint*. With the realists of today, nothing *happens* beyond the story they are telling. The surface isn't alive. It's not *today*."

"Then you think it's impossible," I asked him, "to achieve this kind of visual excitement in our time by manipulating the objective data and the people we know in any kind of a recognizable form?"

"It's a different age we live in. It's an age of indeterminacy, perhaps. Morals are indeterminate compared with other times. You don't call a thing or a person 'good' or 'bad' the way you could once. We know there's good and bad in everyone. This indeterminacy comes out in our painting. Perhaps it's why we're not interested in making portraits. That would be too precise a statement to lend itself to painting as we practice it."

Pollock nodded his head and seemed to go along with this. He did add that when you try to emulate the old masters, as Benton, Grant Wood, and Curry had, and more recently painters like Levine and Tooker, "yes, and Larry Rivers—you get corn, real corn. Bits of Renaissance pastiche are still bits of Renaissance pastiche, no matter how blurred you make them."

I told them of my debate with Jules Langsner of *Art News* at UCLA, and of how his statement that you couldn't paint like Rembrandt in an age of fragmented forms and atomic destruction had made me ask whether Rembrandt's themes—birth, love, humility, compassion, old age, death, etc—were any less concerns of life today. I asked Marca-Relli whether, for example, he was moved by the compassion expressed in Rembrandt's *Prodigal Son*.

"We may feel compassion in it," he said, "but did Rembrandt's contemporaries? Probably they didn't go for it at all. We don't know what Rembrandt felt. And we don't know what emotions people in the future will read into our paintings either."

They asked me whom I had interviewed recently, and when I mentioned Wright and Philip Johnson, Pollock remarked that both architects hated painting. "What's Johnson got in that glass house of his? One painting, a Poussin—if it is a Poussin. And as for Wright, he's a great architect, I guess, but what a ——! That museum! We've had all this trouble in doing away with the frame—and now this. Paintings don't need all this fooling around. The hell with museums! Put the paintings in a room and look at 'em—isn't that enough? You remember that old building where the Museum of Modern Art started? What was wrong with that? I was in a house designed by Mies once; I felt so taut I couldn't say anything."

We were all supposed to meet on the beach but couldn't find each other. I drove back to Springs late in the afternoon to say goodbye, this time accompanied by my wife Maia, who had been at the beach in the morning with the children. The Pollocks insisted we stay for a drink.

"Do you know Katherine Kuh?" Pollock asked me.

I said I did, and that I'd seen her in Chicago a month ago when she was assembling the Biennale show for Venice entitled "American Artists Paint the City," in which he and Marca-Relli had been included.

"What a ridiculous idea," he said, "expressing the city—never did it in my life!"

"I don't think it's so ridiculous," I said. "Aren't you all doing it—consciously or unconsciously? I feel it in your painting, and in Kline's and Bill de Kooning's, not to mention artists like Tobey and Hedda Sterne and O'Keefe, who admittedly are doing it. What are you expressing, if you're not expressing the turbulence of city life—or your reaction to it?"

He thought hard, grimacing with the effort. "Nothing so specific . . . My times and my relation to them . . . No. Maybe not even that. The important thing is that Cliff Still—you know his work?—and Rothko, and I—we've changed the nature of painting."

"You leave out de Kooning?"

"I don't mean there aren't any other good painters. Bill is a good painter but he's a *French* painter. I told him so, the last time I saw him, after his last show. You were there at that party, weren't you?"

"French?" I said.

"You know what French painting is. If you don't, you won't see what I mean. All those pictures in his last show start with an image. You can see it even though he's covered it up, or tried to."

"Why does he cover it up?"

"Style—that's the French part of it. He has to cover it up with style. But why do I say this to you? You're against all this kind of painting, aren't you?"

"I'm against making a cult or a dogma out of it. I'm against ruling out other ways of painting as Hess does in *Art News*. That's what I was trying to say in *The Eye of Man*."

"I'm with you there. None of the art magazines are worth anything. Nobody takes them seriously. They're a bunch of snobs. Hess is scared—scared of being wrong. I hate to admit it, but I prefer the approach of *Time*. I'd rather have one of my pictures reproduced in *Collier's* or *The Saturday Evening Post* than in any of the art magazines. At least you'd know where you stand. They don't pretend to like our work."

"But to come back to 'French' painting," I said.

"Come out to the studio," he said, "and maybe I can show you what I mean."

Maia and I went out with him while the children drifted off into the field picking daisies. The studio was padlocked and he searched frantically in his pockets. No key. We waited while he went back into the house. In about five minutes he returned, shaking his head. "Lee hasn't got one either. There just isn't any key," he smiled wryly. "There's something for the analyst!" he said. "The painter locks himself out of his own studio. And then has to break in like a thief."

Before we could stop him he had smashed a pane of glass.

"Couldn't we force the window?" I said.

He tried, but without success. There were wedges nailed in from the inside.

"Damn!" With his elbow he smashed another pane, and then another, tearing away the wooden strips between them. "Wait. I'll get a hammer and really go to work on this." He ran back to the house while we collected the splintered glass in a pile. Returning with the hammer, he finally managed to raise the lower half of the window and, shoving a table covered with dusty sketches out of the way, stepped in. We followed him. The main studio was an extraordinary sight. Huge paintings, some of them twenty or more feet long, demonstrated clearly enough what he had meant. They weren't French, or even American. They were simply Pollock. Paint laced, slashed, or dripped on canvas after canvas, but always arrestingly, authoritatively, as only he can do it: undeniably the expression of a tormented but vital personality. Even the patterns of paint on the floor itself, where lines and drops of pigment had spilled over from the edges of the recumbent canvases, were recognizably "Pollock."

I asked him how he got the effect of a powdery white line that crisscrossed one brown-and-black canvas dazzlingly.

"Don't tell him," Maia said. "It's a professional secret, and if you tell him he'll start doing it!"

"I couldn't tell him if I wanted to," Pollock said. "I don't know."

Probably he knew very well. At any rate, the stacks of drawings, going back into the thirties, indicated beyond contention that Pollock can draw fluently from nature, or in the realm of nature-derived fantasy, if he wants to.

As we were going out he lifted from the rubble a massive toy locomotive, three feet long, very cunningly made out of iron, but badly rusted. He had found it in a field nearby and wanted us to take it for the children. It was clear that he wanted children, and it was clear that he thought a good deal of the locomotive, and Maia declined it on these grounds.

"I never give away anything unless I love it," he said.

"I'll send you something I feel that way about when I get back," I said. "One of my daughter's paintings, for instance."

"I hate paintings," he said.

As we walked toward the window to climb out, he took a look back into that lair of creative devastation.

"These paintings, the ones I've kept, are my securities. They're all I've got left." He leaned out the window and looked at the view of the distant pond.

"Painting is my whole life. . . ."

A SHY AND TURBULENT MAN
who became a myth

DORTHY SEIBERLING *LIFE* ART EDITOR

NOVEMBER 9, 1959

Even before his death Jackson Pollock had become a myth. With his radical painting style and his unruly way of life, he appeared to be a kind of broncobuster of the art world. When he sped to his death in his second-hand convertible, people said he was "living up" to the myth, a reckless, restless rebel to the end.

Like most myths, the myth of Pollock both simplified and exaggerated the man. Though he threw tradition overboard in his own art, he revered old masters like Rembrandt and spent hours copying Rubens or studying Goya. Though given sometimes to surliness and brawling, Pollock was also a man of gentleness and serenity who liked to garden, chat with the neighbors, and ramble through the woods with his dogs. He was both confident and full of doubt, a down-to-earth Westerner with mystical leanings.

As a child, Pollock had restlessness forced upon him. His father, an inveterate rover, tried his hand at ranching, farming, and inn-keeping all around the West. The youngest of five sons, Jackson worked as a farmhand, milking cows, plowing, cutting alfalfa. With his brothers he explored the rivers and hills and haunted the ancient Indian mounds where the boys staged lively battles, using arrowheads and pottery fragments for ammunition.

Around 1925 Pollock's father took a job as a surveyor and the family moved to Riverside, California. Jackson rebelled against the local school program of football and ROTC and eventually shifted to Manual Arts High School in nearby Los Angeles where he concentrated on sculpture and painting.

In 1930, encouraged by his brother Charles who himself had gone east to study art with Thomas Benton, Pollock moved to New York. To pay for his classes at the Art Students League he worked as a busboy and dishwasher. He also got a job as janitor of a Greenwich Village school which, for $10 a week, he conscientiously cleaned every night, swabbing it down on Fridays. When his brother Sanford came to New York to study painting, they shared the job as well as a loft on Houston Street. (Sanford has since abandoned art but Charles is now an abstract painter, teaching at Michigan State University.)

At art school Pollock created conflicting impressions. Benton considered him "a very fine colorist but not an exceptional student. With anatomy and perspective, he was out of his field. He was incapable of drawing logical sequences. He couldn't be taught anything." His fellow students, on the other hand, were stunned by his drawings. "They were so individual," one of them recalls. "They had tremendous energy. Everyone talked about them." Charles remembers him as a "terrific worker. He turned out a fantastic amount of stuff and it didn't come easy. Jack had none of the facile ability that so many students have. What he had instead was a kind of drive, a fierce intensity."

After leaving Benton, Pollock worked for several years as an easel painter on the WPA art project. Later he supported himself as a museum handyman. In 1941 his work came to the attention of a New York gallery which invited him and two other young painters to exhibit. One of the painters was Willem de Kooning. The other was a young woman named Lee Krasner who became Pollock's most enthusiastic booster and eventually his wife.

In 1943 Pollock was introduced to Peggy Guggenheim, a wealthy avant-garde dealer who took such a liking to his art that she gave him a show, a mural commission, and $150 a month for the next four years. With this security, Pollock and his wife bought a dilapidated house in a little Long Island community called The Springs. Pollock threw himself into restoring the house, tearing out walls, plastering and repainting interiors. Unable to afford a car, the Pollocks rode bicycles everywhere. In 1947 their slim stipend was cut off when Peggy Guggenheim moved to Italy and for the next couple of years they survived on the sale of a handful of paintings.

In spite of the rigors of making ends meet, Pollock was at a peak of creativity. Starting work in the afternoon, he would stay in his studio far into the night, furiously "pouring out" his complex compositions. After several months he would stop painting to recharge himself. During these non-painting periods he gardened, went clamming, frequented local bars, or stayed home and listened to records. An addict of jazz, he sometimes kept the same record playing for a week, generally at full volume. Though usually shy and taciturn, he liked to chin with the local workmen or drop in at the general store to talk politics with the proprietor, Dan Miller. Impressed by Pollock's "sincerity," Miller bought one of his paintings. (He has since sold the picture at seven times the original price.) Pollock himself contributed paintings as well as another of his creative specialties, apple pie, to be auctioned off at annual village benefits.

By 1950 Pollock began to be a celebrated, if controversial, figure in the art world. He sold a dozen paintings to museums and collectors across the country and a coterie of admirers sprang up around him. As his acclaim and income grew, Pollock fell more and more into a state of depression and unease. An off-and-on drinker since he was 18, he plunged into prolonged bouts of drunkenness. In an effort to stay on the wagon, he took up with a health faddist who put him on a diet of raw vegetables and a mysterious protein emulsion, which Pollock often carried around with him to bars. Later he turned to a psychoanalyst, but his anguished mood hung on. Alone in his studio he continued to draw and, spasmodically, to paint, but he would seldom discuss his work with anyone.

In the summer of 1956 Pollock seemed to be putting his house in order, weeding out drawings, occasionally jotting down on paper new ideas for paintings. But at the age of 44 he appeared exhausted from hard living and from the doubts and conflicts raging within him. The night of his accident he was on his way to a concert when, in a wave of fatigue, he decided to go back home. Speeding along the road, he hit a hump, was thrown from the car and killed. His neighbors said it was an accident that could have happened to anybody. Others felt it was inevitable. "He was born with too big an engine inside him," said a friend. "He had to paint to survive. And he had stopped painting."

LEE KRASNER POLLOCK: Statement

Typescript in the Lee Krasner Papers, Archives of American Art, Smithsonian Institution, Reel 3048. This material forms the basis of "Who Was Jackson Pollock?" an article by Francine du Plessix and Cleve Gray, *Art in America*, May–June 1967.

- Insertions for clarity are in [standard] brackets.
- Factual corrections are in {ogee} brackets.

LEE KRASNER POLLOCK

MAY-JUNE 1967

IN a letter of 1929 written from Los Angeles, where Jackson was in Manual Arts High School, Jackson told his brother Sande that people terrified and bored him, that they frightened him and that he could not communicate with them.

Jackson faced his problems. You know, I have so many myths about him to fight, I feel I must at last speak up. The drinking was something we faced all the time; wouldn't I be foolish if I didn't talk about it. No one was more conscious about it than he was. Jackson tried everything to stop drinking, all his life—medical treatments, analysis, chemistry, everything. In the late 1940s he went to a Dr. Heller, a general practitioner who had been successful with alcoholics. He was the first man who was really able to stop Jackson drinking. From 1948 to 1950 Jackson did not touch alcohol. I often asked him what Dr. Heller did, when he saw him every week at the East Hampton medical clinic. Apparently they just talked. Once when I asked him about Dr. Heller, Jackson said to me, "He is an honest man, I can believe him."

He never drank while he worked. You know, he worked in cycles. There would be long stretches of work and then times when he did not work. He drank before and after these stretches. Dr. Heller got killed in an automobile accident—just like Jackson—in 1950, and when Jackson took to drink again later that year there was no Heller to go to.

I remember the day I went to his studio for the first time. It was late '41. I went because we had both been invited by John Graham to show in the McMillen Gallery in January '42. I wanted to meet this artist I had never heard about. Actually we had met about four years before, we had danced together at an {Artists Union} party. But I had forgotten about that first

61

The building at 46 East 8th Street in Manhattan where Jackson Pollock lived from 1935-1945. He shared the fifth floor walkup with his brother Sande and Sande's wife Arloie, and later with Lee Krasner. Pollock's studio room, about eighteen feet square, enjoyed north light from the three windows at the front of the top floor. The buildiing has been demolished.

meeting. When he was invited to the McMillen show I was astonished because I thought I knew all the abstract artists in New York. You know, in those days, one knew everyone. Well, I was in a rage at myself, simply furious because here was a name that meant nothing to me. All the more furious because he was living on 8th Street, just two blocks down from me. He and his brother Sande and Sande's wife had the top floor; each had half. As I came in, Sande was standing at the top of the stairs, I asked for Jackson Pollock, and he said "You can try knocking over there, but I don't know if he's in." I later found out from Sande that it was most unusual for Jackson to answer. When I knocked, he opened. I introduced myself and said we were both showing in the same show. I walked right in.

What did I think? I was overwhelmed, bowled over that's all. I saw all those marvelous paintings, I felt as if the floor was sinking when I saw those paintings. How could there be a painter like that that I didn't know about? I must have made several remarks on how I felt about the paintings. I remember remarking on one, and he said "Oh I'm not sure I'm finished with that one." I said, "Don't touch it." Of course I don't know whether he did or not.

He was not a big man, but he gave the impression of being big. About five feet eleven—average—big-boned, heavy. His hands were fantastic, powerful hands, I wish there were photographs of his hands. All told he was physically powerful. And this ran through from the first time I met him until the day he died when there was quite a change in his physical appearance.

He was not in the war at the time I met him because he had been classified 4-F. He had been in Bloomingdale's [the Westchester Division of New York Hospital] for {three} months when he was {26} years old. And the alcoholic problem had been with him all his life. One morning before we were married Sande knocked on my door and asked "Did Jackson spend the night here last night?" I answered "No. Why?"

"Because he's in Bellevue Hospital and our mother has arrived to New York. Will you go with me and get him?" We went and there he was in the Bellevue ward. He looked awful. He had been drinking for days. I said to him "Is this the best hotel you can find?" At Sande's suggestion I took him back to my place and fed him milk and eggs to be in shape for dinner that night with Mother. We went together. It was my first meeting with Mother. I was overpowered with her cooking. I had never seen such a spread as she put on. She had cooked all the dinner, baked the bread, the abundance of it was fabulous. I thought Mama was a peach. Later I said to Jackson "You're off your rocker, she's sweet, nice." It took a long time for me to realize how difficult she was. You see, at that time I never connected the episode of Jackson's drinking with his mother's arrival. And around then Mother moved out to Connecticut with Sande and his family so we didn't really see that much of her. I hadn't yet seen anything of the hard female.

When we were married Jackson wanted a church wedding; not me. *He* wanted it and he had it. Jackson's mother was anti-religious, that's a fact. Violently anti-religious. I felt that Jackson, from many things he did, felt a great loss there. He was tending more and more to religion. I felt that went back to his mother's lack of it. You know in high school he used to listen to Krishnamurti's lectures.

If I conjure up the gentle part of Jackson, that was one part. But there was the other part, the other extreme, the violent part. Both of them existed in extremes. But Jackson's violence was all verbal. There never was any physical violence. He would just use more four-letter words than usual. Or he would take it out on the furniture. The night that he and Hans Namuth finished the film they were making we had a party. That afternoon Jackson had just started to drink again, after his two years on the wagon. We were having dinner at our long table, Jackson and Hans were at the other end. I don't know what the argument was about, but I heard loud voices and suddenly Jackson overturned the whole table with twelve roast beef dinners. It was a mess. I said: "Coffee will be served in the living-room." Everyone filed out and Jackson went off without any trouble. Jeff Potter and I cleaned up.

I will tell you a story about de Kooning. Jackson and he were standing at the Cedar Bar, drinking. They started to argue and de Kooning said something very nasty to him. There was a crowd around them and some of the fellows tried to egg Jackson on to hit de Kooning. Jackson turned to them and said: "What me? Hit an artist?" He was *not* violent. Angry, yes. Bitter, yes. Impatient, yes. Not violent.

This is how we got to live in Springs: We had friends, the Kadishes, who rented a house out there in the summer of '45. They invited us to spend a weekend with them. Jackson loved city life. I was the one who had an aspiration to live in the country. At the end of that weekend I said to Jackson: "How about us looking for a place to rent and moving out there? We can rent that house we saw for $40 [a month], and sublet our own place." He thought it was a terrible idea. But I remember that when we got back to 8th Street he spent three days stretched out on the couch just thinking. Then on Friday he leaped up and said "Lee, we're going to buy a house in Springs and move out!" Well of course we didn't even have the forty dollars to pay rent, not to speak of *buying* a house, so I said "Jackson, have you gone out of your mind?" His answer was: "Lee, you're always the one who's saying I shouldn't let myself worry about the money. We'll just go ahead and do it." We went back to Springs. The house we wanted had just been sold so, we asked the agent to see what else there was. He showed us a place we liked. The price was $5,000. We could get a $3,000 mortgage and had to raise $2,000 in cash. I went to Peggy Guggenheim but she wouldn't consider a loan and said sarcastically: "Why don't you go to ask [rival dealer] Sam Kootz?" I went to see Kootz, and he agreed to lend us the money but only with the understanding that Jackson would come over to his gallery. When I got back to Peggy's and told her what Kootz had said, she exploded. "How could you do such a thing and with Kootz of all people! Over my dead body you'll go to Kootz." I said "But Peggy it was your idea to ask Kootz." Well, we eventually reached an agreement by means of which Peggy lent us the $2,000. She did this by raising Jackson's monthly fee to $300, deducting $50 a month to repay the loan and having rights to all of Jackson's output for the next {two} years. This, incidentally, was the agreement which gave rise to her recent lawsuit against me.

I think that living in Springs allowed Jackson to work. He needed the peace and quite of a country life. He would have destroyed himself even earlier if he had stayed in the city.

The first two years we lived in Springs we had no car. Later Jackson got a Model A, but in the beginning we had to bicycle to do all errands; that would take a good part of the day.

He always slept very late. Drinking or not, he never got up in the morning. He could sleep twelve, fourteen hours around the clock. We'd always talk about his insane guilt about sleeping late. Morning was my best time for work, so I would be in my studio when I heard him stirring around. I would go back, and while he had his breakfast I had my lunch. His breakfast would not set him up and make him bolt from the table like most people. He would sit over that damn cup of coffee for two hours. By that time it was afternoon. He'd get off and work until it was dark. There were no lights in his studio. When the days were short he could only work for a few hours, but what he managed to do in those few hours was incredible. We had an agreement that neither of us would go into the other's studio without being asked. Occasionally, it was something like once a week, he would say: "I have something to show you." I would always be astonished by the amount of work that he had accomplished. In discussing the paintings, he would ask "Does it work?" Or in looking at mine, he would comment "It works" or "it doesn't work." He may have been the first artist to use the word "work" in that sense. There was no heat in his studio either, but he would manage in winter if he wanted to; he would get dressed up in an outfit the like of which you've never seen.

He often said: "There's no problem painting at all; the problem is what to do when you're not painting."

In the afternoon, if he wasn't working, we might bicycle to town. Or when we had a car he would drive me to town and sit and wait in the car for me while I shopped. When he was working, he would go to town when the light gave out and get a few cartons of beer to bring home. Of course, during those two years he was on the wagon, he didn't touch beer either. We would often drive out in the old Model A and get out and walk. Or we

Jackson Pollock, *Birth*,
ca. 1941. Oil on
canvas, 45 13/16 x
21 11/16 inches. Tate
Gallery, London,
purchase.

would sit on the stoop for hours and not say a word. We hardly ever had art talk. Perhaps some shop talk, but never art gossip like who's going to what gallery.

One thing I will say about Pollock: the one time I saw temperament in him was when he baked an apple pie, and it didn't work. Or when he tried to take a photograph. He never showed any artistic temperament. He loved to bake, I did the cooking, and he did the baking when he felt like it. He was very fastidious about his baking—marvelous bread, cakes, and pies. He also made a great spaghetti sauce.

He loved machinery, so he got a lawn mower. We made an agreement about the garden when he said: "I'll dig it and set it out if you'll water and weed." He took great pride in the house. One of the reasons for our move to Springs was that Jackson wanted to do sculpture. You know, it was his original interest in high school and art school. He often said: "One of these days I'll get back to sculpture." There was a large junk pile of iron in the backyard that he expected to use.

East view, Pollock-Krasner House, 1946. PHOTO: RONALD J. STEIN.

He would get into grooves of listening to his jazz records—not just for days—day and night, day and night for three days running until you thought you would climb the roof! The house would *shake*. Jazz? He thought it was the only other really creative thing happening in this country. He had a passion for music without being really musical. He had trouble carrying a tune and although he loved to dance he was an awkward dancer. He told me that when he was a boy he bought himself a violin expecting to play on it immediately. When he couldn't get a sound out of it he smashed it in a rage.

He was secure in his work. In *that* he was sure of himself. But I can't say he was a happy man. There were times when he was happy of course. He loved his house, he loved to fool in his garden, he loved to go out and look at the dunes, the gulls. He would talk house to Dan Miller, the grocery store owner, he would drink with the plumber or the electrician, those kind of off-beat friends. But he would rarely talk with artists.

It is a myth that he wasn't verbal. He could be hideously verbal when he wanted to be. Ask the people he really talked to: Tony Smith and me. He was lucid, intelligent; it was simply that he didn't want to talk art. If he was quiet, it was because he didn't believe in talking, he believed in *doing*.

There is a story related to this about Hans Hofmann. It was terribly embarrassing to me, because I brought Hofmann to see Pollock. Hofmann spent all the time *talking* about art. Finally Pollock couldn't stand it any longer and said "Put up or shut up!" He meant: "I'm not interested in your *theories*, you've got to make the *paintings*." He had a fanatical conviction that the *work* would do it, not any outside periphery like *talk*.

There is so much stupid myth about Pollock, I can't stand it!

There is the myth of suicide. There is no truth in this. It was an automobile accident like many others. That was a dangerous part of the road; just a while before someone else was killed on that part of the road. The state highway department had to fix it soon after Jackson's death. That speaks for itself.

I'm bored with these myths. Jackson was damn decent to his friends no matter what the situation was. He saw few people; he didn't have a lot of friends. He was not interested in contemporary artists' work, but as it turned out, most of the people he saw had a connection with the arts. Among those who recognized Pollock's work, John Graham preceded everybody. One night when we were walking with John, we saw a little man in a long overcoat; it was [the architect Frederick] Kiesler. John introduced Pollock by saying: "I want you to meet the greatest painter in America." Kiesler bowed low to the ground. Jim Sweeney was the first to go into print for Pollock. It was a fine article, but in it he called Jackson "undisciplined." Jackson got furious. Oh, he was angry, really mad, and he painted a picture, "Search for a Symbol," just to show Sweeney how disciplined he was. He brought the wet painting to the gallery where he was meeting Jim Sweeney and said, "I want you to see a really disciplined painting."

Herbert and Mercedes Matter brought Sandy Calder to see Jackson in '42. After looking at the paintings, Sandy said: "They're all so *dense*." He meant that there was no space in them. Jackson answered "Oh you want to see one less dense, one with open space?" And he went back for a painting and came out with the densest of all. That's the way he could be.

But he had a deep understanding of his friends. One day I asked him "Why is Jim Brooks so terrified of you when you are drunk?" Jackson explained sympathetically to me why Jim might be reacting that way. When I would speak to him about my own troubles with his drinking he would say "Yes I know it's rough on you. But I can't say I'll stop, because you know I'm trying to. But try to think of it as a storm. It'll be over sooner or later."

Jackson Pollock, Lee Krasner (with cow pelvis mask) and unidentified friend, Springs, ca. 1955.
POLLOCK-KRASNER STUDY CENTER, JEFFREY POTTER COLLECTION.

EXCERPTS OF AN INTERVIEW
with Lee Krasner

EMILY WASSERMAN,

JULY 8, 1968

E W: When you met Pollock, what was his attitude toward European painting—what was he thinking and talking about with you?

L K: When I first met him, we didn't discuss painting . . . This starts to take place as we know each other. And his response, to my knowledge (I think he makes this comment on it someplace himself) is that the only two painters who interest him—I believe it's Miró and Picasso—have never been to this country. And I remember him having the latest publication of Picasso, whether it was *Cahiers d'Art* or what, I don't know, thumbing through it and going into a total rage about it, and saying, "That bastard, he misses *nothing*!"

E W: What was his reaction to your work when he first saw it?

L K: Very sympathetic.

E W: Did he in any way criticize you, or give you suggestions?

L K: No, he did not criticize. He simply did this; I'll relate one episode here. This is while I'm in my Ninth Street studio, and we meet, and he's on Eighth Street, and he comes to see me a good deal. I was out one afternoon, and I came in and [looked at] the painting I had on the easel—that I was working, you know—and I said, "That's not my painting," and then the second reaction was, he had worked on it. And in a total rage, I slashed the canvas. I wished to hell I had never done it, but . . . I guess I didn't speak to him for some two months, and then we got through that.

E W: Did you ever talk about each other's work?

L K: To this extent, we did. Let's say, he would come back from the studio, and I'd say, "How did it go?" or something like that, and I'd either get a shrug of the shoulder or there'd be something like, "Come in, I want you to see what I've just done." When I asked him to come to my studio and look at the work, I must say I had to ask him many more times before he responded, than when he asked me. He would come up and speak specifically about the painting in front of him.

E W: In what way?

Lee Krasner, Untitled, 1941. Oil on canvas, 40 x 36 inches. Whereabouts unknown, presumed destroyed. THIS PAINTING WAS INCLUDED IN JOHN GRAHAM'S EXHIBITION, "AMERICAN AND FRENCH PAINTINGS," MCMILLEN GALLERY, NEW YORK, 20 JANURAY-6 FEBRUARY 1942. PHOTO: POLLOCK-KRASNER STUDY CENTER, LEE KRASNER CATALOGUE RAISONNÉ ARCHIVES.

L K: Generally, I would preface it with a big bellyache about something: "I want you to come up and look at what I've done, it's bothering me like hell, because . . ." and then I'd list what was bothering me. And when he'd come into the studio, he'd say something like, "Oh, forget all that, and just keep painting, it's a lot of rot!" So it never went into a so-called formal talk on painting.

E W: What did you gain from each other by looking at each other's paintings, or even talking about them on the level you've explained?

L K: Well, you see, I can say what I gained from Pollock, but it's very difficult for me to say what Pollock could or could not have gained from me. I know only one factor in that respect, and that is that he did keep saying, "Come and look, what do you think?" I mean, that was a constant. So I take it that some part of my response was essential, you know. But the complexity here is because we didn't talk formally about art, so that I would never be in a position to say what he got from me . . . When we met, I responded to his work with wild enthusiasm; he did not respond to my work with wild enthusiasm. He did, however, *respond* to my work. As I get to know Pollock, later on, there isn't very much in painting he responds to with wild enthusiasm, so I'd say his response to my work was pretty good, when I look back on the entire scene. That is, let's say he came to my studio, looked at [the work], and made it clear he thought it was a dud—I don't know if a relationship would have followed.

Excerpt From *OUT OF THIS CENTURY*

PEGGY GUGGENHEIM

1980

WHEN I first exhibited Pollock he was very much under the influence of the Surrealists and of Picasso. But he very soon overcame this influence, to become, strangely enough, the greatest painter since Picasso. As he required a fixed monthly sum in order to work in peace, I gave him a contract for one year. I promised him a hundred and fifty dollars a month and a settlement at the end of the year, if I sold more than two thousand seven hundred dollars' worth, allowing one-third to the gallery. If I lost I was to get pictures in return.

Pollock immediately became the central point of Art of This Century. From then on, 1943, until I left America in 1947, I dedicated my self to Pollock. He was very fortunate, because his wife Lee Krasner, a painter, did the same, and even gave up painting at one period, as he required her complete devotion. I welcomed a new protégé, as I had lost Max [Ernst, my husband]. My relationship with Pollock was purely that of artist and patron, and Lee was the intermediary. Pollock himself was rather difficult; he drank too much and became so unpleasant, one might say devilish, on these occasions. But as Lee pointed out when I complained, "He also has an angelic side," and that was true. He was like a trapped animal who never should have left Wyoming, where he was born.

As I had to find a hundred and fifty dollars a month for the Pollocks, I concentrated all my efforts on selling his pictures and neglected all the other painters in the gallery, many of whom soon left me, as Sam Kootz, the art dealer, gave them contracts, which I could not afford to do.

I felt Pollock had a deep feeling for West American–Indian sculpture, as it came out a lot in his earlier paintings, and in some of those that were to be

73

Peggy Guggenheim with Jackson Pollock in the foyer of her New York town house, ca. 1944.
Photo: Mirko Lion. POLLOCK-KRASNER STUDY CENTER, JACKSON POLLOCK CATALOGUE RAISONNÉ ARCHIVES.

in his first exhibition. This was held in November 1943. The introduction
to the catalogue was written by James Johnson Sweeny, who helped a lot to
further Pollock's career. In fact, I always referred to Pollock as our spiritual
offspring. Clement Greenberg, the critic, also came to the fore and championed Pollock as the greatest painter of our time. Alfred Barr bought the
She Wolf, one of the best paintings in this show, for the Museum of Modern
Art. Later, Dr. Morley asked for the show in her San Francisco Museum [of
Modern Art], and bought the *Guardians of the Secret.*

We did not sell many Pollock paintings, but when he gave us gouaches
it was much easier. A lot of these I gave away as wedding presents to my

friends. I worked hard to interest people in his work and never tired [of] doing so, even when it involved dragging in and out his enormous canvases. One day Mrs. Harry Winston, the famous Detroit collector, came to the gallery to buy a Masson. I persuaded her to buy a Pollock instead.

In 1945, Bill Davis, the collector, who was also a fan of Pollock's, advised me to raise my contract with him to three hundred dollars a month, and in exchange, to take all Pollock's works. Pollock was very generous in giving me presents. At this time I had acute infectious mononucleosis, and during the annual Pollock show had to stay in bed. This distressed Lee Pollock very much, as she said no one could sell anything in the gallery except me, and [my assistant, Howard] Putzel had left to set up his own gallery in New York. Poor man, this proved to be a great tragedy, as it ended in his suicide.

Lee was so dedicated to Pollock that when I was sick in bed, she came every morning to try to persuade me to lend them two thousand dollars to buy a house on Long Island. She thought that if Pollock got out of New York he would stop drinking. Though I did not see how I could produce any extra funds I finally agreed to do so as it was the only way to get rid of Lee. Now it all makes me laugh. I had no idea then what Pollock paintings would be worth. I never sold one for more than a thousand dollars and when I left America in 1947, not one gallery would take over my contract [with Pollock]. I offered it to them all, and in the end Betty, of the Betty Parsons Gallery, said she would give Pollock a show, but that was all she could do. Pollock himself paid the expenses of it out of one painting Bill Davis bought. All the rest were sent to me, according to the contract, at Venice, where I had gone to live. Of course, Lee had her pick of one painting a year. When the pictures got to Venice, I gave them away one by one to various museums, and now only have two of this collection left, though I also have nine earlier ones dating from 1943 to 1946. And so now Lee is a millionaire, and I think what a fool I was.

"SCENES FROM A MARRIAGE: Krasner and Pollock"

GRACE GLUECK

DECEMBER 1981

THE photographs of that period—1942 to 1956—show them in warm communion: Lee gazing quizzically at Jackson as she sits on the floor of his studio; Lee and Jackson smiling across a bouquet of daisies; Lee and Jackson taking a country walk on a winter's day. It was, it might be inferred from the snapshots, one of those idyllic partnerships: artist married to artist, sharing their lives and work, each with a deep and caring interest in the other's career.

"It wasn't a student–teacher relationship, but a relationship of equals," says Krasner today, ensconced in an armchair at her comfortable apartment on New York's upper East Side. "In the beginning, I was much more interested in what he was doing than in what I was doing, which was in the Hans Hofmann–Cubist tradition. By the same token, I had very little interest in what he was breaking with—Thomas Hart Benton and his preoccupation with the old masters. We had a continuing dialogue about our work, although we kept separate studios and didn't visit each other unless invited. We shared one bedroom—there was no problem about that—but not the studio. I honestly don't remember feeling competitive with him. He treated me like a professional painter. If he didn't, we wouldn't have stayed together."

The life shared by these two impassioned temperaments was not all milk and honey, however. Pollock drank off and on, in tempestuous bouts that disrupted his work and disturbed his wife, and as his career took off, hers faltered. Her work was ignored by most of Pollock's New York School mates and the influential critics who promoted their painting. "There were very few painters in that so-called circle who acknowledged I painted at all," she says, "except for Bradley Walker Tomlin and Franz Kline, who spoke with me sympathetically of my plight. But they were the rare exceptions. I never let it sour the relationship between Jackson and me, but, above all, I never let it interfere with my painting. It never became intolerable. I could go into my studio and continue my work. If I'd been career-oriented, I suppose I couldn't have stayed in that situation. But as long as I could keep working, that was it."

A feisty young woman who had worked in the mural division of the Federal Art Project during the '30s and been active in the politically oriented Artists' Union, Krasner

Jackson Pollock and Lee Krasner, July 1950, in the living room of the Pollock-Krasner House, with a rusted anchor they hung as a decoration.
© ESTATE OF HANS NAMUTH.

took up with Pollock in 1942 when he was thirty and she thirty-four. At that time, she was invited by the painter John Graham to participate in a show of young American and older French painters—Braque, Matisse, and Picasso—that he was organizing at the McMillen Gallery. The American painters included, besides Graham, Willem de Kooning and Jackson Pollock.

"I knew de Kooning, but I'd never heard of Pollock and didn't know what the work was like," Krasner recalls. 'I asked around, and then went to an opening where I saw a friend from the project who knew Jackson. He gave me Pollock's address, on 8th Street and University Place, a block away from mine, and I went there. I knocked on the door, and when he opened it, I introduced myself as a fellow participant in the Graham show.

She was, Krasner remembers, "bowled over" by the paintings she saw on the wall of Pollock's studio. "They were Picassoesque, and they moved me to a point that doesn't happen very often. There was a living force in them, and he could see I responded. I later learned he never received visitors, but he didn't kick me out. It ended by his asking where my studio was, and we set up an appointment for him to see my work. When he came to my place, we both remembered we'd met several years before at an Artists' Union loft party."

[TOP]
Lee Krasner, Untitled, 1946-47. Oil on
canvas, 42 x 21 1/4 inches. Where-
abouts unknown, presumed destroyed.
PHOTO: POLLOCK-KRASNER STUDY CENTER, LEE
KRASNER CATALOGUE RAISONNÉ ARCHIVES.

[BOTTOM]
Lee Krasner, *Blue and Black*, 1951-
53. Oil on canvas, 57 3/4 x 82 1/2
inches. Museum of Fine Arts, Houston.
PHOTO: JOHN REED. POLLOCK-KRASNER STUDY
CENTER, LEE KRASNER CATALOGUE RAISONNÉ
ARCHIVES.

Pollock was sympathetic to her painting, Krasner notes, and shortly after the McMillen show, they were dating each other. "Everyone was very poor. You went and sat and had some beers together and talked about art and so forth. Eventually we began living together, though we maintained our own places. But he was ensconced on the top floor of the building on 8th Street with his brother, Sande. At some point, Sande moved to Connecticut, and I was persuaded to take over Sande's half of the loft."

At the time, Krasner worked in the Cubist mode taught by the theorist and painter Hans Hofmann, whose famous school in New York she attended from 1937 to 1940. His teachings stressed abstraction from nature, a respect for the flatness of the picture plane and the necessity of working from a model—restrictions that Krasner began to question when she encountered Pollock's emotive, expressive canvases. Pollock's training, on the other hand, had been completely different. Except for Picasso, he knew almost nothing of the School of Paris painters, such as Matisse and Mondrian, with whom Krasner felt very familiar. His study with Benton had taught him to follow the old masters in compositional effects, and he was also interested in myth, ritual, and the 'primitive' art of the pre–Columbian and American Indians.

"I was much more struck by what he was about; it opened a new channel, a new avenue for me," Krasner recalls. "I started to break away from what I had learned and was involved with." Trying to come to terms with the emotional force of Pollock's work, Krasner began to rethink her own and got into what she now calls her "mud" period—a transitional phase that was to last for several years. "I would work on paintings for months, building up kind of relief slab of no color and getting nowhere. It was all very frustrating, and at that time I didn't really love people or things."

At this point, Krasner had not yet met Benton. "I didn't particularly respond to his work and didn't understand Jackson's involvement," she says. One day, however, Benton came to visit and, in the course of talking with Pollock, turned to Krasner, said he understood she was a painter and asked to see what she did. "I was in the middle of my gray slabs," Krasner recalls, "and so we walked over to my end of the room to look at them. There was an awful silence. Then Jackson said something to break the tension, and that was it. Benton walked out."

To this day, Krasner says, she has a difficult time understanding people "who've moved with such ease in work from figurative to what they call abstract. The fact is, most of it's high decoration, and for me it's not so hard to spot those who've never gone through the transition. It's easy to push paint around, too easy."

Meanwhile, Pollock was gaining recognition, and in 1943, after exhibiting in Peggy Guggenheim's New York gallery, Art of This Century, he signed a year's contract with her that paid him $150 a month in return for his entire output. Later that year The Museum of Modern Art bought his painting *The She-Wolf* for $650. "Jackson was totally determined to live from the sale of his paintings," Krasner notes. "He made a real issue of it. Other painters in his circle—Tony Smith, Barney Newman, Adolph Gottlieb—were all supported by their wives, but he couldn't take that. His attitude was macho; he didn't want me to go out and work and support him. When his work began to sell a tiny little bit, we lived off that. I was able to keep painting that way, so I tried very hard to help him sell."

In 1945 the couple paid a weekend visit to friends in The Springs, a pastoral hamlet on the eastern tip of Long Island. She was so taken with the charms of this rural retreat, Krasner recalls, that she broached to Pollock the idea of their renting the 8th Street studio for a year and finding a house in The Springs. "Are you mad?" he said to me. But back in New York he had a delayed reaction. "We returned to The Springs and through a real estate agent found a house with a barn on five acres—the house I still spend summers in. The price was $5,000. We got it for $2,000 down, let by Peggy Guggenheim on condition that Jackson pay it back at the rate of $50 a month." By that time, Pollock's monthly stipend from Guggenheim had increased to $300, and the $50 was deducted from that.

The year 1945 was crucial in other ways. Krasner's father died that year, and although neither she nor Pollock had wanted marriage at the beginning of their relationship, the loss of her father led to "a total reversal on my part. Jackson and I had been living together for three years, and I gave him an ultimatum—either we get married or we split. He thought about it and then said, 'O.K., but it has to be a church wedding.' I only wanted City Hall, but he said, 'Oh, no. I'm not a dog; I won't go get a license.' He was very traditional and had a high religious streak, which had never really manifested itself."

On October 25, 1945, they were married at the Marble Collegiate Church in New York, with May Natalie Tabak, wife of the late Harold Rosenberg, as their sole witness. Peggy Guggenheim had also been invited as a witness, Krasner recalls, "but she said, 'Aren't you married enough? I have a lunch date.'" Almost immediately the couple moved to The Springs, a move that was to enrich their lives and work.

Every room of the old house was stuffed with furniture, and the barn was solidly packed with farm equipment, Krasner remembers. "It was awful to clean it out. Jackson went up and picked one of the bedrooms to work in. When we had the barn moved, he got that for a studio and I got the room upstairs, because he had to bring in a show for the Guggenheim gallery." The house, heated with coal stoves, had no hot water. "Not until 1949 when Betty Parsons [Pollock's dealer after Peggy Guggenheim told us the Museum of Modern Art had bought a second painting [*Number*

12] did we call Dick Talmage, the plumber up the road, and have heat and hot water put in. The museum never knew what they did by buying that painting. Ever since, I've had a soft spot for MOMA," Krasner says.

Though the Harold Rosenbergs were already summering in The Springs, the Pollocks had the distinction of being the first artists of the New York School to become full-time residents. (Thanks partly to the pioneering Pollocks, the entire eastern tip of Long Island today is crawling with creative types.) "We missed the New York scene to some extent," says Krasner, "but on the other hand, the people we wanted to see we invited out. Moving there meant far more to me than I thought at the time. By 1945 my "mud" period had abated, and out there it broke up. An image began to come through those gray slabs. Also, look what Jackson started to produce. He was living a life he was pleased with. Together we cooked, canned, gardened; it was all a beautiful new experience."

Though Krasner worked every day on her painting, it was up to her to deal with "the domestic part," such as household arrangements. Pollock had such chores as mowing the lawn. At first the two shopped on bicycles, but then acquired a Model A Ford that they could drive to town. "There was this mode to the marriage that was cozy, domestic and very fulfilling," Krasner says. "Jackson had a delightful sense of humor, and when I'd rant and rave about someone being a son of a bitch, etc., he'd calm me down considerably. When I bellyached about my work, he'd say, "Stay with it." We had a continuing dialogue about our work, and he always wanted me to see what he was doing; he was always asking my reaction."

The dark side of the marriage was largely the result of Pollock's drinking bouts. "From the beginning, he had problems with alcohol," Krasner says. "I found it disturbing, but he was constantly trying one thing after another to deal with it, including psychoanalysis. He'd drink in cycles, and when he did, it was rough. When we'd discuss it and I'd tell him I couldn't handle it, he'd say, 'Think of it as a storm, and it will be over.' As long as I knew him, he fought the drinking tooth and nail. He never painted when he was drinking. They weren't routine cycles; the only thing routine was that they were cycles."

Each of them worked in cycles, too. When Pollock was in a "work cycle," Krasner reports, "he'd just get up in the morning, go into the studio and begin. He never talked about techniques or ideas in painting, but he'd call me in to look at what he was doing." Krasner knew when a work period of her own was about to begin. "At some point I'd get fidgety and edgy and I knew I'd have to clear the studio out and start working. I've always worked in that way. Then when I'm through with a whole period, it closes off again, and I get back to everyday putter."

As "part of her process," Krasner says, she has always destroyed a good deal of her work, often bringing it back in other forms, however. In her first show at the Pace Gallery in 1977, for example, the collages she exhibited included snippets of drawings done at the Hofmann school in the late '30s. "Jackson never destroyed his work the way I do. If he had things that didn't come off, he'd put them aside for later consideration. But he had relatively few of these things, where I'd have big cycles of them. What's miraculous is, we didn't destroy each other."

Krasner doesn't remember her specific response when Pollock began to make his breakthrough "drip" paintings in 1946. "But of course they interested me; everything I saw in his studio interested me," she says. But Krasner never, as she puts it, "became a Pollock. I didn't because I wasn't a student of his in that sense. I admired him, but also Mondrian and Matisse. One admires other artists, and I think I'd have admired him whether or not I was his wife. He'd have affected me."

If Krasner responded to Pollock's work, he was an all-important source of support for her own. In 1951 she asked him to speak to Betty Parsons, who became his dealer that year; his intercession resulted in Krasner's first show. In 1953 she began a new cycle, painting in a style related to Matisse, and Pollock wrote to the artist Alfonso Ossorio, a close friend, praising the "freshness and bigness" of her work. "That was the only way he told me about my success," she says. "He wasn't resentful, and when in 1951 I showed a new cycle of collage paintings at the Stable Gallery, he was at the opening, proud as a peacock." She did not, she adds, "hold him responsible for the fact that I hadn't made it before. I felt that was due to many, many things outside of him, including the misogyny of the New York School." And she recalls, "In each case, you knew how threatened they were; one could physically feel the hostility. The whole culture is that way. Pollock wasn't like that; he wasn't threatened as the others were, especially by strong women. He was so damned sure of himself. He knew he was terrific; some part of him knew it. Picasso, at one point, was the only possible threat. After that, forget it."

As long as Pollock treated *her* as an artist, Krasner observes, "that was as much as could be asked for. But I couldn't expect him to take an attitude against the whole culture and his fellow artists. Life was difficult enough."

In 1955 Pollock, now an artist of renown, began a heavy drinking cycle. He re-entered psychoanalytic therapy, and Krasner herself started in analysis. A year later, while Krasner was in Europe "taking a breather," Pollock crashed his car into a tree near their home in The Springs and died instantly. Krasner is still bitter at the therapist "who told Jackson it was all right to drive while drunk." In the shock of grief, her own work was suspended for a while. "But then I realized if I didn't get back to it, I'd enver make it at all."

Asked recently what the years with Pollock had meant to her Krasner took time to reflect. "I gave a whole lot to the relationship, but I received a lot, too," she says. "It's very nice to have someone you can really share things with. We had together a general, big understanding of the meaning of art and what our interests were. And when things were peaceful, there was a quietness and a calm that I haven't experienced since."

JACKSON POLLOCK:

Notes concerning the nature of his drawings and his art psychotherapy.

JOSEPH L. HENDERSON, M.D.
Excerpts from an interview by Jeffrey Potter
[Dr. Henderson, a psychiatrist, saw Pollock as a patient for about 18 months in 1939–40.]

DECEMBER 27, 1982

ART psychotherapy is a recognized aid in treatment of disturbed individuals, but it was scarcely known at the time I saw Jackson Pollock. I knew about it thanks to my work with C. G. Jung, who was among the first psychiatrists to use this method. I did not suggest any such treatment in Pollock's case. His drawings did not strike me as having any therapeutic value at the time he showed them to me. We talked about them as spontaneous products of the collective unconscious, the raw material for the art works he was planning to create. Many showed the influence of other artists.

Only ten years later did I examine them from a psychological viewpoint, and even later began to use them to demonstrate certain psychological principles for my students. I did not mention [Pollock] by name in these lectures until long after his death. The time came when I felt it safe in demonstrating how the drawings represented certain aspects of psychological disturbance. It affected not only Jackson Pollock, but other major artists of his time. It was assumed by Lee Krasner Pollock that it was schizophrenia. Nowhere in my article did I say that Pollock was schizophrenic, but a tendency in this direction was obvious to even a layman's eye.

It was Pollock's devotion to art, and to the Abstract Expressionist movement, that prevented him from going over the edge. I saw his mature work, represented in his action paintings, as providing a partial cure, and an indication of a cure for a certain sickness in the modern art movement. My point of view concerning this schizophrenic trend in modern art of the '30s and '40s is clearly stated in my preface to Dr. H. G. Baynes's classic work, *Mythology of the Soul*. Hence I did not think that Pollock's mature art, any more than his immature drawings, could be judged by personal problems. It became evident to me, and I thought would be evident to others, that I had treated him not as an individual, but as an artist in the process of finding his career. The treatment, therefore, was vocational rather than therapeutic, and could not be judged by medical standards. The words of C. G. Jung sum up this method, as follows:

> The physician should follow nature as his guide, and what he then does is not so much therapy as the development of the creative seed he finds in his patient.

I think that creativity is very close to the edge of neurosis or psychosis. More and more psychiatrists today speak of borderline personalities, that is people who are not crazy and not cripplingly neurotic, but who are creatively motivated. And that brings them very close to the place where you can talk about their neurosis or their psychosis.

Every creative person has a period of incubation, you might say, before they do any big creative work. It's very similar to a kind of agitated depression. They're usually in a very depressed stage, very unsure of themselves, very disturbed indeed, until the creative process gets started, and then it carries them beautifully.

The more I thought back on it, the more I saw that there were elements of greatness in [Pollock] that were always there, and that I must have responded to them. I've often asked myself why I wasn't more strictly psychiatric with him, and I have a feeling that it was because of a certain element of genius that you don't touch with scientific instruments—because you can't.

Jackson Pollock, untitled drawing, ca. 1939-40. Purple pencil on paper, 15 x 10 7/8 inches. Formerly in the collection of Joseph L. Henderson, M.D. PHOTO: POLLOCK-KRASNER STUDY CENTER, JACKSON POLLOCK CATALOGUE RAISONNÉ ARCHIVES.

JACKSON POLLOCK:
Fragments of conversations and statements
Selected, extracted & categorized, from his own notes by

JEFFREY POTTER

1949-1956

PHRASES OFTEN USED BY POLLOCK:
"What are you involved with?" (who are you?)
"Contrived" (dishonest creations)
"Yes, yes" (used by Bonackers–Springs natives)
"It works" (approval)
"Stay with it" (used by Potter)
"From away" (domestic foreigners)
"Finest kind" (Bonac approval)

EAST HAMPTON:
Around here it's backhouse, not outhouse. If I could really *think* instead of only see, I'd think in our two-holer—got it all over one of those "orgone boxes."

This ocean is alive, full of tricks and moods. It can slap you, pat you, and roll you. It's where life began. . . . Since I first saw it, that great source stays with me—nights, city, it follows me.

The West is in it some way—roll of the plains, maybe, a wind in the grasses.

That ground swell is the universe breathing, over and over, short and long. On a good day, my work feels like that—alive, strong, all me.

It's Woman, out there. And it can draw you—suck you out, then down and in, way in. You're home again, where it all began.

That beach is like our life, filling and draining around the clock, kind of bubbling time away.

Horses here, the way they move isn't the same. Comes from the English saddle, could be—used to be for generals so they look good; now it's for girls so they *feel* good.

East or West, if horses aren't plain mean, they're plain dumb. Either way, don't trust them. And don't try leading one out of a barn afire, either. Better they burn than you get crippled.

Gardiner's Bay is sure some fine little piece of water—smells good and all. But I'd never use a power boat on her, too delicate, like a pretty girl you got to take it easy with.

It's for toy trains, the Long Island (RR). Either trip, you wind up at a dead end. And diesels aren't for me, either—got no magic. But steam jobs, all you do is boil water and you got real power. That's just about holy, right?

Bonackers are so squeezed between the ocean and the Bay, they ought to have scales.

DAN MILLER [owner of the Springs General Store]:

Gave me a ride in his old plane, rough as hell. The seatbelt was loose and I didn't dare tighten it—afraid it would strain the crate.

GEORGE SID MILLER [highway equipment salesman, elder brother of Dan]:

He told someone I had a lot of noise in me and I got to let it out. Now, there is one smart Bonacker!

HARRY CULLUM [metal worker]:

Way he can weld—it humbles a guy. He's the best kind of genius: what he makes, *works*.

I like the way he talks, that Harry. Instead of "great," it's "finest kind." And about some guy he met, "I like the way his drawers hang."

Didn't last any longer in school than me, but he didn't have to. Harry was born schooled.

SUMMER PEOPLE:

When they talk, money is in their voice—crisp bills and jingling change—and they think rich, too.

Around here, I'm a "from away" guy. But I always was an outsider. All kinds of levels, too.

JAZZ:

You can stick your symphonies and shit. Jazz is *now*, and that's for me. But so is a cello, all on its own.

JEWS:

They're real outsiders, but they're insiders, too, with their own in a way we can't be. Their women, hey—bed or kitchen, great. But the guys are too quick, you know—too much upstairs. If they were really smart, they wouldn't bullshit each other, would they?

That half-ass collector and his ocean dunes, calls them "living paintings!" Shit, he doesn't have any more feel for them than for art. All he collects are praise and envy.

THE MOON:

You can see it even in bright sunlight, that old moon. Even when you can't, it's up there, all quiet and cold. And something else: that man in the moon? Not so. That's a woman, taking her time, shining on us all.

GOD:

Why give Him—faith—a name? Like titling work—isn't one, or The One, enough?

LOSSES:

(Running over a dog) Happen to anyone.

(Losing a love) Shouldn't happen to anyone.

(Running over a child) Kid knows it all, now. All you know is agony.

RAGE:

When it hits me, I'm not me. I'm it, so watch out.

DEPRESSION:

Being down with it is like I flowed down. Trouble is, I don't know how to flow *up*.

PISSING:

Outdoors, it's what comes natural. In someone's fireplace, it's saying things and nobody interrupts you, either.

Outdoors is the only way, helping out nature. Sometimes a good piss is up there with a good fuck. Both are a release—relief, too.

PARENTS:

Dads beat their young; Moms eat them.

BOOKS:

You don't got to read all the time to know books. I can read by sensing a book—I get what it's saying. Saves time, too.

MOTHERS:

(Being told a friend's mother is small) Lot of shit. All mothers are giants.

THE LANDSCAPE:

I don't look at the view, I watch it. The land is alive, tells you things when you let it.

BULL:

Pure power—got volcanoes in its eyes.

CREATION:

Fuck all the God shit! Way I see it, we're part of the one, making it whole. That's enough, being part of something bigger. Let the Salvation Army take over the gods. We're part of the great all, in our lives and work. Union, that's us.

DEMONS:

(On hearing that Paul Tillich said that JP's demons were not under control, that one day they will kill him)

What about his own demons, ogling young girls on the beach? That holy bastard's as full of shit as [Hans] Hofmann. They ought to geld both Krauts—one for his cock, the other for his hot air. If the Krauts won the war, where do you think I'd be with a name like Pollock? Spelled *Pollack* half the time, anyway.

CREATIVITY:

An artist knows what he's doing, or should. It's not something you talk about, only feel—deep, deep inside.

What I do, I unite parts of union into a bigger whole. With enough, that created whole turns into being.

But I don't talk about it—if I do, I'll lose contact, and with more than just that canvas on the floor. You know, when you lose contact with yourself, living gets to be just jerking off. The creative act has its own life, better had. The unconscious turns it into art, because the unconscious is the source of all art . . . Only you got to let your unconscious be, same time staying with it. . . . I don't know how to say it right, just that it works.

For the rest, let those wise bastards—critics and professors—make a living out of it. That [Harold] Rosenberg, knows it all—my ass!

[Clement] Greenberg at least tried to paint, maybe still does . . . in the dark where he's safe.

89

PSYCHOTHERAPY:

A real artist knows what he's doing on his own, sort of underneath. It's not something you talk about, it's a feel—deep, deep inside. What I do is sneak up on the magic—more than just listen, and you got to if you're going to hear what's coming out. If you try to grab it, it'll stop the creative flow dead—then you too.

The thing is, if you kill off your art, what's left? Except maybe you could be a shrink too, grab some of the action, get what they get every hour on the hour—that forty-five minute hour instead of sixty. I could go for that.

GRANT MARK [who administered a biochemical treatment for Pollock's alcoholism]:

He calls himself a doc but he's more a chemist and smells like a lab. He feeds me these emulsions of shit they dig out of mines, gold and silver, then I got to give him samples of my piss. I don't know what it does for him, just for me: it puts lead in my pencil.

EDWIN H. HELLER M.D. [local East Hampton physician, who kept Pollock sober for two years]:

The white pills could be what they call placebos, dream stuff that's nothing only you think it's something. He talks some and I listen; he really looks at me, or in me.

We kind of chew the fat about me, and—shit, I don't know. What I do know, this is one doc with no shit in his little black bag. When I'm with him . . . it works, that's all.

DR. ELIZABETH HUBBARD [Pollock's homeopathic physician]:

For all I know, her powders maybe come from toad balls. They give me a hangover, only there's no high first to make it worthwhile. Is that fair, paying something for nothing, like getting a hard on and that's all there is?

ALCOHOLISM:

With me it's only my chemistry, not like I'm a drunk or something. Alcohol frees the unconscious if you can handle the stuff. It's a way of making contact—least in the early stages. Later, it's doing things the hard way.

Beer is only a mouthwash, like the French use champagne.

AA:

Sure, sure—I can quit drinking and smoking, only I got better things to do.

Meeting I went to, a bunch of dried out drunks. They're not for me. I only drink when I *feel* like it. Them, they got to.

SUICIDE:

That [Arshile] Gorky! What a way to do it—with a *rope*, crissakes. Franz Kline said it was because Gorky talked so much about being well hung. He was that time, all right.

For me, let the ocean do it—only the right kind of day and ground swell—the kind you rise and fall with, slow and easy. All you do, just keep swimming on out, way out—so far, maybe what's left ends up at Hell Gate.

That way there's no mess to clean up, no guts to lug. . . . Thing is, I'm not a swimmer. Anyway, dying scared is no good for your future.

WOMEN:

They got hooks out for men, but most you can shake loose. The women you got to watch yourself with are the ones that are loaded: rich women's hooks got barbs.

Women are in my work, some way. There'll be women in my death too—bound to be.

A woman with me, she's got to like what I like. What I *think*, too. Sex is great, sure, but only painting is really creative. Sex is for getting your rocks off. What does she get? Lucky.

LEE:

Lee is different: she's a wife, then an artist. She's a base to operate from, sometimes around. She doesn't take any shit from anyone, Lee, even the collectors she's after. She's talented, plenty, but great art needs a pecker. Not even Lee's got that.

RUTH KLIGMAN:

Zog [Wilfrid Zogbaum] calls Ruth "living dangerously," but he's got it wrong. It's living, real living, and new to me. She's free—look at the risks she takes—so I'm free. That's new, too, you bet—free!

When it comes to bed, with an older guy a girl's got something to appreciate. He's been around, knows the scene.

DEATH:

Sleeping late is a kind of dying. We all die a little every day, but sleeping is doing it right. But there's living in that dying—it's like the way we began, asleep. I sure hope it's the way we end, sleep.

Those graves at Green River Cemetery are part of the landscape, and the landscape is part of the sky. So we're all one, that's what.

91

COMBAT:

Fuck war! That's not for artists, goddamit. We don't need to kill to be heroes, crissake. Our kind of heroes—and don't think we're not—create instead of destroy.

ART:

Tom Benton, biggest little man I ever met. Tough as they come, only that was then and this is now.

There are no accidents in painting, mine anyway. That's one reason a camera doesn't make it as art—you take 100 shots, one's got to be good.

Great masters? Balls! Me, I just gotta paint. And famous? That makes you theirs—they own you, so you've lost your you.

Aesthetes, you can have them—bunch of constipated queers. So let Gerald Murphy call me a barbarian, that asshole full of shit. I bet you Picasso's told him off more than once.

These fancy guys aren't all like that. Alexey Brodovitch knows more than they'll ever learn, even if he does go for camera work. And some of it comes pretty close to art: Herbert Matter, Rudy Burkhardt, even old Stieglitz when he cut the shit. They *make* pictures; Hans Namuth *takes* them.

Why does architecture have to be art? It's design, goddamit. Tony Smith is different, along with Peter Blake. They're saying something creatively, not just using building blocks. Bob Rosenberg used to, I guess, but he went all plate glass. His beach house—do any screwing in it, you'd have to wear dark glasses. He ought to stuff all his glass up his ass.

Life and work are one and neither is real for me without the other.

Titles don't work on account they're only labels. The painting's got to say it, hook you so you get in there and feel it. Titles tell it outside and that keeps you outside. You want to know a painting, go *inside*.

A guy shouldn't worry about his talent. Let it be, and if it's there it'll bubble up—maybe more than he can handle. Too much talent can fuck you up good.

The floor is right for me, that's all. I got to move around, so I'm free on the outside. Then I'm free inside, which frees the force which makes the work. Anyway, I like the hardness, the no-give. It suits screwing, too; you can get hold of things.

Know-it-alls claim you can't use housepaint on canvas, won't hold up. They don't know enough to know it doesn't matter how long it lasts. What matters is what is in the work. That lasts, don't worry.

92

There's no feel like it, when a painting comes right. Screwing isn't in it, not in that league. Screwing always could be better, some way. But a painting—*right*, that's all.

Allover works on account it means no limits, just edges. So I work to the edge, on lots of levels, too.

Painting big, mural stuff, is safer. You can let loose with all that room. Feels better—great.

That being "in the painting"—did I dream that up, or Lee?—isn't what counts. It's that the work is *out* of me. If not, you're playing pattycakes.

So what if the old timers had spattered floors in New England? Being walked on is all it's good for.

Sure, art dealers got to live, so do junk dealers. Ass kissing is what it takes, so let them. Junk dealers don't bother, they just stiff you right off. Lee can really handle the art boys, curators and all. Peggy Guggenheim, too. But Betty Parsons—she's too Society to sell much, makes people uneasy. Hard to believe the strength of that little woman.

Teaching can keep *you*, kill your work. Anyway, what can you teach? Not what's inside, which is what it takes.

Why wouldn't I like sculpting? I like using my hands, body too. I figure it's for men, big men—look at Sandy Calder, David Smith, only I mean big inside too. Giving matter life takes power, don't think it doesn't.

Bill de Kooning's *Woman* at Janis . . . that's big time, just right. I get a charge out of it, only how come his *Woman* looks like a guy's wife gets to feel?

Commitment to your work takes guts. If you got them, stay with it. Only don't forget a painter's got to kick the world in the ass, and if he's real he won't even know he's doing it. He's got what it takes, that's all.

Franz Kline said *Life* changed my life, but not yet it hasn't. I bet you *Life* will change my death. It won't be in bed, wait and see.

Somedays, me and the Model A are plain tired. Times like that, I figure I ought to get in and stay there—not drive, just sit. Until we rust away.

JACKSON POLLOCK AND RELATIONSHIPS

JEFFREY POTTER

1998

W H E N I met Jackson, I saw him as something of a mirror image of myself. I thought we had many similarities, and right at the outset I identified with him. Also at an early stage I began to keep notes of our conversations, although not in front of him, so Jackson didn't know I was doing it. I kept tiny notes, in a kind of code, in small blue books that my father gave his children at Christmas. They were ideal for little notes about Jackson, sometimes even as short as a word. This was done for a novel I'd hoped to write called *The Outsider* and although that book never did get written, the original research was very useful when I came to write my biography of Jackson.

The most important thing about Jackson to me is that his story is so American. Where he came from, what he went through—all down the line Jackson Pollock is thoroughly American, and I find that enormously significant.

Jackson was born in Cody, Wyoming in 1912, but not, as is often said, on a sheep ranch. His father had left the ranch and was then working part-time in a gravel quarry. He also worked as a laborer on sidewalks in Cody. Less than a year later the family moved to San Diego for nine months, according to my research, and then started moving from farm to farm. In eight years Jackson lived in six different homes, because as hard as his father worked he was never able to meet the mortgage payments on a farm—in fact he was never able to make it at all. And without question this constant, repetitive failure was very, very bad for Jackson psychologically.

Jackson's father, LeRoy, was not named Pollock originally. McCoy is the family name, which Jackson's brother Sande took after they came to

The Pollock family, Phoenix, Arizona, ca. 1915. Left to right: LeRoy, Frank, Charles, Jackson, Jay, Sande, Stella. PHOTO: POLLOCK-KRASNER PAPERS, ARCHIVES OF AMERICAN ART, SMITHSONIAN INSTITUTION.

New York. LeRoy was an orphan and a neighbor family, farmers out in Iowa, took him in and gave him their name, Pollock. He wasn't really adopted, however, until he was sixteen—old enough that he might go off and they would lose a good farmhand—that's when they legally adopted him. I think LeRoy, a man of very few words, was not strong, and was given to depression. Also, he was a drinking man, and he worked hard to fight it. He was more or less exiled from the family by his wife, Stella. He had to go off to get jobs to try and support the family. He was good about sending money back, but according to Jackson's older brothers he was not entirely welcome because Stella felt threatened by the possibility of his bringing liquor into the house.

In my book, I described Stella as being monolithic, not unlike a bull-dozer at rest. Elizabeth Pollock, who was married to Jackson's eldest brother, Charles, was very fond of her and was outraged by that comparison. She thought I didn't understand Stella, and that was true. The few times I saw her, when she was visiting Jackson and Lee in The Springs, she was very quiet and shy, and may well have had some kind of problem with communication, which Jackson also had. In any case, although her education was minimal, Stella was highly talented in handcrafts and had innate good taste. She was particularly concerned with Jackson, the last born of her five boys. His was a very tough birth indeed—problems with the cord—and I gather Jackson nearly didn't survive it.

So Jackson was Stella's adored baby, and everybody I've talked to in the family agreed that Stella's entire day revolved around this very beautiful, blonde baby, from whom she never really turned away, even when he was sleeping. Therefore you might assume that one of Jackson's problems was

The women of the Pollock family at a family gathering, Springs, July 1950. Standing, left to right: Elizabeth (wife of Charles), Marie (wife of Frank), Arloie McCoy (wife of Sanford), Lee. Seated: Stella, Alma (wife of Jay) with baby Jason McCoy. PHOTO: POLLOCK-KRASNER PAPERS, ARCHIVES OF AMERICAN ART, SMITHSONIAN INSTITUTION.

having a "smother" who so dominated him with love and attention that he had no chance to develop, to express himself, to break out. Elizabeth Pollock maintained, and I think she was right, that that was not the case. What happened instead was that Stella spoiled him. Whatever he wanted, he got, assuming there was any money for it. And he could do whatever he liked. As a teenager he was allowed to smoke cigarettes in the house, and he kept a jug of red wine out back and used it pretty heavily. Stella knew about it, but in spite of her disapproval of LeRoy's drinking she never complained about Jackson's, never said a word. So Jackson grew up under the influence of a very loving but powerful mother, one who was strong enough, in a way, to rob him of his own father—a very unbalanced situation.

Jackson's four brothers were all nice, and they had nice wives. I got to know a couple of them quite well. The eldest, Charles, was much favored by the mother and was given art lessons. He left the nest and headed off to New York as soon as he could. Jay and his wife were good, solid people; he worked in rotogravure for the newspapers. Frank, a very engaging man, married the daughter of a rose-growing family and went into the business. Sande, born three years before Jackson, was very close to him in childhood and became, in a strange way, the father to Jackson. All four older boys were directed by their mother to watch out for Jackson, almost as if he were a cripple. They were constantly having to worry about Jackson in his childhood and youth. Sande, with whom he used to sleep as a kid, was the chief warden, so to speak, right into his adulthood when Jackson was having so much trouble with his drinking.

When they were growing up out West, Charles took Jackson several times to Indian settlements to watch sand paintings being done, and I think the experience marked him strongly. Certainly the vastness of the western landscape did. And yet, although Jackson loved animals, he did not like horses. He could not ride and just did not have much use for horses, period. He had a bad incident when he was very small, riding in a horse-drawn wagon with Stella. She did the milking, the slaughtering, pretty well everything on the farms and ranches except work in the fields—so in addition to doing beautiful needlework, there was Stella out in the yard with an axe to kill the chickens. She also drove a wagon into town with the milk in the morning. On one of those expeditions, when Jackson was five, the horse ran away with them. Apparently he was terrified by it, and I know he had dreams later on about runaways.

Many years later Jackson became interested in interpreting his dreams through the influence of Jungian psychoanalysis. His first therapist was Joseph Henderson, who unfortunately moved to California after working with Jackson for about a year. It's a pity because he did some very good work with Jackson, and he became an eminent psychotherapist on the coast. His views of Jackson are well expressed in my book. Dr. Henderson told me that Jackson was the only patient he really regretted leaving; he was the only one he really liked, and the only one he thought he could really help. I think it was the first time Jackson had an intelligent, informed professional ear to pay attention to his problems, and the first time he was exposed to the Jungian viewpoint about art, which is very appealing to a lot of artists, writers, and musicians. He had somebody who knew what he was talking about creatively and aesthetically. Dr. Henderson meant a lot to him, and he sparked Jackson's interest in the mystical, and in eastern systems of thought.

When Dr. Henderson left, he referred Jackson to a woman, which I think was ideal for Jackson because he liked women. She was Dr. Violet deLaszlo, a Swiss, and had studied under Jung. She was excited by Jackson because of the potential she felt in him, the creative force, and by what she described as a kind of psychic freedom. As she saw it, because of his relative lack of formal education—he never finished high school, and only had about three years of art training under Thomas Hart Benton—he approached things without any preconceptions. Although he wasn't very helpful in articulating his problems, he was able to see things in an uncluttered way that she found refreshing and considered hopeful for his work. They got on very well indeed, and I think Jackson again found a kind of metaphoric home with somebody he admired—an authority figure who was also attracted to him, offering a real sense of companionship.

I think Jackson was beginning to hit pay dirt in Jungian therapy, as he had with Dr. Henderson, but unfortunately the relationship ended soon after Lee Krasner came into his life. According to Dr. deLaszlo, Jackson said that Lee thought he did not need Dr. deLaszlo now that he had her. And I think this was true, to a degree, at the time. Dr. deLaszlo met Lee and agreed that she was quite capable of handling Jackson, but after all that was not what she had been trying to do. She'd been trying to introduce

Jackson to the learning experience called psychoanalysis, as distinct from psychotherapy, and did give him a lot in terms of a widened interest in mysticism and consistency of thought. Dr. deLaszlo admired Lee and respected her forcefulness, which she thought might be a good influence on Jackson's development, but she was not too hopeful about what would happen to him later. And in fact his two further attempts at psychotherapy—much later, when he was in a bad, bad way—did not work for him because he was careful to pick people he could dominate. Or maybe Lee was careful in helping him choose people he could dominate.

Lee was tough but responsible, in the sense that she could use her strength in good ways. You didn't con Lee—even Jackson couldn't, but somehting else was going on between them that was much more important. I would say that Jackson was the first person by whom she was swamped, and in two ways. Number one, the first time she saw his work, she was absolutely bowled over by it, as she put it. Secondly, I think, she was astounded by the man himself, because Jackson had all these forces seething inside him, from rage to occasional joy, and it was all part of his genius. That's the great thing in Jackson's work.

An important element in Jackson's being was the extraordinary child at his core, a flame of pure innocence. With that innocence also came great curiosity and hope. This quality inside him—the seeking, the sense of wonder about life—never changed. And Lee must have been touched by that, just as she was moved by a very attractive young man; also, she was drawn to the troubled child, which indeed he was. I think initially Jackson's drinking didn't worry her too much because she thought she could handle most problems, including those he presented, and she did. For her, he was really a find, totally changing her life.

What Lee brought to Jackson, I'd say, was first of all a broad exposure to painting. She had been trained under the great master Hans Hofmann. She was very good at getting to the right people at the right time in the art world, where she was respected and knew a lot of people, which Jackson did not. Her artistic judgment was important to Jackson, and also she was bright, intuitive, and a good manager of her own life. Lee looked upon Jackson as a full-time job and she made it possible for him to survive as a person. I am convinced that without her, Jackson would not have lived to be forty-four years old; although he was a pretty ancient forty-four when he got there.

Another thing Lee did for Jackson was to support and promote his career. She was even Jackson's editor when he would write an occasional letter or statement, for example when he sent his famous telegram to *Time* magazine. I was there the morning they sat at the kitchen table for an hour just to compose that one short telegram, going over and over it to get

Lee Krasner and Jackson Pollock, 1949. Photo: Wilfrid Zogbaum. POLLOCK-KRASNER PPAERS, ARCHIVES OF AMERICAN ART, SMITHSONIAN INSTITUTION.

it right. It was astonishing to see Jackson pacing up and down like a caged lion—an enraged one, because he couldn't do it himself. Then, too, because right down the line Lee was directing it. I think he resented his dependence on Lee enormously, but there was nothing he could do about it, he was stuck with it. But what he had to accept he could also despise, and that put him in conflict with Lee.

I've been asked if Lee and Jackson were competitive as painters—a good question. I would say that they were not, largely because Lee was so dedicated to his work and to his well-being that she was not going to get into a competitive situation with him. He was quite supportive of her as an artist in her own right, I think, although some of the people I interviewed said some very unkind things about what he thought of her work. But when Jackson was scratching around, trying to put his thinking into words, he'd sometimes come out with things I don't think he meant. His line was, "well, shit, everybody knows women can't paint." I'm convinced he didn't really believe that because I know of some women, like Betty Parsons, whose work he admired. But as soon as Lee began to develop on her own in a sustained way, which coincided with Jackson's decline, I think he resented it a lot.

Jackson was attracted to power figures, but those he was most drawn to were women. If you make a list of the people who were most important in his life, powerful women dominate it. After the woman who gave birth to him, Lee is at the top, then Peggy Guggenheim, who promoted his career in a big way. Of course Dr. deLaszlo, genteel and refined, had a strong influence on Jackson's thinking. There were influential male friends, too, especially Tom Benton, who was a surrogate father as well as teacher and mentor. Benton was a macho type, hard drinking and very handy with his fists, and he became a role model for Jackson. People admired him, were scared of him, and this Jackson liked a lot. In fact for a while Benton more or less adopted him. He and his wife, Rita, took to Jackson and soon he was babysitting for their children, helping with the dishes, doing all kinds of things around the house he never had for Stella. In finding a second home, Jackson also found Rita—a generous, beautiful, very solid woman—a mother figure he could relate to.

When Benton and his family moved back to Kansas City, Jackson was really lost without them. Later, when Jackson began to head toward abstraction, he was careful about Benton, not knocking the man or his work, even if he did say at one point that Tom had taught him how not to paint. Without question Benton was hurt by what Jackson went on to do creatively, seeing it as a rejection of himself and his art. But they did remain friends, if at a distance. In later years, when Jackson was drinking, he made lonely phone calls to Benton, who eventually had all he could take of Jackson's tirades and often would pass the phone to Rita.

Several of Jackson's friends from his youth, such as the painter Joseph Meert—who once saved Jackson from freezing to death when he fell into a snowdrift drunk—and the sculptor Reuben Kadish, remained loyal to him in spite of his behavior. And his brothers, Sande in particular, were his guardians until Lee came along. Jackson was not a man who could stand on his own, ever; he took sustenance from others, not because of greed but of need. It's interesting to speculate what would have happened if he had undergone psychoanalysis rather than attempts at therapy. My guess is that he might have become a well-integrated person, and undoubtedly a much more contented person. Would he have been as good a painter? We don't know. Would he have had a better life? Maybe, but then he wouldn't have been the Jackson we knew.

PERSONAL RESPONSES:
THE ART

GOUACHES AND DRAWINGS

A
R
T

O
F

T
H
I
S

C
E
N
T
U
R
Y

FIRST EXHIBITION

JACKSON
POLLOCK

PAINTINGS

AND DRAWINGS

NOVEMBER 9-27-43

Preview Monday Nov. 8   4 to 6

30 WEST 57   NEW YORK

Catalogue essay, 1943. ARCHIVES OF AMERIAN ART, SMITHSONIAN INSTITUTION.

MALE AND FEMALE

JACKSON POLLOCK

"Talent, will, genius," as George Sand wrote Flaubert, "are natural phenomena like the lake, the volcano, the mountain, the wind, the star, the cloud." Pollock's talent is volcanic. It has fire. It is unpredictable. It is undisciplined. It spills itself out in a mineral prodigality not yet crystalized. It is lavish, explosive, untidy.

But young painters, particularly Americans, tend to be too careful of opinion. Too often the dish is allowed to chill in the serving. What we need is more young men who paint from inner impulsion without an ear to what the critic or spectator may feel—painters who will risk spoiling a canvas to say something in their own way. Pollock is one.

It is true that Pollock needs self-discipline. But to profit from pruning, a plant must have vitality. In art we are only too familiar with the application of self-discipline where liberation would have been more profitable. Pollock can stand it. In his early work as a student of Thomas Benton he showed a conventional academic competence. Today his creed is evidently that of Hugo, "Ballast yourself with reality and throw yourself into the sea. The sea is inspiration."

Among young painters, Jackson Pollock offers unusual promise in his exuberance, independence, and native sensibility. If he continues to exploit these qualities with the courage and conscience he has shown so far, he will fulfill that promise.

JAMES JOHNSON SWEENEY

Introduction to the catalogue of
POLLOCK'S FIRST SOLO EXHIBITION,
Art of this Century

JAMES JOHNSON SWEENY

NOVEMBER 9-27, 1943

"TALENT, will, genius," as George Sand wrote Flaubert, "are natural phenomena like the lake, the volcano, the mountain, the wind, the star, the cloud." Pollock's talent is volcanic. It has fire. It is unpredictable. It is undisciplined. It spills itself out in a mineral prodigality not yet crystalized. It is lavish, explosive, untidy.

But young painters, particularly Americans, tend to be too careful of opinion. Too often the dish is allowed to chill in the serving. What we need is more young men who paint from inner impulse without an ear to what the critic or spectator may feel—painters who will risk spoiling a canvas to say something in their own way. Pollock is one.

It is true that Pollock needs self-discipline. But to profit from pruning, a plant must have vitality. In art we are only too familiar with the application of self-discipline where liberation would have been more profitable. Pollock can stand it. In his early work as a student of Thomas Benton he showed a conventional academic competence. Today his creed is evidently that of Hugo, "Ballast yourself with reality and throw yourself into the sea. The sea is inspiration."

Among young painters, Jackson Pollock offers unusual promise in his exuberance, independence, and native sensibility. If he continues to exploit these qualities with the courage and conscience he has shown so far, he will fulfill that promise.

103

Nov. 3, 1943

Mr. James Johnson Sweeney
120 East End Avenue
New York City

Wednsday

Dear Sweeney—

I have read your forward [sic] to the catalogue and I am
excited. I am happy—The self-discipline you speak of—will come,
I think, as a natural growth of a deeper, more integrated,
experience.
   Many thanks—
   —We will fulfill that promise—

Sincerely,
Pollock
46 E 8th ST.

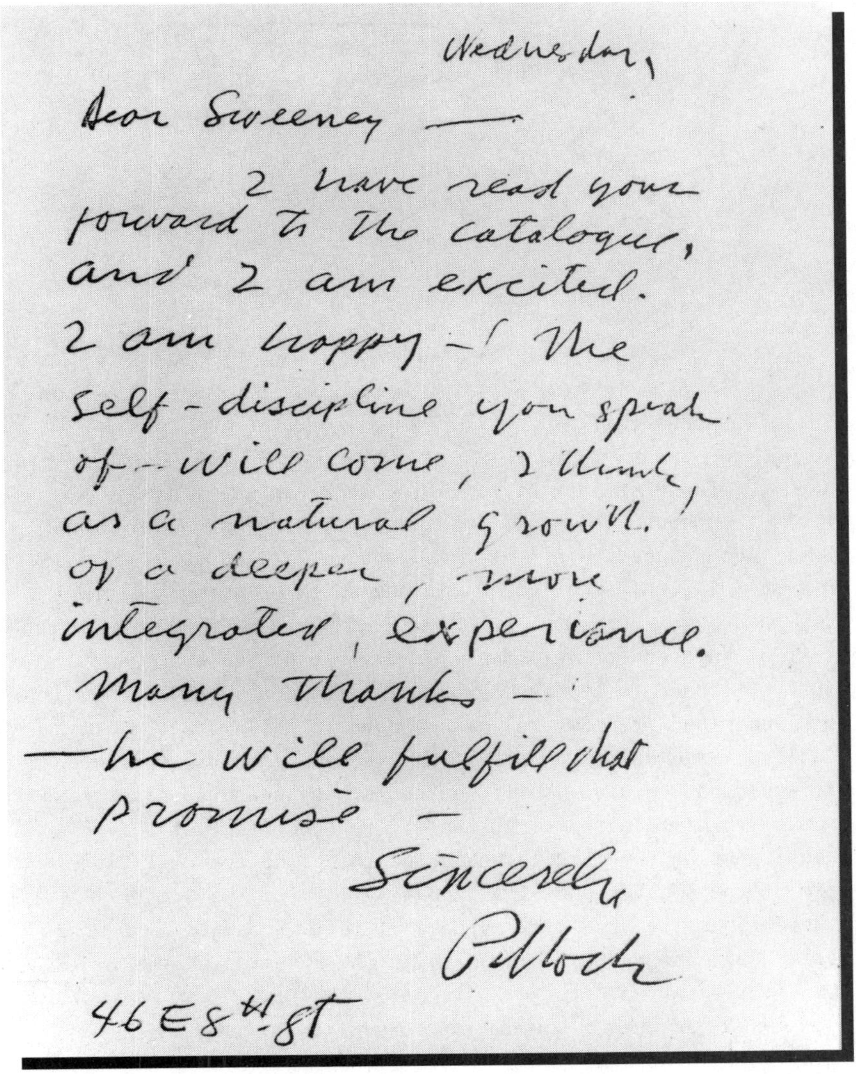

Wednesday,

Dear Sweeney —

I have read your forward to the catalogue, and I am excited. I am happy —the self-discipline you speak of—will come, I think, as a natural growth of a deeper, more integrated, experience. Many thanks —

—he will fulfill that promise —

Sincerely

Pollock

46 E 8th St

Photograph of Pollock's letter.
POLLOCK-KRASNER STUDY CENTER, JACKSON POLLOCK CATALOGUE RAISONNÉ ARCHIVES.

II-9-50

MR. JACKSON POLLOCK
BETTY PARSONS GALLERY
17 EAST 57 ST., N.Y. CITY

DEAR JACK:

Well, I see that I have "my name in the paper" (*Newsday*). People attain fame in many ways: my method is to cling to Jackson Pollock's coat-tail.

You have a terrific show. I did not call you when I was in to see it because of lack of time. [Pollock was staying at Ossorio's town house while his show was on.] Rode in with Julian Levi, who dropped me off at the Downtown Gallery at about 1:15. His show is very nice indeed and seemed to be going quite well.

I think your show far surpasses anything you have done in the last. I enjoyed it tremendously and am wondering what the "critics" will have to say about your "Creation on Glass" I had quite a discussion with some fellow who came in while I was at the Gallery. Said he was an artist and leaving that day for Europe. It would have amused you if you could have heard me blabbering away with him about Art. At the end he conceded that some of your paintings were truly beautiful things—he especially admired two of the smaller ones (#13 and #15) I think. He was still there (in spite of his hurry) when I left. I had to catch the 4:22 train and wanted to drop in at the hospital to see Cynthia Cook while in the city.

I trust things are going well. Everybody seems to have their mind on this blasted [Korean] war and on little else.

Best Wishes and Good Luck
and Regards to Mrs. Pollock

Dan T. Miller

106

Essay for the catalogue of JACKSON POLLOCK'S SOLO EXHIBITION, Betty Parson's Gallery, New York

ALFONSO OSSORIO

1951

THESE paintings are another assertion of the unity of concept that underlies the work of Jackson Pollock. Through the work that he has already done and through these more recognizable images there flows the same unifying spirit that fuses together the production of any major painter; the singleness and depth of Pollock's vision makes unimportant such current antithesis as "figurative" and "non-representational." The attention focused on his immediate qualities—the unconventional materials and method of working, the scale and immediate splendor of much of his work—has left largely untouched the forces that compel him to work in the manner that he does. Why the tension and complexity of line, the violently interwoven movement so closely knit as almost to induce the static quality of perpetual motion, the careful preservation of the picture's surface plane linked with an intricately rich interplay upon the canvas, the rupture with traditional compositional devices that produces, momentarily, the sense that the picture could be continued indefinitely in any direction?

His painting confronts us with a visual concept organically evolved from a belief in the unity that underlies the phenomena among which we

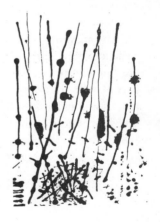

JACKSON **POLLOCK** 19

Original catalogue, Betty Parsons gallery, 1951. POLLOCK-KRASNER STUDY CENTER, GIFT OF THE ESTATE OF ALFONSO OSSORIO.

107

live. Void and solid, human action and inertia, are metamorphosed and refined into the energy that sustains them and is their common denominator. An ocean's tides and a personal nightmare, the bursting of a bubble and the communal clamor for a victim are as inextrivably meshed in the corruscation and darkness of his work as they are in actuality. His forms and textures germinate, climax, and decline, coalesce and dissolve across the canvas. The picture surface, with no depth of recognizable space or sequence of known time, gives us the never ending present. We are presented with a visualization of that remorseless consolation—in the end is the beginning.

New visions demand new techniques: Pollock's use of unexpected materials and scales are the direct result of his concepts and of the organic intensity with which he works, an intensity that involves, in its complete identification of the artist with his work, a denial of the accident.

The present group of paintings is done with an austerity of means that underlines their protean character: thin paint and raw canvas are the vehicles for images full of the compulsion of dreams and the orderliness of myth. Black and white are the sleep and waking of a world where the freedom of private agony and release finds its discipline in the communal basis of these tensions. Forms and images dissolve and re-form into new organisms; like Proteus they must be caught unawares, asleep. They demand of the viewer an alertness and a total involvement before releasing any answer to the questions posed. Without the intricacy of color and surface pattern characteristic of his less immediately figurative work, they are filled with the same combination of strength, sensitivity, and exultant acceptance. Remote from anecdote or propaganda, stripped of immediate material appeal, they both reawaken in us the sense of personal struggle and its collective roots and recall to us the too easily forgotten fact that "what is without is within."

JACKSON POLLOCK

SAM HUNTER

DECEMBER 19, 1956–57

AN uncompromising spirit of revolt made Jackson Pollock the most publicized modern artist of his generation in America, and in many ways, the most influential. In the press he was dramatically identified for the layman with the more expressive and often exasperating contemporary manifestations of artistic freedom. And for a generation of younger artists he had become, before his untimely death in an auto accident last summer, a revered symbol of their new sense of liberation and hopefulness.

With a handful of contemporary painters and sculptors, a heterogeneous group who have been linked in an informal movement sometimes called Abstract Expressionism, Pollock was responsible for injecting into American art a vitality and confidence best compared to that of the period immediately following the Armory Show. His work pointed an unexpected way around the clichés of a doctrinaire non-objective art which dominated advanced American painting in the thirties, and it helped generate new resources in method and released new energies. If Pollock's painting style was aggressive in its self-determination and finally distinctly American in temper, it was also deeply nourished by the radical modern forms of continental painting, and by spiritual attitudes which recognize no national boundaries. One of his significant achievements was to rejuvenate the European sense of art and make it viable again for native sensibility.

Better than any critic or biographer Pollock was aware of his critical role in contemporary American painting history, although he would have hesitated or resisted acknowledging it in so many words. As a man, he appeared driven by some dispossessing, elemental force, and he was given to extreme reticence and long, intense silences which waived any direct discussion of his art. Verbal communication must have seemed at best a clumsy fiat for probing one's innermost feelings through art, and he mistrusted words as a diversion and a possible betrayal. But he needed no outsider to impress on him the revolutionary character of his achievement, which he fully grasped and at times did express in conversation with a terrible lucidity. Pollock himself was the best judge of the size of his painting ambition, and the conflicts, perils, and risks it necessarily entailed. And, because he was so sensitive to his own artistic purpose and fundamentally uncompromising, when the impulse to paint suddenly eluded him, as it did over periods of prolonged inactivity during the last three years of his life, he was desolated by anxiety and by his own self-rebukes. It is idle to speculate whether he would have again resumed painting with some consistency if tragedy had not intervened. The demands he made on himself during what may have been a temporary lapse, and what it is too easy to say should have been accepted as a deserved respite, were as harsh as those he exacted during ten of the most productive years experienced by an American artist of modern times. The drama of his life and his art was their indivisibility; he lived his painting intensely, with a complete absorption, and he painted his life, especially in an early style when he made his own tormented individualism the theme and substance of his art. The problem of painting was identified in a total way in his mind with the problem of existence. In neither were easy solutions admissible. Happening when it did, death may have come as a deliverance from the deep mental anguish of a paralyzing spiritual crisis.

Pollock's serious artistic education began at the age of seventeen when he left Los Angeles to study for two years at the Art Students' League, principally under Thomas Benton. An older brother, Charles, now an art teacher in a western university, had come back to California after working with Benton in New York, and his proselytizing was the first taste Jackson Pollock had of the larger world of American art, and the direct inspiration of what was to become a permanent change in residence from west coast to east. It is curious that an artist as closely identified with the subject matter of American scene painting as Benton should have exercised a formative influence on the rebellious young westerner, if negatively and largely in reverse. (One must add that Pollock himself later acknowledged Ryder as the only American master who interested him at all. And those paintings he did under Benton's influence showed many of the mannerisms and captured something of the emotional atmosphere of Ryder's dream landscapes.) Later the name and style of his most celebrated student were to be synonymous with the free spirit of modernity Benton himself deeply mistrusted and opposed. Yet in Benton's work Pollock might have found hints of that coarseness, rhythmic sweep, and the addiction to grotesque caricature which some ten years later characterized his first original painting style. He won his independence

Jackson Pollock, *Landscape with Rider II*, 1933. Oil on canvas, dimensions unknown. Lost, presumed destroyed. PHOTO: POLLOCK-KRASNER STUDY CENTER, JACKSON POLLOCK CATALOGUE RAISONNÉ ARCHIVES.

finally (and he liked to complain of the intolerable length of the servitude) by pushing his teacher's mannered Expressionism to a point where prevailing interest centered on the expressive pictorial effects themselves apart from anecdotal or representational aims. There remains more than a casual relationship, nonetheless, between such paintings of 1933 as *Landscape with Rider II* and even Pollock's first consistently abstract paintings of 1946, *The Blue Unconscious* and *Shimmering Substance*.

In the beginning Pollock was not primarily concerned with pure pictorial values. His power of communicating and expressing emotion was so elementary that it made him impatient of Parisian esthetics. His own turbulent emotionalism led him to the more strenuous painting manners of his day, to painting which gained an impressive force in an over-sophisticated, over-complex society by its violent, direct handling and controversial subject matter. Thus, in the middle and late thirties he went to Mexican painting for inspiration, drawing on Orozco's blunt, angular forms and mechanistic symbolism to express the romantic protest of the individual against the machine age. Whatever elements of social optimism may have been present in the nationalistic art of the Mexicans were absent from Pollock's adaptions. During the same period Pollock paid at least one call on David Alfaro Siqueiros at the New York studio he maintained during a

111

Jackson Pollock, *The Blue Unconscious*, 1946. Oil on canvas, 84 x 56 inches.
PRIVATE COLLECTION. © THE POLLOCK-KRASNER FOUNDATION, INC./ARS.
PHOTO: POLLOCK-KRASNER STUDY CENTER, JACKSON POLLOCK CATALOGUE RAISONNÉ ARCHIVES.

brief American residence, and to his interest in Siqueiros we may possibly attribute a subsequent thickening and roughening of pigment texture, and a muddying of tonality. The expressionist violence he found in Orozco and Siqueiros confirmed a development that was already proceeding powerfully under its own inner propulsion. As in his relationship to Benton's work, however, Pollock's alliance with these styles was neither superficial nor perfunctory. One has the impression through the early course of his painting that he required fierce and total commit-

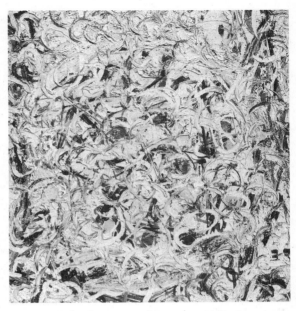

Jackson Pollock, *Shimmering Substance*, ca. 1946. Oil on canvas, 30 1/8 x 24 1/4 inches. THE MUSEUM OF MODERN ART, NEW YORK. © THE POLLOCK-KRASNER FOUNDATION, INC./ARS. PHOTO: POLLOCK-KRASNER STUDY CENTER, JACKSON POLLOCK CATALOGUE RAISONNÉ ARCHIVES.

ments, perhaps to insure a more decisive renunciation at some later date.

The dynamics of the development of Pollock's abstract painting style which was germinating in the thirties would seem to have sprung from a strong tension of renunciation, as if in the role of the revolutionary he had constantly to remind himself of his spiritual chains in order to spur his progress towards freedom. There was also a certain American appropriateness in his manner of arriving at abstraction and in the way he permitted naturalism to re-assert its claims at a much later date; both were part of a related pattern. His most resolutely non-objective manner always carried with it a vague halo of ideas and near-images and intermittently uncovered in its depths some residual ties to natural reality. As late as 1951 there reappeared, almost as involuntary formations, the recognizable anatomical figuration of earlier modes. Yet are not such apparent reversals in style best understood as pretexts the artist has invented in order to be able to re-enact the destruction of natural appearances once again, so that he may arrive at the abstract picture with fresh tension? Out of some qualms of conscience or simply to restore their own convictions, many contemporary American abstract artists still feel compelled periodically to re-experience and bare the origins of an art remote from anecdote and representational subject matter.

Even as he was responding sympathetically to Mexican painting, Pollock's interests were being diverted to Picasso and the fresher formal viewpoints of Paris. The main elements of his first original painting style in the early forties were directly precipitated by Picasso and Surrealism. These were the influences, too, that had so much to do with the whole astonishing, vital burst of energy in American abstract art in the years between 1943 and 1948. Picasso's Cubism gave Pollock his first intimations of the radical nature of modern painting, impressing on him the overriding importance and the transforming function of plastic values. A vivid appreciation of the painting surface as a potential architectonic organism has lent a consistent stylistic logic throughout his career even to Pollock's freest inventions. Equally important were the suggestions he found in Picasso's paintings of the thirties that abstraction could be more than a language of pure esthetic relation, and could embody its creator's fancies, disquiet and passions. By the late thirties Pollock was filling notebooks with fantastic drawings that were free variations on the Spanish master's figuration in the *Guernica* period. But some ineradicable suspicion of authority impelled him to fragmentize Picasso, to create more evenly distributed effects and continuous linear rhythms. These random, undirected doodles supplied many of the aggressive animal motifs for Pollock's paintings of the early forties and also anticipated a later cursive writing which dispensed with image suggestion entirely. Apart from a huge mural painting executed in 1944, however, there was no final commitment to abstraction until 1946.

Pollock's first public exhibition was held in 1943 at Peggy Guggenheim's Art of This Century. It could be said to have taken place in the shadow, if not under the direct auspices, of the international surrealist movement with which the directress and most of the European exhibitors in the gallery associated themselves. And his paintings showed the influence of the "automatism," the attitudes of revolt and the "sacred disorder" which such expatriate artists as Ernst, Matta, and others propounded in New York to the young American avant garde during the war years. To them Pollock owned his radical new sense of freedom, and he spoke more than once of his debt to their unpremeditated and automatic methods. By elevating the appeal to chance and accident into a first principle of creation, the Surrealists had circumvented the more rigid formalisms of modern art. But Pollock and a number of his contemporaries were quick to adapt surrealist strategies to their own artistic needs.

They purged the style of mystification and literary content and applied its quality of freedom to rehabilitating pure pictorial values. In their hands the expressive means of painting rather than associated ideas became the essential content of the work of art. Although American vanguard artists were drawn to Surrealism because its exasperations and atmosphere of scandal suited their sense of crisis, they were not driven into an art of fantasy and private dreams primarily, as might be expected, but one of immediate sensation. They revealed themselves as sensitive materialists even when they crusaded against the materialism of contemporary American culture.

In 1946 Pollock eliminated from his work those medusa images and fearful presences which had been released with such facility in his first two exhibitions. His surrealist symbolism was part of the romantic commitment to the self, but once he had discharged his own rancors, fears, and more disturbing fancies, he was free to break the limits of the self. He then could rediscover himself more coherently in the objective action of the painting and in its internal dynamics. From 1946 to 1951 he painted entirely non-objective works. The painting was now conceived as an intrinsic creation, a work that should stand by a miracle like a house of cards, "sustained by the internal force of its style," in Flaubert's phrase. All emotions, no matter how extravagant, was translated into convincing pictorial sensation. Yet his most abstract flights then and since retained something of the darkling romantic mood of his totemic paintings and betrayed many of the formal obsessions of his figurative style.

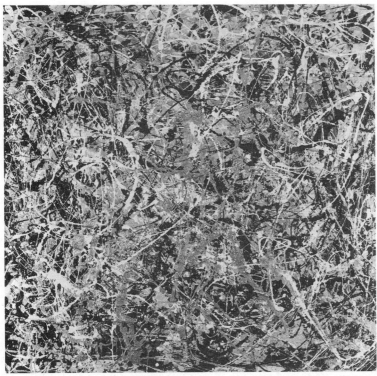

Jackson Pollock, *Number 4, 1949*, 1949. Oil, enamel and aluminum paint with pebbles on canvas, 35 5/8 x 34 3/8 inches. YALE UNIVERSITY ART GALLERY, GIFT OF KATHERINE ORDWAY. © THE POLLOCK-KRASNER FOUNDATION, INC./ARS. PHOTO: POLLOCK-KRASNER STUDY CENTER, JACKSON POLLOCK CATALOGUE RAISONNÉ ARCHIVES.

Jackson Pollock, *Number 14, 1951*, 1951. Enamel on canvas, 57 5/8 x 106 inches. TATE GALLERY, LONDON. © THE POLLOCK-KRASNER FOUNDATION, INC./ARS. PHOTO: POLLOCK-KRASNER STUDY CENTER, JACKSON POLLOCK CATALOGUE RAISONNÉ ARCHIVES.

Perhaps that was because Pollock always saw the painting field as an arena of conflict and strife, on which, according to the stage of his stylistic evolution, recognizable forms or abstract configurations were locked in violent combat. Each picture became the representation of a precarious balance in the play of contending forces. His bursting masculinity had to contend not only with itself, but with a delicate and often exquisite sensibility in line and color. Time has taken some of the sting from Pollock's wrath, and today we begin to see that his paintings seduce as readily as they bruise. Within the general framework of abstraction he could be grave, tender, angry, and meltingly lyric by turns. In any case the motivation of his non-objective paintings remained impure, humanized, one is almost tempted to say, by the pressures of a variety of emotional atmospheres.

Key works of 1946, the turning point in Pollock's career, are *Shimmering Substance* and *The Blue Unconscious*. The rich pigment paste of *Shimmering Substance* points to the densely woven webs of aluminum and enamel paint in such capital examples of later years as *Lavender Mist*, 1950 and *Number 4*, 1949, and also to the thick, pitted surface of *Ocean Greyness* of 1953. It was in 1949 and 1950 that Pollock perhaps attained the ripest expression of his vital material sensibility, building up his surfaces rhythmically by dripping commercial paint from a stick or a can, or spraying it on the canvas with a syringe. Then in 1953, with some relaxation of intensity, he turned back once again to a more conventional use of tube pigment and brush.

The Blue Unconscious uses thinner medium and depends almost exclusively on nervous, broken, linear arabesques to create space, linking it with a more vehement graphic manner which was to come. A cadenced linearism, Gothic in its aspiration, has been one of the strongest facets of

Jackson Pollock, *Ocean Greyness*, 1953. Oil on canvas, 57 3/4 x 90 1/8 inches.
THE SOLOMON R. GUGGENHEIM MUSEUM, NEW YORK. © THE POLLOCK-KRASNER FOUNDATION, INC./ARS.
PHOTO: POLLOCK-KRASNER STUDY CENTER, JACKSON POLLOCK CATALOGUE RAISONNÉ ARCHIVES.

Pollock's style. Did it reflect indirectly the Anglo-Saxon's nagging Puritan conscience, born of some misplaced trust in elevated sentiment over the evidence of the senses? With his great black and white paintings of 1951 and 1952 Pollock came face to face with the radical asceticism which tentatively announced itself in 1946. The results were the most drastic, but also among the gravest and most handsome, inventions of his painting career. An excellent example is *Number 14*, 1951 a work powerful in its plasticity exactly because it has been wrung, under conditions of great intensity, from the narrowest pictorial means.

But Pollock's most critical and exciting artistic contribution was reserved for the period that began with the aluminum pictures such as *Cathedral* in 1947 and continued through 1950. These paintings, a number of them of colossal size, still pose a challenge to advanced styles of our day. Pursuing further the logic of the directions of 1946, he exploded the traditional unities of easel painting. From 1947 his pictorial energies were released centrifugally, no longer respecting either the delimiting spatial boundaries of the picture frame of the traditional uses of paint matter. The applications of silver and enamel paint, and his "drip" methods were designed to destroy the very integrity of medium, to free those forces within it constrained by association with weight, mass and the physical properties of bodies. But all such associations, built into painting by history, custom, and rule, comprise the very flesh of the oil medium. When Pollock broke down conventional painting means with his radical techniques, his works were drawn into a new gravitational system and could unfold a stirring new drama of space.

The special qualities of delirium and rapture he brought to the heightened lyricism of this period, a lyricism epic in its sweep and baroque in its expansive energies, testify to a fresh birth in the realm of contemporary art. In such paintings as *One* and *Autumn Rhythm* Pollock burst through mighty boundaries and attained, momentarily and precariously, a state of absolute freedom. His painting world, which seemed to revolve around some radical new principle of indeterminacy, was remote from the closed and intelligible universe of post–Renaissance art where man cut space to his own measure. It belonged rather to the vast free spaces of modern science and, in pictorial metaphor, showed the limits of the modern individual's rational powers by opening up glimpses of a nature essentially irrational and chaotic.

In the beginning Pollock had felt his artistic mission was to disorient, to unsettle, and to promote disorder, and with an unexampled savagery he proceeded to make of his art a kind of wrecking enterprise. His first exhibited work looked somewhat like a battlefield after a heated engagement, strewn in this case with the corpses of Picasso, the Surrealists, Miro, Kandinsky perhaps, and fragments of American Indian art. The accelerating tempo of his revolt led him to search for a total freedom that would transcend his artistic sources and his own mood of crisis. He created finally an autonomous and sovereign artistic reality, powered by its own dynamism, monumental in its scale and breadth of feeling. Yet the loaded surfaces and aggressive industrial textures of his best work continued stubbornly to point up an attachment to immediate, concrete sensation, as if Pollock partly mistrusted the intangible free spaces to which his powerful imagination had propelled him.

In his unapologetic materialism there are refreshing and unregenerately American qualities, as there are in his effort to breathe spirit into the refractory matter he chose to make the substance of his art. These distinctly native qualities mix matter-of-fact realism with respect to materials, and an innocent idealism. Only a supreme innocent would have felt free to disregard the intrinsic appeals and cultivated uses of the language of paint, and gambled with raw pictorial effects to the degree that Pollock did. And only an idealist of transcendent powers could have won from such patently non-artistic content a deep and moving lyricism.

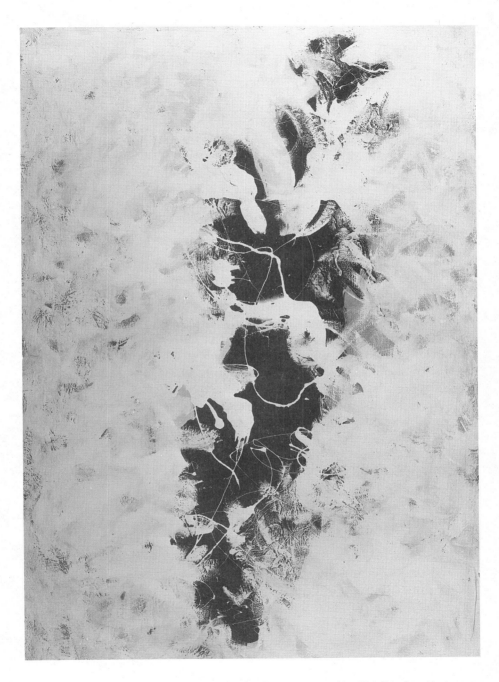

Jackson Pollock, *The Deep*, 1953. Oil and enamel on canvas, 86 3/4 x 59 1/8 inches. Musée National d'Art Moderne, Centre Georges Pompidou, Paris, gift of the Menil Foundation, Houston. © THE POLLOCK-KRASNER FOUNDATION, INC. / ARS. PHOTO: POLLOCK-KRASNER STUDY CENTER, JACKSON POLLOCK CATALOGUE RAISONNÉ ARCHIVES.

THE WHITE CELL

JOHN BERGER

NOVEMBER 22, 1958

In a period of cultural disintegration—such as ours in the West today—it is hard to assess the value of an individual talent. Some artists are clearly more gifted than others and people who profoundly understand their particular media ought to be able to distinguish between those who are more and those who are less gifted. Most contemporary criticism is exclusively concerned with making this distinction; on the whole, the critic today accepts the artist's aims (so long as they do not challenge his own function) and concentrates on the flair or lack of it with which they have been pursued. Yet this leaves the major question begging: how far can talent exempt an artist if he does not think beyond or question the decadence of the cultural situation to which he belongs?

Perhaps our obsession with genius, as opposed to talent, is an instinctive reaction to this problem, for the genius is by definition a man who is in some way or another larger than the situation he inherits. For the artist himself the problem is often deeply tragic; this was the question, I believe, which haunted men like Dylan Thomas and John Minton. Possibly it also haunted Jackson Pollock and may partly explain why in the last years of his life he virtually stopped painting.

The Pollock exhibition, now at Whitechapel, certainly reveals that he was highly talented. Some may be surprised by this. We have seen the consequences of Pollock's now famous innovations—thousands of Tachiste and Action canvases crudely and arbitrarily covered and "attacked" with paint. We have heard the legend of Pollock's way of working: the canvas on the floor, the paint dripped and flung on to it from tins; the delirium of the artist's voyage into the unknown, etc. We have read—and I have often quoted them here—the pretentious incantations written around the kind of painting he fathered. How surprising it is then to see that he was, in fact, a most fastidious, sensitive and 'charming' craftsman, with more affinities with an artist like Beardsley than with a raging iconoclast.

Jackson Pollock, *Full Fathom Five*, 1947. Oil on canvas with nails, tacks, buttons, key coins, cigarettes, matches, paint tube tops, etc., 50 7/8 x 30 1/8 inches. THE MUSEUM OF MODERN ART, NEW YORK, GIFT OF PEGGY GUGGENHEIM. © THE POLLOCK- KRASNER FOUNDATION, INC. / ARS.

Jackson Pollock painting *Autumn Rhythm: Number 30, 1950*, summer 1950.
© ESTATE OF HANS NAMUTH.

All his best canvases here are large. One stands in front of them and they fill one's field of vision: great walls of silver, pink, new gold, pale blue nebulæ seen through dense skeins of swift dark or light lines. It is true that these pictures are not composed in the Renaissance sense of the term; they have no focal center for the eye to travel toward or away from. They are designed as continuous surface patterns which are perfectly unified without the use of any obvious repeating motif. Nevertheless their colour, their consistency of gesture, the balance of their tonal weights all testify to a natural painter's talent, and incidentally also to the fact that Pollock's method of working allowed him in relation to what he wanted to do, as much control as, say, the Impressionist method allowed the Impressionsts.

Pollock, then, was unusually talented and his paintings can delight the sophisticated eye. If they were turned into textile design or wallpapers they might also delight the unsophisticated eye. (It is only the sophisticated who can enjoy an isolated, single quality removed from any normal context and pursued for its own sake—in this case the quality of abstract decoration.) But can one leave the matter there?

It is impossible. Partly because his influence as a figure standing for something more than this is now too pressing a fact to ignore, and partly because his paintings must also be seen—and were probably intended—as images. What is their content, their meaning? A well-known museum curator whom I saw in the gallery said "They're *so* meaningful." But this, of course, was an example of the way in which qualitative words are now

foolishly and constantly stood on their heads as everybody commandeers the common vocabulary for their unique and personal usage. These pictures are meaningless. But the way in which they are so is significant.

Imagine a man brought up from birth in a white cell so that he has never seen anything except the growth of his own body. And then imagine that suddenly he is given some sticks and bright paints. If he were a man with an innate sense of balance and colour harmony, he would then, I think, cover the white walls of his cell as Pollock has painted his canvases. He would want to express his ideas and feelings about growth, time, energy, death, but he would lack any vocabulary of seen or remembered visual images with which to do so. He would have nothing more than the gestures he could discover through the act of applying his coloured marks to his white walls. These gestures might be passionate and frenzied but to us they could mean no more than the tragic spectacle of a deaf mute trying to talk.

I believe that Pollock imaginatively, subjectively, isolated himself almost to that extent. His paintings are like pictures painted on the inside walls of his mind. And the appeal of his work, especially to other painters, is of the same character. His work amounts to an invitation: Forget all, sever all, inhabit your white cell and—most ironic paradox of all—discover the universal in your self, for in a one-man world you are universal!

I have said before that *the* problem for the Western artist is to find themes for his art which can connect him with his public. (And by a theme I do not mean a subject as such but the developing significance found in a subject.) At first Pollock was influenced by the Mexicans and by Picasso. He borrowed stylistically from them and was sustained by their fervour, but try as he might he could not take over their themes because they were simply not applicable to his own view of his own social and cultural situation. Finally in desperation he made his theme the impossibility of finding a theme. Having the ability to speak, he acted dumb. (Here a little like James Dean.) Given freedom and contacts, he condemned himself to solitary confinement in the white cell. Possessing memories and countless references to the outside world, he tried to lose them. And having jettisoned everything he could, he tried to preserve only his consciousness of what happened at the moment of the act of painting.

If he had not been talented this would not be clear; instead one would simply dismiss his work as incompetent, bogus, irrelevant. As it is, Jackson Pollock's talent did make his work relevant. Through it one can see the disintegration of our culture, for naturally what I have described was not a fully conscious and deliberate personal policy; it was the consequences of his living by and subscribing to all our profound illusions about such things as the role of the individual, the nature of history, the function of morality.

And perhaps here we have come to something like an answer to my original question. If a talented artist cannot see or think beyond the decadence of the culture to which he belongs, the situation is as extreme as ours, his talent will only reveal negatively but unusually vividly the nature and extent of that decadence. His talent will reveal, in other words, how it itself has been wasted.

Excerpts from: JACKSON POLLOCK

FRANK O'HARA

1959

Art is full of things that everyone knows about, of generally
acknowledged truths. Although everyone is free to use
them, the generally accepted principles have to wait a
long time before they find an application. A generally
acknowledged truth must wait for a rare piece of luck, a
piece of luck that smiles upon it only once in a hundred
years, before it can find application. Such a piece of luck
was Scriabin. Just as Dostoievsky is not only a novelist and
just as Blok is not only a poet, so Scriabin is not only a
composer, but an occasion for perpetual congratulations,
a personified festival and triumph of Russian culture.

PASTERNAK, I REMEMBER
(*ESSAI D'AUTOBIOGRAPHIE*)

AND so is Jackson Pollock such an occasion for American culture. Like
the Russian artists Pasternak mentions, his work was nourished by international roots, but it was created in a nation and in a society which knew,
but refused to acknowledge, the truths of which Pasternak speaks.

We note that Pasternak puts these general truths in the plural, for culture is capable of entertaining more than one truth simultaneously in a
given era. Few artists, however, are capable of sustaining more than one in
the span of their activity, and if they are capable they often are met with
the accusation of "no coherent, unifying style," rather than a celebration.
Even Picasso has not escaped from this kind of criticism. Such criticism is

panoramic and nonspecific. It tends to sum up, not divulge. This is a very useful method if the truth is one, but where there is a multiplicity of truths it is delimiting and misleading, most often involving a preference for one truth above another, and thus contributing to the avoidance of cultural acknowledgment.

If there is unity in the total oeuvre of Pollock, it is formed by a drastic self-knowledge which permeates each of his periods and underlies each change of interest, each search. In considering his work as a whole one finds the ego totally absorbed in the work. By being "in" the specific painting, as he himself put it, he gave himself over to cultural necessities which, in turn, freed him from the external encumbrances which surround art as an occasion of extreme cultural concern, encumbrances external to the act of applying a specific truth to the specific cultural event for which it has been waiting in order to be fully revealed. This is not automatism or self-expression, but insight. Insight, if it is occasional, functions critically; if it is causal, insight functions creatively. It is the latter which is characteristic of Pollock, who was its agent, and whose work is its evidence. This creative insight is the greatest gift an artist can have, and the greatest burden a man can sustain.

In the state of spiritual clarity there are no secrets. The effort to achieve such a state is monumental and agonizing, and once achieved it is a harrowing state to maintain. In this state all becomes clear, and Pollock declared the meanings he had found with astonishing fluency, generosity, and expansiveness. This is not a mystical state, but the accumulation of decisions along the way and the eradication of conflicting beliefs toward the total engagement of the spirit in the expression of meaning. So difficult is the attainment that, when the state has finally been reached, it seems that a maximum of decisions has already been made in the process, that the artist has reached a limitless space of air and light in which the spirit can act freely and with unpremeditated knowledge. His action is immediately art, not through will, not through aesthetic posture, but through a singleness of purpose which is the result of all the rejected qualifications and found convictions forced upon him by his strange ascent.

But how much clarity can a human being bear? This state may be the ultimate goal of the artist, yet for the man it is most arduous. Only the artist who has reached this state should be indicated by Harold Rosenberg's well-known designation Action Painter, for only when he is in this state is the artist's "action" significant purely and simply of itself. Works of this nature are new in the history of Western civilization, and the spiritual state of their creation is as different from that of previous artists as is the look of the paintings different from that of previous paintings. Action Painting did not emerge miraculously from the void, and it is interesting and even comforting to make not-too-far-fetched analogies with the works of predecessors because art is, after all, the visual treasury of man's world, as well as of individual men. Nevertheless this new painting does have qualities of passion and lyrical desperation, unmasked and uninhibited, not found in other recorded eras; it is not surprising that faced with universal destruction, as we are told, our art should at last speak with unimpeded force and unveiled honesty to a future which well may be nonexistent, in a last effort of recognition which is the justification of being.

It is, of course, Pollock's passion as an artist that kept his works from ever being decorative, but this passion was expressed through scale as one of his important means. In the past, an artist by means of scale could create a vast panorama on a few feet of canvas or wall, relating this scale both to the visual reality of known images (the size of a man's body) and to the setting (the building it would enhance). Pollock, choosing to use no images with real visual equivalents and having no building in mind, struck upon a use of scale which was to have a revolutionary effect on contemporary painting and sculpture. The scale of the painting became that of the painter's body, not the image of a body, and the setting for the scale, which would include all referents, would be the canvas surface itself. Upon this field the physical energies of the artist operate in actual detail, in full scale; the action of inspiration traces its marks of Apelles with no reference to exterior image or environment. It is scale, and no-scale. It is the physical reality of the artist and his activity of expressing it, united to the spiritual reality of the artist in a oneness which has no need for the mediation of metaphor or symbol. It is Action Painting.

This is a drastic innovation hitherto unanticipated, even in the mural-size works of Picasso and Matisse. No wonder, then, that when these paintings were first shown in the Betty Parsons Gallery the impression was one of inexplicable violence and savagery. They seemed about to engulf one. This violence, however, was not an intrinsic quality of the paintings, but a response to Pollock's violation of our ingrained assumptions regarding scale. So impressively had Pollock expounded his insight into the qualities dormant in the use of scale that when seen only a few years later at the Janis Gallery or in The Museum of Modern Art the violence had been transmuted into a powerful personal lyricism. The paintings had not changed, but the world around them had.

Nor is the meaning of these paintings ambiguous. Each is a direct statement of the spiritual life of the artist. Each is its own subject and the occasion for its expression. There is no need for titles. This was, in fact, the "spiritual climate" of the New York School in those years, and most of the painters involved in it simply used numbers for identification of canvases, though many had previously used titles and would return to them again, as did Pollock.

MYTHIC ACT

HAROLD ROSENBERG

MAY 6, 1967

Jackson Pollock's chief public statement about his work, a three para-graph note written in 1947, is devoted entirely to method; it contains no reference to the paintings or to what he was trying to achieve through them. Apparently, he assumed that the value of what he did lay in his way of doing it—an assumption common to scientists and to celebrants of sacred rites. He had found the means, he believed, to generate content beyond what the mind might supply. A work could be initiated without idea or subject by a simple act of will—the will to make a painting. Any gesture with paint or crayon was sufficient to set up a situation that would then engage the artist's latent impulses. Once reciprocating action had begun between the artist and the canvas, an image laden with meaning for both the painter and his public would be brought into being; Pollock, who had been psychoanalyzed, often spoke of "reading" a painting. What was essential in creation, he declared, was to maintain "contact" with the total-ity that was in the course of being formed. So long as the contact was sus-tained, the picture would take care of itself. "I have no fears about making changes, destroying the image, etc., because the painting has a life of its own. I try to let it come through. It is only when I lose contact with the painting that the result is a mess." The action of the artist thus blends into the "activity" of the canvas in a kind of feedback process that excludes error. Later, Pollock claimed that his method also excluded chance or accident—a claim that is logical if one conceives of a painting as an invis-ible being, a kind of demonic form, that uses the artist and his strokes or casts of paint to materialize itself in the visible world. Correcting mistakes and abolishing chance, "contact" also eliminates conflict. As long as the

129

silver cord holds, "there is pure harmony, an easy give and take, and the painting comes out well." As Kierkegaard might have put it, the teleology or destiny of the painting suspends the ethics of the painter and his need for a principle of choice. For Pollock, the aim of painting was to achieve not a balance of antagonistic factors, as in de Kooning, but a state of grace.

Pollock's way of working raises the problem of the role of consciousness in art. "When I'm *in* my painting," he wrote, "I'm not aware of what I'm doing." As an inhabitant of the alienated realm of the canvas in progress, the artist exercises his craft, as it were, blindly, like a woodcarver working from inside the wood. More abstractly, he resembles an organic force; Pollock's wife quotes him as saying in reply to an observation about working from nature, "I *am* Nature." The implication is of being almost completely obedient to automatic impulses (though miraculously beneficent ones), like a person caught in the sweep of an event or moving under the influence of drugs. Pollock is thus an ancestor of Happenings and of psychedelic art. He himself provided the basis for derivations of that sort by declaring that "the source of my painting is the unconscious." Since, to those who accept the Freudian theory, all art originates in the unconscious, this could only be his way of repeating that he painted without being aware of what he was doing. One is invited to see his paintings as gigantic doodles. Or, in more romantic terms, as direct products of being carried away or inspired. The element of involuntarism, of being possessed by the work as by the fetish with a "life of its own," cannot be excluded from Pollock's art without violating the artist's purpose and falsifying the content and meaning of his creations. To picture Pollock as the solver of certain formal "problems" of art history is precisely to blur his part in the history of painting and the desperate efforts of artists in the twentieth century to revive art's ancient powers. The concept of the doodle as the "model" of Pollock's paintings is, naturally, an oversimplification: doodles are not done in a condition of alert intentionality, any more than images are conceived in a state of narcosis. But even a doodle ought not to be mistaken for a product of pure automatism. Automatic drawing by a person who is wide-awake inevitably absorbs into itself some degree of imitation and judgment. If the doodler is an artist, his image-forming will draw upon the whole range of his experience of art. Moreover, the longer one "works" on a doodle the more one sees in it and the more possibilities arise for conscious intervention. Disturbed children, encouraged to let themselves go in drawing, were soon found to be painstakingly copying examples of spontaneity presented to them by their teachers.

Pollock designed his method as a means for resisting mental calculation. With him, automatism served in the first place to unlock the activity of painting and release it from dependence upon concepts. Once the artist had entered into motion, his transaction with the canvas would carry him through varying stages of awareness. Though his painting began with random gestures, his consciousness of it would grow as the work progressed. "After a sort of 'get acquainted' period," Pollock explained, ". . . . I see what I have been about." But to maintain spontaneity as a power of continual refreshment, it was necessary to hold himself aloof from rational or aesthetic decisions. Only in the arena of the action could the artist's psyche be wound up to the unrealized demands of the picture. Thus, having declared that in his painting "there is no accident," Pollock completes his credo by adding, "Just as there is no beginning and no end." In photographs of the artist at work, he wears an expression of extreme concentration, on occasion almost amounting to anguish, and his body is poised in nervous alertness, as if he were expecting signals from above or behind. He seems about to dart into movement; in the most eloquent of the photographs (one by Hans Namuth) his feet are crossed and his right arm is flexed to fling the paint in a gesture that belongs unmistakably to dance. With his paint-saturated wand, he will draw lines in the air, letting flecks of color fall on the canvas as traces of his occult gesticulations. His consciousness is directed not toward an effect determined by notions of good painting but toward the protraction and intensification of the doing itself, of the current that flows between the artist and his marked-out world and whose pauses, drifts, detours, and tides lift him into "pure harmony."

Obviously, Pollock was an artist with a secret. He knew how to make magic—a peer of the Navajo sand painters (invoked in the statement I have been quoting), who rolled their patrons in their glittering compositions as a cure for disease. His colleagues talked; Pollock had, as he liked to put it, "something to say." Being a painter was to this medicine man to some degree a masquerade. He preferred to play the laconic cowboy—a disguise that both protected him from unwanted argument and hid his shamanism behind the legendary he-man of the West.

To conceive of art as a form of incantation is not unusual in modern thinking—especially since the Symbolists, *The Golden Bough*, and the writings of Freud. Why Pollock's magical procedures should upset people, including those of his admirers who wish to transform him into a hero of technological progress in painting, is a problem not of art criticism but of the deficiences of American education. The notion of the artist as a "seer" guided by outside forces is implicit in the classical conception of the madness of the creator—a conception resurrected by Rimbaud in his celebrated axiom "I is another." Pollock read Rimbaud in translation, and a quotation from (if my memory is correct) "A Season in Hell" appeared in large letters on the wall of his wife's studio in the early forties. The principle of the displaced ego of the creator, adopted by the Surrealists as a primary article of belief and disseminated by them in New York in the years before the war, provided sufficient hints for Pollock's "When I'm *in* my painting, I'm not aware of what I'm doing."

The originality of Pollock lay in the literalness with which he converted theoretical statements into painting practice. What to others was philosophy or metaphor he dealt with as material fact. Since in his view the driving force in painting was "contact" between the artist and his canvas, he concluded that creation could be dissociated from the formal history of European art and brought about through concentrating on techniques for making that contact more immediate and complete. In order to be literally "*in* the painting," Pollock renounced the easel and tacked his canvas to the floor. His other innovations stem from a similar substitution of contact for tradition. Pouring the paint from the can or dribbling or throwing it off the end of a stick was a means for gaining closer touch with the medium than was possible through applying paint with a brush. Refusing to work from preliminary drawings or sketches was an assertion of the primacy of directness in each individual composition. From the desire to be totally encompassed by the work came the wall-size dimensions of the drip canvases, so suggestive to later 'environmental' painters and sculptors.

Leonardo, the Surrealists liked to point out, had called the attention of painters to the significant shapes evoked from the unknown by cracks in plaster and water stains on paper. Yet painting had lagged behind poetry in resorting to free association. Words, in their immateriality, are more responsive to psychic states than are mediums requiring the use of tools. Pollock's modifications of painting tend toward an emulation of writing. In throwing, dribbling, and blotting his pigments, he brought paint into closer approximation of the resiliencies of verbal utterance. The essential form of drip painting is calligraphy. In tying to the picture surface color layers of different depths, Pollock produced the visual equivalent of a play on words—a standard feature of oracular pronouncements. Masterworks like *Full Fathom Five* and *Lavender Mist* transform themselves from sheer sensuous revels in paint into visionary landscapes, then back again into contentless agitations of materials. Their immediate derivation is not the work of any painter but Pollock's favorite readings, from Rimbaud to *Finnegans Wake*. The thought of being influenced by other artists made Pollock uneasy, and he shook off his teachers with an impressive degree of success, but he eagerly identified himself with Hart Crane and with Joyce and Dylan Thomas.

Pollock's most spectacular accomplishment is his large drip paintings. Since they almost go over the brink into non-art, these works have provided a bonanza for post–Dada critics engaged in shuffling paintings into various patterns of aesthetic evolution. Thus the drip paintings have been separated from the inner continuity of Pollock's creation and the drama of his adventure with mythic powers. Happily, the current exhibition at the Museum of Modern Art, the biggest ever assembled of Pollock (or of any American painter there), restores the drip paintings to the context of Pollock's effort. That the core of this effort lies in the tradition of art as ritual is made explicit by the titles of the chief works of Pollock's early maturity—*The Guardians of the Secret, The She-Wolf, Night Ceremony, The Night Dancer, The Totem,* all done in the first half of the forties; among the paintings of this period not in the show are *Masked Image, Magic Mirror, Circumcision, The Key*. Typical of most of these paintings is a curious rectangular or circular structure suggestive of plaques or medallions. The paintings tend to be crowded with incomplete shapes, vanishing faces, and arbitrary emblems, and are sprinkled with inchoate writings, signs, and numbers. Forms are contoured or cut by thick black lines, and the dark and heavy pigment upon a ground of rather sinister gray creates an atmosphere of primitivism and psychological disturbance not unlike that in some of Klee's last paintings. For an artist just turned thirty in the wartime United States, these paintings show a remarkable inner sophistication and sense of purpose; they emanate from a region of Pollock's imagination to which he was to return in his last years. The totems, masked mirrors, and night ceremonies adapted from Mexican mural painting and the Left Bank poetic kitchen are replaced in 1946, a year after Pollock moved to East Hampton, by the nature mysticism of compositions like *Sounds in the Grass: Shimmering Substance, Sounds in the Grass: The Blue Unconscious,* and *Eyes in the Heat* (which is not in the show), in which hidden creatures peer out between ridges of high-pitched yellow and blue paint.

It was from these apprehensions of presences and energies in nature that Pollock passed into union with them through releasing paint in fluids that directly record his physical movements. In the drip paintings, his striving toward an overwhelming symbol is loosened and breaks down into the rise and fall of rhythms rebounding from the canvas on the floor. He has discovered the harmony of the "easy give and take" and has condensed it into a style belonging exclusively to him. The state of abstraction into which Pollock has entered, as well as its origin in the flowing of natural energies, is, as before, conveyed by his titles; with a few exceptions, like *Autumn Rhythm* and *Lavender Mist,* which look back to the intuitions of 1946, the drips are identified only by numbers or are called simply *Painting* or *Black and White*.

Bringing the drip paintings into focus with the earlier totemic compositions provides a measure of both their strength and their weakness. What was radically new about the method of the drips was that the method was all there was to them. By discarding all traces of symbolism or visual mythology, exemplified by Surrealist dream pictures and the abstract figures of Gorky and Klee, Pollock pushed toward a purging of the imagination—or even its elimination. The catharsis implied by this technique established a connection between the matted undergrowths of *Blue Poles* and *Full Fathom Five* and the expansive vacancies of the work of Pollocks' friends Barnett Newman and Tony Smith or the unyielding surfaces of Clyfford Still. It was myth without myth content—a pure *state*. It joined painting to dance and to the inward action of prayer, as Cubism had joined it to architecture and city planning.

What proves most remarkable in the Modern Museum retrospective is Pollock's variety, an effect of temperament, physical ebullience, and integrity of purpose. For this "sand painter," the painting was medicine for the artist himself, not for a patient brought out of his tent to be cured for a fee of two goats. Contact was Pollock's salvation, and he tried to make it appear afresh in each painting. Whatever slackness and repetition occur are attributable Jess to Pollock's character than to his method. In its "easy give and take" the artist could only win or lose, without struggle. Its goal of "harmony" induced a settling down of psychic method into aesthetic process; this is clear in the work of Pollock's followers, for most of whom relaxed floatings or daubings of paint produce a mere simulation of the Master's outer-controlled tension. Drip-painting contact contains no principle of resistance. It offers the temptation to roller-coaster thrills. A painting like Pollock's *Number Seven, 1950*, analyzed layer by layer, amounts to a record of glides and turns whose major quality is headiness. Lacking Pollock's magical mission, such paintings fulfill themselves exclusively in the aesthetic and represent his jazz music for the avant garde art world.

The Modern Museum retrospective makes it clear that Pollock himself, after the first excitement of his plunge into the abstract world of liberated pigment, found its harmonies less than satisfying. Already in 1949, only two years after lighting upon his new method, he deliberately defaces a typical drip painting with cutouts of flat, sharpedged shapes and entitles the work *Out of the Web*, intimating an escape from the tangle of unmitigated responsiveness; in two other works executed in the same year—*Cutout*, a painting distinguished by his peculiar gracefulness, and *Shadows*—he repeats the motif with human shapes emerging out of the jungle of interwoven vines of paint. Turning to the rigors of black and white, to collage and massive drawings of classical heads, he signals his awareness of the limits of visual "gorgeousness" as represented by *Lavender Mist* and other joyous isles gleaming with shreds of blue and aluminum. By 1953, the year of *Blue Poles*, a painting attractive because of a degree of naturalistic grossness, Pollock is in full swing back to the denser intuitions and more refractory images of his early-forties paintings. The flow of paint gradually dries up; his works take on references to paintings of contemporaries; execution becomes tighter and more tentative. He begins consciously to display skill—a necessary preliminary to a new departure but bound at the start to act as a handicap. Abstract titles like *Number Twelve* and *Black and White Painting* give way to a new set of riddles: *Four Opposites, Easter and the Totem, Portrait and a Dream*, until the list ends, with uncanny appropriateness, in *Search*—apparently the last oil painting he completed before his death.

on pollock's paintings

FRANCIS BACON, Painter to Melvyn Bragg

They do look like bits of old lace,
don't they?

JACKSON POLLOCK: An Artists' Symposium

APRIL 1967

BY BARNETT NEWMAN

The paintings of Jackson Pollock? The time has come to praise a colleague, not to bury a hero.

Let us hope it is not too late, for he has already been thrust into art theory—drip, all-over, stain, gesture, performance, wall-painting, etc.

Is this all that the admiring theorists and the self-serving dancers on his grave see in him—Pollock, "the picture-maker," the inventor of "styles"?

Is Pollock the prophet of our fate?

Pollock was more than a great "picture-maker." His work was *his* lofty statement in the grand dialogue of human passion, rich with sensitivity and sensibility. But it must not be forgotten that moving through the work is that revolutionary core that gave it life.

Before the art historians succeed in burying that revolution, let us remember what happened. In 1940, some of us woke up to find ourselves without hope—to find that painting did not really exist. Or to coin a modern phrase, painting a quarter of a century before it happened to God—was dead.

The awakening had the exaltation of a revolution. It was that awakening that inspired the aspiration—the high purpose—quite a different thing from ambition—to start from scratch, to paint as if painting never existed before. It was that naked revolutionary moment that made painters out of painters.

137

Jackson Pollock raises all sorts of questions—the relation of the artist to his public image, to psychoanalysis, to his self-image, to critics and collectors, to words, to booze, to success, and to the present that was his future. Today's situation in art was foreshadowed by Pollock's conflicts.

Pollock's fierce, twinkling bull eyes and great shoulders are there in his work. Some artists' faces are embedded in their work in this way, as a kind of personal resonance, others not: Picasso's face is in his work, and Modigliani's, Klee's, van Gogh's, Delacroix's, Raphael's, but not, say, Soutine's, Mondrian's, Seurat's, Grünewald's. This resonance—a trace of the personal—is an attribute which doesn't add meaning to nor detract from the work: in fact it invites false values. It is the attribute—much prized by hucksters in the entertainment world—that makes readers of movie magazines regard the roles of stars as an adjunct to their private lives. The serious audience for art has not vanished, it has merely been deluged (for how long?) by the fan-magazine mentality of a much larger, spurious audience, as is evidenced by the coverage in the press, whether it be Louella Parsons or John Canaday: How much does Liz Taylor get for a picture? And how much does Andy Wyeth get? The proof's in the pudding, ducks.

Thus Pollock's vivid personality invited recognition before his painting did. He was the first American artist to be devoured as a package by critics-and-collectors (whom he cowed), by *Life* magazine in the late '40s in a spread which asked, somewhat wryly, if he were America's "greatest artist," and subsequently by the fashion magazines and gossip columns and the rest of the paraphernalia.

Serious artists can enjoy the W. C. Fields aspects of this kind of success, as Franz Kline did when he went from being totally broke to instantly solvent, whereupon he strolled into a Park Avenue automobile showroom and said, pointing, "I'll take that black Thunderbird," or, like Jackson, when he strode into the Cedar Tavern, one night and, tapping his bulging-wallet, announced, "J. P.! Those are the right initials for an artist." He was greeted with a burst of hilarity and hugs and no hard feelings. Success was not unimportant to Jackson and he was constantly testing his position and prone to put-down competition, several times coming close to blows after delivering himself of detrimental opinions of other artists' work to their faces. He tested the way a child does, and as innocently. When he approached Gorky at a party in the spring of '48 with some unflattering comments about Gorky's painting, Gorky responded with a dangerously affectionate smile, took a pencil out of one pocket, a lethal looking jackknife out of another, and, without removing his eyes

138

from Jackson's face, slowly sharpened the lead to a point an inch long. "Pardon me, Mr. Pollock." purred Gorky, "you and I are different kinds of artists." Jackson studied Gorky's face and the pencil point alternately, weaving a bit, then gave Gorky a small, sly, approving grin and wheeled away, satisfied.

When Pollock's work was shown for the first time at the historical exhibition chosen by John Graham in 1942 for the MacMillan Gallery (including de Kooning, Stuart Davis, Lee Krasner, Graham himself), he was immediately recognized by other painters as wise in the ways of School of Paris art—hardly a distinguishing characteristic at the time. What did distinguish the man and the work was a unique and astonishing energy. There was no existing framework for this energy and it was not until 1947 that, throwing away what he *knew*—the preconceived forms which hampered him—he arrived at what he *was*—which he didn't know, finding paths impassable for anyone else in his own labyrinth. Hunched over his huge canvases, completely in control of his new-found whiplash skeins of paint, he evolved his radiant panoramas that inspire relief along with a lurking sense of disquietude characteristic, it seems, of all great art.

The beautiful poet, Frank O'Hara, who now lies a few feet away from Pollock in the graveyard at The Springs, East Hampton, wrote of the artist in 1959 in answer to his own proliferating questions and insights: "This new painting does have qualities of passion and lyrical desperation, unmasked and uninhibited, not found in other recorded eras; it is not surprising that faced with universal destruction, as we are told, our art should at last speak with unimpeded force and unveiled honesty to a future which may well be non-existent, in a last effort of recognition which is the justification of being."

BY ROBERT MOTHERWELL

"A man's real mistress is life."
Céline

I first knew Pollock at the beginning of the 1940s. As the result of a bitter quarrel between our wives, Lee and Maria, in East Hampton, in the mid 1940s, we were forced to break off relations. Then in the late 1940s and early 1950s, Pollock and I met in New York several times by chance, amicably. Sometime before his death, he came uninvited to my house to a big party I was giving for Philip Guston and behaved cordially, though fiercely baited by Kline and de Kooning (I suppose because of some past history, perhaps the episodes at the Cedar Bar). I marveled at Pollock's

For Motherwell: Jackson Pollock, Untitled, ca. 1943. Colored papers, with brush, ink, crayon and colored pencil brushed with water, 15 1/2 x 13 5/8 inches. PRIVATE COLLECTION.
© THE POLLOCK- KRASNER FOUNDATION, INC. / ARS. PHOTO: POLLOCK-KRASNER STUDY CENTER, JACKSON POLLOCK CATALOGUE RAISONNÉ ARCHIVES.

restraint, because I had often seen him violent; and at Kline's brutality, because I had never seen him anything but gentle (as he always was again when I saw him). I was glad that Pollock left as cordially and quietly as he had come. I never saw him again. I think. I did meet him at the Schrafft's men's bar the Friday of the weekend before Tomlin died; I remember this distinctly because Pollock was to meet Tomlin later that afternoon at the train for East Hampton. Pollock that day talked angrily of how in American one never permanently "makes it," that each new show is a new absolute test, despite whatever one has done in the past. But whether this was before or after my Guston party, I do not remember—I think before.

Anyhow, in the early 1940s I knew Pollock professionally, we even collaborated together on several projects. Which I regard as something of a miracle, when I think of what a "loner" he was. I first met him in the late winter or spring of 1942, about a project which is too long to relate here, but which had to do with a group of young artists jointly experimenting with (and exhibiting the results of) what the Surrealists called "automatism," a project which, in my view, marks the real beginnings of "Abstract-Expresionism." (Baziotes, who knew Pollock from the WPA, introduced us. It is a pity that Baziotes, who had almost total recall, was never taped about those early days, before his untimely death.) The project was never realized, though Pollock, Baziotes, myself and our wives made "automatic" poems together and Pollock and I made our first collages together one day in his studio. But as I said, all this is a long story, and not the proper place for it. I should mention that we all were in our twenties then, and poor.

Pollock then was a deeply depressed man, as well a man with his aesthetic aspirations might be in those days—of the Depression, World War II, the WPA, the prevalence of Marxist intellectuals and painters, and so on—

and like most depressed men, rather reticent. His wife often spoke up for him, in a protective but not always feeling way: one sometimes wondered if Pollock himself would have replied in the same words; and beneath his depression you could often sense his potential rage. I talked a lot, filled with ideas I had gleaned from the Parisian artists then in exile in New York City. I have always detested chauvinism, even as a young man, and one of the first things that impressed me about Pollock when he did begin to talk was his lack of chauvinism. (You must remember that in those days American artists with the tendency towards "modernism" were very much under the shadow of the Europeans, including some then in our midst, overshadowed not only economically and socially, but esthetically as well. Indeed, the whole problem of American modern artists was to find a creative principle that would allow us to create on terms of equal "originality"—the "quality" was already here—with the modernist movement abroad. That principle, in my view, turned out to be "automatism"; but we did not fully realize it then; and some who arrived later doubt it now.)

Pollock first began to talk a lot to me when he was asked, a year or two after I met him, by a California art magazine to produce a statement of his views. He obviously wanted to accept, but was shy about his lack of literary ability, like a diffident but proud Scots farmer. We finally hit on the scheme of my asking him leading questions, writing down his replies, and then deleting my questions, so that it appeared like a straight statement— though there is a brief passage in it on art and the unconscious that does come from me, with Pollock's acquiescence.[1] It was during this time that his lack of chauvinism came out clearly. When questioned on which American painters he liked, he could only think of Albert Pinkham Ryder. He felt, as I did, that anything "American" in one would simply come out, and was not a conscious issue to take a position on—in those days, the literary and political intellectuals wanted you to take a position on everything except what interested us most, our own personal art, to which they were indifferent. (Pollock in fact had very Leftist political views that seemingly had little to do with his art.) Rather than the question of "Americanism," Pollock was much more eager to talk about a piece John Graham had written somewhere asserting that the essential colors of Mediterranean art are green and white. Earlier here I compare Pollock to a Scot, and I used to think of him, as I still do, as an essentially "Celtic" artist, characterized by a lyricism that, in its labyrinthine line, surge of feeling, formal complexity and nakedness of impulse is typically Celtic—think of the makers of ancient Irish carvings, or Robert Burns, or Yeats, or the bagpipers and sword-dancers of Scotland. Whether that image is true or not, certainly one of the things that Pollock's work has meant to me is a large and airy lyricism, whose authenticity of impulse cannot be doubted.

I was also stuck by how his artistic affinities—his admiration for Ryder, his study with Thomas Hart Benton, his involvement in Orozco and El Greco and, lastly, his immersion in the Picasso of the 1930s—were invariably for artists, however else they might differ, who had in common an overriding emphasis on an intensely Expressionist rhythm. I think he responded to rhythm more than anything else in art. Indeed, perhaps it is not too much to assert that his greatest works are marked by the intensity and violence of his rhythm, modified by an incorruptible respect for the works' flat surface, an art masculine and lyrical and, as in a Celtic dance, measured, despite its original primitive impulse. That he also meant to me, his rhythm.

Pollock was very interested that I too, painted on the floor sometimes, and he had adopted the procedure for himself more consistently than I did. To a non-painter, this may seem like a mere detail, but it has important aesthetic implications. For one thing, painting on the floor on an unrolled, long piece of canvas allows one to crop, which in turn can lead ultimately to the overall picture, one of the basic contributions, on the scale on which it was done, of Abstract Expressionism. For another thing, working on the floor in some magical way solves a lot of spatial problems—one loses the sense of the horizon line that so often sticks in one's head with a vertical canvas—and the space can be three-dimensionally penetrated without losing the flatness of the floor when the painting is uprighted, as with a Persian rug hung on a wall. For a third thing, Pollock's famous "drips" could be better controlled; if he had been working vertically, the drips would have become up and down rivulets (as in Sam Francis), and he would have become a vertical rather than horizontal painter, with the subsequent loss of his landscape reference. Finally, working on the floor, the automatic drips would not further spread or move, and he could paint "contrapuntally," that is, in layer after layer, and reach a physical complexity that none of his colleagues could. Certainly one of the beauties of Pollock's art is how complex it is, given its high degree of abstraction. As A. N. Whitehead used to say, usually the higher the degree of abstraction, the lower the degree of complexity. . . . To put my general point here in another way, working on the floor allowed Pollock the utmost spontaneity of automatic drawing with an *ipso facto* controlled space. Of those painters who came after him, perhaps only Helen Frankenthaler (though intuitively, not conceptually) grasped this; and she brought with it a color-sense that he could not match. Though when I wrote about him in *Partisan Review* in the mid-1940s, I thought he would be a colorist—he so loved Mediterranean art. But his color rarely radiates as his line does. Though brother, what a beautiful overall space! This he also meant to me, the beauty of space.

My next to final notion here has to do not only with Pollock, but, given present Gaullist attitudes towards America, with the ironies of history, and the indestructibility of the human, whatever the historical situation. In those days, the great French poet and chief of the Surrealist tribe. André Breton, used to walk the streets of New York. (I think that he earned his living broadcasting to the free French, then under Pétuin.) Breton used to say that the art of the future would be "convulsive"; but certainly it never occurred to him that one of the makers of that convulsive future art was Jackson Pollock, who also walked the streets of New York. Pollock loved then the violent Picassos of the 1930s, such as the drawings for *Guernica* and the *Woman with Knife and Cock*, owned by Mary Callery (which was well-known to us). Indeed, I think then his deepest aspiration was to make a parallel and personal version of such imagery, but he could not. It came out too Picassoid. With convulsive violence, Pollock then splashed out, or struck out his human image. Then I think a time came when he abandoned the original human image, *realizing that his negative striking-out was image enough*. It is true that, in one of his last shows, Pollock tried the human image again. But that was not where his power lay. It lay in a force of negation that was part of his character. What Pollock stands for, perhaps most of all, is that in the end there are no art rules, or that the rules are no good, that only when a man really asserts his identity, even if to the point of convulsion, dues his medium rise to the character of style. *That* Pollock meant most of all to me; that is, the creative power of anger and negation. The destructive side of these we know too well, Abstract Expressionists perhaps most of all, with many of us prematurely in the grave.

Perhaps Pollock at last learned the lesson of most modern artists, that what one is most gifted at is not necessarily how one most wanted to paint, that one's mature style is as unexpected to oneself as to everyone else.

Whatever his profound inner conflict was, I think personally that it was never wholly resolved, despite the great lyrical works that are the by-product of that conflict. Pollock makes me think of Picasso's remark about Cézanne, that what is great in Cézanne is not the beauty of the painting, that academic painters' painting is often as beautiful, but that it is Cézanne's anxiety that counts. I think that in the end the human price of Pollock's inner conflict became too great for him, a common artistic phenomenon that people on the outside seem to find difficult to grasp. It is a hard thing to say, but it is probably true that Pollock ultimately destroyed himself. Perhaps here is where he is closest to the American myth. (I remember Hans Hofmann reported as saying, when he first heard of David Smith's violent death, "how American.")

All this, and certain infantile acts, have led to the public image of Pollock as a very active man, as an "Action Painter," in the current jargon. All this, and certain infantile acts, have led to the public image of Pollock as a very active man, as an "Action Painter," in the current jargon. But I would suspect the opposite, that Pollock was an essentially passive man, who occasionally, at an emotional price that it frightens me to contemplate, overcame his passivity through a convulsion of activity that became transcendant when coupled with his sensitivity to painting as a medium. No artist can do more. Artists who *do* do it are heroic, and Pollock *was* a hero. Not an essentially American one, like Gary Cooper, but a modern and international one, as it turned out. Which, given the place and time, is even more heroic.

Therefore I hope that the Pollock exhibition at the Museum of Modern Art will not be taken by the cool younger generation as just a moment in American art history, but as a celebration of the force of man's spirit. All the rest is politics, of various painters trying to force themselves onto history's stage.

BY PHILIP PAVIA

He invented the One-two-three Experience

Jackson Pollock imprints inside a working artist an odd pyramidlike space. The pyramid is not a concrete delineation of a pyramid, but rather a satisfying loaded feeling which he plants squarely on the *site* of our sensibility. His plane hugs the flat canvas and the space spins out at you as if you were looking down at a pyramid. Minor movements on major movements, all aggregating and interlocking onto a basic underlying plane. It is as full and complete an experience as one ever has in abstract art. The *straight* artist today, young and old, after withstanding the first onslaught of anti-art wars, embraces Jackson Pollock more than ever. He was the real pioneer for inventing ways to make the complete experience in abstract art.

It's not surprising that today you say 'full experience and abstract art' in one breath, because that combination is the problem that he solved. Today both are being attacked—abstract art and, more important, the full experience. Before Jackson Pollock, abstraction, as practiced by working fine-artists (with only a few odd exeptions) rarely passed the decorative stage of incomplete and weak experiences. It was at this unformed time that Jackson Pollock's solution began penetrating the whole art community in New York. That abstract art could encompass a complete experience, as figurative art could, was his point. What a revolutionary statement he made!

In the 1930s, when I first met Jackson at the Art Students League, our schooling was geared for the complete experience through an old-fash-

144

ioned "one-two-three" (shop talk from representational painting and sculpture): the tradition enumerated number one as the line, number two as the form, number three as color. They were equivalent to the reading, writing, 'rithmetic of primary school. A work must have the three elements before it can encompass a complete experience. Representational work of the '30s shows a conscientious application of the one-two-three solution. Some, for instance, overemphasized line by subduing form and color. In others, the lines were hazy, and emphasis was put on distinct *form* accompanied by "white-hair" color (the inference was old color, a color mixed with a lot of white). Another instance of the '30s, to pick at random, might be to subdue the first two and press "color on color" until it looked like Cézanne's idea of a Mexican village with multi-colored planes. No matter how the one-two-three was juggled, the experience was completed as far as representational imagery was concerned. How significant at this point to recall Jackson Pollock's intense schooling, spanning seven years, of almost constant attendance at the Art Students League.

Pollock's genius simply substituted the first one-two-three with another one-two-three. Through them he elevated abstract art to a noble fine art, independent and persuasive. Abstraction attained equality alongside traditional art in his canvases, because the depth of experience was as full and complete.

The importance of completing the experience has come into prominence only since the recent decline of anti-art. Anti-art's sloganing of a non-experience art was its sick premise. It started a disease that attacked the whole pragmatic basis of American art. The French, who are more knowledgeable, always suppressed anti-art—to a reasonable degree.

The polemic in Jackson Pollock's invention deepened the abstract experience more than we knew way back in the '40s. Instead of line he used the *movement* of massed lines; instead of form he projected a new aggressive *space*; and instead of color he hit on the abstract sense of *light*. From his example of deepening the sensibilities, other artists caught on and succeeded in their own individual expression. Everyone knows how the great abstract movement has been replete with format and invention.

Jackson's three subtle ideas rubbed off on artists who didn't know the exact words for them. Nonetheless they spread like wildfire—their new way produced many variations and formats and images. It was not his technique, but the connection to the three basic rings in our sensibilities that anchored the revolution. Only once or so in fifty or sixty years do we discover a new area in our sensibilities. Jackson Pollock did exactly this to us. The term "expressionism," according to the dictionary, is a *way* of expressing. To paraphrase this, he raised abstract art to a major way of expression.

Unique is not a general word if you underline its root meaning: one and individual. Jackson Pollock makes you conscious of one unique core in his personality. Despite the gentle randomness of weaving and under-weaving lines and drips, they always maneuver around the core. He made a situation in which the slightest change in line came directly from a choice in his sensibility. A flying dripping line swings this way, then that way, at the command of subtle impulses in his one-two-three language. His line masses move around a delicate compass with the needle pointing to the lodestone of his personality.

Jackson Pollock's space was new and unique. His sensibilities reversed the old perspective idea that the nature of space was to recede and never stand still. By terrific power in projecting his mass movement of lines and his distribution of light, he drove space into the room *at* the onlooker and he never let the space recede beneath the back of the canvas. The onlooker himself became the turning perspective points, the apex of the pyramidal feeling that I spoke of at first. The space was not only new, but very convincing.

His last invention towards a new *way* of expression was in his sense of light as opposed to color. He tried to make color more abstract, but did not reject it. As in a Mondrian, subtler divisions of light substituted for color sensations and passages. Pollock's black-and-white and silver paint, operating as color, completed the substitution of light for color. He was careful of overemphasizing color, as was Mondrian, because it made space recede.

Why do we embrace Jackson Pollock more than ever today? Because the majority of social forces have coerced the art community with the idea of non-experience and anti-artist. This should be the last straw. Non-experience asks the outsider to make a complete experience—within himself; to be the other half of the artist: a sort of audience-participation because *you,* as the audience, become the participant expected to furnish one-third or two-thirds of the experience on your own. The anti-art artist in his new role of anti-artist gives the work of art a minimum or minimal scaffolding. Gestalt rationalizes this idea: you attain the final experience within yourself. Gestalt psychology says your mind will complete configurations in after-images of "ambiances." But after-images do not make an aesthetic experience—they belong to the optics or mechanical actions of our body and are not related to our sensibilities. When the Gestalt minimal artist presents one color, have no fear; you, the participant, are expected to finish two-thirds of the experience with your own favorite color combinations. You, the participant, are qualified to sign your name to the work of art. When the Gestalt anti-artist leaves you with plain ordinary air space, have no doubt, you are expected to finish off the experience with any location and with your movements and the light you choose. The Gestalt artist gives you the trigger, as he says, meaning to start you off on your own sweet, unaccompanied, lonely, arty, individual way. The pragmatic fact remains, that a Gestalt art is a non-experience, therefore it is anti-art. The Gestalt idea does not apply to esthetics and therefore cannot substitute for, or compete with, the pragmatic idea of raw expression.

Another school of non-experience revives the Occult art of England. An emblem or geometric outline, they say to you: you, again the audience–participant, should summon some mysterious meaning in your experience, don't be such a flatfoot onlooker. In an art work as plain and dry as a textbook, you—invoking the powers of William Blake—should immediately cite magical and allusionary meanings. Even if the participant—English or not—brings a sense of awe and a book of occult geometric meanings, the work of art fades away *within* the onlooker because it is an incomplete experience—love-making without a crescendo.

These learned schools of anti-art are fading away, but the breed of artists who stick with the *straight* experience will survive. Their aim is clear—a full, clear experience. The techniques and the images of Jackson's work may be bypassed as the countenance of each decade changes, but his unique invention of a *way* toward a full experience will persist throughout the changing decades. The '60s, in spite of the help of a brilliant audience-participation, seem to have lost half of the decade in the fading away of non-experience art—but I feel the Pollock tradition persists and will emerge on top. The '70s will be the decade of most surprises, because by then we will have forgotten anti-art's army of occupation, and the great Pollockian excavations of the experience will liberate great, great surprises.

BY ADOLPH GOTTLIEB

During the 1940s, a few painters were painting with a feeling of absolute desperation. Pollock was one of these. The situation was so bad that I knew I felt free to try anything, no matter how absurd it seemed: what was there to lose? Neither Cubism nor Surrealism could absorb someone like myself: we felt like derelicts. The American establishment was obviously lacking in seriousness. There seemed to be an enormous vacuum that needed to be filled: but with what?

Therefore one had to dig into one's self, excavate whatever one could, and if what came out did not seem to be art by accepted standards, so much the worse for those standards. This meant that one had to establish one's own values in the face of that huge vacuum, and a few critics eventually talked about art as being on the brink of an abyss.

Obviously with this effort to establish some sort of values, everyone was on his own, and though it seemed as if certain artists were loosely banded together, actually there was a strong spirit of individualism. Pollock was one of the individualists, and like a few others at that time, who also found themselves at the edge of the abyss, I am sure he felt alone.

BY JAMES BROOKS

Jackson's break into the irrational was the most violent of any of the artists', and his exploration of the unconscious, the most daring and persistent. A highly responsive draftsmanship swept his work through a world of revelations and frights, and he was always past the point of no return.

Perhaps there was no immediate Pollock school of painters because his work acted in a very different way—as a destroyer and a liberator over a wide spectrum, fertilizing seemingly opposite expressions by its disgust with the threadbare and by its strong assertion of life.

BY LARRY RIVERS

Helen Frankenthaler and I visited the Pollocks in The Springs in the spring of 1951. We saw his large light studio: tremendous canvases piled up on the floor, perhaps fifteen one on top of the other. He lifted the corners so we could peek. We had lunch in his house. The amount of work combined with his serious talk and the monastic lack of housiness moved us. About an hour after the visit Helen and I were standing on a deserted beach with drawn faces looking into the ocean which by now had become the ancient abyss, promising to devote ourselves ever more determinedly and forever to ART. By 1954 this had all changed considerably :He had tried to destroy a piece of sculpture of mine commissioned by Castelli that stood in Castelli's driveway by running it down with his Ford. He made many offending remarks about my work, some published, some just brought by mouth, and some directly. What I had seen in his work as depth of involvement now seemed narrowed simply to his point of view. My devotion to Art and a life of Art had taken on a distinctly anti-Pollock tone. What was obviously gorgeous in his work was becoming infused with a mindlessness impossible to separate form his social personality. I was so put off by him and the applause that surrounded his work I could hardly look at it. Mostly I kept my opinions to myself; I couldn't bear the sour grapes. I wouldn't attend his funeral. I thought it false: that if I went I would be trying to appear as an accepted member of a certain community of sentiment. His death, ten years, thousands of works later, mine and everybody's, a realization of how impossible everything seems and must have seemed to Pollock, have made me more open to his work and him. My piece of sculpture deserved to be run down and Pollock's work still gives me a good deal of assurance that there is some virtue in "keeping at it" in the middle of the contradictions, difficulties, and uninteresting absurdities of being alive.

BY ALEX KATZ

I was in a state of intoxication. I had found myself. I had discovered direct nature painting. I was bothered by the way my paintings looked. I remember painting sunlight coming toward me through trees, and ending up with contained planes. When I saw Pollock, I realized he had sensation, energy and light, and it seemed much more like the motif I was painting than my paintings. He opened up the areas of sensation painting and gestural painting, which wiped out the rules I had been painting by, and opened areas that I'm still following. The paradox with Pollock is that as he questioned twentieth-century French painting he made me reconsider other European artists: Tintoretto, Fragonard, Valesquez, and Watteau.

The modern art that thrilled me was all European. It was impossible to consider it as having anything to do with my life. Impossible for me to be a part of it. I could paint in their manner as a provincial or paint in a personal style that was provincial. Pollock made it possible for me to participate. The establishment of sensation painting was something I could relate to my experience, and questioning the standards of the great twentieth-century painting made it possible for me to accept myself. It became evident it was my sensation, my picture, and either I was there in the present tense or it was all wrong.

The establishment of a grand personal style offered many possibilities for a large number of artists.

BY AL HELD

Pollock converted me to modern art.

First saw his paintings in the late 1940s when I was a student Social-Realist, and hated them. They were everything art wasn't supposed to be about. The paintings made a fantastic physical impact on me. I couldn't shake them off. After much rationalizing, I decided that Pollock was *the* Social Realist (sounds naïve now). I even dripped paint for a while.

149

Attitudes about art keep changing and Pollock's paintings seem to be able to absorb them.

BY ALLAN KAPROW

Scholarly techniques applied to an artist's sources are valuable aids to knowing what he is all about. It is quite helpful, for instance, to investigate Jackson Pollock's roots in Impressionism, Cubism, Dadaism, Surrealism, and Navajo sand painting: possibly even in Soutine's expressionism, certainly in Benton and the modern Mexicans: Orozco, Rivera, and Siqueiros. The critical task thereafter is to emphasize the most relevant of these derivations, for him, for his milieu, and for us. Relevance clearly is a shifty affair, but it is necessary to account for what Pollock seemed to be involved in, whether we care for it or not.

So far as present taste is concerned, I share the view of some critics that the automatic writing and drawing of Dada and Surrealism, added to the sand-rituals of the Southwestern Indians, are primary. For it was such stimulants that evolved into the most important of his works, the large drip-paintings. But even so, his concern with the unconscious, with primitive myth and ceremony, with the crisis of self-realization, in short, with the romantic urgency of creativity, are surely not factors in today's art.

What is relevant to painters now is Pollock's whole surface rather than his imagery or impulses. Artists' conversations and the evidence of their work point to an interest in surface as *sufficient value*, not as a "mere" surface covering over a truer, "inner content": that is, surface as in no way bound up with its verbally implied opposite, in no way "superficial." Contemporary surface breathes, bugs you, warps, declares itself directly. Pollock's surface is particularly moving in this respect.

Alfred Brunelle calls this phenomenon *Skin Freakism*. In his essay, "Bunny Head Infinity" (from a pamphlet printed by F. Castle, N. Y., 1966, on the Guggenheim Museum's Systemic show), he suggests a psychedelic analogy. Skin Freak is: "An experience induced by using a pleasurable hallucinogen . . . [is] an individual who prefers to structure his sensory experience to center on physical sexuality when under the auspices of a pleasurable hallucination." He says of Abstract-Expressionism: "Being innately physical, and directed by personal pleasure because of the remoteness of the prevailing (European) traditions, the flatness of the surface was perceived in the new art not as a passive wall, but as a skin automatically suggestive of possibilities for visual stimulation . . . As more and more extraneous European elements were eliminated, the conception of

American painting as skin became classic, that is, supreme and ordained . . . For there, skin ruled, not by force, but by right, its secrets were unattainale, ultimately sublime. [This] work celebrates in an epic way the palpable source of mysticism, which is feminine mystery. The idea of skin as the totality of all aspects of all things and their indeterminate but always correct identity, is now crystalized . . . Skin, which was once only paint, is everything which ignores information and professes delight. Bunny Head, which might be postulated as the ensemble average of sensual joys, is what is happening." Thus, Jackson Pollock helped point the way to Bunny Head.

A film of the artist at work indicated the close bond between his body movements and the track left by them on the surface of the canvas. Then Harold Rowsenberg's article "The American action Painters," in ART-NEWS, Dec., 1952, completed the growing idea: why not separate the *action* from the *painting?* First make a *real* environment, then encourage appropriate action. The expanding scale of Pollock's works, their iterative configurations prompting the marvelous thought that they could go on forever in any direction including out, soon made the gallery as useless as the canvas, and choices of wider and wider fields of environmental reference followed. In the process, the Happening was developed.

Whether it is Skin Freakism or Happenings, such uses of Pollock's example can be criticized by the strict scholar as *misuses*. Surface, divorced from anxiety and crisis, may be called a parody of the full range and power of the older man. And Happenings have in fact been considered an unwarranted exaggeration of the myth of Action Painting.

But it could have been argued some years back—and perhaps it was— that Pollock didn't understand Impressionism because he had no sense of sunlight or nature, and his color was acrid; that he didn't learn anything from Cubism because his forms were too loose and weren't founded on an analytic methodology; that he didn't know anything about Dadaism since he lacked the cultural exhaustion of the Europeans, their political outrage and their sense of humor; that his interest in the unconscious was corny compared with the intellectual refinements of the Surrealists; that he couldn't have gotten a thing out of the Navajos because he was ignorant of the religious meanings of their painting rites; that he couldn't maintain the rural American imagery of Benton; and that, as far as the Mexicans were concerned, he was a poor bet for a political propagandist . . . It could have been argued—and I remember very clearly that it was—that Pollock didn't even know how to *paint* because, according to Continental criteria, he had no grasp of negative-positive space relationships.

Well (lights up, music), now he is accorded the honor of being an expert: notice how deftly he places his marks, how brilliantly he controls his format, the critics (including myself) say. But it is not my intention to imply that thus he has proven his real understanding of his sources. Nor that Skin Freaking and Happenings will be vindicated similarly. Quite the contrary, I wish to propose, instead, that Pollock really misused his sources by all conventional standards, taking from them rather marginal attributes or tones of feeling, rather than developing their central principles. Pollock may be the first major artist who, after a pathetic apprenticeship to older art, was able to become major by ignoring *demonstrable* familiarity with existing models.

Picasso, after all, proved his mastery over a variety of styles, historical and contemporary, as steps along the way to both innovation and virtuosity. And Picasso was the archetypal modernist. But Pollock's realized works of 1947–51 bore none of the direct resemblances to predecessors that Cubism bore to Cézanne. The reasons for this change in creative possibility are too complex to go into here, but a principle was set for a generation to follow: namely that insight and growth in art lie less in certain lineal developments that are synthesized at some later point, than in a numberless range of arbitrary attractions and repulsions to and from things in *and* out of art. These may or may not be crystallized in the medium first begun with. An artist may like the smile on the face of a 6th century B.C. kouros, and the smell of gasoline, and the result could be musical. In other words, art may now be a discipline of deliberate "misuses" (or free interpretations and combinations) of source material.

A tentative awareness of this new atmosphere is already apparent in critics who are otherwise traditional in their thinking. For instance, William Rubin, in an informative article on Pollock (in *Artforum*, Feb., '67) refers to the continuity of the Pollock concept in Frankenthaler and Louis, among others, and then mentions Johns, Poons, Stella and Warhol as painters who also benefit from his single image and all-over method. Now at the very least, these four artists can be said to misread Pollock's "hot" treatment of the canvas, if all other differences are ignored. But if criticism has become so sophisticated that observations like Mr. Rubin's can be made—correctly, I think—then it should be easy to list as Pollock's heirs not only Skin Freak painting and Happenings, but much more.

If an artist wanted to make the connection, he could say that some of the underground discotheques come straight out of Jackson Pollock—and he'd be right. Look at the action! It's all-over; it's intense; when you're in it you don't know what you're doing; it seems to go on without beginning or end; the noise and the lights assault you; the pulsations, changing ever-so-slightly, come in waves; you are surrounded; it's overwhelming . . .

/

[1]Only a fraction of the whole material was used, I think

BY CLAES OLDENBURG

Egomessages about Pollock.

1. Following his call to directness got me out of art school and unlocked the use of paint. The school system was to have the student choose a favorite French Impressionist or Post-Impressionist to follow. After a few weeks with Cézanne, I switched to Pollock, i.e., chose the living, which meant trouble. For example, I brought to class a palette of store paints in a cardboard box. I put them on the canvas and they ran off on the floor, because I didn't know that Pollock painted straight down.

2. Pollock acts in my work as a fiction. I objectify him: American Painter, Painter of Life, Painter of New York. I honor all the stereotypes about him. This extends to edge of magic procedures of identification, with which the stereotype receiving machinery more or less cooperates (for example, pp. 110–111 in Kaprow's recent book on Happenings). Here I've got the thing down on the floor though usually I had it on end and the paint found its own way through gravity.

3. Pollock's paint immediately suggested city subjects, the walls, the stores, the taxicabs. I don't know if he cared about that. In Happenings, which owe something to him, the world is smeared with paint or its substitutes. I used that kind of paint to entangle the objects in my surroundings. Later I used paint-like material, like water, for dipping people in. The vinyl I now use is still paint, the objects dissolving now in paint. Pollock is a paint-legend because, unlike Picasso, he turned the Sapolin loose.

4. His statement in *Possibilities* is the model of truth and unsentimentality, exactly what an artist can say about what he is doing. It seems strange to hear him speak of "my painting," which suggests a small piece of property, or ground, which he is standing on. How hard to stand on other paintings of the time—in fact his were very large by comparison. The canvas on which I now (a post–Pollock painter) am standing on not only stretches as far as I can see or hear, but has layers, roofs, floors, basements, etc. Seeing gold frames around Pollocks now is funny and also hurts.

5. The big symbol energy that vibrates in Pollock's lightcords is painful now, but also unnecessary. Every simple thing is so engaged in its own vast symbol production that it seems better to switch off. That was a time when no thing spoke for itself and the landscape was full of noisy monuments. But now everything speaks for itself.

6. New York scares the hell out of me. When I ran for death to Los Angeles, I made the Bedroom as a demonstration of my necrophilia. On

the walls are pseudo-Pollocks, yardgoods from Santa Monica. Whatever else this act suggests, I intended at the time to use Pollock as a symbol of Life, and photography, as the symbol of Death.

BY KENNETH NOLAND

I really haven't much to say about Pollock. As you know, along with David Smith his position, attitude, and work mean a great deal to me. But I don't consider it my responsibility to take a stand. His work and what he tried for are great for me. Other people can write about why Pollock is great or not great, or use his work and position to make whatever point they need to make, but most writing about art including writing by artists is art-world junk.

BY DAVID LEE

For this new confidence in his senses, it is right to say that Pollock broke significantly with the classic history of painting. It is not of much interest however to speak of subsequent breaks. It is a change which he did and we are doing. Drips of oil are not more information than a sheet of acrylic, painted or pressed. It is stupid to formulate what happens from year to year by employing evolutionary schemes in which artists are treated as if they were empirical scientists constantly reducing a problem toward its solution. It is not progress, it just happens that an artist will lose interest in what has preoccupied him when it has become information. Artists always appear to perceive that technology, when it is any use, returns the circle of man's achievement to where it begins—at spirit. Representation, for example, was not a "problem" and it was not "solved," but artists put it to the side with other labor-saving devices when the technical institutes succeeded in making it accessible to any hard-working applicant.

Pollock, a past-master of formal design, put aside that technology and its abstractions and rationalizations. He put design theories (which the technologians called "basic" from the same unitarian impulse that now has them call structure "primary") in their place beside air brushes and reducing lenses. He put those very reasonable theories of how to balance line and space and color and so on out of art (which is not to say he forgot them). What he did concern himself with, and what is now our concern, is the selection and the manner of presentation of the parts of material which one sees in the finished painting. He chose oil and canvas. The oil, itself in parts, he laid on the face of a shallow box covered with canvas.

And, as any philistine can tell you, that is all there is to see. Ask an artist, or someone else, about his attitudes, but don't look for them in a painting. It alludes to none. It has no images but the one in your eye. It is a bewitching decoration—an artist made it. He devoted his entire self, including what he remembered, to making it, but he did not put that information in it. Explanation is something else like this. A painting is only symptomatic of an artist's attitudes. It is real and not any abstraction. It is only an obscure and personal demonstration. Pollock's paintings are not *important* to you, they are important to him. If you are affected seeing them, well you know, that's your trip, not his. You can't go on his trip except metaphorically. And *that* is a trivial trip, a pleasant indulgence for the readers of art books.

BY AL BRUNELLE

Jackson Pollock is legendary because it is a traditional response to value rarity. Perhaps not one man in a million is capable of *personal* activity; the others are merely communicative or self-communicative, dealing in information. Pollock's paintings are incomprehensible, perfect settings for private reveries which will not resemble Pollock's. They will be an affront for spectators lacking the self-confidence to enjoy it.

The familiar conception of Painting is based upon Painting as a language, with individual activity existing within an established syntax. This painting still exists in Europe in a decadent form, but can hardly be said to ever have existed in this country. Many of its stylistic devices and techniques, including some of the latest, have been preserved by documentation. These form the basis for the business of commercial illustration. They are also practiced as a pastime by retired Kansas farmers, Queens housewives, Andrew Wyeth and others. Any Frenchman with a tongue (langue) will gladly say that all this has nothing to do with Painting.

The arts have always been supplementary communication systems, reflecting and reinforcing the characteristics of the chief system, Language. Changes in and adjustments between all systems resulted from, or were mitigated by, desire rather than necessity. They were formal rather than informational. The only art which has an effect is Poetry. Poetry gives form to language.

The technological revolution initiated a ravenous demand for information, exceeding the capacities of the existing systems. A permanent state of emergency resulted, causing a neglect of form. Necessity birthed new supplementary systems, which were, of course, more efficient in manipulating information than the older ones. The old systems decreased in importance. Painting, even in its halcyon days, was known to be an imperfect medium; and its incomprehensible aspects, largely pleasurable, were defended more and more often with the term decoration.

With technological demands supplanting the formal gist of language, poets, the makers of language, were shouldered aside by the minor literary professions, the users of language, who speedily infiltrated technology. This situation, aided by heterogeneous immigration, overwhelmed the barely established provincial culture of the United States. The result was the ideal climate for technology, language, and customs so informal and flexible they can hardly be described as culture. Pollock and his four contemporaries, Still, Newman, Reinhardt, and Rothko, unable to connect to the remnants of the European tradition, created an entirely new type of painting out of their personal desires. Ted Castle has written: "painters don't love painting, but they do love something abstracted out of it which we call Art". A *dignified* self-expression, non-compulsive and understood, IS the content of their art activity. It IS NOT the content of their work, which is personal and non-expensive, alluding to nothing.

The New American Painting is not a communication system. It is not a school, nor does it recognize historical necessity, avant-garde evolutionary schemes or any fabrication traceable to the most vulgar and informal knot of critics, those characterized by jargon, which is the antithesis of poetry. I refer to those described, ironically enough, as formal critics. More than the others, Pollock seemed especially vulnerable to speculation and he dominated the scene because of this. He exemplfies the idisyncratic nuture of the new painting and the critical failure to deal with the visible remains of this adventure.

There are more painters now whose activity is personal, and has correspondences with Pollock, than there were 15 years ago. After the original five, at least 14 others, and there will be more in increasing numbers.

BY JANE FREILICHER

I am trying to think about Jackson Pollock from a hotel room in Barbados, West Indies. Through the window, which by coincidence is curtained in a sleazy-looking "Pollock-inspired" fabric print, comes the noise of a steel band playing its version of the hit tune of the Caribbean season, the "Lara" theme from the movie *Dr. Zhivago*. So much for cultural fallout.

If the themes, shapes, ideas, the "content" of art can be so quickly ground down and redistributed throughout the world in the form of curtain material or jukebox tunes, then what is it that does remain alive, essential, and durable in a work of art? Much as one may try to reject the idea of art as mysterious and unexplainable, how does one explain what gives a work of art its vitality and expressiveness when its technical or conceptual innovations no longer arrest us.?

Fairfield Porter once said of Pollock's paintings that they looked to him like tracings of thornbushes in the snow. They perhaps can be seen as evolving from a kind of American naturalism which was transformed into something new by Pollock's fierce and gorgeous doodling. The statement "the medium is the message" might have been invented to describe his work.

Pollock's achievement brought a glamor and authority to American painting which inspired younger painters in the late 1940s and 1950s with a kind of "new frontier" excitement. If you could bring it off, "make it work," it might be possible to do anything and, indeed, by now "anything" has been attempted. In my own mind I think this atmosphere almost of elation which pervaded the art scene in the heyday of Abstract Expressionism while contributing a sense of esprit-de-corps and purposefulness, a kind of group spirit which was pleasant and no longer exists, made me want to stand a little to one side, where I was anyway, and go on with what I was doing.

BY JOAN MITCHELL

I feel very content to remain "a speechless and helpless manufacturer of art objects" [See *The New Art Selection Process* by Irwin Fleminger, A.n., Jan. '67], and reluctant to comment on, or try to explain, the greatness of Jackson Pollock and what he meant and continues to mean to me. Undoubtedly his enormous generosity and lyricism of feeling are frightening to the non-feeling reductionist school so prevalent and popular today.

Frank O'Hara's own lyric generosity and greatness expresses what I cannot in words. In his monograph on Pollock, he wrote: "In *Blue Poles* he gave us one of the great masterpieces of Western art, and in *The Deep* a work which contemporary esthetic conjecture had cried out for. *Blue Poles* is our *Raft of the Medusa* and our *Embarkation for Cytherea* in one. I say *our*, because it is the drama of an American conscience, lavish, bountiful, and rigid. It contains everything within itself, begging no quarter: a world of sentiment implied, but denied; a map of sensual freedom, fenced; a careening licentiousness, guarded by eight totems native to its origins (*There Were Seven in Eight*). What is expressed here is not only basic to his work as a whole, but it is final."

BY DAVID NOVROS

Blue Poles, Number 1, 1950, Lavender Mist, and *Autumn Rhythm;* if I say that these paintings are "totally resolved"—what do I mean? I mean that in describing my appreciation of *Blue Poles* I cannot separate colors, color drawing, composition, space, shape and describe the ways in which these elements are independently deployed in the painting. If I write about the "colors" in the painting (ultramarine, black, white, orange, yellow, aluminum) and how they are juxtaposed then I will be writing about the "drawing" which at the same time will describe the "space" which will describe the "composition" which will describe the "scale" which will describe the "total color quality." This meaningless verbal circle suggests the complex visual unity of *Blue Poles.* Yes—there's that orange next to that aluminum behind blue just on a plane with the black, no—behind the black, no—in front of the black, no—. Those *Poles,* no, they are blue paint, no, they are drawing, no, they are the "compositional" structure of the painting, no—what are they? The physical size of the canvas defines an area and determines the scale that goes on inside it—no, the canvas appears to be in heroic scale because of its content, no—why is that painting so big—not just large in scale—but absolutely big? Is this confusing? When written, yes, but when standing in front of *Blue Poles,* there are no contradictions, the painting transcends all paradox—it is a unified object—a painting—and that is something I know, but can't explain.

BY GEORGE SEGAL

I never met Pollock. Everybody spoke of him when I was going to art school at NYU in the late '40s. They told me he was violent, deep, inarticulate, he drank too much, was passionate, revolutionary, put HIMSELF in his paintings. I had an image of Marlon Brando's brooding pouting profile looking down while Stella ripped his teeshirt from his sloping shoulders with gouging fingernails. But Pollock's creased forehead in his photographs intrigued me. He had the agonized look of a man wrestling with himself in a game of unnamable but very high stakes.

I was reeling under a barrage of words when I first saw Pollock's paintings. The words said: you can't talk about or explain art; suppress figures; read French Symbolist poetry; look at Cubism; look at Surrealism; forget about Cubism; forget about Surrealism; pick up a paintbrush and take a hero's stance in a monk's cell; be as tough and earthy as a New York cabbie.

What shocked me about Pollock's paint was that he bought it in the corner hardware store and used it like a prehistoric magician or medieval monk.

It didn't matter to me whether the paintings were abstract or figurative; the pure lines tangling looked like the path of cosmic forces, the bugs looked like they were coming out of primeval ooze. She-Wolves, Totems, the man was excited over myths. How much did he believe in Jung? Where was the beginning, middle, and end of his pictures? How could he fly and still be rooted to cigarette butts and his own handprints?

But where was my own beginning, middle, and end? I was on an endless shuttle between a chicken-farm in New Jersey and downtown New York. The coops were the city simplified to a nightmare: rows of brown wooden rooms, old tenement doors, slimy brown muck on the floors, hysterical wind impact of white wings. Train rides and city buildings were grey and the only color seemed to come from electric and neon light. The colors in Impressionist paintings looked as made up as a Hollywood Technicolor movie. The first de Kooning Woman I saw looked like fragments of a rosy Rubens floating in a sea of garbage and I roared with the laughter of recognition.

All this new work fascinated and disturbed me. How could these paintings catch the feeling of how and where I was living, then change and become places of the mind? I felt earthbound, walking into a loft, aware of paint peeling off bricks, galvanized ¾-inch unions screwed cockeyed on gas lines, paint drips on rough splintered wood floors, then a big painting, all lines and marks. What was impressing me? The painting? The climb up the long dark stairs and coming into an unbelievable expanse of pure white walls? Both?

Years later I saw a Rothko show at the Modern Museum where the paintings were hung close together in small cubicles and people looked incredibly good surrounded by this single glowing world. When I heard that Rothko had hung the show himself, I was secretly pleased that he understood this need for complete envelopment. The big Pollock paintings were something else. He painted them on the floor and gestures near the edges were completed off the canvas and people were talking about endless continuum. But he picked them up and mounted them on wooden stretchers, bending the gesture around the edges, and hung them on a wall. After staring at them, the violence and turbulence ebbed and a strange evenness emerged.

Two things struck me. One had to do with the liquidness of body movements. When I lifted a sack of feed, I felt the pressure on my ankles and belly and the weight on my back. When I dreamed of lifting my panel truck wedged down a flight of stairs, the movement was easy and liquid. Walking, breathing and being felt liquid, and I said yes to Pollock.

The other thing was more tenuous. He implied endless continuation, but chose to contain his image in a severe geometric rectangle. An intelligent man, he couldn't be called wrong. Like all of us, he accepted the plane of the canvas psychologically as a metaphor for his private universe. Like a book, the painting became an object in the world, a special object

that afforded a glimpse into the interior of a man. Why hang my own wishes and doubts on Pollock? I found his work uncanny in being able to project his sense of being. But I couldn't separate my own sense of being from the place where I was. Shouldn't the work flow from yourself out into the real world and return because it was the same thing? But how do you do that?

I stopped painting for two years after that and felt very courageous when I resumed.

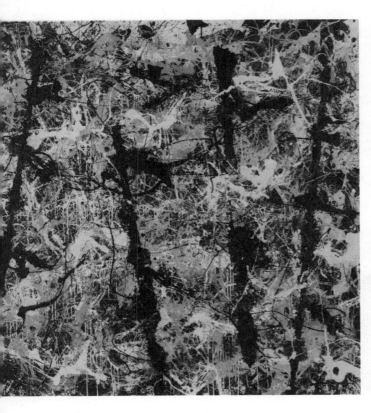

For Novros: Jackson Pollock, *Blue Poles: Number 11, 1952*, 1952. Enamel and aluminum paint with glass on canvas, 82 7/8 x 191 5/8 inches. NATIONAL GALLERY OF AUSTRALIA, CANBERRA. © THE POLLOCK-KRASNER FOUNDATION, INC. / ARS. PHOTO: POLLOCK-KRASNER STUDY CENTER, JACKSON POLLOCK CATALOGUE RAISONNÉ ARCHIVES.

ANDY WARHOL

1962

You mean I don't have to drip?

Andy Warhol to Ivan Karp

Improvisations: NOTES ON POLLOCK AND JAZZ

ANDREW KAGAN

MARCH, 1979

In a large sense, Jackson Pollock's epochal innovation consists in his having created high art through the act of direct improvisation. This feat had no complete precedent in the history of what we call high art. That Pollock was able to win such stature for absolute painterly improvisation was the consequence of a particular set of conditions formed by his background, temperament, taste, social milieu, and historical context. In the literature on Pollock, the improvisatory character of his art and techniques was noted very early and has been mentioned often, but its causes and origins have scarcely been examined.[1] Some critics have even gone to great lengths in an attempt to demonstrate that Pollock was really more composer than improviser, but such misguided apologias only serve to obscure the true character and significance of his achievement.

Somewhere in the distinction between composition and improvisation, an imperfectly defined distinction, lies the threshold which Pollock crossed to attain his success and renown. At present there is no way to demarcate accurately the point at which improvisation leaves off and composition begins, though we know well enough what we commonly mean by "impovised" and "composed." A better understanding of this distinction would lead to a better understanding of Pollock's achievement. I do not propose to offer conclusive definitions here, not to explicate exhaustively the course of artistic evolution by which Pollock arrived at his celebrated, liberating "drip" technique. I would like, in this brief essay,

[1]Cf. William Rubin, "Jackson Pollock and the Modern Tradition, II," *Artforum*, V (March 1967), pp. 30, 32; "III," *Artforum*, V (April 1967), p. 29; B. H. Friedman, "Profile: Jackson Pollock," *Art in America*, XLIII (Dec. 1955), pp. 49, 58–59; Alfred Frankenstein, review in *The San Francisco Chronicle* (Aug. 12, 1945).

only to draw attention to some heretofore neglected causal factors which made possible the creation and acceptance of Pollock's art.

Since the Renaissance, the fine art of painting has been dominated by the concept of the picture as a *composition*, i.e., as the precisely calculated, balanced, carefully analyzed and premeditated arrangement of pictorial elements in a harmonious order. The end products of this system of composition have usually evolved through a serious of experimental studies used to determine the proper values, proportions, and location of specific elements within a general, geometric scheme of design. Renaissance aestheticians such as Alberti were so taken with the order, principle, and proportion of ancient Greco–Roman architecture that they viewed the application of tectonic canons to pictorial art as the only logical course by which that art could progress or be revitalized. The grid was an especially revolutionary invention, and it came into standard use as a means for conceptualizing, structuring, and analyzing the picture surface, for breaking it down into more manageable components, and for projecting and measuring more specific design ideas such as perspective.

While these developments were underway in painting, similar tectonic principles were being applied to music, and the art of musical composition began to take form in similar fashion. Music theory and practice were being revolutionized by the refinement of notation, the standardization of compositional devices such as staff, meter and tempo, and the gradual elaboration of counterpoint—the system of theme-and-variation structures that grew into the monumental, soaring architectures of J. S. Bach.

Both high music and high painting retained the ideals of freshness, vitality, and spontaneity such as are found in good improvisation. There has always been praise for that sense of something continually discovered anew, the uninhibited flow of original thought which harkens back to the creative play through which our primitive ancestors gave birth to the arts. An improvisatory style was, for example, kept alive in the Renaissance *tocatta* for solo keyboard. But pure improvisation was effectively excluded from the Renaissance high art tradition, which held it to be too primitive, casual, ephemeral, naive, and juvenile—or not sufficiently stable or monumental—for the sublime expressions of advanced civilization.

Between the period of Baroque and the late nineteenth century the arts underwent a gradual process of readmitting improvisatory elements. From Hals to Watteau to Delacroix to Monet, the spontaneous, bravura brushstroke lent increasing freshness to the strictures of static pictorial composition. In music, improvisation slowly gained acceptance as a semi-serious branch of performing art. In the nineteenth century, it even found a place in the high art of composition, as the concerto cadenza became a conventional opportunity for virtuosos to show off their skills. Nevertheless, the basic Renaissance principle of composition as the standard criterion of high art continued to reign supreme and was not seriously contested. Periodic reactions against the loosening trend—such as the Davidian Classicism of the late eighteenth century—served to reaffirm that principle. And even in the "age of sensibility" the keyboard improvisations of such masters as Scarlatti and Mozart were admired at least as much for their structure as for their expressive and inventive immediacy. That is, their improvisations sounded almost composed.

One of the most profound reactions against the loosening of compositional principle resulted from Cézanne's vision of building Renaissance-type structure into the impressionists' *plein-air* renderings of light and color. The Cubist system of composition, which Picasso and Braque developed from Cézanne's Ideas, held sway over much of the high art produced in the first half of the twentieth century. Through Cubism and Constructivism the grid and plastically distorted versions of the grid came to exert a grip on painting of this century as firm or firmer than the grip held by the perspective grid on Italian painting of the Quattrocento.

For many serious, young American painters in the 1940s, the grid concept must have come to seem a kind of obstacle or *terminus post quem*. The most ambitious among them sensed that they held in their hands the destiny of a new American art, and possibly the destiny of the whole western high art tradition. Highly conscious of their potential historical role, they had rejected American provincialism in favor of European modernism in its recent manifestations of Cubist and Constructivist composition. But they also came to understand that whoever intended to become the next Picasso or Matisse would have to invent a brand new pictorial language as those men had, a fundamentally new approach to picture-making that would be both universal and characteristically American, as French painting had for two centuries been both universal and characteristically French. One obvious point of attack was against the grid and the practice of composing formal elements in relation to that rectilinear framework. Another large target was the very notion of pictorial composition itself.

Pollock was the first to make this breakthrough, going beyond grid composition with his convincing demonstration that high, ambitious painting, even heroic, monumental painting, could be produced by straight improvisation. In his works from 1947 to 1950 he embraced the elements of accident and chance in pictures that record his free, dynamic gestures of applying pigment to canvas. In so doing, Pollock became the first American artist to be recognized for the creation of a distinctively American art that was unquestionably international in its consequence. Among the forces which guided his steps along the path toward improvisatory painting, none, I think, was more specifically decisive for his art than the improvisations of jazz music, which he loved and followed closely. It is strange that this connection has received so little attention, because Pollock was a true jazz addict, and jazz, the invention primarily of black Americans, was the first indigenous American music to receive international acclaim and appreciation. Even now it remains identified with the United States in most of the musical world.

According to Pollock's wife Lee Krasner:

> He would get into grooves of listening to his jazz records—not just for days—day and night, day and night for three days running, until you thought you would climb the roof! Jazz? He thought it was the only other really creative thing happening in this country. He had a passion for music . . . He told me that when he was a boy he bought himself a violin expecting to play it immediately. When he couldn't get the sound he wanted out of it, he smashed it in a rage.[2]

All accounts of Pollock's character describe him as an angry, almost suicidally repressed man, given to fits of violence and alcoholism. He himself spoke of "the wilderness in me."[3] It is not surprising that his taste in music should have run to a form of immediate emotional expression, and improvisatory form in which authenticity of feeling mattered even more than technique, though virtuoso technique was essential. Jazz voiced the passions of a passionate people. In "hot" jazz, the emotional extreme was the desiderata, not the state of inhibition, temper, and balance. "Cool" jazz also allowed for the discharge of intense feeling, but in a more restrained manner. Pollock evidently found release for his torments in this music, and he dreamt of finding a similar catharsis in visual art.

At the age of eighteen, when he was just beginning to explore art, Pollock was already bemoaning the lack of "freedom and rhythm" in his drawing.[4] In the early 1940s, contact with Surrealism led him to experiment in the direction of "automatism," but the focus of those experiments was on unconscious image manipulation, as in automatic writing. In paintings such as *Search for a Symbol* (1943) and *Blue Unconscious* (1945) he was trying unsuccessfully to paint out his craziness with a combination of Cubist technique and pseudo-psychological, Jungian Surrealist imagery. Not until he managed to abandon the Cubist way of approaching the picture and to grasp fully the modern idea of painting as an absolute, not an imagistic medium, was he effectively able to pour all of himself into his art. For Pollock the two problems—grid Cubism and

[2]B. H. Friedman, *Jackson Pollock: Energy Made Visible* (New York, 1972), p. 88.
[3]Ibid., p. 228.
[4]From a letter to his brother Charles, dated Jan. 31, 1930. Quoted in Francis V. O'Connor, ed., *Jackson Pollock* (Museum of Modern Art, New York, 1967), p. 15.

Jackson Pollock, *Autumn Rhythm: Number30, 1950*, 1950. Oil on canvas, 105 x 157 inches. Installation view, Betty Parson Gallery, 1950. Photo: Hans Namuth © Estate of Hand Namuth. Pollock-Krasner Study Center, Jackson Pollock Catalogue Raisonné Archives.

the production of artistic symbols—may have been indistinguishable. In any case, both were solved for him simultaneously when he figured out how to adopt jazz improvisation as a model for painting.

A variety of sources served to sanction Pollock's consultation of music as a model of artistic absoluteness and helped him to form a specific connection with jazz. One very important source was the example of the German artists Klee and Kandinsky, whose improvisatory drawing techniques were made familiar to Pollock when he studied printmaking with Stanley Hayter in 1945.[5] Both Klee and Kandinsky were well known for their use of musical models in art theory and practice. Klee must have been of special interest to Pollock because of that earlier artist's exploitation of the furious linear energies found in the scribblings of young children and his pioneering explorations in what he termed his "field of psychic improvisation."[6] Klee's improvisatory drawing technique also strongly influenced the "automatic" drawing of Miró and Masson whose work also entered into Pollock's thinking. However, the music from which Klee and Kandinsky took inspiration and direction was primarily Germanic serious

[5] Andrew Kagan, "Paul Klee's influence on American Painting: New York School," *Arts Magazine*, 49, 10 (June 1975), pp. 58–59.

composition of the eighteenth and nineteenth centuries, music with little personal relevance to Pollock. Another significant source linked to serious composition was the painting of Janet Sobel, an American autodidact, whose work Pollock saw and admired in 1944.[7] Sobel's picture entitled *Music* was an absolute work with a veinous, marbled texture claimed by the artist to have been inspired by symphonies of Shostakovitch.[8]

The well-known early 1940s "Broadway Boogie-Woogie" series of Piet Mondrian may also have counted for some influence on Pollock. Though these works are characteristic of Mondrian in their composed rectilinearity, their nominal tribute to a form of jazz and their absolute, syncopated ecstasies might well have planted a crucial suggestion in Pollock's mind or acted as a catalyst. Picasso, who was Pollock's idol, was probably helpful as an authoritative precedent for reference to primitive black art. We know that Pollock had been much concerned with the issue of primitivism at least since 1937, and he was no doubt seeking a personally valid point of contact.[9] There was nothing primitive about progressive jazz, but it was a black art-form, and it was generally seen as beneath or outside the western high art tradition. The example of Picasso provided reassurance that such references could be acceptable in high art.

Finally, Pollock must have found additional support for his interest in jazz in the field of art criticism where the issues of absoluteness (or abstractness), primitivism, and pictorial musicality were extensively aired. It is especially interesting to note that in 1945, two years before Pollock unleashed the expressive forces of his drip technique, the critic Alfred Frankenstein made the following not-quite-accurate but highly prophetic analogy to Pollock's work:

> The flare and spatter and fury of his paintings are emotional rather than formal, and like the best jazz, one feels that much of it is the result of inspired improvisation rather than conscious planning.[10]

The act of improvisation has been characterized by one writer as "a lightning mystery . . . the creative mystery of our age."[11] Pollock's successful turn to improvisation raises questions far broader than those which

---

[6]Ibid., pp. 54–56; also Andrew Kagan, "Paul Klee's 'Ad Parnassum': The Theory and Practice of Eighteenth-Century Polyphony as Models for Klee's Art," *Arts Magazine*, 52, 1 (Sept. 1977), pp. 101–2.

[7]Clement Greenberg, " 'American-Type' Painting," in *Art and Culture* (Boston, 1961), p. 218.

[8]Rubin, "Jackson Pollock and the Modern Tradition, III," p. 29.

[9]Friedman, *op. cit.*, p. 150.

[10]Frankenstein, op. cit.

[11]Alec Wilder, quoted in Whitney Balliett, *Improvising: Sixteen Jazz Musicians and their Art* (New York, 1977), p. vi.

concern only his personal sources. For example, what was going on in American culture that enabled it to take improvisatory painting seriously? And what was going on in the larger traditions of western civilization that enabled Pollock's highly spontaneous, gestural art to be heralded as the new standard of high painting? To answer these questions requires an awareness of the role of black people—and particularly of black musicians—in the formation of American culture.

America has long looked to its black population for popular culture and diversion. Blacks have provided the white socio-economic mainstream with innovations in culture and diversion to an extent grossly disproportionate to their numbers in the society. The white spin-off from black humor and music has been a familiar part of American life since the middle of the nineteenth century. From the minstrel shows to Al Jolson to Amos and Andy, Janis Joplin, Leon Redbone, and countless others, white performers have borrowed from and imitated their more inventive, less inhibited, less cautious black counterparts. Scores of white performers have attained eminent success by rendering black innovations palatable to the white multitudes. For the past two decades, genuine black music and the exploits of black athletes have been staples of the American entertainment diet. This dependence of white upon black is one of the most important cultural phenomena in our history.

Why have blacks so disproportionately influenced American culture? There appear to be three main causes. To begin culture, whether high or low, has rarely been taken very seriously by the mainstream of white American citizenry. "The business of America has been business" and work related to business. The business of pleasure, amusement, or cultivated diversion has been suspect, viewed askance from the position of our Puritan work ethic. Such pastimes have until recently been accepted as necessary evils, but fundamentally decadent, and not a real "man's work," at least when pursued on a full-time basis. The commercial exploitation of cultural innovations was not quite so disreputable because that is real business. But for a "respectable" white person to give himself over to the single-minded concentration and dedication necessary to expand culture at its roots was extremely problematic where music, entertainment, and visual art were concerned. (Literature has for some reason, probably our strong English heritage, always held a greater aura of respectability in this country.) Here we said "time is money," not "leisure" or "culture." Moreover, America has had no system of monarchical or state patronage by which art could, through economics, be bound to the official values of the society. In other words, there was a vacuum of cultural power and leadership. These conditions left a very large field very largely open to blacks of talent and ingenuity who had the time, lack of guilt, lack of inhibition, lack of social and emotional restraint, and the freedom to indulge passion—all necessary ingredients for pioneering fresh, new approaches to cultural expression.

Second, most blacks were effectively barred from education and other fields of economic competition. So their talents and aspirations naturally tended to turn toward the only avenue where there was real hope of success. They also could afford more easily to be daring, experimental, and uncautious—gamblers out of desperation—because they had so little to lose.

Finally, there is the simple fact that because of slavery, caucasians were exposed for the first time in large numbers to the black genius for rhythmic syncopation, an innate sensitivity not nearly so prevalent among whites. Forcibly removed from their native jungle environments, many blacks had and have not yet lost what most whites lost long ago via interference with natural processes of selection and the complexity of life in civilization: that is, an attunement to the fundamental rhythms and motions of the body, an attunement which is the ultimate basis for all musical expression. The races share common origins, and as a result of the exposure, many whites eventually came to feel the lack of that primitive rhythm within themselves. Hence the simultaneous repulsion and attraction, and the increasing dependency on black musical thought. Hence also the pervasive clichés about "jungle drums of passion" and "natural rhythm" in our literature.

Primitive African music is dominated by rhythmic ideas, from the most elementary repetition of percussive sounds to the most complicated syncopations in vast rhythmic orchestras. In contradistinction to western music, melody is virtually inconsequential. Melodic elements reside In simple chants repeated over and over and in the tweeting, chirping sounds of rudimentary plucked and blown instruments. There is an "allover" character to the descant and an absence of thematic development. But when blacks of high intellect, talent, and musical ingenuity encountered western forms of music in their new American surroundings, some remarkable things happened. First, from American folk ballads and hill music of Irish, Scottish, English and German descent, there crept into African-style field chants the idea of melody and theme. Protestant church hymns gave rise to the gospel-spiritual style. From out of these two lines of development was born the blues, with its plaintive, powerful, directly emotive expressions—tragic cries of pain and alienation—and its distinctive harmonic idiom and chord progressions—elementary stuff, but unknown in African music.

Later, more sophisticated black musicians such as Scott Joplin started to write down their compositions in ragtime. Here the black feel for syncopation was merged with the European concepts of counterpoint, key modulation, and theme and variation. From its early forms of lively, semi-improvised honky-tonk, ragtime was distilled into a composed, distinctively American music of serious interest and national importance. Then, out of these three source elements—the free emotional expressions of blues, the driving, pulsing rhythms of African racial memory, and the free-flowing, swinging, but tempered and developed melodic lines of ragtime—there was born an altogether new form of music, jazz. The essence of jazz was the development, on the part of individual virtuoso performers, of characteristic, highly individual and distinctive styles of improvisation. It may have been the black sense of felt rhythm—the subconscious mastery and control of rhythmic pattern in time—that made the best of black musicians so extraordinarily brilliant at the art of improvisation. Because they didn't have to worry about the rhythmic structure, but simply felt it, they were freed to expand their range of expression in wild cascades of melody. Here was precisely the "freedom and rhythm" for which Pollock yearned.

An important feature of jazz which it borrowed from western music and which set it apart from its earlier black sources was the concept of forced, rapid evolution, i.e., ambition. As change and variation are internally essential to western music, so stylistic, conceptual change has been its major external aspect. This has segregated it from the folk music of primitive cultures which usually changes only minimally over centuries. But in certain styles of jazz, the African concept of "allover" melody—melody as a constant, uniform texture—began partially to supplant the western concept of theme-and-variation. This caused some western composers such as Stockhausen to rethink the role of linear, thematic development. It may also have been some kind of determinant in the widely remarked "allover" quality of Pollock's improvisations.

Jazz has never been considered a truly high art, and its practitioners have not tended to see themselves in competition with Mozart, Bach, and Beethoven. But as an extremely sophisticated form of popular music it quickly captured the imagination of large segments of western society. A number of symphonic composers, such as Copland, Stravinsky, and Gershwin, started to incorporate jazz elements into their music as a kind of folk reference. This gave jazz a certain cachet among the arbiters of culture. However, it remained for Pollock to turn the *act* of improvisation to the purposes of high art.

For Pollock it was the improvisation, not the harmonic idiom, that mattered most in jazz. And ambitious improvisation was precisely what made jazz such a significant novelty in Europe. There it came to symbolize the wildness and freedom associated with the new world, and the "noble savagery" which had so titillated the fantasies of many Europeans since the time of Rousseau. As some types of jazz might loosely be interpreted as the blacks' celebration of their freedom from slavery, so jazz in general came to suggest to Europeans the imagined freedom of life in an optimistic young nation. The very same factors were essential in gaining European acceptance for Pollock's paintings, Pollock was especially well suited to this fanciful vision of "noble savage" because of his slightly brutish appearance, his violent temperament, and his upbringing in the "wild west" of Wyoming. The fact that Pollock was wilder, more passionate, and his art more electric, more immediate, and more improvisatory in character than that of his contemporaries, surely aided him in becoming the first American painter to win that kind of acceptance.

Moreover, by clearly visualizing painting as the product of intense, powerful, direct physical action, Pollock helped to solve a major American artistic dilemma, i.e., that question about the inherent seriousness of the visual arts. It must be stressed that this dilemma was not entirely a function of middle-class antagonism to art. Many young artists during the 1930s and 1940s were caught up in a guilt-producing proletarian work ethic, in many ways not so different from the Puritan work ethic. Both viewpoints tended to condemn effeteness, delicacy, and frivolousness in art. One of the great achievements of reputedly macho, he-men artists like Pollock and David Smith was to reconceive absolute art as rugged labor. For Smith, whose art consisted in welding huge masses of steel, the problem was not as complicated. In the case of Pollock, I do not think that success on so grand a plane would have been possible had not jazz improvisation already gained so much acceptance in our society and in western civilization at large.

Like the styles of many great improvisors in music, Pollock's was a very personal style and difficult to emulate effectively. Unlike static composition, such as the highly copyable works of Mozart or Ingres, Pollock's improvisations are strongly flavored with accident, which is virtually impossible to recreate.[12] The doors he opened were not to a school of style, nor of artistic improvisation as such, but to the idea that an American art could be high art. To Europeans who recognized a lapse in their own artistic innovation and leadership, he appeared as a new prophet to revitalize and save the western tradition in art. Through his heroic striving for excellence he helped make it possible for his fellow artists to see themselves as respectable human beings, worthwhile citizens, and serious *American* artists, creating emblems and standards for a courageous new empire of freedom. His was no bogus, depicted, pseudo-heroic social realism of muscle-bound factory workers, but rather the authentic expression of hard, passionately dedicated personal labor. The major artists who considered

[12] Rubin, "II," p. 30; "III," p. 29; Friedman, "Profile," p. 58.

themselves his followers, such as Morris Louis, created art less improvisatory in feeling and totally unlike Pollock's in aspect. But they learned from Pollock, as he had learned from jazz and other sources, that improvisation does not necessarily mean indolence, laziness, or lack of serious direction. When it is motivated by high purpose and "high anxiety," it can yield art with a claim to the great tradition of Cézanne and Van Gogh.

Several critics partial to Pollock, but steeped in Renaissance structural theory, have attempted to defend his work by claiming that it is composed and designed, not improvised. It has been asserted that Pollock's linear improvisation was in fact an inevitable outgrowth of late Cubist design, and was predetermined by the evolution of Post-Renaissance pictorial tectonics and its exclusively internal formal logic.[13] This belles what we feel in Pollock's work and what we know of its origins. The conditions in which it arose were conditions which very strongly implied the necessity of denying or consciously breaking away from the Renaissance notions of composition based on grand schemata of design.

To be sure, like all masters of improvisation, Pollock thought out his strategies and sketched an outline in his mind before entering the arena to perform. He thoroughly knew his format and chosen rhythms, colors, and tempos. He owned a superior talent and a dexterous physical machine well coached in certain idiosyncratic movements by long study and practice. But what happened in the creative act when all was going well was "the lightning mystery," not precisely determinable before the fact and not precisely duplicable after it. At his best, he was "blowing" in paint. To say that his work sometimes appears almost composed is mainly to say that, like Mozart or Scarlatti, he was a masterful improviser who retained a sense of structure and form even at the extremes of emotional intensity.

It is also possible that Pollock, in studying the bare canvas and preparing his thoughts, mentally cut up the surface into a grid, for that is how he was trained, and that may have been a convenient means to project measure and rhythm into the work. But the observation that Pollock had assimilated grid-thinking cannot sensibly be extrapolated into classifying his art as a logical development within late Cubism, against which it is in fact a reaction. Pollock did indeed choose to affiliate himself with the mainstream of western art, and he did so triumphantly. Yet in at least one crucial sense he stands apart. Like the great virtuosos of jazz, he grew to feel rhythm and structure so strongly inside that his mind was freed from those concerns, and thereby liberated to explore uncharted territories of the creative impulse.

[13] E.g., Greenberg, op. cit., pp. 217–19.

THE ARABESQUE AND THE GRID

PAUL JENKINS

JANUARY 1984

To me, Pollock's gestural poured paintings did not derive from Surrealist automatic writing but were purifications and perfections of the arabesque. The intertwined skeins are integrated with the grid and not floating or resting on it in an ambient state. The elaborate twistings and turnings which came from chaos achieved great painterly simplicity with a sense of wholeness. He consummated what came from the fire and drew from the kiln the finished and the resolved.

I am indebted to Jackson Pollock on many levels, personal and aesthetic, objective and emotional. One thing about Jackson's painting was the breaking up of shapes and forms which let the light in, the bringing of opposites together, formal and informal, the formal seems random and the informal is dictated to. Jackson evidenced the strictest laws in the most seemingly random chaos.

One night in 1956, I was sitting with Jackson at the Cedar Bar, where he was creating his own table. Addressing an irate comment about Mondrian by another painter, Pollock screwed up his face and growled, "You mean you don't see Mondrian in my work?" I grew to see, not just feel, the utmost rigor with inspiration in his painting, and this was a profound influence on my life humanly, not just as an artist.

Jackson Pollock brought out of chaos his visual order and proved in our time, his time, that the enigma could be manifested and discovered in painting. Unlike the sophisticated European Surrealists who delighted in shocking but did nothing to alter painting itself, he was not interested in shocking and revealed that the very structure of painting itself had to be changed if the other, the enigma, was to be revealed.

My impressions of Jackson Pollock need space to move in because it is the very spirit of this man which has affected so many of us in a profound way. He was able to reveal a kind of psychic energy with absolute certainty without falling into the peculiar quagmire where Surrealism seemed to entrap most of the European painters, painters who derived from Dada but who became essentially employers of shock motif, combined with academic perceptions in painting.

As a painter, he was able to make the Jungian archetypes that he was involved with viable, and transcended being a symbolist. Underneath the forms were his own imperative grids of total consciousness. In the most abstract paintings he did, the presence was always hovering. Through skeins and poured pigment, Pollock was further able to equalize the foreground, middleground, and background, not unlike Tobey in his *white writing*, through what Tobey called his *moving focal point*. In *No.1* and *Lavender Mist*, Pollock created his own means for the eye to traverse the canvas and take in the mass and the total sense of oneness. With Jackson's grid underneath the informal pouring, the informal evidence kept the painting up front and away from leading you to distant horizons. What is significant is his sense of mass, rather than shapes, in the painting. The shapes are implied and are like subliminal optical after-images. In making the painting come forward, the frontal tactile awareness of the surface was ever-present—the paint was impacted. It was not just poured on, laid on, dripped on, skeined on. It became an amalgamated *à la prima* mass which was not a one-shot but a total involvement. A painting first and a referential to what Tom Hess would call the "Big Subject" afterward. It was not encumbered and did not rely on heavy-hitting symbolist notions such as with Edvard Munch, Max Beckmann, André Masson or in another context, Odilon Redon's allegorical imperatives.

With the Surrealists, painting was an illustrating feat with which they could shock the bourgeoisie and yet placate them at the same time with the knowledge that there was a traditional foreground, middleground, and background. They would not give up the Venetian opera backdrop and ended up being illustrators for the dashing poets whom André Breton led with such authority. They used the unconscious as a theatrical zone and Ernst, Tanguy and the more metaphysical DeChirico would not give up the exaggerated traditional optics. There was no true rupture with the familiar as they had always been able to perceive it. The Surrealists relied primarily on subject matter which titillated and intrigued, and extolled the paradox of opposites colliding in order to create fascination. They did not contribute to formal or informal discoveries relating to structural possibilities of growth in painting itself. They ignored the lessons Gauguin so generously offered, and had no willingness to see the varying planes in the reflections of Monet or in the architecture of Cézanne. For the Surrealists, the canvas remained a window through which they were to peer. And in the main it was the window of a *voyeur* with cold cynicism and no compassion. It was not outrage at the human condition, as in Goya and Daumier, and in George Grosz's *Ecce Homo*.

For Pollock, the canvas was a humanistic wall of the world—possibly a greater world than we know it to be, but one that has furthered our aspiration and belief in the tragic stature of the individual. He was the one that Motherwell remembers as having said, when put to the wall, "Yes, it does belong to the unconscious." But you've got to turn the unconscious into a painting and not make it an illustration of someone's fantasy. And he was able to do that.

Manet, Cézanne, and Monet were all painters, not idea men like Duchamp or Picabia. Surrealist ideas did not evolve in pure abstract terms—there was a lot of war between the pioneer Abstract Expressionists and the Surrealists.

Kline, Gorky, de Kooning, and Pollock went through the door of Cubism and came out the other side with their own kind of discovery. They were fighting the French European influence; they were fighting for their own identity. It may be true that Matta and Gorky walked hand in hand expressing their ties with Surrealism as they understood it. But the Surrealists did not take to the others so much, with the exception of Robert Motherwell, who understood possibly better than anyone the intention of Dadaism, Surrealism, and Cubism. Motherwell was able to evidence it when he talked about figurative painting. At one point, I remember he said, "Figurative paintings are difficult because you end up with an effigy." Think of the portrait he did, *The Homely Protestant*. And the portrait paintings of Jean Dubuffet in the late forties and early fifties which were shown at the Galerie René Drouin at the Place Vendôme. Drouin was among the first to show the obscure Wols and the very strange Fautrier, whose figures certainly had the look of primordial earth mothers. To me these portraits are effigies of psychic content. They weren't done for patrons, and they weren't done for religion. They were done out of the artist's necessity.

In Pollock's figurative instances, such as his totemic stick figures, these figures were caught in a visual exorcism, as in *Guardians of the Secret*. Then, later in *The Deep*, there is the enigmatic implied figure. There remains more to be said about the figurative urgency in Jackson Pollock's work.

He was mythic like Orpheus. He ventured into the unknown of his own labyrinth. But no matter what his large subject, no matter what unknown reef he might have discovered, he never forgot for an instant that he was first and foremost a painter.

Paul Jenkins
January 1984

JACKSON POLLOCK: Down to the Weave
a Commentary on a Selection of Key Works

FRANCIS V. O'CONNOR, PH.D.

ELEVENTH ANNUAL POLLOCK–KRASNER LECTURE, AUGUST 16, 1998, GUILD HALL, EAST HAMPTON, NEW YORK

Lᴇᴛ's get right down to the weave about Jackson Pollock by starting with one of his early drawings.

PHOTO: POLLOCK-KRASNER STUDY CENTER, JACKSON POLLOCK CATALOGUE RAISONNÉ ARCHIVES.

Untitled Drawing
c. 1934–38 (JPCR 3:388)
Crayon, brush, and pen and ink on textured paper, 8½ × 11¾in.
Metropolitan Museum of Art, New York

177

This is a surprising and disturbing sheet, about the size of a piece of business stationery—but of a texture and quality you wouldn't type upon. The surface of the paper, with the crayon and wash just touching the peaks of its handsomely irregular topography, is visible overall, and lends unity to the images on its surface. The colors are rich, complex, beautifully prismatic. A wash of pale blue surrounds the image, balancing the red flames. It is as if Pollock wanted to seduce the eye away from his ominous subject.

Set out on a locationless, desert-like plain are an irregular hole with what appears to be a ladder set in it, and a bonfire. It is unclear just what the purpose of the ladder and the hole is. The shape of the hole is nothing human hands would dig; it suggests a sinkhole. It is equally unclear what the round form beneath the fire might be. Feeling through this work is a bit scary. The images are vaguely threatening. They compel one's own narrative—which can be even scarier. They conjure primal reactions: to things burning, oneself plunging into a hole, or worse, something emerging from a hole. . . . One can even smile at that sick joke of a ladder: the rungs have been erased—and the remaining two poles are red and blue, echoing the work's tonal polarity.

You realize the entire drawing is about being above and being below—from the deep texture of the paper which shows through the elegantly applied medium from below, to the import of what is below the fire or in the hole—or what caused that wind-whipped fire at the top of the composition, or what might be in that hole, which is below the fire. So in this simple set of relationships a very complex, ambiguous, emotion-laden directionality can be perceived.

You wonder if Pollock, being the youngest and most coddled of five boys—it was Charles, Jay, Frank, Sanford, with Jackson last—had something to do with this sense of above and below. This declension of siblings was one of reality dimensions that contributed to his insecurity and anxiety. Being at the bottom often makes an individual seek out what is lower in order to be higher. Fortunately for Pollock, lower came to equate with "deeper." This was an aspect of his essentialist nature, as I shall discuss later.

Toward the end of his life he provided a clue to what this drawing means when explaining to Jeffrey Potter why he never went to the movies: "Movies keep you outside looking at the outside. I want to look in, like a personality or soul X-ray. . . ." (Potter, *To a Violent Grave: An Oral Biography of Jackson Pollock*, New York, G. P. Putnam's Sons, 1985, 140) And he also fantasized about holes in the ground, telling Potter in 1955: "What I'd really like is a dry well to live in down at the bottom." . . . (223) Later he told Potter this dream:

> Down in [the well] everything was dark and quiet, just the way I wanted. Then the sand walls started running, a cave-in, but I wasn't buried, just out in the open with all the darkness and quiet that ever was. (226).

Pollock's later statements make you realize that this drawing can be construed as an allegory of his art in this sense: just as there is something happening on the surface of his works—so also just below the surface.

Rare is the Pollock in which you cannot, at some point on its surface, see right down to the weave of the canvas or the texture of the panel or paper or whatever the ground is—or at least sense through glazes of color and varnish, its underlying painterly stratificatons.

Pollock's work builds up an archeology of facture that he always reveals. In this he practices art as Freud conceived the unconscious in terms of the city of Rome: as an accumulation of historical events eventually buried by others, that retain significance in the psyche's underground realm—and that build pressure toward conscious revelation. Further, Pollock's Jungian analysts gave him a sense of being rooted in nature as well as determined by repressed experience. His work, in consequence, always has an literal "interior" as well as a figurative "depth." The subtle dialectic between these conceptualizations of psychic temperament and artistic space became his essential subject.

Pollock's drawings, however, make you conclude that this drawing is an atypical sheet. While often surprising in their details, few arrest attention both by the stark strangeness of the images and their symmetrical arrangement on the page. Here, the whole configuration attracts attention—as does its arched top.

That suggestion of architecture sets you thinking about murals. Pollock was a student of the great American muralist, Thomas Hart Benton. His acquaintance, through Benton, with the Mexican muralist José Clemente Orozco from his first year in New York suggests Orozco's influence in this drawing. The flames and that hole resonate with the Mexican's expressionism, and their piling up on a flat surface beneath an arch suggest the formal strategy of a wall painter thinking about architectural scale and sightlines and filling irregular surfaces with legible images.

Pollock had done this in two rough mural studies about this time, possibly for a New York settlement house, the most developed depicting music makers—a work that can also be related to Tom Benton's weekly country music evenings in which Pollock participated.

Two of his brothers, Charles and Sanford, were WPA muralists—as was his old friend from Los Angeles, and the future Abstract Expressionist, Philip Guston. He was an assistant on a WPA mural undertaken by one of Benton's students.

It is known that he watched Diego Rivera paint his ill-fated mural at Rockefeller Center in 1933 and was employed for a time in 1936 by the youngest of the three most famous Mexican muralists, David Alfaro Siqueiros, in his "experimental workshop." There he probably saw the first random application of paint, splashed on May Day floats; Charles recalled the floor of the workshop looked "like a Pollock" because of this.

The mural was the era's most glamorous art form, and Pollock never had the opportunity to paint a wall in the 1930s—a fact that would determine later ambitions toward large scale work, and achievements of facture that are anticipated *in micro* by this mysterious, elegant drawing.

Before discussing other works by Pollock, let me describe the method I am employing.

Pollock was an individual impatient with anything other than the most direct route to a goal. This is typical of someone severely injured early on by life. Pollock was born strangled by the cord, an event that left him with mild learning and motor disabilities, and most probably, a precocious vulnerability to alcohol. Such persons tend always to be seeking, at least unconsciously, the cause of their affliction. The outward manifestation of this is what I call an aggressive essentialism. It is the psychological equivalent of political radicalization: that is, when a person is so afflicted by injustice that life is meaningless until equity is restored. Restoring equity, for Pollock, then, was to get to the bottom of things at the cost of all intervening superficialities. In Pollock's art, this is symbolized by the laying bare of the historical process by which each work was created. Its stages are clearly visible, most often literally "down to the weave" of the canvas.

No artist among the Abstract Expressionists is more open about revealing the stages that led up to the surface we see. This vertical directionality down to the weave, distinct from any device of perspective (though at times contributing to the spatial drama of the work), is a hallmark of Pollock's facture.

You might still ask what "meaning" means when interpreting Pollock. Here meaning is the sum total of three things:

1) what you feel on first encountering the work,
2) what you can see of the qualities of the work that made you feel as you did,
3) what you know about the work's imagery and intent, and the historical origins and context from which and in which it was created.

The point to stress here is that the first levels of relevant information in the quest for meaning are *visceral and visual, not verbal*. These are the realities that I think have been forgotten in the current "literature" on Pollock and most serious art. Indeed, one must come to the sad conclusion that for many historians, biographers, and critics today, the works of art *are not real as objects*—only the theory of explanation is real. This *lack of empathy*—this inability to share in another's emotions or feelings—this inability to see, and through perception, to feel through what is actually there in the art work, but instead to assert only what theory requires to be there—makes all too much recent art commentary tendentiously distortive, unenlightening, and ultimately useless.

But enough; let us go West.

Going West
1934–38 (JPCR 1:16)
Oil on fiberboard, 15 ⅛ × 20 ¾ inches
National Museum of American Art, Smithsonian Institution, Washington, D.C.
(Gift of Thomas Hart Benton)

This is a small work, heavily painted, dark. A night scene lit by the full moon. One's first impression is of a strange turbulance—of unnaturally elongated hills, a roadhouse and windmill set askew, and a storm-swept sky leading the eye from lower right around to upper right in a great crescent-like swoop. The lower curve of this oval serves as road for an odd conveyance composed of an unlikely team of five long-eared beasts pulling what seems to be a log on wheels, and a rather small covered wagon. A figure in a wide-brimmed hat riding one of the animals looks back over his left shoulder as if to see if the rear wagon is making the turn. A large rock in the lower left balances the quite solid-looking cloud in the opposite corner. The overall surface is rough yet strangely transparent, as if the moon's luminosity has penetrated its every detail. There is an eerie quality about this quiet, involuted scene.

The overt subject: the team, its rider, and the wagons, which the title tells us are "going west," suggests, first off, that the time of night depends on the turn ahead in the road. If it is to the left, then the evening is young and the low full moon is rising in the east; If it is to the right, then the moon is setting in the west. The work's composition would suggest the latter, as does the title. But the darkness up ahead does not reveal the road's direction, so this must remain ambiguous.

You see three things immediately.

First: The undulous landscape, the oddly angled roadhouse and vane, and those long-eared beasts all come right out of any number of works by Pollock's teacher, Thomas Hart Benton—who once owned *Going West*. It is an odd mixture, nevertheless. The steep hills resemble the talus heaps Benton locates next to mine shafts—and which Pollock used in several watercolors, both of which depict teams and wagons. The roadhouse plus windmill is another of Benton's recurring motifs.

Second: If the terrain and animals are Benton's, then that agitated, moon-lit sky is the hallmark of Albert Pinkham Ryder—the only artist Pollock said he ever really liked, and whose work Benton's dealer in the 1930s, Fred Price, handled as well. The moon, and a team and wagon going in the same direction, can be found in Ryder's *The Sentimental Journey* of before 1898, though the animals are clearly horses and their cargo a hearse.

Third: There is a suggestion of Picasso in the brightness around the moon. It is visible in the very carefully painted meeting of that area and the profile of the hills just above the roadhouse. One of Pollock's later themes would be that of the "Moon Woman," a figure that appears in the imagery and titles of a number of Picasso–influenced drawings and paintings (here, reversed). Here the profile with a classical nose and the sweeping cloud of hair—with the moon set as an earring—latently broods over this mysterious scene.

We can be sure that Pollock was thinking, while painting this complex work, of the dominant woman in his life at this time: his mother Stella (whose very name connotes, among other things, the night sky). We can deduce this from two facts. First, "going west" for Pollock in New York during the mid-1930s would have meant to go home to his mother in Los Angeles. He had done this several times since coming east in 1930. But, second, that curious team, whatever its roots in Benton and Ryder, was most likely derived from an old photograph of the site where Pollock was born: Cody, Wyoming. This is especially true of its double cargo. This photograph belonged to his mother. It is likely, on the evidence of motifs from them appearing in his work, that he had seen them. Since his family moved from Cody just eleven months after his birth, these photographs became his visual memory of that landscape. In this one, a team of four pulls a double wagon along the road to Cody Bridge. Other such teams can be seen elsewhere in the photograph.

This explains the strange, log-shaped wagon, which may well be some sort of a tank, and the miniature Conestoga wagon. You drove them sitting on the buckboard. But Pollock's can just about make the turn as he watches from the back of the right rear member of his curious—one would think undrivable—team of five.

If we identify the rider with Pollock, and I think we can, it is to be noted that he points ahead yet looks back, as do two of the five beasts. At this time—the mid-1930s—of the five men in his family, two lived East; three lived West. Pollock is going West, yet looking back to the undersized covered wagon where the pioneer's family would have ridden. But it is not yet around the bend, and conveys no people. Finally, one notes, that the team is standing still while everything else—the land, the clouds, and the moon itself—move around it.

This involuted little painting can be read as an allegory of Pollock's ambivalent artistic and familial relationships—and as the precursor of all too many stmied motions in his future life.

Mural
1943 (JPCR 1:102)
Oil on canvas, 7 ft. 11¾ in. × 19 ft. 9½ in.
Museum of Art, University of Iowa, Iowa City
(Gift of Peggy Guggenheim)
(see color plate no.3.)

As with so many of Pollock's works, the first impression facing this huge painting is of chaos—a surging mass of vaguely figurative elements that seems to progress from right to left with meaningless abandon. It is a hard work to sort out visually—a matter emphasized the more by its scale and your proximity to its complexity. Within five feet you cannot see the outer edges; it totally envelops you. The most comfortable distance is about its length away: twenty feet. From there the remarkably turbulent imagery comes into focus, and one begins to realize that the overall effect of this work is as much the result of its sophisticated color as its radical structure.

Aside from black and white, red, yellow, and blue predominate—but in dualities of brick red/pink and a deep blue/blue-grey with about three shades of yellow from gold to lemon. All of these colors are interlaced with great skill—with the blue-gray being used as a masking device. While there are no poured elements, there is much splatter and occasional delicate brush trailings in pink and yellow. In places the ground shows through down to the weave of the canvas. Areas of sky blue can be found at the top and other areas of flesh tone here and there suggest a vestigial "figures in a landscape" theme. Interpretors of this painting have claimed it represents everything from a herd of wild horses to Native American flute players—but it is wiser to keep to what the eye can see, and feel that through.

While the vestigial figures seem to march from right to left, a closer examination of the surface reveals that it was painted from left to right—as are almost all of Pollock's large canvases. He was right handed, and tended to "write" out his big, allover paintings, whether they were vertical against the studio wall, as this was, or, starting about 1947, spread out on the floor. If you feel through the sweep of the black forms to the far left, and follow them as if your own hand were striking them out with a wide, loaded brush, you can get a sense of how the painting happened.

It is characteristic of a Pollock that the left edge almost always begins with an elegant encounter of curves, which then move, with increasingly formulaic variations, across the width of the work, to an abrupt termination of verticals—as here, where three strong uprights bring the rightward movement to a conclusive stop. If you look carefully at the left third, it is also plain that many of the forms there are more varied and tentative than those at the center or right, where the circular and oval forms and the blue-gray masking become more regular than earlier.

Historically, this painting was commissioned by Pollock's dealer, Peggy Guggenheim, early in 1943 for the lobby of her New York townhouse on 61st Street. He stretched the canvas for this work—removing a wall in his 8th Street studio to fit it in—in July, and intended to have it ready for his first one-man show that November. Instead, he spent the summer and early fall painting smaller works, such as *Guardians of the Secret.*

After brooding over the blank canvas for six months, sometime around the turn of the year Pollock locked himself in his studio and created *Mural* in one day of furious activity. This, at least, is how Lee Krasner recalled it. From photos of the painting just after completion, it is obvious he touched it up later—and then dated it 1943, the year of conception if not completion.

Three aspects of his experience during the 1930s contributed to the gestation of this painting and its rapid execution, once begun: the emphasis on mural painting he had known since coming to New York in 1930; the mural technique Thomas Hart Benton taught his students; and Picasso's exiled *Guernica.*

Pollock's first, and only, training as a muralist came from Benton. It is not surprising, then, to find that *Mural*, like all his other wall-size canvases through the 1952 works *Convergence* and *Blue Poles*, was composed in accordance with his teacher's methods. Benton's central tenet was to stabilize curves and diagonals around verticals when painting mural-scale in order to establish a rhythmic structure across the wall plane. While Benton integrated this system into representational murals, Pollock took it literally, paring the system down to Benton's abstract diagrams in this and others of his large paintings. This is a good example of Pollock's instinctive essentialism, trying to x-ray a situation, to get down to the weave of the experience, down to the grounding of anything he tried to do.

Finally, the presence in New York of Picasso's famous mural without a wall, the *Guernica*, had an enormous influence. First exhibited at the Valentine Gallery in the spring of 1939, it traveled the country that year. It is plain from the drawings and paintings Pollock did at that time that he was eagerly appropriating motifs from the exiled mural into his own work. Lee Krasner recalled that she and many of her fellow WPA artists sat for hours in the gallery mesmerized by this vast and utterly radical work.

A crucial point here is that *Guernica* was a mural that had become an easel painting. Movable murals were not unknown to artists during the 1930s. Both Thomas Hart Benton at the New School for Social Research, and Diego Rivera at the New Workers School, had painted on removable panels, and these works received great attention in the art community. Further, the great majority of Treasury and WPA murals were painted in the artists' studios on canvas and later installed *in situ*.

Pollock's achievement in *Mural* was to take all these precedents and influences and fuse them into the first major large-scale painterly—as opposed to geometric—abstraction ever created in America. He had achieved one of the most powerful, innovative, and prophetic paintings of it era.

Mixed Media Drawing
1946 ((JPCR 4:1011)
Spatter, pen, black and colored inks, gouache, wash and
graffito/paper, 22 ⅜ × 30 ⅜ in.
Private Collection
(See color plate no.4)

In 1945 Pollock and Lee Krasner moved to The Springs. This change of environment from city to country had a profound effect on his work—it opened it up to light and color and a certain joyfulness that was absent in his city creations. This is best seen in the contrast between *Troubled Queen* and *The Key*—as well as this marvelous untitled mixed-media drawing.

One senses here, but on a much smaller scale, the same antic exhuberance that went into the crafting of *The Key*. The colors are bright and mostly primary: red, yellow, blue, orange, set over a delicate baby–blue wash articulated with the inevitable black and white. The standard composition of a

JACKSON POLLOCK'S NEW YORK STUDIO at 46 East 8th Street, 1933 to 1945

JACKSON POLLOCK'S EAST HAMPTON STUDIO, 1946-56 (Schematic Reconstruction)

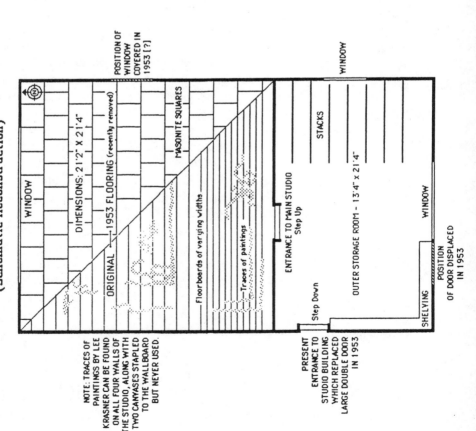

central mass flanked by vertical figures is operative, but with far more simplicity, openess, and transparency. Here there seems to be quadruped movement—very definitely to the left, if that big arrow at the top (or the blue one entering from the right), or the direction of that pointed snout and thrown back ears parading forward, mean anything. But this is a very strange beast indeed, with its curved feet in front echoing those two crescent-crowned shaman staffs behind, which may or may not be the hind feet. Here the the beast's body is red with yellow udders that recall *The She-Wolf*, but doesn't quite. Are those feathers attached to the hindquarters? And are they tickling that arrow-pierced blue moon so it grins?

To answer these questions, keeping with the previous point about ambivalent directionality in Pollock's work, and following an intuitive suspicion that there is more here than meets the upright eye, turn this drawing upside down. Now, in what might be loosely interpreted as a high-steppng, red, mule-drawn wagon, with a blue wheel, hauling a very large yellow bird (covered with a red lacrosse net?), that may or may not be laying an egg we can construe an image of Pollock carting his new bride, Lee Krasner, off to East Hampton.

Seriously, looking at this sheet reversed, you gets the very real kinesthetic impression that most of it was made from this point of view—most of the feather strokes work to the eye this side up, as do the brush–handle scratches in the black over yellow of the bird. But turned back so the signature and date are legible, it makes better sense formally: the space at the bottom gives it a setting, and stability. As in *Going West*, Pollock is never exactly going anywhere when he depicts travel. All real motion, for him as an essentialist, is internal. That is perhaps worth thinking about.

It is plain from this and the other works of the spring and early summer of 1946, that Pollock was elated to be in the country, working on his new house, and painting. The dark city moods had been exorcised by the fresh country atmosphere. By June he had been able to move the barn away from blocking the view out the back door of his house, and set it up as his studio. Then he was really home.

The point here is that there was not much difference between the front-room studio on 8th Street and the studio he made out of the East Hampton barn. The old studio was about eighteen feet square and the two windows faced north. The main room of the barn was about twenty-one feet square, and Pollock immediately added a big window in the north wall. Given a few work tables and stacked paintings around the periphery, the new studio was just about the same floor area as the old; the only difference was its height—and its transparency: he could see outside between the wall boards, so ramshackle was the ancient structure. Being in the country offered no more elbow-room than being in the city.

This delightful drawing, started out as a raucous hauling of his bird-like bride to the country in a wheelbarrow, ended up as a figure of internal

Dining room of the Pollock home, Cody, Wyoming. PHOTO: COURTESY PF FRANCIS V. O'CONNOR.

motion, pointing in two directions, but not moving. Nothing essential had really changed.

The new studio was to see the creation of all of Pollock's famous poured paintings starting in 1947. I want to make two points about these works. First, to say something about the peculiar shape of some of them. Second, to suggest an obscure origin for the pouring technique itself.

Of the 144 paintings created between 1947 and 1950, over one third are horizontal, and of those 53 works, 25 percent are extremely long in respect to their height. This is a shape that is peculiar to Pollock, and finds its origin in the same family photos of Cody that influenced *Going West*.

When I first saw this picture of the dining room at Cody in mother Pollock's trove of keepsakes, I exclaimed—look at the Pollocks on the wall. They turned out to be oleolithographs of pansies that housewives could mail order with boxtops—ready for framing.

If one thinks about *Summertime* of 1948, that is eighteen feet long, or Alfonso Ossorio's *No. 10, 1949*, one can see what I mean. And if you looks at the oval mats in the photo of the living room, some surrounding photos of Pollock's brothers, there may well be a visual origin for his device of masking images with gray paint—as in *She Wolf*, or The Ossorio Foundation's *Dancing Head*.

Comparable in peculiarity to this eccentric shape is Pollock's use of metallic silver paint. In the late 1920s Pollock attended the camp meetings of Krishnamurti, the former guru of the Theosophists. Krishnamurti's

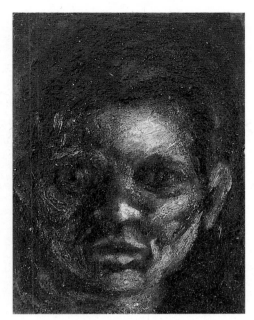

Jackson Pollock, Untitled (self portrait), ca. 1931-35.
Oil on gesso on canvas, 7 1/4 x 5 1/4 inches.
Courtesy Joan T. Washburn Gallery, New York.
© THE POLLOCK-KRASNER FOUNDATION, INC./ARS

Jackson Pollock, *Flame*, 1937. Oil on canvas mounted on composition board, 20 1/8 x 30 inches. Museum of
Modern Art, New York. © THE POLLOCK-KRASNER FOUNDATION, INC. / ARS.

Jackson Pollock, *Mural*, 1943. Oil on canvas, 95 3/4 x 237 1/2 inches. University of Iowa, gift of Peggy Guggenheim. © UNIVERSITY OF IOWA ART MUSEUM, IOWA CITY. PHOTO: POLLOCK-KRASNER STUDY CENTER, JACKSON POLLOCK CATALOGUE RAISONNÉ ARCHIVES.

Jackson Pollock, *Mixed Media Drawing*, 1946. Spatter, pen, black and colored inks, gouache, wash and graffito/paper, 22 3/8 x 30 3/8. PRIVATE COLLECTION.

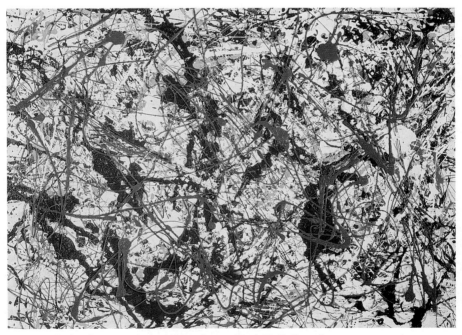

Jackson Pollock, *Silver Over Black, White, Yellow and Red*, 1948. Enamel on paper mounted on canvas, 21 x 31 1/2 inches. Musée National d'Art Moderne, Centre Georges Pompidou, Paris. © THE POLLOCK-KRASNER FOUNDATION, INC. / ARS. PHOTO: POLLOCK-KRASNER STUDY CENTER, JACKSON POLLOCK CATALOGUE RAISONNÉ ARCHIVES.

Cecil Beaton, photograph for the March 1951 issue of *Vogue,* taken at the Betty Parsons Gallery, November or December 1950. The model is posed in front of *Autumn Rhythm: Number 30, 1950.* © CONDÉ NAST.

Norman Rockwell, "The Connoisseur," cover for *The Saturday Evening Post.* © 1962 THE NORMAN ROCKWELL FAMILY TRUST.

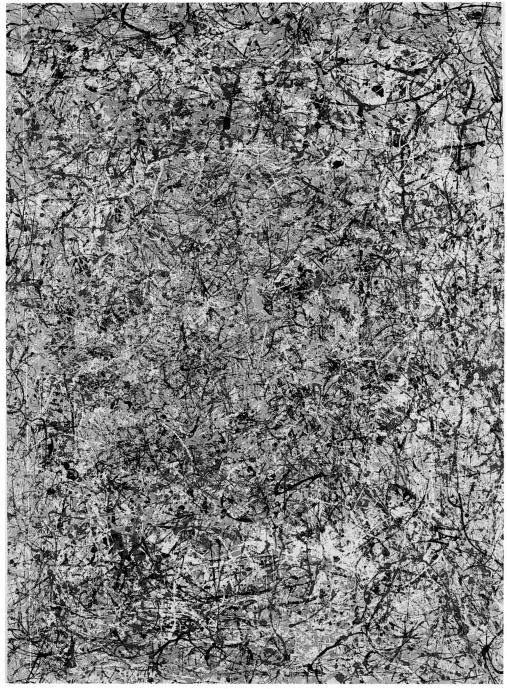

Art & Language, *Portrait of V.I. Lenin in the Style of Jackson Pollock,* 1979. Oil and enamel on board mounted on canvas, 69 1/4 X 50 inches. COURTESY OF GALERIE DE PARIS, PARIS.

"God! Your Jackson Pollock always puts me in a frenzy."

Colors that appear in Pollock's 1952 canvas, *Convergence*, decorate his studio floor.

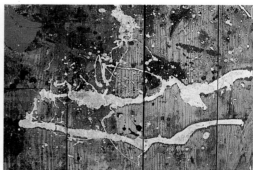

A Pollock gesture on his studio floor. The aluminum and orange paints are from *Blue Poles*.

While painting *Blue Poles*, Pollock walked barefoot across the canvas. His footprints remain on the studio floor.

The colors and gestures on Pollock's studio floor from a rich document of his work from 1947-1952.

book, sold at those meetings, had covers decorated in all-over patterns of metalic silver and gold inks; when the silver receded the gold was dominant, and vice-versa. Add later the paint spattered floor of Siqueiros's Experimental Workshop, Max Ernst's dripping paint pot, and maybe Stanley William Hayter's endless line, among other over-determining factors, and you have the pouring technique.

The interpretive principle here is that if you are going to go down to the weave—that means more than just the canvas—but down to the texture of the artist's life all the way to the beginning, down to the first contiguous influences. Then the later ones will take on a greater meaning, especially if you realize that an artist cannot be influenced by something that is not somehow meaningful to him or her in the first place.

PHOTO: POLLOCK-KRASNER STUDY CENTER, JACKSON POLLOCK CATALOGUE RAISONNÉ ARCHIVES.

Poster
c.1951 ((JPCR 4:1090-P26)
Serigraph, 16 $^{11}/_{16}$ × 20 $^{3}/_{16}$ in.
Black on white printed edition issued as poster for
Pollock's exhibition at the Betty Parsons
Gallery, November-December 1951
The Museum of Modern Art (Gift of Lee Krasner Pollock)

After the poured paintings of 1947–50, Pollock took to pouring in black. In 1951 he had a show of these works at Betty Parsons Gallery, and designed a poster for it. One's immediate reaction to this image is puzzlement and confusion. It is difficult to read the imagery. It flickers, conflicting the eye. Something is going on, but it is not immediately apparent what.

This is the only poster Pollock ever designed. If you think about it, posters are, in effect, miniature murals—and murals are meant to speak to an environment, to define the purpose of a space. In thinking about doing a poster, Pollock seems to have associated with murals very easily. The linear grid across the center of the work resembles the "squaring up" muralists use to enlarge a design to wall-size. But the most specific association to murals is to be found in the central, horizontal figure, which reflects Pollock's lifelong dialectic with the work of José Clemente Orozco.

If you turn the poster so the right side is to the bottom, there is an unmistakable resemblance to the Aztec sacrifice panel in Orozco's Dartmouth College murals. Looking carefully at the poster from this perspective, it is clear that some of the heads depicted can plausibly be seen as deriving from the heads of the priests in the fresco. Further, the central splayed figure is almost a direct transcription of its ritual victim.

Looking even more closely at the design turned the first way suggested, the central victim is flanked by two female figures. Their heads are about parallel to the victim's and their bosoms just opposite the victim's slashed chest. The woman to the left wears a high-heeled shoe that almost steps on one of the victim's feet.

This motif of the shoe can be found in the blatant image of Woman, that was obviously influenced not only by Orozco's Prometheus mural at Pomona, California, but by his early series of drawings of Mexican prostitutes, and satires of rich Capitalist women, where high-heeled shoes take on the symbolism of decadence and imperialist indifference to the poor. The high-heeled shoe becomes for Pollock a symbol of female aggressiveness.

The emergence of Orozco as an influence here suggests that his role in Pollock's art ought to be reassessed. The conventional wisdom would have us believe that the two main influences on Pollock were his teacher, Thomas Hart Benton, and Picasso. That is true as far as it goes, and the influence of David Alfaro Siqueiros remains vestigial. Certainly Pollock's formal strategies in his largest paintings are derived from Benton, and there is a perpetual dialogue with the inescapable Picasso. But it is the influence of Orozco that colors—one is almost tempted to say darkens— much of Pollock's iconography. For all of Picasso's protean inventiveness in his aggressions against the female form, he never quite approaches the power of Orozco's concentrated and often quite rhetorical expressiveness on all fronts. Picasso never gets that serious—because he is incapable of a passionate ideology.

It is perhaps worth noting that Orozco's last mural cycle, painted in 1940 at the Gabino Ortiz Library at Jiquilpan, appears to have had a definite influence on Pollock—who would have known the walls from the press and from photographs and studies exhibited at the Delphic Studios gallery run by Alma Reed.

The mural on the nave wall depicting *After the Battle*, which shows old women scavenging among the dead, seems a plausible antecedent for Pollock's famous 1947 drawing of *War*.

Indeed, the murals in the chapel, painted exclusively in black on white plaster, with touches of dark red, would seem to be directly related to Pollock's black pourings, and would be a precedent for the use of a similar linear complexity and dark red in such works as *Number 11, 1951*.

Page from Sketchbook
1956 ((JPCR 3:906)
Ink and wash on paper, 5 × 12 in.
J. Pierpont Morgan Library, New York (Gift of Eugene V. Thaw)

The drawing is just a few free, attenuated brushings of wash and ink. The image is of a female animal made out of long lines. Its head—whether horned or just bearing long ears is unclear—is to the upper left, its feet to the base line, its udders central. To the upper right is a dot and an arc—perhaps an eye, perhaps the moon and Venus.

The sheet is one of many in a long Japanese paper sketchbook. Up to a certain point it was used as a scratch pad on the telephone table in Pollock's house; then there is the sequence of wash drawings from which this one has been selected. The point of transition from jottings and doodles (many of the latter over the former) to these works of art is of some interest, since the page contains what is probably Pollock's only dream recorded in his own hand:

Paul [abstract drawing of a dog]
["U" shape] divining rod—two nites
[Drawing of tank-type vacuum sweeper with hose]
vacuum sweeper becomes my dog which attacks me

---

two cars—the one I am driving rams into the first car
which my wife has left and run away from. between the two wrecked cars is a dead
boy.

Such a dream can only be interpreted now in terms of what is explicit—just as the details in the works of art discussed here can only be explained in terms of what we can feel, see and know.

"Paul" was Pollock's first name; he had always been known in his family as

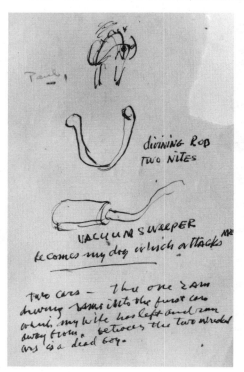

Jackson Pollock, page from a sketchbook, undated. Ink on paper, 5 x 12 inches. PHOTO: POLLOCK-KRASNER STUDY CENTER, JACKSON POLLOCK CATALOGUE RAISONNÉ ARCHIVES.

"Jack"; he dropped Paul when he came to New York, thinking "Jackson" more manly. The image of the dog looks more like a cat with its back up. Below that is Pollock's image of a divining rod, the device psychics use to find water. Pollock, it would seem, had some skill in this. Below that is a vacuum sweeper with its hose rising like a threatening cobra; Pollock says it became his dog and attacked him.

This first half of the dream (marked off from the second by a line) can be construed to refer to Pollock's birth strangled by the cord—Paul's birth: the dog, the rod, and the sweeper all have elongated, flexible shapes that for him are threatening. Indeed, the sweeper sucks in, keeps in, engulfs, and devours—as do animals and mothering women, whose household tool is about the size of a dog. The dream, to this point, is a microcosmic biography of all those factors in his life that led him on.

In the early spring of 1956 Pollock made three attempts to sit through the American premier production of Samuel Beckett's *Waiting for Godot*. The play proved so moving for him that he burst into tears and fled at the entrance of Lucky. Most interpretors of this incident refer to the existential alienation of the play's protagonists, Vladimir and Estragon, as having affected Pollock. I would suggest that it was rather the sight of Lucky on his leash of rope, bound at the neck, staggering onstage under the weight of Pozzo's luggage, and struggling to its center before Pozzo appears—the length of rope is thus emphasized. This image is what Pollock found unendurable. Later the two tramps notice that the rope has caused a running sore in Lucky's neck. Given what we know of Pollock, his retreat at about this point to the theater's bar, his later emotional breakdown during the second act that forced him to flee the auditorium, and his wild fit of weeping later, are perfectly understandable. Beckett had touched his rawest nerve. Pollock could only flee his identification with Lucky. He told Potter: "Okay, I went to that play. Only I couldn't take it. I walked out . . . I felt my guts being pulled out backwards every time. Like one of those births they have to drag you out, cut you out" (229). That Pollock's associations were to a birth trauma, however deflected from his own, tells all.

Experiences such as these in the early months of his last year point to the agony of his psychosomatic decline. All testimony about these final months offers a picture of a hopelessly lost and emotionally needy human, weeping, hypersensitive, perversely drunken, reaching out, irresponsible and uncontrollable. There was no hope—everything began to appear as that barren, moon-dominated stage, where time and motion were arrested in an eternal cycle of repetitive stasis—where the promise of Godot never materializes—and where even suicide by one's own hand seemed beyond available energy. The protagonists sit. They say . . . let's go. But they do not move, just as none of Pollock's journeys ever got him anyplace different.

The second half of his dream, about the auto accident, is uncannily premonitory. If it seems too good to be true, it isn't. All big dreams seem overly obvious unless you know the dreamer; it is the sign of their authenticity (and their embarrassing lack of literary decorum). The dream anticipates the fatal car accident that would take Pollock's life, but with one blunt difference. It involves two cars, when in fact his car skidded on a turn and crashed without contact with another. Every dream, Freud teaches, contains a conflict and a wish; here the conflict was with his wife, who had indeed run away from the hell on wheels her husband had become; the wish contained his rage against her for that abandonment. Jung, on the other hand, sees every dream as symbolic of the present state of the dreamer.

The victim is a dead boy—Paul—Jackson's way, perhaps, of deflecting death back to his first persona. In his first and only full-face self-portrait, he depicted himself as a boy, not the young man of nearly twenty he was when he painted it. He had once referred to his mother as both a womb and a tomb, which are the symbolic poles of this dream. It tells us that Pollock had looked down to the weave of his life and his imagery and knew what his wife and friends already knew watching his reckless driving, that a car would be his bodkin.

All he needed was to be drunk enough, depressed enough, and angry enough—and that day soon enough came, just down the road.

AN ANECDOTE

LEROY NEIMAN

2000

WHILE a student at the School of the Art Institute of Chicago (1946–50) there was, of course, a lot of talk about Jackson Pollock and the Abstract Expressionists. I had been impressed by a strong pre-drip Pollock canvas in the 1947 58th Annual Exhibition of American Painting and Sculpture at the Art Institute of Chicago Museum.

Then, in October 1951, now as a member of the faculty of the SAIC, I saw a half-dozen Pollock drip paintings in the exhibition of the Art Club in Chicago. It felt like being hit over the head with a sledgehammer.

Six months later—a happy accident. One late afternoon looking out of the sidewalk level window of my basement studio on Wabash, near Chicago Avenue. I saw Louie, the building janitor, hauling out to curbside one wheelbarrow after another, full of half-empty enamel paint cans. I charged up onto the street and inquired about what was up. Louie said the cans were left over from tenants' decorating efforts and he was cleaning out the basement. I asked it I could relieve him of the whole works. "They're yours," he said, "just lug them into your basement yourself." That's how I started. Times were lean—the enamels just acquired represented a year's worth of paint supplies to me. I could drip and slop around as liberally as I wanted at no expense. My objective was to let the paint run and drip as I'd slap it around, trying to harness its fluidity to arrive at some semblance of control, a la Pollock.

Thank you, Louie, and thank you, Jackson.

Jackson Pollock, *Lavender Mist, Number 1, 1950*, 1950. Oil, enamel and aluminum paint on canvas, 87 x 118 inches. One of the paintings exhibited at the Arts Club of Chicago, 2-27 October 1951. NATIONAL GALLERY OF ART, WASHINGTON, DC, AILSA MELLON BRUCE FUND. PHOTO: HANS NAMUTH © ESTATE OF HANS NAMUTH.

"BEING A GREAT MAN is a Thesis Invented by Others"
Peter Busa on Jackson Pollock

CHRISTOPHER BUSA

MAY, 2000

> Although I never met Pollock, here I have put together a picture of him and the aesthetic concerns of his milieu gleaned from my father's journals and sketchbooks. I transcribed those tattered pages a few years after my father's death in 1985. The raw transcript is available through the Archives of American Art, Smithsonian Institution.

1. SURREALISM AND FORMALISM: AN UNHOLY ALLIANCE

In 1946, the year I was born, my father had his first show at Peggy Guggenheim's gallery, Art of This Century. He wrote a brief explanatory letter to this important patron: "For Peggy: the first impression you should have of my work is the feeling of a symphonic orchestra playing at full blast, but controlled by a Toscanini of color, resulting in unbelievably beautiful combinations, with strange passages of subtle color." Guggenheim stimulated the free and random attitude by showing artists whose work emanated from the automatic impulse. Since 1941, my father had worked to reconcile chance with order, Surrealism with Formalism. "As far as my own development is concerned," he later wrote, "I was never happy about this aesthetic marriage [between Surrealism and Formalism] and I thought it was an unholy alliance that betrayed my formalistic Indian influence."

My father grew up in Pittsburgh and attended Carnegie Tech for three years. He described himself as "an intense, hardworking student who used

197

to take the skeleton home to work on the anatomy." In 1933 he moved to New York and enrolled in Thomas Hart Benton's class at the Art Students League. Benton's theory of bumps and hollows was very matter of fact. Nevertheless, my father appreciated it as one of the great ideas about form. "In all of us," he said, "it instilled our own notion of rhythm." Pollock was in the group, along with his brothers Sande and Charles, who was monitor of the class. "On an intimate level," my father recalled, "Pollock touched everyone. He always needed a family and he always had his own brothers and the family of artists. His circle of friends belies the story of his being a loner."

In the mid-1930s, for the downtown artists, E. A. Gallatin's Gallery of Living Art at New York University was the place to go and see modern art. "The gallery was situated in a library area, so the atmosphere was quiet and casual," my father said. "I remember the students studying and looking up once in a while at us, the strange artists in dungarees. We were the first people to wear those clothes. At the same time, we were involved with looking at Léger's *The City*. My generation was not naïve or self-taught. We had to work hard to become innocent."

2. CUBISM AND INDIAN SPACE

Beginning in 1935, my father worked with Hans Hofmann when his school was on 57th Street. As he recalled, "Hofmann used to refer to the 'force-impelled void,' which was considered full of vitality, a manner of painting in which the object is dissolved partly in a lost-and-found effect with the background. The idea stood out that there was such a thing as nothingness. Annihilation gestures in history have a short existence, but they stand out. Miró. Newman really ruined Pollock. The hidden history of American art is to see how minimalism and pure abstraction could destroy all Pollock stood for. Some of us had read [Henri] Bergson and Bergson says that in order to get to zero, you have to go through ten, nine, eight, seven, and so on, until at zero you are faced with everything. Pollock, at one end of the stick, made the work too busy even as he faced the idea. He literally told me that the kind of space he was interested in was like a hedge, which was his description. And [Roberto] Matta and Gorky would say it's like smoke. Matta would blow smoke, which is the space, the space in between. But Pollock's idea, the hedge, which he mentioned often, is frontal."

Hofmann's was then the only school in America in which one could study cubism, where the emphasis fell on discriminating positive and negative space. My father and some of his friends developed an alternative approach to pictorial space, based on American Indian precedents, which was later dubbed Indian Space painting. In an interview with the art historian Ann Gibson, my father said, "What was of interest to artists like Pollock, myself, Steve Wheeler, Will Barnet, Norman Daly, and others you may mention, was not the idea of the symbols but the structure of the space. The structure of space reflected by American Indian art was all positive, without negative space. This was a unique idea. Cubism dealt with positive and negative space. The artists who developed from American Indian art elevated so-called primitive art to the same level as accepted art. We did for American Indian art, you might say, what Picasso did for African art.

"But more precisely what I got from Hofmann was in the notion of *transformation*, where the impression is being carried by an artistic vehicle. Hofmann was very interested in the chancy idea of polarities, that is, having some climax with the adjacent opposite, rather than keeping them at quite a distance. Van Gogh might have an orange touch and a blue touch, but they will be at two opposite ends of the canvas, rather than adjacent. We were very interested in those things."

3. CHANCE

My father was employed on the WPA Federal Art Project from 1936 to 1941. Those five years, he said, were "like a graduate school of advanced training." William Baziotes introduced my father to drip painting early in the project. If the WPA had brought artists together at the height of the project, the "strange thing," my father said, is that it also did so at the demise of the project, when the purpose of serving starving artists was deferred to the urgency of war. He remembered: "We were supposed to make armbands and posters for recruiting agencies. But after we'd do that, we'd spent an hour or two together. That's when I saw a real interest in working with automatic drawing and painting. Lee Krasner, if you can imagine, was you might say our supervisor—John Ferren, [Gerome] Kamrowski, Baziotes, Pollock, myself—what a group!

"We would spend the afternoon doing these automatic things. Jackson used a tube of paint because he couldn't get brushes then, squeezing the tube almost like frosting. On the last dredges [sic] of the project, after we did our work for the government, we figured we were just doing this for ourselves because we had a little time. I sensed a breakdown with the war. We were isolated without materials. Something essential was in the air. When Jackson did that {20}-foot mural for Peggy, that was the breakthrough, like the Ladies of Avignon [for Picasso]. Pollock painted it in one day, broke all sense of time. When I first saw it I had a shock of great anxiety. Today it looks graceful, a tranquil yin and yang rhythm, as if you are sitting under a tree and looking up at the leaves moving in the breeze. It was done on the wall, before the drip."

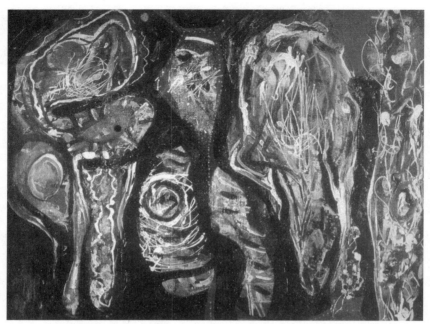

Jackson Pollock, William Baziotes and Gerome Kamrowski, untitled collaborative painting, 1940-41. Oil and enamel on canvas, 19 1/4 x 25 1/2 inches. COLLECTION OF GEROME KAMROWSKI.

My father came to understand that a Dadaist would rent a whole floor of a hotel without enough money to tip the chambermaid; Surrealists, going to a further edge, entirely abolished the concept of talent. Somehow my father also felt that the art of painting is essentially conservative and has little to with the historian's dream of a logical progression. The idea that painting can continue only if it becomes something else—not painting!— is a curator's idea. His idea of authentic self-expression is not based on novelty, but on acceptance and rejection, "a very long-winded process, grounded in knowledge of accumulated experience rather than in feeling great or feeling lousy."

In the forties my father's work became more and more involved with American Indian art. Surrealism was a sidetrack. The automatic images, he felt, were bound to dominate, "because one can only do these so much before they become mechanical and repeat themselves." He began to recognize a schism between a formal or plastic approach to painting and one engendered by the unconscious, where private or personal symbols would control the work. He saw this early in Miró's amoeba shapes and later in Gorky. At the same time, he loved the idea of Mondrian, the god of neo-plasticism, going to Harlem to dance.

Ultimately, he perceived that Surrealism's value was heuristic and utilitarian. Speaking at a forum organized by the art department at New York University, where he taught, my father was interrupted by a question from

Ad Reinhardt, who was in the audience. Reinhardt asked, "What good are the automatic gestures in your work? What good is it to scratch and spill?" My father replied that the method assumed "the biggest order in the area of chance." Reinhardt said he liked order, but he couldn't see the analogy. So my father said, "Let's compare automatism to the act of love, not caring where one starts the process." Reinhardt still wanted to know what good it was, so my father compared it to "a football game where you flip a coin to decide how the game will start."

Automatism is supposed to be unpredictable, yet my father wondered why the forms were often the opposite. So he asked if automatism was really automatic. Art enters paths not preconscious and for this reason my father preferred to work with a certain speed of activity, saying, "here is the hand, minus the I." Matta preached that "the cardinal principle was not to cheat chance," as my father put it. One day my father said something to Pollock about Matta's smoke drawings, and Pollock told him, "This is an a priori condition. I already know that I'm going to drip. That's what makes it automatic." My father saw how conscious Pollock was of his ability to engage his mind, not just his arm. What my father loved about the art of painting is "the moment of the exact look that the painter freezes for us." He believed that Pollock's subject matter was not automatism but his temperament. Besides, he wrote: "There is no such thing as pure automatism; one always needs an expressive, gestural objective."

"Matta," my father said, "wanted to gain some support for his point of view, but that movement didn't last very long because the Americans didn't want to be used. We didn't want to belong to a group and we never thought of it as a group. But we had a big flirtation with Surrealism. Rubbing against our innate antagonism to Surrealism was the very stimulus of our interest. Five of us used to meet on Saturday at Matta's or [Robert] Motherwell's studio. The exchanges were very interesting; some of the comments were like an advanced seminar. Side by side with our endeavor was the stimulation we received from the exchange of paintings. Matta would look at our work and make comments about what dimensions we were reflecting. He had an organic attitude about whether you were reflecting a rhythm that would be associated with water or fire or rock and so on. Pollock's work was exuberant, really outstanding, with a natural access to the unconscious.

"Kamrowski was the exception who became an orthodox Breton Surrealist and sort of broke with us on that basis. Baziotes, who had been very close to the Surrealists, decided to move away. Later Fernando Puma had a gallery on 57th Street and he hung a Kamrowski. Pollock went up to take a look, and told me that it was 'too slick' and looked too much 'like a polished Matta.'"

Still, he insisted: "The enthusiasm of fellow artists, collaborating, was genuine. I'll never forget the one time Motherwell and Pollock spent an afternoon doing collages together when they were going to submit some collages to Peggy Guggenheim's gallery, which was more or less the head-quarters and where we all had one-man shows. She was very gracious. She opened her arms to Pollock, her number-one man. She was very tough, very harsh on Alfred Barr when he didn't want to write anything on Pollock."

4. FORM AND FEELING

In a notebook from 1974, my father wrote: "Ever since the '40s I have understood abstraction in art as the basis for revealing feeling. Today the laziest banalities are extolled. Banalities are considered on the same level as an invented expressiveness. All works of art have structures that reduce experience to forces. The only thing of value is what touches you in your own experience. It is a private odyssey with our public parts, if we can believe [Alfred North] Whitehead who said that a thought was capable of having form. And so form can form us when feelings are transformed into concepts that have form.

"With Pollock there was always this relationship to his sense of doubt, and that is what killed him. It is also what kept him alive—his sense of existing in one's time with the ability to break through the chaos into the character of form, and that form, in turn, changing him. If you were to look back, the work was greeted with cries that it eliminated all resemblance to the figure. But his involvement was humanistic, and he was not afraid to give configuration to his painting. As a matter of fact, in the late '30s he was rejected from the AAA [American Abstract Artists] group for his reference to the graphic inventiveness of Picasso and for his overtones of subject matter.

"In retrospect it seems to me that Abstract Expressionism is the last gasp of academic art in the 20th century. And that seems like a strange thing to say. But I think it's quite true. When history is written we'll look upon Abstract Expressionism as being one of the most naturalistic efforts of our century, not only in terms of the image but also in terms of the invention of forms tied to tradition."

Pollock walked into a class my father was teaching at Cooper Union, and he said he needed a job and wanted to teach. My father looked around at the traditional exercises the students were doing, and said, "What the hell would you teach here, Jack?" Pollock said nothing. He knew my father was right, so he turned around and walked out. The experience of seeing a great artist not having a social use disturbed my father. He wondered if art education should be eliminated: "I'm sure the careerist could find another job, or if some were really interested in art they would get a chance to prove it. Long ago I knew there were two roads in art, Picasso and Matisse. So when Pollock said there were only three great artists—Picasso, Matisse, and *himself*—he showed he understood this, anticipating the polarity of the opposition between these two roads. Pollock's problem was not so much to be ahead of his time, but to be ahead of himself, and on several occasions he spoke about 'being ahead of myself'."

"You rain a series of blows upon the subject and it begins to weaken—do you paint the picture or does the picture paint you?" my father asked, and answered: "Pollock proved there was great strength in the idea that what is peculiar to you is not necessarily alien to other men. Jackson's remark to Hofmann—'I am nature'—crystallizes that so beautifully. Real growth in art is achieved by the barest of means. There is no greater discipline than artistic discipline. There is no greater battle in life than that of narrowing one's scope in order to increase it and witness it."

Jackson Pollock: IMAGES TO THINK WITH

WILLIAM S. WILSON

MAY, 2000

As a painter, Jackson Pollock was using visual thinking to express some of his thoughts. While his thoughts are visual, rarely verbal, both verbal and visual images can be used to think about the implications of his paintings, and about his stance as a painter. Images can be used like tools to probe themes onto an observable plane.

Around 1946 Pollock painted a picture he titled *The Little King*, refer-ring to a ready-made image—a comic character drawn by Otto Soglow—that carried many ideas. The image had a power before Pollock quoted it, and he could not have controlled its meaning in a painting. That is, he couldn't control the implications of the image suggested by the title, at least not as those would combine with other implications, constructing ideas separate from his visual thoughts. Even the word "little" in *The Lit-tle King* has suggestions that overflow, if only because Pollock's actual first name, Paul, means "little."

In 1947, Pollock painted over *The Little King*, which can stand for a process of canceling an image with paint, but not with a different legible image. The image and idea of "king" belong to a socio-economic culture, so that painting over a reference to "king" with a "galaxy" shows how a negative cancellation of an image helps Pollock, as the positive of the negation, toward expression of responses to the Cosmos. As he told his friend, Raphael Gribitz, of the cosmos, "That's influencing our lives. Goddamit, of course heavenly bodies influence our psyche!"

Reuben Kadish remarked to Jeffrey Potter that his friend Pollock had a "pantheistic quality, giving him a link with a kind of creative continuity." Such "pantheism" cannot be made specific, but it can be clear enough to

Jackson Pollock, *The Little King*, 1946. Oil on canvas, 43 1/2 x 34 inches, Painted over.
PHOTO: POLLOCK-KRASNER STUDY CENTER, JACKSON POLLOCK CATALOGUE RAISONNÉ ARCHIVES.

be used to separate Pollock from the Surrealists. The unifying thought in European Surrealism is that the Cosmos is the Dream of a Larger Consciousness. At significant moments, an image in the unconscious of a person coincides with an object in the world, an object that is an image in the dreaming cosmos. For Pollock at his most thoughtful, the Cosmos is the action of a Larger Consciousness, and the action of the unconscious and conscious minds can participate in the larger action. The apparent world can be seen, heard, and felt as the projection of cosmic forces toward a sensory plane.

Thus a painting made within those forces is an expression of those forces. Such a painting means what it is: an expression of the Cosmos through a visual elaboration of the very forces which leave their marks in paint on canvas. The marks can be read back toward the forces enlisted in their construction (production), but when they are read back toward the painter, difficulties arise in crediting the man with the product of natural forces that pass through him as a painter. A painter can be understood as

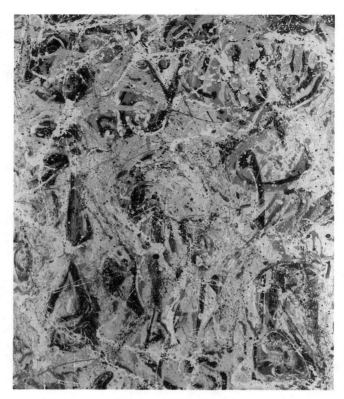

Jackson Pollock, *Galaxy*, 1947. Oil and aluminum paint, sand and gravel on canvas. Painted over *The Little King*. Joslyn Art Museum, Omaha, Nebraska, gift of Peggy Guggenheim. PHOTO: POLLOCK-KRASNER STUDY CENTER, JACKSON POLLOCK CATALOGUE RAISONNÉ ARCHIVES.

thinking not only about natural forces, but as thinking with natural forces which shape him as well as his paintings.

The terms that are available, like animism, can't be specific or persuasive enough that anyone could be committed to them. To paint like Jackson Pollock, however, one had to believe like Jackson Pollock, and he undoubtedly believed in "one life within us and abroad." In Jeffrey Potter's oral biography, Pollock is quoted making a characteristic statement: "Churches are okay if you got to belong to something to feel safe, but artists don't need that . . . they're part of the universal energy in their creating. Look—existence *is*. We're part of all like everything else, we're on our own" (154).

Pollock left visual evidence with which to think about him. He had shown drawings to two psychoanalysts, using the drawings in sessions that became activities more than confessional sessions probing for meanings that could be applied in therapy. He bought a house that was originally finished with clapboard, but later, about 1950, he had the house shingled

East View, Pollock-Krasner House. The house, built in 1879, was shingled in 1950. Pollock had the pile of glacial boulders collected from the property in 1956. PHOTO: PRISCILLA BOWDEN.

in natural cedar. Those shingles were cut by a retired circus clown whose skill Pollock envied. "I'd give a lot to be as old as that circus clown and split shingles like him," he told Potter (180). When he had the studio renovated in 1953, he had the ex-clown install the shingles on that building too.

The meanings of the shingles can be drawn closer to the meanings of the paintings. With shingles, the undetermined minute changes combine into an all-over (over-all) impression, a sum of unplanned changes that occur within a predictable range of accidents. Shingles and unpainted siding allow for a range of accidental effects, the weathering that changes the surfaces. At a certain point, as one approaches a shingled wall, the wholeness of the wall dissolves. Then particular shingles become visible as such, not as subordinate to the whole. The familiar process is like looking at a painting, which can be seen as a whole, when the surface as such can't be seen. Yet when one moves closer, the surface can be seen as a tactile surface of separate units, and the wholeness disintegrates into parts.

In the yard behind the house, raw boulders—a statement of what glacial forces can carry only so far—lie near the raw shingled buildings. Pollock had them collected from the property and piled there so he could study them. Such images were for Pollock a visual poetry, taking the poetic quality of visual phrases, as George Santayana put it, "to be due to their concentrating and liberating the confused promptings left in us by a long experience." When he died, Krasner had one of them moved to the grave in Green River Cemetery to become his tombstone, but she later replaced it with a bigger one. On what grounds does one judge the right boulder? One constructs such criteria as one works.

No criterion–idea of a good or beautiful boulder exists; it is always being improvised. Nor has rectilinearity been imposed upon the boulders as a sculptor or stonemason might shape them. Archetypes and patterns exist for brick or for cut stone, but not for boulders. The expression of the boulders, as an arrangement of specific objects, combines self-reliance, purposelessness, and in case the house looked too comfortable, aggression against bourgeois complacencies, with clock-time and wristwatch time shrinking from glacier-time. With an image like this, I am suggesting that Pollock, like a boulder, loomed large in the landscape, and that his house and studio were images of himself as an obstacle to ordinary social conventions.

Criticism and attempts at histories of art, even biographies of artists, tend to underplay the images with which artists and other people think. Pollock thought with specific and concrete images, and his friends have tried to convey some of his qualities in verbal pictures, as when the bartender at the Cedar Bar described him as a teddy bear outside the bar, but a grizzly bear when he was inside, and Robert Motherwell likened him to Marlon Brando in scenes from A *Streetcar Named Desire*. Whether or not such images hold clues to interpretation, Pollock was aware of the ritual of a Native American bear dance, and knew Tennessee Williams, the author of *Streetcar*, in Provincetown. Pollock's teacher, Thomas Hart Benton, painted Brando in *Streetcar*, an image that was reproduced on the cover of an early paperback edition of the play.

So often the work of a son is a criticism of false illusions in the work of the father. Pollock's father worked as a surveyor, and Jackson had co-operated with him in taking measurements of the land. He seems not to have taken away with him the abstract operations of a surveyor, using abstractions like numbers and ideally straight lines to impose a grid on a landscape. The abstract operations of a surveyor pass frictionlessly and effortlessly through the landscape. Pollock took the side of the natural objects against the surveyors, admiring the freedom of forms within the forms of boulders, shingles, and the natural world around him (and, offered his choice, picking the runt of a litter of pups). His philosophic thoughts — animistic, pantheistic — had, and have, such a "freedom of form within form" that they go unrecognized as philosophy. Yet David Sylvester, discussing the recent Pollock retrospective exhibition at the Tate Gallery in London, writes in *The Times Literary Supplement* of the movement of forms in his paintings as "a metaphor for the universe. It's metaphysical, perhaps an incarnation of the concept of the Heraclitean flux."

Rather than thinking to produce a survey, Pollock entered processes within which any product was open to reconstructions. As he moved toward an appreciation of the actions in a landscape that resist loveless calculations, he savored the animations in the weather, and the weathered surfaces and shapes produced by such processes. He freely repainted within his own canvases, working at repair, as a negation of damage, until it became positive, an emergent novelty. Recall that he repainted *The Little King* as *Galaxy*, a title that brings him closer to his themes of absorption in the cosmos.

"Ever try listening up there at Green River?" he asked Jeffrey Potter. "You can feel what I'm trying to say, maybe."

PERSONAL
RESPONSES:
THE MAN

JACKSON POLLOCK

BRYAN ROBERTSON
1960

As a man, Pollock was taciturn and contemplative by nature, though he was drawn to violence by fatality and, at last in his death, by finality. He was absorbed all through his life by the structure of violence: an essentially twentieth-century speculation. The inner springs and tensions of violent action or a dramatic situation moved him and aroused his imagination rather than the violence itself as an emotional display.

If this attitude had been reversed, he would almost certainly have been a brilliantly gifted mannerist artist instead of an inventor. For our mannerist society has only elaborate standards of exterior behavior and superficial style to inject into life, with no beliefs to harness or subordinate these standards to. Our creations do not stem from any guiding belief or faith other than the cult of the individual. Development in this direction is restricted because we do not react emotionally to what we apprehend mentally. Such a human condition paraphrases mannerist art.

In looking and seeking beyond the façade of life, Pollock tried to unite his intellect with his emotional reserves and reconcile flesh and spirit. The spectacle, wherever it occurred, touched him less than the unfolding motives which disclosed the spectacle. He strove continually to formalize, to rearrange, and to transcend actuality. The Kabuki Theatre would have excited him more than a theatrical production of Berthold Brecht. He saw constantly the archetypal principles at work behind human gesture, action, and common behaviour.

In nearly all Pollock's pictures which contain specifically human references these are transformed and held at a considerable stage from reality, partly by the sheer intensity of his recreated conception of life in terms of pigment and formalization, but frequently by complete translation into terms of ritual forms or archetypal masks. These relate on occasion to the ancient mythology of Greece, to the primitive cultures of Mexico, and to the folk art and decoration of the American Southwest, where he spent part of his youth, though the derivations are not precise or specific in any literal sense. In this way, as an artist, Pollock kept life and the ravages of existence at a certain remove, though he explored style voraciously, for style in America is a perpetually burning question for everyone and an answer, eagerly anticipated, to inner uncertainties.

For artists are lonelier and more isolated in America than anywhere else. Their recent elevation to what is practically the status of film stars in pre-war years has not lessened the problem of living in a community which lacks a self-engendered tradition in the visual arts and is now striving, at high speed, to create one. A high proportion of American artists live in New York, and the febrile background provided by that beautiful and heartless city combined with the enforced self-consciousness of their situation give a special edge to behavior as well as to work.

Pollock was occasionally exposed to the craving for violence which animates all of us at times and suddenly flares up in American life. When he was drunk and unhappy, and involved in trivial bar squabbles, weapons were sometimes thrust into his hand by avid onlookers.

Because of alcoholism he was sometimes violent in an off-hand manner for the hell of it. Even when this occurred, the still dormant interest in inner motivation gave his conduct a certain point and meaning. He would sometimes lose patience with the dragging time flux, with that remorseless inevitability of pace and flow and rise and fall of human encounter. When he became impatient in this way he could be intensely disturbing to any group of people, even to a gathering of friends, for in his work Pollock grew more and more to like only the formality that might be produced by spontaneity. This pursuit was reflected in his life. He may have considered Rilke's line. "Did not the circumspection of human gesture amaze you?"

As a double-edged means of visual discovery and personal liberation Pollock sought to trap the transience of human gesture and to isolate it from anything that the gesture might depict. He saw the spectacle, or the situations of life in visual terms; explored the motives or inner springs of action which determine the spectacle; and then scrutinized, as autonomous marks or movements in space and time, those gestures which finally implement the spectacle. In doing so, he sought also to extend the usual boundaries of gesture and its formal implication as an activity in itself, and to magnify and illuminate its action. In this way, he forged a style that was free of mannerism because it sprang from life.

When Pollock tried to precipitate a new situation in his attempt to go against the momentum of life which produces circumspection, it was as if he crashed an immensely heavy object onto a table and sent flying in all directions some sticks that had been lying in carefully arranged groups. This was his attempt to disrupt the time flux and to invoke a new contingency. To throw his own presence into the smoothly modulated pattern of existence. Or violently shake an all too predictable kaleidoscope.

Jackson Pollock outside his studio with *Number 9, 1952: Black, White, Tan*.
POLLOCK-KRASNER PAPERS, ARCHIVES OF AMERICAN ART, SMITHSONIAN INSTITUTION.

Jackson Pollock
AN APPRECIATION

FRANK A. SEIXAS

OCTOBER, 1963

JACKSON Pollock was physically big, larger than life-size; not only tall, but broad, deep-chested, well-muscled, and well-proportioned. His hands were immense, with thick fingers—the hand of one who had known phys-ical work. His features, too—thick, fleshy, one might say, as if hewd out of rock, save that there was a softness and a placidity about them. Above this his bald pate, framed with brownish hair which later had streaks of gray. A strong jaw below completed a face which one might see on a brutish day-laborer. One would notice him on entering a room—he seemed out of place indoors.

When he spoke, it was quite different. His {hazel} eyes would light up with the most intense humanity. He was interested in people, and he was amazingly warm and gentle. Diffident, shy—almost to the point of embar-rassment—he spoke in short sentences or phrases. Sometimes obscure or tangential. He was quite often silent, letting Lee speak for him.

We met him in The Springs at the home of some friends who were his neighbors. No one then knew where Springs was—the world of abstract art had not descended on it. I think he was the first professional artist I had met, and this made the meeting a great excitement for me. Shortly there-after, we visited the barn which he used as his studio and saw his work. The canvases were not as large as they would later become, but the intri-cate interweaving of lines and blobs of thick paint was there, giving a sense of constant movement, of three dimensionality, and of chaos which are characteristic of all that followed.

A week or so later, we were pleased that he accepted an invitation to come to our cottage. Something had moved me about his painting, and I had tried to fit it in to my own experience. As a medical student, I had been impressed by a thought common enough to be banal, that the microscopic architecture of the body showed the immensity of the beauty of nature. Jackson's paintings had reminded me of one aspect of this—the microscopic structure of the nerve cell with its expanded neurone, extending out to the filament-like axons and dendrites. This thought made it possible for me to enjoy his painting, because it captured a part of nature, unlike the angular and architectural fragments of other non-objective painters.

When I communicated this to him, Jackson became very excited. He was eager to see pictures and diagrams of nerve cells and I had the opportunity to show him some of these, with their beautiful stains by Cajals and Nissl. He had never looked into a microscope although I suppose, as all art students, he had studied gross anatomy. He had a mystical sense that he had discovered something intuitively; that he had seen as a microscope does and that in nature everything is open to those who put themselves in the position of receptiveness to it. He told me of seeing in a rock or a tree many things that others had not.

There followed several other visits to the studio and to his adjoining house. On one of these he showed us an early sketchbook of the time before he had developed his current style which showed a mastery of draftsmanship and form which were classic. They reminded me most of etchings by Blake, with whom he had much in common. Another time he told us a little about his home in {Wyoming} and showed us the hostile notice that a show of his had garnered in the local papers.

That winter we received an invitation to his exhibit at Betty Parsons Gallery. It was a small show, and his paintings were modestly priced, some going for {$300,00}. We talked about buying one, but somehow we didn't. We weren't really aware of the extreme poverty they were living in. We heard later that winter they had no heat at all, and finally traded a painting for the services of the heating contractor. Other paintings went for groceries and an ancient car was obtained, after some bargaining, for another painting. I don't think there were many connoisseurs among the tradesmen, but Jackson was a man who inspired friendship and respect among men. He was known as a man who could do things with his hands, other than painting, and they trusted him.

The next summer the old standard farmhouse was being transformed, Jackson had decided to tear out some walls. His architecture and his carpentry was as good as his instinct for art and he made massive structural changes, making the first floor into one large open room, painted white, with plants and beautiful old solid furniture in balance with light modern chairs. The outside, too, was changed. Flowers and a vegetable garden were planted.

One day that summer we went with some friends, an attractive looking couple, who, while they are far from being Philistines, approach the world with very common-sense eyes. He was by then doing the immense canvases spread out on the floor and dripping the paint directly from the tubes onto the canvas. He described his method of painting, and then there was a period of silence. Something had to be said, and our friend's wife finally inquired, "But Mr. Pollock, how do you know when you're finished?" Jackson drew himself up to his full, impressive height. He was very serious, as he replied softly, "My dear, how how do you know when you're finished making love?"

A year or so later we heard that he had changed galleries, and he was now exhibiting with Sidney Janis. He had been told (he didn't say this) that people wanted larger canvases, and now the huge works with which he is associated, were being shown. The gallery was thronged, and there was an excitement in the air. The paintings were selling for {$5,000} or more; and museums were buying them.

People we knew in Florence said that all the art students with Guggenheim Fellowships who were there to study the old Italian masters were talking only of Jackson Pollock. *Life* did an article. A movie was made satirizing his style. But the paintings were thought about and talked about.

One can conjecture why; perhaps because the complex network of threads reflect awareness of the infinite simultaneous stimuli to which our nervous structure dances—perhaps because we see no order in the chaotic random motion of the human particles and electronic particles in today's world. Perhaps he reflects our atomic, post–Freudian age, in which we scurry for security, fleeing the dissonances that not only surround us but struggle to emerge from within. Perhaps in the decomposition of form, his intuitive microscope was being turned on an impending explosion in himself and warding it off by externalizing and magnifying it.

Each spring when we arrived in the country, changes were evident at his house. Instead of one ramshackle car, three or four sleek foreign cars would be parked in the driveway. De Kooning was in the vicinity, and Ossorio. We would visit the lust yet airy interior to find a number of people dressed in the latest resort wear discussing abstruse themes. Jackson, now bearded, of course, in old dungarees, was showing some external signs of an internal struggle. He was on the wagon and drinking only coffee, or had taken up vegetarianism, or Zen Buddhism seemed to be important. Always, with the shyness, the sincerity, the basic honesty and forthrightness that seemed his quality—and behind that a sense of terrible struggle with the forces bigger than himself.

We went with him on a beach picnic—with the de Koonings and others whom I don't remember. The wildest picnic—that is not a sexual wildness—but the flinging about of great bodies with great energy and muscular freedom which seemed almost to want to physically encompass the interminable stretch of beach and sand and the entire ocean that lay before us. This was one of our last visits with Jackson.

Finally, we heard the news—the tragic accident on the familiar stretch of road that led from his house to East Hampton. As we drove down that summer, we were confronted with a large sign,

THIS IS IT

SPEEDING VIOLATIONS WILL BE

PROSECUTED

I don't recall the words that followed the title, but it was evident that the remorse and sense of loss that all of us felt was shared by the authorities, who I suppose had been known to overlook a little speeding on the part of a prominent citizen.

For the funeral the little church near Jackson's house was so full of people from all over the world and of flowers, that as many stood outside as were contained within.

We valued Jackson Pollock highly—as a human being. We had the feeling he valued us too. As a matter of fact, he made us a gift, and for a man who communicated so much more in symbols than in words, we have treasured that memory.

You may think he gave us a picture. No—it wasn't that; it was the largest, deepest purple, most symmetrically formed eggplant that I have ever seen. He had grown it. It was delicious.

That's what I know about Jackson Pollock.

Excerpt from an Interview with REUBEN KADISH

JAMES T. VALLIERE

CA. 1965

POLLOCK was going to be top. He was going to show Benton. But painting was even before his ego. Sometimes he would blow off about his greatness, but if he saw a good painting by somebody else he made sure others saw it too. He had a great faith in himself that people couldn't destroy. He would often challenge your relationship with him. He would test you; put up a barrier to see if you would say to hell with him. But he was just testing.

Jack made his presence felt. Sometimes it was negative, other times not, and there was frequently a touch of theatrics. He had a way of firing the situation. One time we were playing poker, using matches for chips. The discussion turned to art and Jackson, making a point, hit the table, which set the box of matches on fire. Things like that would happen often. He wanted the final say.

He wasn't an intellectual giant, but he had a sharpness and was very discriminating toward painting. You see this in his work, both the great feeling and intelligence is there. Among his contemporaries, de Kooning is a man of similar intelligence. Jack mentioned that de Kooning was a truly great painter, "a damned good painter, but he never finishes a painting."

Jack was out to paint the best god-damned picture that could be painted. Tremendous ego—he wanted to see a movement take place here. The general feeling of the time was always that American painters were inferior to Europeans. The Europeans were the best, and art was really happening over there. So he resented them. Someone asked him once if he was ever going to Europe. He answered, "Hell, no. Those Europeans can come look at us."

He was pleased that the Europeans were the first to recognize him, and excited that they respected his work. That was very important to him.

The Impressionists had the same idea—of putting their painting on the map—when they wanted a French national art. I'm not using the term national in a regional or provincial sense. Impressionism is French painting, and Abstract Expressionism is American. They both have a locale without being local, an identification without being provincial. It's not like the "international art" of today; you can't tell whether something is Japanese or Italian. A Pollock is definitely recognizable wherever you see it. It's Pollock, and it has something of the American spirit.

An Interview WITH TONY SMITH
AND PAUL FEELEY

JAMES VALLIERE

AUGUST 1965

THE following conversation with sculptor Tony Smith took place quite by accident. We were introduced one morning during August of 1965 by Lee Pollock, and were soon discussing Pollock's work. Paul Feeley, a painter who had studied with Thomas Hart Benton, was also present. As we begin Tony Smith is speaking about his first contact with Pollock and his work.

What was your first encounter with Pollock?

I first saw one of his works, I believe it was *Flame* at the Pepsi-Cola Exhibition. I don't remember the exact date of the exhibition,* but it was a huge show with about two to three thousand paintings. I remember that I didn't like *Flame*, it was too tight and oppressive, it gave me a feeling of claustrophobia.(See color plate no. 2)

I think it was in 1940 that I probably met Pollock for the first time, because, I remember his hair was still quite strong and low on his forehead. But then I really didn't get to know him until he had his first show at Betty Parsons Gallery.† He contacted me because he wanted advice on how the show should be hung. I saw him several times before and after the show and then maybe once or twice a year until 1950–51. I know that when I left NYU I had seen a lot of Jackson.

---

*The exhibition was held in 1943 at the Metropolitan Museum in New York City.
†1948.

So you didn't know Pollock in the 1930s but rather during the late 1940s onward?

But Jackson spoke to me about his early years in New York, in fact he did say that he originally came to the City with a desire to learn to make sculpture. I can remember, very clearly, his telling me that he came to New York to learn "to sculpt like Michelangelo." He was disappointed when he arrived because he found there was nobody to study with. In those days, 1930–33, you didn't have much of a choice—you could either study with someone who was tied up with the "Ten" or you could study under a European. For instance, I studied with George Grosz.

Did Pollock ever say why he studied with Benton?

It's very easy to talk about the American Scene and the subject matter that Benton was concerned with, but there was more in him than that, at least there was something else that an art student would see in him. Although I never studied with Benton I was at the Art Students League while he was there. When Jackson came to New York—he was interested in the Baroque, that's what he told me when I knew him in the late 1940s. In the early 1930s there was only one man who thought it was important to study the 'Grand Manner'—that was Benton. Jackson told me that he studied with Benton largely out of default, as he was the only one, at that time, who thought anything of the Baroque.

Paul studied with Benton, maybe he can tell you more about him.

When did you study with Benton?

(Paul Feeley) Sometime during 1933.

What kind of class did you take with Benton—was it mural, figure drawing, or what?

(Paul Feeley) It was just the Benton class. I don't recall that it had any special title. The whole thing was very loosely organized. There were no lectures, or anything for that matter that would give the impression that he was following a rigid format. You just went in and began to work. Everybody seemed to be doing pretty much what they wanted to. You paid your month's fee and entered the class. You could start or stop anytime you felt like it. So there were some people who had been there a long time mixed in with others who had just arrived.

As a student what did you think Benton was trying to teach?

(Paul Feeley) Benton had several spiels. He hated the French, especially the Cubists. It's difficult to say exactly what he was trying to get across. He had this idea that you were supposed to work out the composition for a painting in three-dimensional models—before you painted it.

223

Barnett Newman, Jackson Pollock and Tony Smith, Betty Parson Gallery, 1951.
PHOTO: HANS NAMUTH. © ESTATE OF HANS NAMUTH.

He would make these wooden models, with the space receeding on an angle, an inclined plane, then he would locate figures on it. He also had ideas about how you were to locate figures in a painting. I didn't go for it. Don't you remember him Tony?

(Tony Smith) All I can remember is that we used to refer to Benton's paintings as "prairie Picassos." But you do have to give him credit for emphasizing the Baroque and the painters of the "Grand Manner"— Rubens and others. He was the first American that I know of who did so in this century. It's quite possible that his emphasis on the "Grand Manner," as a teacher, will be far more important than his own work.

For instance, I can remember a black and white painting of Pollock's, probably 1950 or 1951, with a great Rubenesque figure in it. I asked Jackson where he learned to draw like Rubens. He answered "Tom Benton." He just threw the answer out—no hesitation "Tom Benton." Jackson was like that, his answers were direct.

As you probably know Pollock was intensely interested in the American West. Did he ever, in conversation, mention to you anything about the West?

(Tony Smith) Jackson and I had both been in the Southwest. When I was young I had TB, so I went there for health reasons. Jackson was very proud of the fact that he knew the Indians of the Southwest. That's the way he put it, he knew the West as it really was, whereas he considered that I had been there as a dude. He made quite a bit of the fact that he knew the people, the Indians, at first hand.

Did he ever speak about specific experiences that he had while he was in the West?

He told me stories about things he'd done in the West, but I can't specifically remember any of them. I can remember that he took me to see a film called *Racon Pass*, just because he had been through that pass. He had a tremendous sense of identification, a strong personal association with the West—his past. I always had the impression that he thought the West had a certain sense of freedom, perhaps that it was in some way more real than the effete East. He had a rapport with this—the authentic life of the West.

I also think that Jackson's feelings about the West profoundly affected his general behavior. It showed in the way he would walk around—well he walked like a cowboy. And it showed especially in the way he would relax. He would let his body sag in a chair, much in the way you would imagine a cowboy would. I remember that I was particularly struck by this because none of his brothers behaved like that, so I knew it wasn't something that he'd inherited. Whatever it was he picked it up himself. For some reason or other he strongly identified with both the West and especially the idea of the cowboy.

You mentioned that he was proud of the fact that he knew the Indians. Did he ever say anything to you about what he specifically liked about them?

I can remember one very remarkable experience. Jackson and I were walking in the village and we came to the corner of 8th Street and 5th Avenue. The building on that corner had just been torn down to make way for a new hotel. Naguchi, the Japanese artist, had been living there and in the debris scattered about the ground you could see pieces of bamboo and other things that indicated that an Oriental had been living there. Jackson went over and picked up a bamboo rod and held it over his head—slightly bent—and raised his face towards the moon and began to utter something that, to me, sounded like poetry—the type the Indians of the Southwest were known for.

It was not precisely Indian poetry that he was speaking, rather the tone and the meter, along with the way he was standing—made me immediately think of the Southwestern Indians. I asked him if he knew of the poetry of these Indians, and he said "Yes." I later sent him an anthology of Southwestern Indian poetry.

225

Jackson was also quite aware of Mexico—he would allude to Mexico and the Southwest with a knowledge, which struck me as being romantic as he obviously thought that life in those areas was more authentic than life is here.

Another thing that I recall is that for years Jackson talked of building a huge dirt mound in front of the house here in East Hampton, one that would be quite high and long. When asked why he simply said, in jest, "to get some privacy." He was quite insistent on this mound and it struck me as very funny because there is *very* little room for such a huge mound to be built between the house and the road. He claimed that the Indians built mounds around their villages.

When you spoke to Pollock did he speak freely, that is, was there an easy give and take. I say this in reference to the impression that many people had that he was non-verbal?

All the talk about his being non-verbal is false—when he had something to say—he said it. He didn't waste words, in that sense he was laconic—he came directly to the point.

Also in the strict sense of the term you didn't have a conversation with Jackson. You would ask him a direct question and he would give you an answer. Although he wasn't a talker, he wasn't evasive either. Occasionally when he didn't want to answer a question he would just smile.

Did he speak about art very frequently?

No. Jackson would go up to a painting and look at it very intensely—he would be standing no more than a foot away—then he would move his hand in a gentle swirling motion in front of the canvas but not on it. When he confronted a work he wasn't inclined to talk about it.

One time I asked him what he thought was the greatest work of art in North America. He thought for a few minutes, then he said "the Orozco fresco at Pamona College."* He had a quick mind and when he spoke he always came directly to the point—sometimes embarrassingly so. I can't remember any other specific conversations about painting—except he would maybe talk about the way Orozco drew isolated subjects, something like that that was very specific. I can remember looking at some early Mondrians with Jackson. There was a time in New York when you could go around to various galleries and see early Mondrians that were quite close to what Paul Klee was doing. Mondrian seemed to interest him—especially in works where the lines were not so rigid. He seemed to like the way Mondrian handled the surface in these early works.

*The fresco is entitled "Prometheus" and was completed in 1930.

I've always felt that there was some kind of similarity in the way both Mondrian and Pollock strove to keep the visual intensity of their works on the surface. The whole trend of painting in the twentieth century has been towards the surface, much in the way one might say the dominant theme of the Renaissance was the exploration of space in art.

An interview
WITH DANIEL T. MILLER

JAMES T. VALLIERE
1965

THE Daniel T. Miller General Store is just a short walking distance from the Pollock house. It looks today much as it did during the 1940s with its air of stark neatness ringing of Calvinist New England. There are no neon lights or cardboard posters to obstruct its plain white facade or its impeccably placed rows of foodstuffs. The only changes have been in policy—Miller no longer sells beer and since August of 1965 he no longer carries charge accounts.

I had been warned that during the interview we might expect interruptions as Mr. Miller employs no help and he would still have to tend to the store even while we conversed. The Bookmobile which arrives promptly every Thursday afternoon at three o'clock stood as the only real threat that would attract people who might drop in. Mr. Miller, an extremely polite and gracious man (few have ever seen him without a white shirt and tie although he pumps gas daily) ushered me into a small office which adjoins the main room of the store. There we spoke for over two hours—with the door left open in case "customers called."

Were you living in The Springs when the Pollock's first moved here in November of 1945?

Yes, this was my home. I was born here and this is where I've spent most of my life and my people on both sides have been here for generations. We kind of like it here.

Has the general store always been in your family?

No, I started this store. This building was built over two hundred years ago and it was built for a store. When I bought it in 1945 it was pretty well abandoned. It had been a store for a long time, people had lived here and rented part of the time. I guess squatters had lived here part of the time and by 1945 it was pretty well battered. But it was basically a wonderful building.

You are one of the people who wasn't an artist and who knew Pollock. Also I take it since living here most of your life you must know the community pretty well. Was there any reaction when the Pollocks first arrived to the idea of an artist coming here and settling down, a man who made his living in such a different manner from the local people?

You have to understand that when the Pollocks first moved here, they perhaps rented first then bought an old house, they were in many ways different from the common concept of an artist. They did not dress or act or do anything to their appearance that was different from ordinary people. They rode up and down here on a couple of bicycles for several years before he got an old Model A Ford. I might make the point here that Jackson Pollock didn't basically move to Springs—he was moving away from something more than he was moving to something. He told me that himself openly and hinted at it several times. There were conditions in New York that had developed that he wanted to get away from, associations to a certain extent. He wanted to get away. Jackson Pollock was in many ways a very, very conservative man. I don't know whether you can follow with that.

In what way do you mean "conservative"?

Jackson Pollock in his art—perhaps I'll use the wrong words—was not an innovator but an explorer and discoverer. He was reaching out, he had something in him that he had to express differently than had been done. That is what I believe. In his art and in his belief in himself he was very sincere and honest. And I think one of the things that he was moving away from was the tendency to be surrounded by people who were not as sincere or as able. In other words he wanted to get away from the fraud, the foam, and battle the waves himself. Now that's what I honestly think.

You started to tell us the reaction of the local people when he first appeared here.

He was liked, he was accepted, no problem. He wasn't belittled as a man but his art was not understood. People wouldn't take one of his paintings for a gift. I had one of his paintings. Hung it on the wall in here for many long years. He sort of traded it off for a grocery bill. But most people who looked at it wouldn't give it room in their outhouse. Wasn't malicious, though, it was just their opinion.(See color plate no. 5)

Now my brother had a farm hand working for him, Charlie, an old man who didn't know much but who could drive horses and mow. Sometimes in the summer he mowed the leaves along the side of the road for the Town. He was in here one day, the team was out in front. Pollock drove by here—he had acquired his beat up old model A Ford by then—and Charlie liked Jackson. He liked him, worked for him some, mowing around the yard. "That old Pollock," he said, "lazy son-of-a-bitch, ain't he Dan?" And I said, "Charlie what do you mean he's lazy?" "Why I never see him do a day's work, did you?" he said. That was pretty much the local reaction; not bitter, not evil or vicious, but it was just the way he would talk about anybody else around here. See at that time Jackson wasn't considered wild-hide or anything.

The local people misunderstood the nature of his work, the ways of a painter being unfamiliar, whereas they probably thought of work as something physical, something you do every day for eight or ten hours.

Charlie did—do you see what I mean. If he didn't see a man out there he didn't see him working. At the same token he didn't see me working either. I told Jackson what Charlie said. I've known many artists and wonderful people but a good many of them I couldn't have told that story to, but I told Jackson and didn't he laugh. Instead of being offended he loved Charlie all the more. That's the kind of guy he was—he was a tremendous man.

I understand that you have a rather distinguished career out here yourself—that you were one of the first men on Long Island to fly and own your own plane. Did Pollock ever go flying with you?

That is a bit exaggerated but I did take Pollock more than once. I laughed the first time I took him to Block Island. We were coming home, and we sat there in this place you know. We wheeled up over the creek here and started to go across those light wires over the field there and I could feel his knees banging up against mine. When we hit the ground I said, "Jackson, one of your legs is nervous, isn't it?" He grinned and said "By God I didn't know what you were going to do."

Was it a single-engine plane?

Yes. Just a small single-engine plane. You'd sit side by side quite close together, he had his leg right against mine. He went with me more times than that.

Did he ever discuss his feelings about the New York art world?

You know one day we were talking and it was a time when he was having sort of a hard time. He was beginning to get recognized, there had been a write-up in some magazine or other, and that had opened up the

*A nickname for the inhabitants of East Hampton which is derived from the name of the original residents of the area—the Acabonic Indians.

criticism of people who were supposed to be critics and writers and it opened up the criticism on the part of the Bonackers* who didn't know much about painting, except that what he did was something different.

I can tell you a very amusing thing about that. He came in this day and he was speaking of a few things and was a big mad and discouraged—discouraged isn't the word. He talked a bit about it and as he was going he stopped in the doorway and said to me "Dan I want to tell you something— I am a great artist. I don't give a damn what anybody said, I'm a great artist and I know it." And do you know I believe him. I believed that he was.

Life magazine came out with a long article, "Is Jackson Pollock the Greatest Living Artist in America," which was quite a shock to the art world. How did the people around here react to this story?*

The native people around here weren't ready to admit to themselves that they were wrong. Of course I guess that a good many of them made peace with themselves by figuring that *Life* magazine was crazier than Pollock. As for me the article was no surprise because people from *Life* magazine had been over here and they took a few pictures of Pollock and his grocer.

How do you think Pollock felt about the Life article?

Well he was proud of it, of course. Say what you want, we have certain things by which we measure our efforts in life. Money is one of them, gratification is another. People many times use the word "notoriety" in speaking of Jackson and I do not believe that word was ever well used. I don't believe that whatever notoriety there may have been gave him a bit of pleasure. But that *Life* article did signify achievement, some recognition of what he was trying to do and succeeded in doing. Obviously it wouldn't have been there if he hadn't.

I remember one day Julien Levi came in here and we were talking about Pollock. He said "Dan, you're right, Jackson Pollock is a great artist." and I said "Mr. Levi I do not understand very much about that type of painting." And you know, Mr. Levi said 'Dan, very few people do—and a lot less number are able to do it. But Jackson is one of the few in the world" that's what Julien Levi said "Jackson is one of the few in the world who are really great artists and know what they are doing."

You mentioned that the word "notoriety" was frequently used by people when they were speaking of Pollock.

I keep coming back to the image that was set forth—that Jackson was a wild-eyed radical or something like that. Well in his paintings, the emotions of his paintings, that was all that was wild.

*'Is he the Greatest Living Painter in the United States,' *Life* August 8, 1949.

Then you think that Pollock's public image was inaccurate?

Probably necessary but while he was a part of it, it was not a part of him. I am sure that while that might have been done for various reasons to promote paintings I do not think he used anything in his paintings to do that. Although he was a part of it it wasn't of him. That's my feeling.

Do you think his problem with alcoholism had something to do with that public image?

Well his big problem with alcoholism comes right on back to the basic conservative man that he was. He sought answers to problems in the same way it's been sought since recorded history began. When I state things I state them talking here with you as a positive fact. They are positive as far as my own thoughts are concerned. I am sincere in thinking that Jackson among other things got to the point where there was something inside of him that he was not being able to put down on canvas the way he wanted to. And it was frustrating, that's what I believe. Then without going into detail there arose a certain set of circumstances and conditions that he had to strike out at, that he had to get relief from, and what did he do? Just the same as generations for hundreds of thousands of years—he turned to women and alcohol. It's been done a million times. That's basic—there's nothing new in that reaction.

His problem was not the alcohol but frustration, the frustration that there was in him that he might not be able to express. I believe that with Jackson it drove him nuts. Am I crazy or am I talking some sense?

You're making a great deal of sense.

Alright then. I believe that alcohol brought out a Jackson Pollock that was one hundred percent different than the Jackson Pollock when he was sober. I have seen it in other people reveal the vilest part, the part that all of us try to keep hidden and subdued. When he'd been drinking he was immediately foul-mouthed and irresponsible and he got himself kicked out of almost every gin-mill around because he was offensive.

Now I've thought of that many times and my belief is that because he was a great artist that there were things in him that had to bust out and that's the way they bust out. Things that I might have been able to cover up and control and maybe the ordinary man could, but in Jackson Pollock they could not be kept down. I presume the time came when his wife probably tried to correct him and it probably just made things worse. Evidently things were going to pot to some extent. But there is nothing unusual in that, that was no unusual thing. Lord we've seen it a thousand times the same way.

Now I've heard say, after Jackson passed on, that he knew himself to be a faker and a fraud and was perhaps driving himself to admit it, that he couldn't live with himself with that knowledge. If I know anything that is wrong that is as wrong as anything could be. That is not in any way the right answer to Jackson Pollock and why he was being driven nuts, to use the expression. It was a frustration that if he could have lived and gone beyond that point, he would have been able to grab that paint and put it down. But he didn't live to that period of time.

In what way did he change as the years went on?
Well the first number of years life was pleasant, seemed to me. It appeared in general that he was doing what he wanted to do and needed to do. I suppose it was a frustration of some kind that seemed to enter the picture. I felt that up to a point he could do his work and was apparently satisfied with it. Whether other people were or not, he was happy with it, and he began to get recognition. Then there was something that began to bother him and he was not as happy with his work and he was not happy with his home.

Was this after 1949–1950?
Oh I would say within a year or two of when he was killed.

I see, 1954–1955.
I might not have sensed this thing right off the bat but he did begin to change. It was a frustration that led not only to a breaking out, but an eruption, a violent reaction seeking relief. It also led to an attitude on occasion of "to hell with it." But I say no reaction different from what had been with men throughout the centuries, except that some people are able to contain and hide it, if not to overcome frustrations that in others are apt to erupt. And perhaps the more able and sensitive a person is the more they tend to be that way.

This is me all over. You ask a question or two and I'm off. I am not ordinarily that garrulous, but I have thought many many hours after Jackson went on to come to peace with myself as to what happened. I liked Jackson personally, I liked him very much indeed. I'd like to add a little thing here about Mrs. Pollock. I've seen him drive up here to these gas pumps for gas and get in and drive away with Mrs. Pollock sitting beside him, and wouldn't have sat beside him in that condition he was in but she did. There was a quality there or love or however you want to put it. But the point I wanted to make is that she didn't just get up and run when things got a little bit rugged. She sure didn't. I thought to myself more than once "Well Lee I wouldn't drive with that son-of-a-gun—I'd get up and walk off" but she didn't. I like her a lot too.
In what way did his financial success around 1949, 1950 seem to affect him?
It might have made a difference but I do not think it was one of the basic

things that changed him. He drove up here with a Cadillac one day and said "Well Dan," he says "I traded this for one of my paintings." To him it was an enjoyable thing, he wasn't bragging exactly but he had reached the point where somebody gave him that car for one of his paintings.*

Did he ever come over and sit down to talk during the later years?

No, he never got to that point. I don't think I appreciated at the time what I have since, as I've thought it over. I knew it wasn't the Jackson Pollock I knew—that man who was running around here foul-mouthed and drunk. That was not Jackson. There was something that was doing it, that I know. If we could look back steadily and turn the clock back how different we would do sometimes, wouldn't we?

When he first came here he was almost, you could say, a happy man, and he was not happy when he died. He was not happy at all, he was frustrated.

Did he ever say this to you?

No, never. I cannot say that he ever said this.

During the time in which you knew Pollock what did you think he was trying to do in his painting?

I never fully understood just what he was trying to do, but I did get more of the picture eventually. Many people pretended to understand but didn't. I remember one time after Jackson had been here many years. I received an invitation to attend a lecture in New York on modern art by a man that was beginning to be recognized as a critic and a writer. I mentioned it to Jackson. He came in, I had the letter and he looked at it and said "Dan what the hell does he know about it." Those are the words he used— "What the hell does he know about it." Jackson had in him a knowledge and an ability, a power, that was honest. I know he was a great artist because he told me so.

You see I had begun to understand a little bit about what he was trying to do and it was evident that he was destined to become a very controversial man.

When you say that you were beginning to understand to some extent what he was trying to do, did you gather this from conversations with him?

Yes. Some of the things that Jackson told me if I repeated to you wouldn't sound just right because he was only speaking in a way that he would try to make me understand in my limited understanding.

---

*The agreement to trade a painting for the Cadillac never materialized. The owner of the automobile returned the painting for the car.

Like one day we were talking and he oversimplified the thing and said "Dan for an artist it's no use to reproduce something. A camera, a color camera, could do it better. It's no use for him to paint something for other people to see when everybody can go around and see it for themselves. The artist should reflect along the line of the time and the age in which he lives—he should strive for something different." And I said "Well Jackson this painting that I have of yours, it has balance, it has line—I can see that much. But it represents a whole mass of things churning up and unsettled and we cannot see one part of it but that it leads to the next. Yet the whole picture does make sense. Now is that what you say that maybe reflects the world we live in?" And he didn't contradict it nor answer it. I could see that I had an idea but I still didn't have the whole picture. But after looking at that painting and studying him and his works for a dozen years I could in my own mind bring out this fact. Although, like the present day world, no man could see where the confusion, the upsets, and the changes were leading, still when you put it all together in a painting as Pollock did there was nothing displeasing about it. It made a picture, the whole thing did.

In my own thinking it all adds up and makes something. I carried on from there, of course, the painting is something that you have to put in a good deal of what you want to take out, don't you know.

Had you thought much about painting before you met Pollock?

He opened an entire new world to me, him and talking to other artists around here. That's where my information has come from—talking to people like Pollock.

AN INTERVIEW WITH
James Brooks

JAMES T. VALLIERE

NOVEMBER, 1965

JAMES and Charlotte Brooks live in a small single story house in The Springs and since both are painters they have two studios which can only be partially seen from their back porch. Throughout this interview which took place on a chilly morning in early November of 1965, Mr. Brooks sat quite relaxed on a couch in the far corner of the living room. He rarely changed his position during our lengthy conversation and only occasionally were his long and thoughtful comments punctuated as he leaned forward to re-fill his pipe.

When did you first meet Pollock?
    I don't remember exactly when, but it was in the Project days.* I met his brothers Sandie and Charles before I met him and for a year or two I knew them a little better than I knew Jackson. And then somehow Jackson and I got to seeing more of each other, but it was not much before the War.
    I returned from the War in the fall of '45 and lived in New York around several places—with friends. I needed a place to live. At that time Jackson and Lee were moving out of their place on 8th Street where they had an entire floor. They were in fact moving to East Hampton. Jackson let me have the front part of the apartment and his brother Jay took the rear. I suppose that's really how Jackson and I became friends.

---

*During the Depression the Federal Government sponsored various relief programs under the Works Progress Administration (WPA) one of which, for artists, was called the Federal Arts Project.

You are one of the few major painters of this post-war period that served in the armed forces. Have you ever thought about this?*

I've thought of it a great deal although I never knew exactly how many of the guys were in or out. I knew that a great many were not in the service. When I returned to New York in 1945 with my wife Charlotte, it was a job in itself just to find a place to live let alone keep track of what everybody else was up to. The art scene was set really—the galleries were showing this certain group of young painters and they were already pretty well known.

Jackson Pollock and James Brooks in Brooks' studio, Montauk, New York, 1950.
PHOTO: HANS NAMUTH © ESTATE OF HANS NAMUTH.

*Pollock, Guston, de Kooning, Baziotes, Kline, Motherwell, Rothko, and Still did not serve during World War II. All of them had their first New York solo shows before 1948 (with the exception of Kline)—Pollock was the first with a show in November of 1943.

Then there was a big change in the art world when you returned after the war?

Yes, certainly, that's when it had its biggest change. The artists who didn't go to war were a talented bunch. It was a small field and they were encouraged more than they had ever been. And so they made tremendous strides and really did some great work. I think it was a great period. It was just unfortunate for some of us who were really in the cold when we came back. We didn't feel that way, but actually in retrospect, I'm sure that things were pretty well set, kind of an historical fact.

What were your thoughts about Pollock's work when you first saw it in 1945?

I was very interested. It was invigorating, very liberating. You see for a while after I came back I painted in kind of a synthetic cubism; it was rather tight and there was something else I needed to do. The whole atmosphere after I came back had started to change with Pollock, Motherwell and others. That helped me a good deal. I do remember that Jackson had *Gothic* and *Pasipháe* hanging in the apartment. I particularly liked *Pasipháe*, I thought it was a great painting.

So you liked the work you saw right after the war?

At that time it was intensely interesting to me. Sometimes the individual work was not so successful, but his whole attitude towards it was. I recognized that it was something that I needed at the time. I felt it as an expression of a thing that was somehow happening all around. It was in the air. Everybody seemed to be feeling it. I thought he was doing a lot, more so than most people. I didn't think of the actual lasting quality of his work, but rather I thought of him as a painter who was deep into something that interested me a lot.

When you say "he was deep into something" what exactly was he deep into?

He was breaking the space concept that had bound us before. He made it easier for me and probably for many other people. His unconscious came through to a point where we didn't think so consciously about how a picture was made, or how space should be constructed. In a sense he kind of walked right into another world.

Did it occur to you at that time that perhaps Pollock had simply picked up most of his ideas from the Dadaists and Surrealists, that he was just repeating something that had already been done?

No it didn't seem that way to me. I wasn't perhaps very familiar with the European developments, but it wouldn't have mattered anyway. With the awareness of the unconscious opened up by Freud and others and the way it affected the literary and aesthetic environment it seemed to be just a natural thing for him to be doing.

I recognized that there were influences, which I respected him for, but despite that his work did seem different and very much his own. I don't think there is such a thing as a complete individuality or originality and so it would never bothers me. If the work uses all the influences in a way that transcends them, then it's a mutation—which is the basis of change in art forms.

Anyway I didn't think of it that way—he was just a guy really trying to test into something. His compulsion and forms interested me more—which is probably because I was open to it at that time. Many of us were ready for something like that, we felt the same need but expressed it differently.

This was your impression in 1945. Pollock, however, was leaving New York then. Did you go to East Hampton to visit him after he moved out there and did you continue to see his work?

I can't remember exactly when we first began to come out—we did come out with friends to hike around Montauk. But we did visit the Pollocks once in a while and we would spend the weekend at their house. We liked Montauk pretty much, soon after we rented a place there for a summer and then bought a small house. I believe that was in 1949.

You must have seen Jackson then when he came into New York?

Yes, Jackson would come in for his shows or just on an impulse and we would get together. He liked to come in—it got pretty lonesome there. They were poor and couldn't travel much. I think they had a pretty tough life.

At times he drank heavily and at other times he didn't drink at all. But he would come in and it would get pretty wild sometimes. There is a story that Bill de Kooning tells of having a dream where he is in the Cedar Bar with all the gang and the doors fling open and Jackson is standing there and says "I can paint better as any man in this room." Real cowboy stuff. It seemed to me that he got a little more like a cowboy as time went on and legends were built up around him.

So you think he acted more like a cowboy as the years went by?

I don't think he acted differently, really, maybe a little, but he dressed more that way and I think he was almost forced into it by this legend that was building up around him. I think this public image is also partly responsible for his death. I think he just couldn't withstand it or couldn't fight it. He worked best when there was no value to his work, when an impulse would go down without any premeditation of it being valuable or not valuable. But when it got valuable and every stroke was worth money, or was famous, I think it paralyzed him. He became very self-conscious.

His strong forte was his unselfconscious action. He had this release—everyone had it—but not as much as he had it. That's the way he acted with real meaning and when he wasn't able to act with that kind of abandon I think it destroyed his impulse to work or it paralyzed him in relation to the world around him which was building him up so strongly. I just feel it was dangerous.

What did Pollock talk about, that is when you would have a conversation with him?

He was an intensely self-conscious man, one of the most self-conscious that I've ever known. When he'd had a drink or two he became a very interesting talker, very trenchant. He could talk about painting quite beautifully. It was good to talk about your painting with him because he attacked it in a structural way, not bringing in other meanings that a painter has that you can't talk about too much. Other times he would go into a very interesting monologue about things in painting that you'd done that had provoked him in a psychological way—the images—the strange formation that you were bringing out or were repressing. Even things such as bulls' heads or goats' heads he would mention in a combination of mystical and psychological knowledge.

Did he use psychological terms?

No. He did not.

But you say that he did have a knowledge?

Well he had been analyzed or there had been attempts to analyze him. It's my assumption that he had read and had had conversations with analysts and was therefore conscious of symbolism. I don't think that he ever used it directly in his work—I think he just saw it later—if it occurred. He was actually very involved in it. I believe, after the fact.

Did Pollock ever speak about the criticism that was written about his work?

No, almost never. I don't remember any definite things. He would be affected or hurt by something and he would say "do you know so-and-so—the guy who wrote it" and I would say yes or no and he would just drop the subject. But you could tell he was thinking about it. I remember when *Life* came out with that article in 1949 . . .

The one that asked if Pollock were the greatest living American painter?

Yes. Bradely Tomlin and I read it on the way out on the train to visit Pollock. I don't think Bradely had met him before then. We brought the magazine out to him and he was very embarrassed. He couldn't read it while we were there.

What is your reaction when you see a Pollock now—is it the same as it was originally?

No, it's not the same as it was originally. At the time there was always some shock mixed in, but now it's more set in history, I know it already, I've seen everything before. Now it still seems good. It seems very good—very interesting with a great deal of intensity and variety to it. It looks like good painting.

But when you first saw it it was quite a shock to you?

Yes. Quite often, although I saw it so often that it hardly ever happened that I had that strong a reaction. But I can remember a show that he had at Peggy Guggenheim's Art of This Century Gallery, that was the year he did *Eyes in Heat.** It was kind of shocking to me. Now it looks classic.

You think they look quieter, less turbulent to you now?

Oh yes. Yes the things that had seemed very violent now seem quite lyrical to me.

How do you feel about his importance today. As a painter do you think he really is as important as his reputation would have him be?

I think he is under a slight veil now. He isn't of such importance to younger painters coming up, but it still looks important to me. Jackson never had the kind of influence like a Hofmann did. Jackson's influence is a different kind of thing, it was more open and couldn't be used in a strict technical sense.

More on an idea level?

Yes. It was more of an attitude towards things.

How do you feel about Pollock, the man, today. Do you think his works have overshadowed him as an individual?

I think Jackson has been remade since his death, very consciously, into some kind of an historical figure. It doesn't seem to me to reflect anything of him at all. It doesn't seem like Jackson Pollock. His close friends can't feel of him as that kind of a man, or even a great man, they felt him as a friend.

Also there is a falsification going on, their stressing one thing to serve certain interests and letting other things go, things that might adversely affect the image of Jackson Pollock. But there are so many things that would affect him adversely if told—that if not told, leaves nothing of him. In the end it will all make him a much bigger and a much more interesting man.

*1946.

29 Depot Avenue, Falmouth, Mass.

Dear Lee:

A friend has forwarded to me the recent (March 26) article by John Gruen entitled "A Turbulent Life with Jackson Pollock," which seems an admirable piece of reportage, a very human and sympathetic statement.

Actually I had very little contact with Jack—never saw him except at the Cedar on one of his benders. I do recall asking him for the loan of a painting for the first show at St. Mark's in the Bowerie and being gently refused—he wouldn't say why. I also seem to have got his signature for a reproduction of his work in Hess's book—*Abstract Painting*—when it first came out.

But I didn't cease to think about him. And when Seymour Franks came down here and demonstrated his version of Pollock, I took it up and developed it in my own way by painting in between the spilled lines of paint as if a kind of cloisonné, perceiving as never before the figure-ground possibilities of flat areas of color in non-overlapping free forms (Color parallels the pic-ture-plane, but does not of itself say which is forward or back—Stuart Davis) until I could dispense with these dripped outlines. To me it seemed that the remote control of dripped-paint was virtual rather than direct, and somewhat de-person-alised, constituting a record of the natural tensions and viscosities of paint and without the manual character that is the direct imprint of the psychology of the artist at work, at that particular time and place of his being—as Ehrenzweig points out in his *Psychoanalysis of Artistic Vision and Hearing*. As far as I was concerned Pollock's role was liberating and this seems to have been the general consensus of opinion, for then as now there was little direct imitation—it was considered reprehensi-ble. In a way this was ridiculous. It is as if Clyfford Still for example had sewed up all of Chinese painting as his private domain. And like so many others, I couldn't help but feel that [Pollock's] death was suicide, at a moment of doubt and despair.

Fresh fuel was added to this idea by chancing upon Pollock's statement in {Sidney Janis' book, *Abstract and Surrealist Art in America*}, saying, "Anything I might have to say about my paintings would only destroy them." I asked myself, for whom? and concluded that this was in line with Hofmann's "I want not to know what I am doing but what I am feeling." Gruen's article stresses Pollock's non-verbalization. You will well recall how the speakers at the Club floundered around with words, sometimes in a literate-illiterate manner with aphorisms and observations probably elaborated while painting (e.g. de Kooning: "Space is like walking into a dark and empty room and stumbling over a dead body"), or else stream of consciousness (Resnick—"the symbolic rationale of irrational thought") or sometimes in a defensive, flippant, smartalecky manner. One of the best—not heard directly but related to me—was an observation by Kline about his own work: "The Dark is where you are, the White is where you want to be." I asked him about this and he replied, "Did I say that?" thought it over a moment and said: "Sounds all right to me." But in general they did appear to be holding their cards close to their chest, as if self-knowledge would be destructive and cut the ground from beneath them, and not-to-know was a protective self-indulgence.

Thus Pollock could have become a person named Jackson Pollock, compelled by his insistence upon non-verbalization or conceptualized untitled awareness of himself—to paint works by the celebrated painter Jackson Pollock, and become totally fed up with this situation. The inhibiting doubt was self-recognition in this present phase of himself. This is self-consciousness—which implies awareness of others rather than knowledge of oneself, and is often characterized by biting one's nails in indecision, being beset with uncertainty and seeking self-liberation through self-destructiveness. The attitude is, "I'm going to throw myself away, and then you'll be sorry." Thus I would contest the statement that "Actually; no one knew as much about himself as Jackson did. He knew what he was about, and he knew how riddled with doubt he was." I would agree he was riddled with doubt but that one must discriminate between self-consciousness and self awareness.

I would agree with his statement that art and life are one and inseparable, but add that life is a going concern—a power in the realm of Becoming, ever in transition and not susceptible to any ultimate definition or determinism.

In terms of this constant fluctuation of who one is Now—the solution to me in any present way has been to make the painting a process in a state of figure-ground ambivalence, where these

co-exist as alternatives. Only in a state of satori do these
have simultaneous force, equal but opposite, equivocal. One sees
ordinarily an either-or rather than a both-and-neither. This of
course does not absolve me from seeking a fresh statement in
some new unknown way that I come across while working that seems
plausible and knowable. I cannot predict my evidences and am
highly suspicious of plans, programs, intentions, and purposes
allegedly fulfilled, that are pretexts arrived at by *a posteriori*
hindsight. Nothing turns out as planned, but tends rather to
fulfill itself by its own coherence of simultaneous harmony and
contrast, in the multiple realms of colors, shapes, areas whose
interactions are both form and content. There is but one cate-
gorical statement that one can make about what *Art Is*—that it
composes a self-sufficient entity, a total situation, of itself
so. It is a fiction in the guise of an absolute.

W. H. Littlefield

de KOONING ON POLLOCK

AN INTERVIEW BY JAMES T. VALLIERE

1967

Valliere: In 1942 you and Pollock exhibited along with others in a show called "French and American Painters." It was held at the McMillen Gallery.

de Kooning: Yes. It was a very little show—not outstanding. The critics liked it and were sympathetic so it was written up nicely. The Americans looked very good; they were different from one another, but nobody paid attention. It was not like today. People just weren't buying American painting.

Valliere: But why were a group of almost completely unknown Americans like yourself, Pollock and Lee Krasner shown with highly recognized Europeans—Picasso, Braque, Rouault, etc.?

de Kooning: Because of John Graham. The owner of the McMillen Gallery asked him to arrange an exhibition and he picked us. Graham was very highly regarded. He had written a book called the *Dialectics of Art*. Also, Graham, Stuart Davis, and Arshile Gorky at that time were known as the Thrèe Musketeers. They were the three outstanding modern artists. Graham was very important and he discovered Pollock. I make that very clear. It wasn't anybody else, you know.

Valliere: You think Graham discovered Pollock?

de Kooning: Of course he did. Who the hell picked him out? The other critics came later—much later. Graham was a painter as well as a critic. It was hard for other artists to see what Pollock was doing—their work was so different from his. It's hard to see something that's different from your work. But Graham could see it.

Valliere: Had you ever seen any of Pollock's work before the McMillen exhibition?

de Kooning: No. That was the first time. Pollock was about nine or ten years younger than I. I knew Graham as early as 1927 and through him met Gorky and Davis; but I got to know Pollock only after the group show at McMillen.

Valliere: After you knew him did you speak about painting very often?

de Kooning: No, not much conversation. He didn't like to talk. I remember that Mercedes Matter once told me a story of how Pollock and her husband Herbert met when Lee and Jackson had them to dinner. Jackson and Herbert spoke a little to each other upstairs and when they came down they just sat for the rest of the night. Not a word was said. When they left, Jackson told Lee that Herbert was a "nice man, a nice fellow." Mercedes said Herbert said the same thing about Jackson. They were each taken with the other—they had a nice feeling between them. They didn't have to talk.

Valliere: What about the Club? Was Pollock involved in that?

de Kooning: No. That started after Pollock had moved out to East Hampton. He was very suspicious of it.

Valliere: Why was he suspicious of it?

de Kooning: The Club was always misunderstood. We always wanted not exactly to start a club but to have a loft and for years I had it in mind. The Greeks and Italians each have their own social clubs along Eight Avenue. We didn't want to have anything to do with art. We just wanted to get a loft, instead of sitting in those god-damned cafeterias. One night we decided to do it—we got up twenty charter members who each gave ten dollars and found a place on Eighth Street. We would go there at night, have coffee, a few drinks, chew the rag. We tried but couldn't get a name so we called it the Club.

Valliere: Pollock didn't like that.

de Kooning: He was suspicious of any intellectual talk. He couldn't do it—at least not while he was sober. But he was smart though—oh boy—because when he was half-loaded, that in-between period, he was good, very good, very provocative. But he had contempt for people who talked—people who taught.

Valliere: But don't you think that might have been part of his belief that art could not be taught and only phonies tried?

de Kooning: Maybe. He never taught, although many of us had to, and he felt superior about that. He felt that he was a very important artist and that most of us weren't so hot.

Valliere: He tried to make it known that he was *the* painter?

de Kooning: Oh yes. He was *it*. A couple of times he told me, "You know more, but I feel more." I was jealous of him—his talent. But he was a remarkable person. He'd do things that were so terrific.

After a while we only used the Club on Friday and Saturday nights. The rest of the time we'd all go to the Cedar Bar as we were drinking more then. So when Pollock was in town he'd come to the Cedar too. He had this way of sizing up new people very quickly. We'd be sitting at a table and some young fellow would come in. Pollock wouldn't even look at him, he'd just nod his head—like a cowboy—as if to say, "fuck-off." That was his favorite expression—"Fuck-off." It was really funny, he wouldn't even look at him. He had that cowboy style. It's an American quality with artists and writers. They feel that they have to be very manly.

Valliere: I've heard that you wrestled with him at the Cedar Bar.

de Kooning: Oh yes. It was a joke, very friendly. He'd go berserk—like a child—a small boy. We'd run, fight, jump on each other. Such joy, such desperate joy.

But there was another side of him too. When he had money he spent it and he began to dress with a great style. He had a nice physique—tall with muscular arms that hung away from his body. Tweed suits looked very good on him.

Franz Kline told me a story about one day when Pollock came by all dressed up. He was going to take Franz to lunch—they were going to a fancy place. Halfway through the meal Pollock noticed that Franz's glass was empty. He said, "Franz have some more wine." He filled the glass and became so involved in watching the wine pour out of the bottle that he emptied the whole bottle. It covered the food, the table, everything. He said, "Franz have some more wine." Like a child he thought it was a terrific idea—all that wine going all over. Then he took the four corners of the table cloth—picked it up and set it on the floor. In front of all those people! He put the goddamn thing on the floor—paid for it and they let him go. Wonderful that he could do that. Those waiters didn't take any shit and there was a guy at the door and everything. It was such an emotion—such life.

247

Another time we were at Franz's place. Fantastic. It was small, very warm and packed with people drinking. The windows were little panes of glass. Pollock looked at this guy and said "You need a little more air" and he punched a window out with his fist. At the moment it was so delicious—so belligerent. Like children we broke all the windows. To do things like that. Terrific.

AN INTERVIEW WITH
Clement Greenberg

JAMES T. VALLIERE

1 9 6 8

CLEMENT Greenberg was the only critic who consistently championed Pollock's work through the 1940s. Writing in the *Nation* in 1946 he called Pollock "the most original contemporary easel-painter under forty"; in 1948 he wrote that "Since Mondrian no one has driven the easel picture quite so far from itself," and that he will in time compete with John Marin "for recognition as the greatest American painter of the twentieth century." He wrote that the exhibition of *Number One* in 1949 justified "all of the superlatives" with which he "had praised Pollock's art in the past."

But by 1952 Greenberg was no longer writing superlatives about Pollock's work. Many have waited for his re-appraisal of Pollock's paintings which has never come. Thus the objective of this interview was primarily defined by Mr. Greenberg's sixteen years of relative silence about works which he had previously applauded without reservation. Our conversation began with Mr. Greenberg commenting on an interview which I had made with Willem de Kooning on Pollock which was published in the fall of 1967 in the *Partisan Review*.

CG: I read your interview with de Kooning on Pollock when it first appeared last fall. I even toyed with the idea of writing a piece about it. De Kooning's version of what went on at the Cedar Bar glamorizes his own past. At the time nothing was romantic, it was ordinarily dailiness and it's a bitter irony, because at that time Jackson was destroying himself.

Jackson would go down to the Cedar to a den of enemies. He was accepted as a figure but not as a painter. Phil Guston wished he'd go back to painting the way he did before 1947. I know that de Kooning,

Hofmann, Gottlieb, Motherwell and the rest of those guys couldn't make anything of Jackson's post-1946 pictures. They didn't know what the hell Pollock was about in his all-over pictures. When Pollock went to the Cedar he had to show them, and when he was drunk he felt that he had to shock them.

JTV: Then he wasn't accepted as a great painter?
CG: No, and he knew it. But he wouldn't talk about it. It never came up—what the guys at the Cedar thought about his work. It didn't shape up as an issue to talk about because it was almost too much of an issue.

I knew that Jackson didn't like de Kooning and he didn't like Kline and all the horseplay. He never indulged in horseplay with people he liked as far as I know. There may be exceptions, but I can't imagine him kidding around with Tony Smith, Jim Brooks, or Barney Newman. It was only with "the boys," and then there was a lot of unavowed aggression on Jackson's part, more than on de Kooning's or Kline's part. But they were also great ones at concealing their feelings. It was no accident that Jackson broke his leg twice in this horseplay. He had never broken a bone in his body before.

This gets chewed over again and again, the talk about the heroic generation. I'm sick and tired of talking about it. But I'm not sick and tired of emphasizing what washouts most of these people were as human beings. And they were washouts. At the Cedar Bar there were people that I liked, but the collectivity was awful and squalid.

JTV: Did you feel this way about the Club as well?
CG: Yes. Again it was squalid, maybe the word sordid is better. Doomed artists. Whenever artists herd apparently they're doomed. Where are they now? Kline's and de Kooning's reputations remain inflated, not entirely but considerably.

JTV: During the 1940s and early 1950s were painters aware that they were living during a significant time in the history of American art?
CG: I was always pessimistic when someone would say, "American painting is going somewhere." The main feeling was—and this was shared by Lee and Jackson—was that "we're up against it, the big world won't recognize us." And Pollock wasn't selling during the late 1940s and the fact that he did sell two shows in 1949 was just a drop in the water. He didn't sell much from his best show, which was in 1950.

JTV: Then there wasn't a steady building up of optimism.
CG: We knew that there was something going on, but thought that it would take decades before it would come through.

JTV: *When did the breakthrough come?*

CG: If you talk in terms of money, it was 1955. That's a matter of record. You can talk to the dealers about that.

JTV: *During this time did Pollock look as though he were the leading painter?*

CG: No, not at all. There was always a star that was brighter than his. If it wasn't Matta Echaurren it might have been someone like Emmerson Woelffer. Then de Kooning and Kline came up fast. And don't forget that Jackson wasn't accepted as a great painter. Down at the Cedar he was thought to be a freak. Charlie Egan thought that de Kooning and Clyfford Still were the two great painters. I remember taking a bus ride with Charlie to Provincetown in 1955 and he said to me, "You don't really take Pollock seriously, do you?"

JTV: *Do you think that Pollock's reputation is inflated?*

CG: No, but it's based partly on the fallacy that he stepped outside of art and that he was the first to do so. He didn't step outside of art and the idea was absurd to him.

I know that Jackson did not think that he was breaking with the past in any hyper-revolutionary way. He had a very keen awareness of what was going well and what was going badly. He didn't believe in accident. The automatic drawing was commonplace in New York before the Surrealists arrived in 1940. We knew about it from Miró's practice and a little bit from Masson. We didn't know Masson's work very well, but we could see it in Paul Klee and it wasn't an issue. It's true that very few people practiced automatic painting and yet then they did. Gorky's Miró- and Picasso-influenced pictures were involved in it.

JTV: *Did Pollock admire artists like Miró and Picasso?*

CG: Very much. I never used to think that an artist's taste mattered except in a very private relation to his art. But since then I have changed my mind. In the fifties I noticed that any artist who admired de Kooning without very great qualifications was doomed in his art. De Kooning was the Pied Piper who led a generation of artists over the hill. And at that time anybody who looked even a little bit like Pollock looked a hell of a lot too much like him. But time would have taken care of that, just as Gorky's Miróesque and Picasoesque pictures no longer look anywhere near as derivative as they used to. When you're too close, certain salient common features get reduced.

JTV: *Did Pollock ever speak to you about the paintings that his contemporaries were doing?*

CG: He succumbed to Clyfford Still's work around 1951 or 1952 and he became part of the faction around him. It was the first time that he'd ever joined up with a group. The first time he became one of the boys. Jackson was just beginning to lose his stuff, and the fact that the two things coincided I don't think was accidental.

He had great admiration for de Kooning's hand, but he wasn't sure about his art. The competitiveness between them was more personal than artistic. It was more in terms of prestige and acceptance. Jackson figured prestige was something that you had to have, but it wasn't like a lodestar as it is with de Kooning.

Jackson was one of the first artists I knew who gave up going to museums. One night at my place on Bank Street, which dates it as post-1947, I showed Jackson a book of colored reproductions of Rubens' landscapes. He looked through it and said, "I can paint better than this guy," and I was appalled—as I still am. Don't be so sure of that, even as checkered as Rubens's quality may be. Jackson didn't go near the Old Masters as far as I know during the 1940s and 1950s, unlike other artists like Gorky.

It was in that same living room that I remember showing Jackson the first Mark Tobey that he'd ever seen. It was a colored reproduction of *Tundra*. Jackson had been said to have been influenced by Tobey, and I knew that he'd never laid eyes on one before.

JTV: In 1948, when you wrote that Pollock will in time compete with John Marin as the greatest American painter of the twentieth century, did you have any idea that it would be picked up and thrust into national prominence as it was by Life *magazine during the following year?*

CG: You don't have any idea at all of what's going to happen. I was accused by everybody of making rash, reckless, extravagant statements. Well I did. I said that David Smith was probably the greatest American sculptor to come along, and that Pollock was probably the greatest American painter at the time of the twentieth century and maybe the greatest American painter of all. Well now people feel differently about what I said then.

JTV: How did they feel then?

CG: They said that Greenberg just specializes in rash shockers. Read what Alfred Barr said about me in his Matisse book. Well OK, you look at all the rash statements that I made. I said that Dubuffet was probably the best painter to come out of Paris since Miró. That's commonplace now. When you see something happening you record your reactions.

JTV: How do you feel about this particular statement about Pollock now?

CG: Marin gets better and better, damn it. He's an unexportable fine painter. I still don't think Marin will export, whereas Pollock has been and is being exported.

JTV: *Why, after 1952, did you write so little about Pollock? I don't believe after that time that you ever called him a great painter in print.*

CG: There were two reasons. One was that I thought that Jackson lost his stuff around '52, in my opinion he lost his inspiration. The other thing was that he had become, if not famous, at least notorious and I suppose the battle had been won. I get a kick out of yelling about people who are not up there yet.

JTV: *Do you see this as your role as a critic?*

CG: No. I don't see any role at all. This is my inclination. No policy. And it's not altogether laudable either. It just wasn't necessary to praise Pollock anymore. It had been said.

JTV: *In 1948 Louis Finklestein challenged you to defend your espousal of Pollock. You replied in the* Nation *that "I happen to enjoy Jackson Pollock more than any other painter."*

CG: That's right. But enjoy is not the right word. I'd been sent by Jackson Pollock more than any other painter in our time.

JTV: *What was it about Pollock that you liked?*

CG: You can't demonstrate esthetic judgement. It was just great. After I saw the [Peggy Guggenheim] mural which he did in 1943 I had such confidence in him. I thought that his first solo show in 1943 was good, but when I saw that mural, I felt that he was going to be a great artist.

JTV: *In your 1955 article on "American Type Painting," you mention the works of de Kooning, Hofmann, Pollock, Tobey, Newman, and Still—in that order. Why didn't you attempt to evaluate these artists in terms of their importance?*

CG: I think that I was getting a little self-conscious about ranking. I've remained self-conscious ever since then. Art in this country has eventuated into a scene. Now you're said to be pushing someone if you praise them. Although it's known who I think makes the best art now, I'm very diffident to saying it as loud as I did in the forties.

JTV: *The critical climate has changed.*

CG: There is more of a milieu, there is a milieu now. In the forties you were writing out into a vacuum and you didn't know how well off you were. Then there was less factional difference. In the forties I also used to write denunciatory reviews. I would pick someone whom I thought had an inflated reputation. I don't do that any more either.

JTV: *You never quoted Pollock when you wrote about his work.*

CG: It simply never entered my mind. I don't think I quote living painters. And I don't pay any attention to what they say in connection with their art. Jackson never talked crap, but then he never talked about his art the way many painters do. And he didn't joke about it either. It was either good or bad. It worked or it didn't work.

JTV: What do you think of Blue Poles?

CG: That and Governor Rockefeller's painting, *Number 12, 1952,* they were teetering. I can remember walking into Jackson's studio in East Hampton and I had the feeling that this was the first time that I'd seen, not bad paintings, but paintings where the inspiration was flagging. With *Blue Poles* people thought the bars helped them make more sense of it—than with the earlier all-over works. There are many admirers of Pollock today who prize him for being way out, for almost taking leave of art, and not because they can tell a good Pollock from a bad one.

JTV: You consider his work to be vigorous right up through his black and white period in 1952.

CG: After that Jack began to teeter. His 1953 show was the first bad show that I'd ever seen.

JTV: Which paintings do you consider to be his finest works?

CG: *Autumn Rhythm* and *Lavender Mist* are two of his best. I dubbed *Lavender Mist* and also one called *Lowering Weather.* Jackson was willing to go along with the latter but Ben Heller thought that that wasn't profound enough, *Lowering Weather* being just too descriptive. Ben pressed him to find a real significant title and Jackson sat around, squirming, and said "just call it "one'".

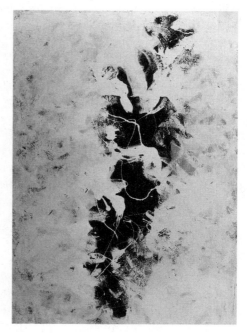

His best show was in 1950. After 1952 we parted company artistically. I felt that he had come to a dead stop. He knew that I didn't like his '53 show. I liked *Easter and Totem* and

Jackson Pollock, *The Deep,* 1953. Oil and enamel on canvas, 86 3/4 x 59 1/8 inches. Musée National d'Art Moderne, Centre Georges Pompidou, Paris, gift of the Menil Foundation, Houston. © THE POLLOCK-KRAS-NER FOUNDATION, INC. / ARS. PHOTO: POLLOCK-KRASNER STUDY CENTER, JACKSON POLLOCK CATALOGUE RAISONNÉ ARCHIVES.

Grayed Rainbow. Jackson asked me what I thought of *Easter and Totem* which was exhibited in the 1955 Carnegie International. I just nodded. He went on to talk about some of his other pictures in the 1953 show. He said that in *The Deep* he was on to something there, but he just missed it. He never talked that way before. I don't think there was any question in his mind that he had lost something.

JTV: Do you think that it bothered him?
CG: Yes, I do. He thought that his only justification was to be a painter.

JTV: Did you see Pollock quite a bit while he was in East Hampton?
CG: I started visiting him in 1946, just after he bought his house.

JTV: Did you have any discussions with him about art?
CG: Lee and I and Jackson would sit at the kitchen table and talk for hours—all day sometimes. Jackson usually wouldn't say much—we'd drink a lot of coffee. I know that this sound like part of a myth. We would sit for hours and go to bed at three or four in the morning.

Jackson Pollock being interviewed at his retrospective exhibition, Bennington College, November 1952. The session is being filmed by The March of Time for a television documentary.
PHOTO: POLLOCK-KRASNER PAPERS, ARCHIVES OF AMERICAN ART, SMITHSONIAN INSTITUTION.

He said to me once, "I don't know where the pictures come from—they just come," with a look of surprise on his face. And he expected me to be surprised. I knew then that when things go good for you, you don't know where they come from. But Jackson was so surprised that he didn't figure the picture out. It came without having to be figured out, as if works of art ever really succeeded by being figured out, whether it be Mondrian, or Poussin or Rubens. But that kind of remark would lead half-literate people to say that action painting is accidental. I do remember Jackson saying in the movie that was made of him painting that his pictures have no beginning, no middle, and no end. A half-year later I said to myself, you idiot don't pick up what other people say about you. I'd written that in the *Partisan Review* and it's not true. I didn't say that to him because I was too embarrassed. At the time I was so mortified, so ashamed of myself for having prematurely interpreted, and to have him pick it up.

Pollock was a pure guy. He was. I'm not idealizing him. It was inconceivable for him to do something because it would get him somewhere. When he was drunk he was intolerable. When he was sober he was a pure guy, and that was the real Pollock. He was self-centered, though. You could say to him, "Jackson you're not paying enough attention to what's going on in me," and he would jump.

For a while there was a coolness between the Pollocks and me. I think Jackson had his first retrospective at Bennington College in November of 1952. He had been drinking, and he turned on me and called me a fool. I got sore about that. Then for about two years I didn't have much to do with him.

JTV: *What do you think was his most radical innovation in terms of the space and pattern of his works?*
CG: It wasn't the space. I think the shallow illusion of depth had Cubist antecedents, and of course there was Miró's indeterminate space. When Bryan Robertson writes about a new kind of space he's full of shit. It's the all-overness that's gotten into contemporary taste. It's become what one demands of advanced painting. Jackson brought this to a head more than anyone else.

JTV: *How do you feel about Pollock now?*
CG: I think he's better than I thought he was.

JTV: *How do you see him in relationship to his European contemporaries?*
CG: I don't think that the best painters Paris produced during the early forties—any of them are as good as Pollock. Not Dubuffet, not Hartung, not Wols.

JTV: What about the Surrealists?

CG: The only big painter they had was Miró, and I think he will probably add up to more than Miró.

JTV: How do you feel that he now compares with other 19th and 20th century American painters?

CG: I think he's the greatest painter that we ever had. The other great Americans—Eakins, Homer, Marin, the early John Sloan—didn't change the course of art. They didn't add in the sense that a major painter does. Now the mainstream must go through Pollock and others of his generation.

Excerpt from an Interview with
MATSUMI "MIKE" KANEMITSU

MARJORIE ROGERS

JANUARY 14, 1976

In 1956, in the summertime, my wife and I were in East Hampton to go grocery shopping in the supermarket, and my wife said she has to get gasoline. So I stand in front of supermarket, and here is Jackson Pollock with Ruth Kligman—that's his girlfriend. And they both wave to me when they pass me. Then they come back again, and they say, "Are you coming to Ossorio's party tonight?" So I say I might go there. And he says, "Maybe I see you there." And in Ossorio's party that evening, they have some kind of music they play—kind of boring. So I left. I go home, and then suddenly somebody knocks on my door frantically. So I open, and it is that old-time painter named Julian Levy. And Julian Levy says, "Mike, hurry up, Jackson has died." I say, "What?" "Yeah," he says, "his car has crashed!" So he drives me up to Springs, and I see the car, and that's he's dead. And Ruth Kligman's girlfriend, she died. You know, she's a completely innocent person. Ruth Kligman is the only one alive, but she is in hospital, too. This was a big shock for me. That was a big story; we had a funeral.

Jackson Pollock's wife—they were separated at the time—was living in Paris. Lee Krasner is also a fine painter. Jackson and I became much closer friends during the time that he was separated. I used to go to the East Hampton railroad station, and right across they have a bar, a local bar, I think called Cavagnaro's. Anyway, bartender looks exactly like Mussolini, you know, so we used to call him Mussolini. Often Jackson Pollock and I met [at] that bar early in the morning. Jackson Pollock, if he don't drink, is the most quiet and shy person. Then, if he starts [to] drink, he changes the whole personality. So I used to meet him about ten o'clock in the morning in the bar, and he was just sitting alone and sad. I remember his face very well; he just sat there. Then he was drinking beer or scotch, then slowly he's an alive person. But early in the morning, he's a very sad man. And, of course, Jackson Pollock's most fear is his mother, he is scared to death of his mother. When his mother used to visit him, he hid. You never find him—terribly, terribly frightened of his mother.

But anyway, just before he passed away, I become most closest to Jackson Pollock. And I used to go to his studio and see his painting. And he always give me one: "Take this, take that." But I never took them because he was drunk. You don't do that kind of thing. Anyway, late in his life, just before he passed away, I was very close to him.

Matsumi Kanmits, Jackson Pollock, 1955. India ink on paper 18 x 14 inches.
COLLECTION OF LAWRENCE W. LAZARUS, CHICAGO.

PHOTOGRAPHING POLLOCK

HANS NAMUTH

NOVEMBER 17, 1979

I am looking at an old snapshot of Jackson Pollock standing with his wife and mother in the kitchen of his home in East Hampton. Someone had taken the picture a year or so before I met the artist. Pollock seems to be preparing a salad dressing as the two women look on. A towel thrown over his left shoulder makes him look like a waiter in an Italian restaurant, or a bartender. What is so amazing is the utterly peaceful, self-assured expression on his face. He is beautiful—Jackson at his best—in command of the situation, and the women admire him. This is what he was like when we first came to know each other—peaceful, in harmony with himself, in control, often silent.

My most lasting impression of Pollock was his silence. He was perhaps too shy to speak; he could not express personal feelings in conversation. In contrast, his face was vivid. His eyes brightened when you spoke to him, and his smile was captivating. His face was the reason I learned to like him sooner than I learned to appreciate his work; it took a while to get to that. The feelings that he could not vent in words were expressed in his painting. To me, Harold Rosenberg's term "action painting" really meant that it was during the act of painting itself that Pollock engaged in the act of communicating.

I first saw Pollock's work in 1949 at the Betty Parsons Gallery in New York City. My first reaction was hostile. The paintings seemed disorderly and violent. I could not tear myself away from my old loves: Vincent Van Gogh, Franz Marc, Paul Klee.

I had heard about Pollock before seeing the exhibition. I might not have gone a second time had it not been for Alexey Brodovitch, who was art director of *Harper's Bazaar*. Brodovitch also taught at The New School

Jackson Pollock at work on *One: Number 31, 1950*, from Namuth's first photographic session with Pollock, July 1950. © ESTATE OF HANS NAMUTH.

for Social Research. One day in class he mentioned Jackson Pollock. Brodovitch had a caustic wit and constantly chided students for lack of *awareness*. He asked, "Does anyone here ever go to galleries? Who of you, for instance, has seen Pollock's work at Betty Parsons?" I was the only one to raise my hand. He glanced at me, and added: "Pollock is one of the most important artists around today." I went back. Again I found the pictures difficult, but after more visits I began to come to terms with them. I wanted to meet the artist.

Our meeting took place six or eight months later. In the summer of 1950 my family and I had decided to go to the Hamptons and had rented a house in Water Mill. I knew that Pollock's work was to appear in a group show at Guild Hall in East Hampton. There was to be an opening on July 1st, a Saturday, which I decided to attend. Someone pointed Pollock out to me. He was standing in a corner near his paintings, and no one was paying any attention to him.

I went up to him and said, "Mr. Pollock, my name is Hans Namuth and I have wanted to meet you."

He said, "Yes, why?"

"I'm a student of Alexey Brodovitch and I also take photographs for *Harper's Bazaar*. I thought it might be a good idea if you let me come and photograph you while you are painting."

At first Pollock was reluctant, but at last he said, "Well, why not?" He promised he would start a new painting for me, and, perhaps, finish it while I was still around. Then we arranged to meet at his studio on a weekend.

When I arrived at the appointed hour, I was met by Pollock and his wife, Lee Krasner. He looked exhausted. Shrugging his shoulders he said, "I'm sorry, Hans, there's nothing to photograph because the painting is finished." I was crushed. No photography? Hesitantly, I suggested going into the studio so that I might at least see what he had been working on. He looked at his wife, who nodded. We went into the converted barn that served as his studio.

The large barn was filled with paintings. A dripping wet canvas covered the entire floor. Blinding shafts of sunlight hit the wet canvas making its surface hard to see. There was complete silence. I looked aimlessly through the ground glass of my Rolleiflex and began to take a few pictures. Pollock looked at the painting. Then, unexpectedly, he picked up can and paintbrush and started to move around the canvas. It was as if he suddenly realized the painting was not finished. His movements, slow at first, gradually became faster and more dancelike as he flung black, white, and rust-colored paint onto the canvas. He completely forgot that Lee and I were there; he did not seem to hear the click of the camera shutter. I wore two Rolleiflexes with 80 mm lenses around my neck. Both cameras were loaded, and when one was finished I quickly switched to the other. Then I reloaded both.

My photography session lasted as long as he kept painting, perhaps half an hour. In all that time, Pollock did not stop. How long could one keep up that level of physical activity? Finally, he said, "This is it." Later, Lee told me that until that moment, she had been the only person who ever watched him paint.

I rushed back to my darkroom to develop and print the pictures. The following weekend I returned to the Pollocks with the proofs. At the time I was not working as a photographer. I had a full-time job, and it was a difficult feat to make so many prints in the evenings. When I started enlarging my negatives I realized that some pictures were not sharp due to a defect in one of my cameras. At the time, I was very disturbed by this, and I showed none of these images to the Pollocks. It was not until years later that I understood how exciting these photographs really were. Many other pictures had blurred body and hand movement because I had had to use relatively slow shutter speeds—1/25th and 1/50th of a second— as Jackson moved swiftly around the canvas. In all,

Jackson Pollock at work on the concrete pad behind his house, during the filming of Namuth's documentary, fall 1950. © Estate of Hans Namuth.

I shot only four or five rolls of Tri-X. Today I would make ten times as many exposures and, with luck, find one or two good pictures on each contact sheet. In those days every shot counted. If I did not have six or eight good pictures on a sheet of twelve I was devastated.

When I showed the Pollocks the prints from our first session, they were pleased, and encouraged me to come back. The ice was broken; the awkwardness had disappeared. Almost every weekend throughout the summer I returned. We worked whenever Pollock was in the mood. I made about five hundred photographs. We didn't talk much—he was absorbed in his painting and I in my photography. The proofs, then as today, reveal a collaboration, a silent trust.

After that first session, Lee no longer came. She had begun to trust me. The Pollocks were very close; he was dependent on her approval, judgment, and friendship. Had she opposed my working with him, I am certain that it would have been the end. She sometimes became a little annoyed that I broke into their lives when it was not completely convenient, but in the end she allowed me to do what I wanted.

My impression of Lee was that she was there to help Jackson work, to help him stay alive. Her own painting was secondary to her. The arrangement of their studio space reflected the extent to which she kept herself in the background. Jackson's studio was in the large barn; Lee worked in a small bedroom where she painted small pictures. After Jackson's death she moved into his studio and her paintings became larger. She had probably always been an artist who required a large area to work in. At times it must have been difficult for her not to be able to spread out, especially during the later periods in 1954 and 1955 when Jackson was very inactive.

When I met the Pollocks, although Lee's work had been shown, it was not well-known. I believe her first major exhibition took place in 1951 at the Betty Parsons Gallery, and a year or two later she showed at Eleanor Ward's old Stable Gallery. I photographed that show. I also photographed about twenty of Lee's canvases, mosaics, and collages. For nearly two years I was the Pollocks' "house photographer."

Lee was charming and intelligent; she created a welcoming atmosphere, gave wonderful dinner parties, and my wife Carmen and I were often their guests. The Pollocks were generous despite limited means. The meals were delicious. The conversation, stimulated by Lee, was always good. Jackson never talked much, and never expounded on theories of art. He would make statements from time to time or answer questions.

Architects Marcel Breuer and Peter Blake, who designed and built a model for a museum of Pollock paintings, were often at the Pollocks'. So were artists who spent summers in East Hampton: the Saul Steinbergs, Gina and Alexander Brook, the John Littles, Wilfrid Zogbaums, James and Charlotte Brooks, Tony Smith, Tino and Ruth Nivola, Corrado and Anita Marca-Relli, the Clyfford Stills, and so on. Pollock attracted a great many artists because he was considered a master, especially among people who were not competing with him. Other visitors included critic Clement Greenberg, who brought Helen Frankenthaler, the painter. Greenberg came to look at Jackson's new canvases, and I saw him there occasionally. He was extremely good company, but I think that his influence on Jackson is exaggerated. Jackson listened to Clem's deliberations and read his essays in the *New Republic*; then he continued to follow his own voice and directions.

My own relationship with Jackson revolved around our work together. Our aim was to make photographs that had validity and performance, and eventually to make films. We did not talk about each other's hopes, disappointments, or personal lives.

In those days my photography with artists was not commercial. As a youth in Germany I had wanted to become a theater director, and had political circumstances not dictated otherwise, I would probably have pursued that course. Later, photographing an artist gave me the feeling of being in a theater, of watching and directing. I took to the art world with ease, and was accepted. Pollock was not the first artist I had worked with, but he was a key person. Through him I met Franz Kline, James Brooks,

John Little, Ossorio, Barnett Newman, and others. Through Newman I met Clyfford Still, and then came Willem de Kooning, Robert Motherwell, Ad Reinhardt . . . an unending chain. I became part of that world and I was happy there. I felt excited and enriched in the process. When questioned about my motives I would say that the pictures were needed "for my files."

The Pollock photographs produced that first summer were not well received. In October 1950 I showed them to Edward Steichen, curator of the photography department at the Museum of Modern Art. Steichen was not an easy man to see. He had photographed a number of artists in his day, including Matisse and Brancusi, and had formulated a few theories of his own about the process. Looking through my portfolio, he dismissed the pictures, saying, "You know, Namuth, this is not the way to photograph an artist. The nature and personality of such a complex human being are only partially revealed when you show him at work. Spend some time with the man, take pictures of him as he wakes up in the morning, brushes his teeth, talks to his wife, eats breakfast . . . follow him through his day. . . ."

Stuart Preston, art critic for the *New York Times*, was kinder. He looked carefully at my pictures, and then said: "I feel quite alien to this art." To explain his lack of interest he took me to a room filled with small 17th-century paintings, exquisitely framed. My interest in Pollock grew. We had documented the process of painting to its fullest extent, but only in still photographs. To make a film was the next logical step. Pollock's method of painting suggested a moving picture—the dance around the canvas, the continuous movement, the drama. However, if no one was interested in the still photographs, would anybody be interested in a film?

At the end of summer, 1950, I suggested to Pollock that we use a movie camera to record his movements. He agreed, and one weekend I brought my wife's camera, an inexpensive Bell and Howell "Turret." As with the still photographs, I used available light and black-and-white film with a hand-held camera. Pollock started to work. I moved around him and then went up to a platform (a hayloft) to film from above. All the still photographs had been done at ground level, although sometimes I climbed on a chair or held the Rolleiflex above my head.

I ended up with seven minutes of film that are quite exciting. The beginning is awkward (for a moment the camera lens intrudes into the frame and I accidentally cut off the top of Jackson's head), but soon the viewer is caught up in the artist's actions. The film reveals the continuity of Pollock's method of working—the white, empty canvas, the hesitant start. The paint flows from the can onto the whiteness. Next, a pause, as if Pollock were at a loss about what to do. He stirs the paint for a moment, and then, suddenly, returns to the picture on the floor and his dance becomes quicker and more erratic. There seems no end to the dance as the fever of painting takes hold of him. His movements are abrupt; his pace staccato. Finally, in the fading daylight, a sudden ending. There was no more film.

I had mixed feelings about the results; I left the film in a drawer for years. Eventually, a friend, Jim Fasanelli saw it and described his reactions in a letter to me: "It taught me to respect Pollock in a way I never had before. For one thing you could see, literally see, he was not dripping. That word simply does not suffice. What you saw was Pollock take his stick or brush out of the paint can and then, in a cursive sweep, pass it over the canvas, high above it, so that the viscous paint would form trailing patterns which hover over the canvas before they settle upon it, and then fall into it and then leave a trace of their own passage. He is not drawing on the canvas so much as in the air above it. He must have loved the forms and lines he could make this way. This is what is really on the canvas, at least the first stage. The armature stage, you might say. The sign of the passage of something fleeting . . ."

The painting he created during the black-and-white film was particularly beautiful; no one knows today where it is or what became of it. His wife later exclaimed as she saw the film, "My God, where is that painting? It's lovely." It is conceivable that he destroyed it or painted over it.

Recently I added a soundtrack to the black-and-white film, using excerpts from a radio interview conducted by William Wright in 1950. In it, Pollock says that his painting bears a kinship to the sand paintings of the American Indians; that he works directly, without sketches or drawings, that nothing in his work is accidental; that he controls the flow of paint. In his writings and interviews, he stressed these and other themes over and over. To see Pollock at work in the film as he expresses his thoughts on his method is an extraordinary experience.

I took the first test film to my friend Paul Falkenberg, a successful film editor who had worked with Fritz Lang, Georg Wilhelm Pabst, and other well-known directors. He suggested that we work together. I would do the filming and directing; he would make suggestions and edit. We decided that this film *had* to be in color.

We couldn't afford lights, so the solution was to make the film outdoors. We found a cement platform nearby where a house had once stood. Jackson placed a canvas on the cement and started to paint. I began to film. We continued to work for five or six weekends during the months of September and October of 1950. As Paul inspected the footage he made suggestions on close-ups needed for the editing. He never interfered. He simply advised from a distance.

I soon found out that a film, like a short story, needs a beginning, a middle, and an end. It wasn't enough to show the painter painting. I wanted more; somehow a main ingredient was missing. I realized that I wanted to show the artist at work with his face in full view, becoming part of the canvas, inside the canvas, so to speak—coming at the viewer—through the painting itself. How could this be done?

One evening it came to me: the painting would have to be on *glass* and I would film from underneath. When I broached the idea he liked it and replied that yes, he had often thought about working on glass. Pollock, a marvelous carpenter, built a large platform; we bought a sheet of glass (we could afford only one) for $10. After many unsuccessful attempts, I finally figured out how to lie on my back with the camera on my chest and photograph him from below.

Jackson had several false starts before he hit on what he wanted to do. In the film there is a moment in which he wipes paint off the glass to begin again, and says, "I sometimes lose a painting but I have no fear of changes, because a painting has a life of its own."

The scene begins with Jackson standing on the glass, pouring paint out of a can. Interestingly, when white paint hits the glass it turns black. It becomes silhouetted because the rays of the sun cannot bend around the glass, an unexpected visual effect.

As Jackson works on the painting, he scatters bits of wire mesh, glass pebbles, shells, string and plain glass onto the surface. This use of foreign matter was not unusual in his work, as he mentions in his narration. The layers of paint in which these objects were embedded were very thick, requiring a week to dry.

The final version of the film lasts for about eleven minutes, but it seems longer. The film starts with Jackson painting as his {border collie, Gyp} sits nearby. Then there is a short transitional passage that shows Jackson's shadow flinging paint dramatically onto a canvas. The scene was actually simulated and I periodically consider deleting it because it is not convincing. In the next sequence, a long painting, *Summertime*, is pulled slowly beneath the camera. The canvas appears to be floating past the viewer. Next, Pollock is seen tacking the same painting onto the wall of the Betty Parsons Gallery. There are other paintings in the Gallery, and a visitor (actually his wife). The music of a cello leads into the last section of the film, the painting on glass.

We filmed during the height of autumn, when the leaves were changing. One day as I was driving from my home in Water Mill to Pollock's house, I glanced up and watched the way in which the leaves of the elm and maple trees blurred as I was passing them. Squinting my eyes, pictures seemed to form above. It seemed to me that this was what Pollock was trying to do. His work was close to nature.

Tony Smith, the sculptor, a friend of Pollock's, said in a 1967 interview (*Art in America*): "I think that Jackson's feelings for the land had something to do with his painting canvases on the floor. I don't know if I ever thought of this before seeing Namuth's film. But he was shown painting

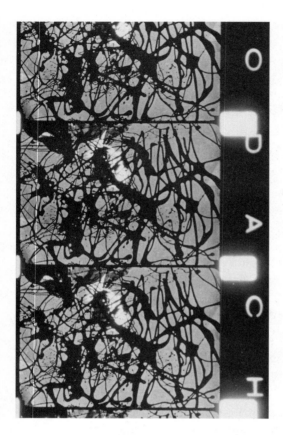

Frames from the film of Pollock painting on glass, fall 1950. © ESTATE OF HANS NAMUTH.

on glass seen from below, and it seemed that the glass was earth, that he was distributing flowers over it, that it was spring."

We used Jackson's own voice for narration. The text was a communal effort. The three of us took bits and pieces from Jackson's writings and interviews and put them together. Long after the film itself was shot, Jackson came to New York and recorded the narration.

We made the film with very little money, $2,000.00 at the most. Expenses were incurred in the laboratory with the developing of film, dubbing of voice, and recording of music. Today we probably could not have done it for fifteen times that much.

Our prop for the film, the painting on glass, stood outside for weeks. Rain fell on it, leaves collected on top of it, ocean winds weathered it. Then one day Jackson decided to take it inside. It is now in the National Gallery in Ottawa, Canada, *Number 29, 1950.*

The film was finished and ready for distribution in early 1951. In June of 1951 it was shown at the Museum of Modern Art, and in August of that year at an art film festival in Woodstock, New York. Aline Louchheim, reviewing for the *New York Times*, wrote: "On most counts, the films did preserve the integrity of the work of art, with the outstanding exception of Jackson Pollock who belittled and denigrated his own work by a precious and pretentious presentation."

The film was offered for rental for a small amount of money to colleges and art schools all over the country as well as abroad. At first the distribution went very, very slowly, but then in 1952 it took off. By 1956, the year Pollock died, thousands of students here and abroad saw the film.

It was not easy to find outlets for the still photographs. Alexey Brodovitch was one of the few who understood and liked them; he published a selection in 1951 in *Portfolio*, a magazine he edited with Frank Zachary. About a year later *ARTnews* published some of the photographs. In 1957 they appeared in the ASMP Annual, and later still in some Museum of Modern Art publications. At the time of Pollock's death many periodicals called me; they wanted photographs only because of the "event."

There is a postscript to the making of the color film on Pollock. The last outdoor scene took place on a chilly day in October of 1950. I was lying down in the damp grass with the camera on my chest, shooting up at Jackson, who was working in the wind. Watching the film, one can see the force of the wind distorting Jackson's face. It was cold. There were many technical delays, and when we finally finished it was 4:30 in the afternoon. Our hands were like ice—we could barely move them. We needed something to warm us. I went inside the house and stood by the fire, but Pollock headed straight for the kitchen; minutes later he called me. I saw him there with two large glasses filled to the brim with bourbon. I protested, but he had already emptied his glass, his first drink in two years. It was not long before he had a second.

Later he took a string of heavy cowbells from the door that led from the dining room to the living room. Playfully—and perhaps not completely playfully—he threatened to hit me with them. Startled, I said, "Jackson, put those back!" This made him angry. My wife, who had come into the room, said: "For heaven's sake, Hans, leave him alone." Jackson quieted down, and put the bells back in place.

Lee was giving a dinner party that evening. Carmen and I went home to change, returning at eight o'clock. Jackson was very drunk. There were about fourteen dinner guests and everyone was trying to ignore his condition. We were dismayed. We knew what a great struggle it had been for Jackson to stop drinking.

Each guest had chipped in some part of the dinner. I had baked bread for the occasion and Lee had roasted a turkey, others had brought salad, wine, dessert. All of a sudden, without warning, Jackson, who was sitting at the head of the table, abruptly lifted the table. Down went the turkey—dishes, wine, and all. It was the end of a lovely dinner party.

I have asked myself why Jackson chose this point in his life to resume drinking. In part, of course, it was the result of the circumstances of that last day of filming. There was a heavy air of crisis hanging about. I recall that on that chilly October day I was overcome by a feeling of nervousness and depression. The weather was getting too cold to continue working outdoors . . . we were running out of money . . . the glass painting was finished and could not be done over again—this *had* to be our last day of shooting. Jackson must have been full of tension, too; it was not just the cold. When we suddenly said, "*We are done! It's great, it's marvelous!*" we embraced and we were happy. Jackson had to express that release with a

269

Jackson Pollock holding his painting on glass after the completion of filming, fall 1950. A still from the out-takes of Hans Namuth's film. PHOTO: POLLOCK-KRASNER STUDY CENTER.

drink of bourbon, then another; just like the ex-chain-smoker who reaches for "just *one* cigarette," and then finds that he is back at chain-smoking.

One can, of course, speculate on the deeper reasons. I wasn't aware of it at the time, but in retrospect I think he had reached a transition point in his work; he had traveled to the other end of his rainbow. The last few years had been his best and his fullest, years in which he worked feverishly, every day, and often at night. He had, I think, only a certain allotment of time. By 1950 and 1951 he was slowing down. He was unhappy. He needed a change of pace, a drink. If he had not taken it on the day we finished the film then it would have been the next week, the next month, or the next year. His working patterns altered. He painted less frequently, less intensely. He did not drink every day. Sometimes periods of time went by without his touching alcohol. Then, suddenly, he would start again.

It was his wife, Lee, who had found Jackson the doctor who had helped him stop drinking for two years. She had been through a great deal even before their marriage, when they lived together in New York. To me, she always seemed to manage to take his bouts with a grain of salt, even when Jackson was so drunk that he would demolish the furniture. She knew that he had to be left alone until it blew over. And it always did.

I recall an evening in 1953 when Carmen and I were visiting the Pollocks. Jackson had been drinking but not too much. He had a Model-A Ford, which I had photographed him in, and he said, "Let's go for a ride, Hans." I accepted. Carmen and Lee remained behind. He took me on a wild ride through the woods. We visited a few friends, returning about an hour and a half later. Carmen was very upset, but I had experienced no fear being next to him. I felt: I have to be with him, to protect him, to be good to him, and to bring him back home again. Someone had to be with him.

I photographed him from time to time after 1951 but there was no continuity. At times he called me when he needed some of his work documented. A slow deterioration set in with his return to drinking and in time I did not really feel like taking pictures of him anymore. I strongly believe that each person should be photographed at his best, be it at the age of twenty, or forty, or sixty. I did not wish to show a great and tragic artist in his declining years.

The last time I saw Jackson alive was at a small party at his home. By this time his health was failing. I had stopped by one evening to say hello without knowing that eight or ten other people were there. Lee was in Europe. Jackson was with a young art student and model named Ruth Kligman. Everybody was having a good time, laughing and talking and drinking beer. Jackson was sitting quietly in the midst of it all, completely isolated, with a can of beer in his hands. After a while there was an exchange of words between Ruth Kligman and Jackson. In a moment of anger Jackson said something to her that made everybody pause.

Ruth just looked at him, and said, "Don't brag, Jackson."

His face reddened and he fell silent.

Everything seemed strange that night. The guests were talking animatedly to each other; no one seemed concerned with Jackson. In the midst of all this noise and laughter and talk, and indifference to Jackson, I asked him, "Jackson, why do you do this? Why do you destroy yourself?"

He replied, "I can't help it."

Jackson's nature and art were not inherently violent. There was overwhelming anguish in him at times, but there was also poetry and there was love. Jackson was capable of great love. He loved his wife deeply, and in a way he loved me and his friends. (I think of his gesture of affection at the Betty Parsons Gallery in 1951. As I came in, he said to Lee, "Where is that picture for Hans?" and then handed it to me, with a big smile, as if he had painted it specially for me.)

His love for others is not the only kind I wish to mention. There was his love for the canvas, the way he handled brush and paint, letting the paint flow so lovingly onto the linen. He knew well what needed to be done: he also knew that there was little time to do it.

271

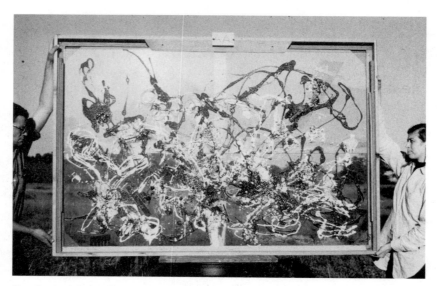

Sheridan Lord and Ceil Downs Lord holding Pollock's painting on glass, *Number 29, 1950,* behind the Pollock-Krasner House, ca. 1956. Pollock-Krasner Study Center, Jackson Pollock Catalogue Raisonné Archives.

Pollock died in a road accident in Springs in 1956. I was away in California at the time, and came back the next day. When I went to the funeral parlor in East Hampton I asked to be alone with him. He was lying there silent and beautiful. I felt a strong urge to photograph him. I explained to the undertaker that my deepest wish was to take one last picture. He replied that he could not allow it without the widow's permission. Lee was in Paris at the time of the automobile accident and had not yet returned. And so the matter rested. My last photograph of Pollock exists only in my memory's eye.

EXCERPT FROM AN INTERVIEW
with Patsy Southgate

JEFFREY POTTER

1980

NEITHER Peter [Matthiessen, my husband] nor I knew anything about abstract art. We were completely liberated by discovering it, and we talked endlessly about the theory behind it. We argued terribly.

It was thrilling to learn about abstract art [from Jackson]. First of all, he hated anything that had to do with French painting in particular, and European art in general. He felt this was the American contribution to art, and it was much better than anything that had ever been done because it was more visceral and personal and soul-searching and romantic and imagistic and almost sacred. To break the image down and re-form it in your own image — that's a very creative act.

I always found images [in his work], because I'm a literal person. I think they were there. He did, too, I think. What he said was that he took the image and broke it up and put it together again in his own image. It scared the pants off me at first, and I resented it. Finally I just loved it, of course, and I couldn't bear anything else.

I remember he asked me to name his paintings, and I would name them something or other and he would say, "That's exactly what I was thinking about when I was painting it, so I am communicating with you." He always named his paintings with numbers, so that was what really got to me. One that I named was called, I believe, *Easter [and the Totem]*. I don't think my names were used often. I think it was just the idea, to prove to me that he was communicating, because Peter and I were accusing him of throwing up this obscure wall of paint and defying people to try and see through it or see into it, and he was saying that's not what he was doing. He was opening himself up, and all you had to do was look.

Jackson Pollock, *Easter and the Totem*, 1953. Oil on canvas, 82 1/8 x 58 inches.
THE MUSEUM OF MODERN ART, NEW YORK, GIFT OF LEE KRASNER IN MEMORY OF JACKSON POLLOCK. © THE POL-
LOCK- KRASNER FOUNDATION, INC. / ARS.

From a symposium,
"JACKSON POLLOCK: PORTRAIT AND A DREAM,"
Guild hall Museum, East Hampton, NY

PAUL BRACH

JUNE 8, 1986

I didn't know Jackson at his very peak. I did know Jackson when it started to fall apart for him in the early and middle '50s. The man I knew was silent at times, glowering with suppressed violence, with sudden strange moments of tenderness, always off balance and keeping you off balance. That strange quality is very hard to apprehend.

I think there's part of Jackson's art that is also very hard for people to get. Once I gave a lecture about what the literal subject matter of abstract art might be, if it had any. When I got to Pollock, I showed two pictures: one was of the Assyrian hero-god, Gilgamesh, who holds two lions apart—a forerunner of Hercules, in a way—the other was a Monet Nymphaed. I said that what was incredibly exciting about Jackson's work was that he managed to get Gilgamesh into the middle of the water lilies. That violent struggle is what's so clear in the paintings like *Pasiphaë*, those that are influenced by Masson, and Picasso, his more surreal paintings.

What's fantastic about Pollock is how he expressed that sense of the classic hero fighting the beast (the beast in himself), embedded in this amazing, shimmering, lyrical world. Not an anthropomorphic world, but a pantheistic one in which "every prospect pleases and only man is vile." And he got those two together in the heroic work, from 1948 to 1951.

Now, that isn't the good stuff of myth. Jackson drunk; Jackson terrorizing his fellow artists in the Cedar Bar; that's the stuff of myth. Jackson and Ruthie and her friend in the car; that's the stuff of myth. Somewhere along the line, you see, if the life is interesting enough, we don't have to look at the art. Art isn't that easy. I'm not sure it's available to everybody. As an aside, I want to quote Franz Kline talking about Van Gogh. Franz

275

said, "You know, he never cut off his ear in his art."

What do we love about the idea of the artist? That he's not like us. Other artists are much more likely to be suspicious, not on a sour-grapes level, but we are much more likely to be suspicious of the mythicizing of one of our fellows. Just plain suspicious. You get up in the morning and you go to work. And sometimes it's hard to work. Sometimes your life takes good turns and sometimes it takes bad turns.

I want to quote two of Jackson's contemporaries. What they said was overheard by me, so it wasn't said for an audience. Bill de Kooning was at the Museum of Modern Art's retrospective that turned into a wake for Jackson because it came only four months after his death. Bill looked at all this and thought about the media turning Pollock into the comet that went across the sky and crashed. Bill said, "Fuck this shit. I want a long life in art." And he got it. That's number one.

The other is a little more ethnic. Philip Guston and Jackson were close and on and off. They'd shared teenage years in Los Angeles. Philip was at the opening of the retrospective and he looked around and said, "My grandmother, my old Jewish grandmother, always used to say, 'football is for the goyim.' " That was a marvelous analogy. He saw the Pollocks, even the best of them, as the antithesis of the slow, sober coaxing of art out of every day and every day and every day.

And what each man was saying was a deeply held psychic polemic. It wasn't really trying to put Jackson down. De Kooning has publicly acknowledged what Pollock meant to him, but he rejected the phenomenon of Pollock. So did Philip. Both these men sensed that there was the seed of myth in this phenomenon and recoiled. That's my guess. They recoiled because there's something very uncomfortable about watching the reality of someone's life and the reality of the art being turned into myth and eventually, somehow, losing its probity, losing its intactness. It just balloons out, and there's a set of automatic responses, and the work gets lost as the artist becomes a celebrity. How did McLuhan describe a celebrity? "Someone who's well known for being well known."

How many days did Jackson spend in Cody, Wyoming? Around three hundred, all told. How many horses did he ride? Zero. He couldn't ride. He had no interest in riding. He didn't project himself as the archetypal Westerner, except that he did have an affinity to open spaces. He had an affinity to mean, hardscrabble poverty—the farming that they did when he was growing up—he talked about that. He talked about a very different kind of hardness and rawness and poverty than the children of immigrants experienced. It's not the clamorous populated poverty of city life.

I think I once wrote that "Jackson shot up the frontier town of modern art." That's what the Europeans thought, you see. They thought he came in and turned every convention upside down. And that's partly the trivializing of Jackson, especially in terms of his technique. I asked him once, "Why did you start to throw the paint?" "I don't know," he said. "Someone tried to talk me into using a dagger striper," it's a paint brush used for pin-striping automobiles, "but the sucker didn't hold the paint long enough. I just wanted a longer line." Simple. An artist would understand that. I did. Not, "I wanted to dance with the wolves," but, "I wanted a longer line."

That's what makes those of us who go into our studios every day very uncomfortable about the mythicizing, because it overlooks, "I wanted to make a longer line. I wanted to keep it going." You see something and you go back into your studio and little by little, you find a way to do it, or you find a way to do it and then you see the "something." Well, that's interesting to me, but maybe only because I'm an artist and the rest is fascinating bullshit.

EXCERPTS OF A SYMPOSIUM

PAUL JENKINS

1986

WHAT I would like to do, inasmuch as this event took place almost fourteen years ago, is look with asides at the narrative as it stands. These asides can help me to translate objectively what I tried to say about a man whom I grew to like as a person. I think I understood his pain and his anxiety, which in fact helped him to discern many things about himself. He looked into it and, as we all know, sought outside help.

Let me give you a precise example of what I mean. This is something that Lee Krasner told me about him when she was staying at my atelier in Paris just before the fateful accident in 1956. Lee and Jackson used to go into New York City to see their own separate individuals who would try to help them.

Lee told her tale to this doctor and it was one of the most terrifying nightmares anyone has ever told me. When she came back to the hotel, Jackson was there waiting for her, and he turned white when he saw her. He walked up to her and clasped both of her hands and they sat down together. "What happened, Lee?" "Jackson, please, I am all right." "Please tell me. You are completely different!" Lee went on to explain Jackson's astonishment and how she could not get over it. Even in our day and age, what happened can be compared to a kind of exorcism. A kind of monster that had dwelt in her childhood had dissolved, vanished—and Jackson knew it, he did not just sense it. In Lee's dream, a frightening total monster lived in her cellar when she was a child and it was real in her psyche, not her imagination.

When she was staying with Esther and me in Paris, she thought of Jackson constantly. One day, her eye caught sight of an upright roll of canvas I had just bought. She broke out into a laugh, "As poor as Jackson and I were, we always had art materials."

Let us say that this serves as an introduction to the forthcoming asides. Now we can start off with the first paragraph.

First and foremost, Pollock was a painter, then he was a Jungian, an alchemist, a voyager. But he did a paradoxical thing for me that will always reign supreme. They talk of his prima materia, which he was able to bring forward, and then transform into his own kind of glistening, alchemical gold. But what is this psychic gold? It is something of the spirit. Something that cannot be seen but is made seen by the will of this man.

As the first aside, there was the time someone was expressing and extolling the virtues of one of his recently finished works, and he turned and said, "Yeah, but is it a painting?" He had an imperative sense of self honesty.

We must remember that although Jackson died thirty years ago, he is not about to perish in the memory of those who knew him. [and then I veer off to say—] For those who did not know him, he still fires some kind of aspiration, imagination—and what is imagination but real estate of the soul that one can claim as one's own? Are we going to look at Jackson's paintings, or are we going to look at his life?

In his life we could equate the two as being meaningful but we have to be careful. Take the quiet and seemingly contained life of Bonnard. There is nothing all that quiet about his paintings. He had great conviction and on emanating light. Those self-portraits seem to convey a neutral presence, but there is nothing neutral about his climactic paintings. With Jackson, he wears well the myth of Icarus who flew too close to the sun. There are other artists who can compare to this, but they didn't leave as much behind. They were quite quickly forgotten ashes. So let me say to young artists, don't die.

We all have our own versions of Jackson, whether we knew him personally or have read biographies or deductions made by others. I think his own statements and explanations hold up in time. For all of his well-recorded outrageousness, for all of his vulnerability, he was a constantly giving spirit, an energizing spirit. And others responded to him.

This was a man who was helped. We have accounts of how John Graham furthered his work, and even Mondrian looked favorably at the work by a man who could be seen as on the other side of the moon. If anything, Jackson was not misunderstood. He was leaned into by numbers of people, diversified in opinion, and even those who were more sharply critical of him, gave him his due. One man whom I respect and who could be extremely sharp about Jackson as a person and Jackson as a painter never questioned his dedication. That was clear, abundant and final.

What then follows reads like a eulogy but before I set sail on the sea of fourteen years ago, I want to say it was Michel Tapié, Alfonso Ossorio, and Paul Facchetti who made possible the exhibition of Jackson's work in Paris in 1952.

Before I left New York for Paris in the early spring of 1956, I reached out to Jackson and Lee and urged him to come to Paris. The more I talked with him, the more his head sank down and then his hand reached out toward me. I thought I heard him say that it was too late. I was talking to a man forty-four years old—what the hell could he mean? I wanted him to see and feel how the attitude had transformed. From the day his work was first shown in Paris in 1952, this man from Cody, Wyoming—Timbuktu or Katmandu, it didn't matter where he came from—stirred a new awareness and he still shakes things up.

You could say I have reason to career into a kind of eulogy when that message was announced over my telephone in Paris. Lee was there staying with me and Esther. Lee had returned to Paris after visiting Charles Gimpel in Menerbes and Douglas Cooper in Menton. The telephone rang. I got on the phone. It was Clem. Lee did not even have to hear it, she sensed it, knew it, and screamed "Jackson's dead!" I grasped her and held her against the wall. She was heading for the open balcony and we lived on the sixth floor. Then, as if a magic switch had been turned on, she said, "I have to go back," as I led her back to the couch. I told her I understood. "No, you don't understand. I have to go back now." It was a Sunday in 1956. I called Darthea Speyer who was U.S. cultural attaché and the flight was arranged for that very evening to return to New York, where she would be met at the airport by Barnett and Annalee Newman. To make the time pass, we drove to the Bois de Boulogne and then to the Luxembourg Gardens before she boarded her plane that night.

Lee Krasner-Pollock protected and fostered his painting after he died—and look what she was able to do, not just for Jackson and for herself, but for other artists as well.

While she was in Paris, we saw painters, met old friends like John Graham at the Deux Magots. . . . Maybe if Jackson had gone to Paris, it might have turned everything around. But that is the positive side of nature. I can remember the times when the permanent shadow almost took over, then something happened to turn it around and one went on. He deeply disturbed numbers of people and caused them to waken from the depths of their own souls to a new kind of awareness.

Well, as I said, we all have our versions of Jackson—The last retrospective at the Modern showed us his staying power and could not have been better presented. What it abundantly evidenced was that here was a struggling artist who worked through the ways of Thomas Hart Benton and the lure of Picasso's drawings until he was able to dictate to himself what his true necessity was. He gave ceaselessly, he took, and thankfully there were those who knew the secret of how to give to him.

I almost forgot. Just before returning to the city from my visit to his place in Springs, he said "If just five people understand what you are doing, that's enough."

Lee Krasner in the studio soon after Pollock's death, 1956. Their dog Gyp lies at her feet.
PHOTO: MAURICE BEREZOV. POLLOCK-KRASNER STUDY CENTER, JEFFREY POTTER COLLECTION.

CONVERSATION

BERTON ROUECHÉ, *New Yorker* columnist, and
ENEZ WHIPPLE, Director Emerita of Guild Hall

APRIL 6, 1989

BR: My wife Kay and I wanted to move out of the city. In 1949, through a
local realtor, Ed Cook, we found a beautiful old house, the Parsons
house, in Springs. It had no heat, no light, no plumbing. We rented it
for $25 a month, and we put in a furnace, we put in plumbing, we put
in electricity.

EW: You got to know the artists pretty intimately down there in Springs, I
should think, because that house is right in the heart of Springs, near
Pollock's.

BR: We got to know Pollock simply as a neighbor, and we became friends
for several reasons. One, he had a deep suspicion of Easterners, and my
coming from Missouri made him feel more comfortable with me. Also,
I had known Thomas Hart Benton, under whom he had studied, so
that was another link, and we got along very comfortably together. That
was the period when he had pretty much stopped drinking—this was in
1949–52—when he did most of his best work and wasn't the problem
that he became later on.

EW: I remember once we invited you and Kay and Jackson and Lee over
for dinner, and we all went to see Bea Lillie at the theater afterwards. It
was in the summer, and I had a box [at Guild Hall's John Drew The-
ater]. We all sat in the box, and Jackson seemed to be perfectly all right.
He seemed to enjoy her performance very much.

BR: I remember the performance, but I don't remember that Pollock was
there. It seems an unusual thing for him to do.

EW: Well, he was fine that night. He certainly wasn't drinking at that point, but I remember that people around town sort of warned us not to get too friendly with him, because he would walk into the house and raid your liquor cabinet and get into a big fight and so on. I guess because of that we were a little bit wary of getting to be too close to them.

BR: As I say, our relationship for a long time was very informal, neighborly. We went clamming together, and all that sort of thing. I'd finish work in the late afternoon, and Kay and I would walk up to their house. I remember we would sit around the kitchen table and drink coffee and talk in a non-artistic way, just about the local affairs. He was very much interested, you know—he wanted to be as local as he could.

I wanted to do a profile of him for *The New Yorker*. I mentioned it to Bill Shawn, who was then the editor, and he said, well, let's wait, let's see if he really amounts to anything. So we compromised, and I did a "Talk of the Town" interview with him. ["Unframed Space," August 1950] And he liked it well enough so that we continued to be good friends.

EW: It's too bad you didn't do the profile, because it probably would have been one of the best . . .

BR: Oh, it would have been a disaster, because I really had no idea what he was doing, and not much sympathy, really. I was just beginning to see the Abstract-Expressionist paintings and they were a puzzle. I'm afraid that I would have made a mess of trying to explain what he was doing.

EXCERPT OF A STATEMENT

GRACE HARTIGAN

SUMMER, 1993

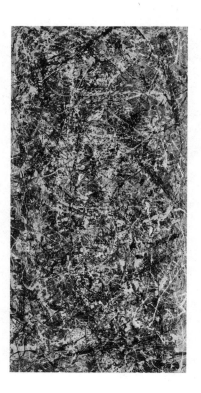

Back in 1948, I was helping Jackson Pollock hang a show at the Betty Parsons gallery. Pollock's friend, the artist Alfonso Ossorio, had bought a Pollock. In the center of the work, a chunk had fallen off—a chunk almost as big as the palm of your hand. So Pollock said, "I'll get some paint and fix it up. He'll never know the difference."

When the show ended, Pollock sent the painting to Ossorio. Ossorio knew the difference, and he called Pollock. Jackson said, "Send the painting over to the studio, and I'll do a good job on it." When Jackson had the painting in his studio, he repainted the whole work. Pollock said, "He'll never know the difference." He sent it back. Again, Ossorio knew the difference. Pollock told me later, "He likes it even better."

Jackson Pollock, Number 5, 1948, 1948. Oil, enamel and aluminum paint on fiberboard, 96 x 48 inches. DAVID GEFFEN, LOS ANGELES. FORMERLY IN THE COLLECTION OF ALFONSO OSSORIO AND EDWARD F. DRAGON, EAST HAMPTON, NEW YORK. © THE POLLOCK- KRASNER FOUNDATION, INC. / ARS. PHOTO: POLLOCK-KRASNER STUDY CENTER, JACKSON POLLOCK CATALOGUE RAISONNÉ ARCHIVES.

THE END OF THE AFFAIR

WILL BLYTHE

OCTOBER, 1999

AT summer dusk in her studio, the light fading to a monochromatic New York gray. Ruth Kligman is listening intently to Ruth Kligman. She is reading aloud a love letter she has recently written to a man who has been dead for forty-three years. "Jackson, Jackson, Jackson," she begins, her voice trembling with a certain actressy gusto. "I loved you so much and I made you the promise to keep that love always, and I did just that, kept my word, for me, for you." She reads on, stopping periodically to look up at me and exclaim, "It's beautiful, isn't it?" Barefoot, recumbent on her bed in a tea-length black dress, propped up on pillows, she looks every inch the professional (if funkified) widow.

She's actually not the widow: not literally anyway, but such details are for the small-minded—for Ruth Kligman loved him last and best, and had he lived, they would have been married. She assures me of that.

At one point, the curtains flare into the studio with an explosive pop. "Did you see that? That was him coming in," Kligman tells me. "He protects me. Whenever I give interviews, doors swing open, the electricity goes off, engines shut down." The "he" in question is Jackson Pollock, perhaps the greatest American painter, tagged "Jack the Dripper" by the wits at *Time* magazine, a homegrown manic genius who flung his psyche full-force onto the canvas, pouring out lyrical, spooling traceries of desperate energy.

Given the force field that surrounded him in life, it doesn't seem so implausible that he might exert poltergeistic powers after death, especially in this bedroom so largely devoted to his memory. It has the feeling of a shrine, a Spanish botanica filled with candles and images of the saints and

Ruth Kligman at the Pollock-Krasner
House, March, 1994.
PHOTO: HELEN A. HARRISON.

the dead. Pollock, of course, is both saintly and dead, an icon of purity for this era of hype, and in the way of purists who live (and drive) fast, die young, and leave a pretty (bloated) corpse, he is soon to be the subject of a major motion picture, directed by and starring Ed Harris. Pollock was the first American celebrity artist, and naturally, the first celebrity artist to flee from his celebrity. Hold his story up to the light, turn in whichever way you will, and it can serve as an object lesson for almost anything—the ravages of demon rum (or six-packs all the livelong day), the devouring of the artist by the wolves of commercialism, a foreshadowing of the perils of celebrity culture, the comedy of psychoanalysis in its American heyday, and on and on.

But for Kligman, his story is her story, a love story. An acquaintance, the composer Ned Rorem, describes her account of the romance. *Love Affair* (being reissued this fall by Cooper Square, with her love letter to serve as the introduction), as "one narcissist depicting another." ("I think that's because *he's* narcissist." Ruth says.)

Above the doorway to the bedroom is a photograph of Kligman astride Pollock's knee. A painter herself, she has embroidered the border of the paint with her own squiggly brushwork. The effect is somewhere between a grown-up's handmade memorial and a high school sophomore's doodling around the yearbook picture of a crush. On the day of the snapshot—August 11, 1956—Pollock had been drinking since early that morning, and Kligman had been working hard to lighten his mood. But in this moment, at least, sitting on a boulder in the broad summer light of the Hamptons, they're putting on a spirited face for the camera. The picture was taken by her friend Edith Metzger at two o'clock in the afternoon of Pollock's "death-day," as Ruth calls it.

On the floor elsewhere in the studio sits a painting of Pollock's entitled *Red, Black & Silver* that she calls the last he ever did, which he gave Ruth just weeks before his death. She's thinking about selling it. At sixty-nine,

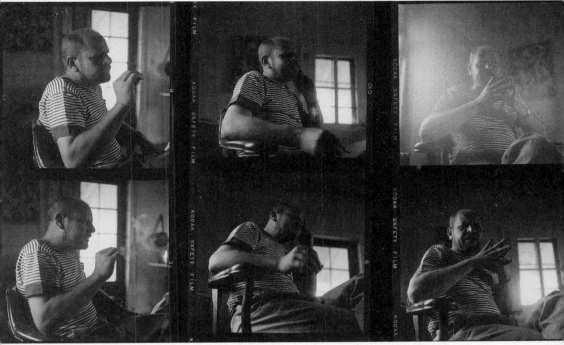

Jackson Pollock in his studio, August 1956. FROM A CONTACT SHEET OF PHOTOGRAPHS BY JOHN REED. POLLOCK-KRASNER STUDY CENTER, JEFFREY POTTER COLLECTION.

having been a painter and a lover all her life (sadly; there are no pensions for those pursuits), she could use the money.

The earthly aspect of Kligman and Pollock's romance expired at its rocky peak on Fireplace Road in East Hampton. Long Island, on the night of the picture, when Pollock, drunk, took a curve too fast and cartwheeled his convertible into the trees, killing himself and Metzger and severely injuring Kligman. Pollock was forty-four, Kligman twenty-six, they had been in love only months. "At the moment he died, I believe his soul went into my body," Kligman says. For her, the divide between the spirit world and this one is about as thick as a stretched canvas. "And when I was convalescing in the hospital, he came and visited me."

The New York art world, where there had been much disapproval of the liaison, sometimes reacted as if the wrong person had lived. In the wreck's aftermath, the poet Frank O'Hara nicknamed Kligman "Death Car Girl," a sobriquet that apparently stung. (When O'Hara died, says a friend who knew them both, Ruth composed a poem that went like this: ("You called me Death Car Girl/But look who's dead now.")

Here in Kligman's apartment, the light in the room grows dimmer, encouraging more confession. We are, fittingly, turned into abstractions of ourselves, little blobs of luminosity, telling our woeful tales of love. Kligman picks up the letter to read on. Despite her self-absorption, a quality of which she's well aware: "I'm fascinated by myself and I know it," she says; the performance is moving. The narcissism of adolescence is charm again from one approaching seventy.

In the near-darkness, Kligman looks in my direction. It seems that she is crying, but it's hard to tell. "You never stop," she says. She means, I'm sure, you never stop loving, even after forty-three years of irrevocable absence. She taps on the lights, leads me to the door. We pass through the narrow kitchen, where a Larry Rivers drawing of Ruth rests atop the counter. Then we arrive at what can only be called The Wall of Kligman, an entire gallery's worth of photographs devoted to herself. That's Ruth and Willem de Kooning in 1959, sunning themselves on a Long Island beach. That's Ruth and Jasper Johns in 1986 at her gallery show: their arms around each other, beaming at the camera.

("She was good," says an acquaintance. "She didn't just stop at straight guys.") There's Ruth with Franz Kline, whose studio this once was. There's Ruth looking remarkably like Elizabeth Taylor, to whom she's often been compared. Here's Ruth in 1980, photographed by Robert Mapplethorpe. That's Ruth by Irving Stein, by Timothy Greenfield–Sanders, by Bert Stern, by Rudy Burkhardt. It strikes me as very impressive, if not a little prematurely posthumous.

The next time we see each other, after upbraiding me for not calling her when I said I was going to ("You're a man, you probably didn't even know you did it," she says teasingly), Ruth Kligman gets right to the mystery that is haunting her: "Why did Jackson want to know me? Why did they *all* want to know me? Why was I there?"

It's a karmic question, to be sure, with a pardonable touch of preening. After all, her little black book could pass for a guide to twentieth-century painting.

Tonight, in a flowing white dress, Kligman positively radiates queenliness. The staff at the restaurant where we're having supper treats her with a sort of vexed deference, unsure whether she's someone they should know. She had lobbied the Four Seasons or Le Cirque, but we have ended up downtown at Il Candinori, a restaurant in Greenwich Village, scant blocks from where she met Pollock one evening in 1956 at the Cedar Street Bar (despite the name, then located at Eighth Street and University Place), a now-legendary artists' hangout where, as is customery in such places, thousands of masterpieces were painted by hand in the smoky air following nights of drunken talk, then never quite re-created with the same bravura the next hungover morning in the studio. With Pollock then occupying the Ernest Hemingway Papa Bear Chair of the art world, his arrival had electrified the joint. Patrons, themselves enlarged by a genius in their midst, secretly hoped to witness a brawl—Pollock was known to randomly punch people out, often famous artists—or some other memorable atrocity, such as the time he ripped the bathroom door off its hinges. (And before that, on the Upper East Side, he had wnadered into a cocktail party at the collector Peggy Guggenheim's, peed into the fireplace, and wandered out again. Drunken genius has always had its privileges, especially when it's not your fireplace.)

On that night, Pollock locked eyes with Kligman, then working as an assistant at an unnoticed midtown gallery for $25 a week. He blustered over to her table, pulled up a chair, and sat down with Ruth and her friends, a group of aspiring artists. Pollock was, in fact, a shy, inarticulate man, often so monosyllabic that he was described by the painter John Ferren as the ultimate "ugh artist." Social occasions were hell for him. One of Kligman's companions introduced Pollock to Ruth, saying, "Jackson, this is Ruth Kligman . . . she's new on the scene . . . she's going to be somebody . . . isn't she pretty?"

"You sound like a goddamn ass," Pollock thundered. "I'm not impressed with those things." He turned again to Kligman. "You have such warm eyes," he said.

"Thank you," she said.

"Don't thank me. It's true. Who are you?"

It was a good question. Twenty-six years old, a former Seventh Avenue model, Kligman mainly knew what she wasn't, or didn't want to be. And that was middle-class. No more nights at home watching TV (as she had back in her modeling days, while living with her mother in Newark). No children. No making money just to make money. (Her grandfather, a merchant, was known as the "Apple King" of New Jersey.) No big extended Jewish clan to suffocate her. "Middle-class women get fat, they get sick," Kligman says. "It's a terrible life, not what God intended."

Her parents had divorced when she was young. Her handsome father adored her, her mother doted on her twin sister, Iris (at present, a composer living in Malibu). She and Iris stayed with their mother. Ruth was the shy one. Her identical twin overshadowed her throughout their childhood, then got married at twenty-one and moved out. Now Ruth was alone. "I took the idea of family," she says, "and put art in its place." When she was seven, she had fallen in love with Beethoven. "It was his face," she says. "I saw an etching of him in a book. I saw those eyes and that forehead, and that was it."

Now, in February 1956, Jackson Pollock, with his big bald brow jutting truculently into the world, had lurched in her direction. Here it was again: the phrenology of genius. Despite her fragile sense of self, Kligman did know that she was beautiful. 'I had confidence in that, and in the intuition I had developed from having been overshadowed,' she says. She admired that Jackson liked her quite a bit. A week after meeting him, she called the Cedar Bar at 11:45 one night, sure that he would be there. He rushed over to her apartment on 16th Street and proceeded to have a weeping fit—not exactly a standard seduction technique but, in the spirit of abstract expressionism, un-phony. And it worked.

They fell in love, Kligman pumped the bellows to inflame Pollock's ego with hot gusts of adoration, trying to fill his psychic hollows with the kind of praise she one day hoped to merit, as either a genius in her own right or the soul mate of one. This came at a time when Pollock was lost, his great paintings done, his artistic momentum flagging. He was drinking too much. His eleven-year marriage to the painter Lee Krasner was unhappy. And his longtime champion, the critic Clement Greenberg, was dumping on his new work. Along came this brash, good-looking woman who told him he was a genius—and let's not underestimate the fact that it was a good-looking woman saying this.

"He was having a hell of a time," Jackson's friend, the painter James Brooks has said. "Lee was pretty good at bringing him down. . . . He felt good about [Ruth]—you know, a pretty, voluptuous gal, thinking he was the greatest man in the world, and in love."

Even today, Kligman purveys an oxymoronic blend—the hauteur of an alluring woman who knows her own beauty with the child of divorce's eagerness to please, especially Daddy. For someone so admittedly electrified by the high voltage of self, Kligman nonetheless inspires those around her to shine.

"The minute I saw Jackson, I knew him better than anyone in the world," Kligman says. "I already knew his work. He was expressing the way I feel. I said to him, "You are the greatest painter in the world. Why are you crying?" He would be stunned. I would say to him, "Don't you know what you've done?" He didn't undersand how I knew what he'd done. I mean, it wasn't Clem Greenberg saying it. It was me. He knew that I knew something. Bill de Kooning knew, too. They all did. That's why they gravitated to me. See, I thought it was my appearance, but it was this other quality—my intuition."

That spring, Pollock and Kligman would meet in bars and her apartment whenever he would come into the city from his home in East Hampton in order to visit his shrink. As the affair progressed, they began spending more time together on Pollock and his wife's home turf, the Hamptons, which in those days was not the posh celebrity summer camp it is today but a sort of rural Greenwich Village, where artists could find a cheap house and work in relative isolation under the high Atlantic light. Early one morning that summer Krasner caught her husband and

Ruth Kligman in the 1960s. PHOTO: CARLOS SANSEGUNDO.
POLLOCK-KRASNER STUDY CENTER, JEFFREY POTTER COLLECTION.

Kligman sneaking out of a barn next to their home, giggling as they went, and delivered Pollock the usual ultimatum: her or me. Krasner then departed to Europe for six weeks, perhaps hoping that the affair would cool off when the two paramours had each other all to themselves.

Pollock immediately installed Kligman in the farmhouse he and Krasner shared. As Pollock's friend, the late Hamptons fixture Patsy Southgate, told his biographer Jeffrey Potter, Pollock's "dream was to have both" women. But he sensed the local community's disapproval, an attitude encapsulated in one wife's depiction of Kligman as an "art bobbysoxer." The couple were thrown back on their own company. Yet as claustrophobic and harrowing as their East Hampton sojourn often was, Kligman has largely colorized the stark film of those weeks.

"I'm like Cleopatra," she says, "and Jackson was like Marc Anthony. I think I had met him before; he was a very deep soulmate. Nothing else could explain why I've been involved with him over the years. He died in my arms."

"He died in your arms?" I had been under the impression that Pollock had been killed instantly when he slammed headfirst into a tree, ten feet up the trunk. When rescuers arrived, they found Ruth, who had also been thrown from the car, pulling herself down the road on her stomach, calling for Jackson.

"Well, what I mean is, an hour before he died, he had been in my arms, crying."

"What do you think would have happened had he lived?"

"If he hadn't died," says Kligman, "we would have gotten married. That's what he wanted. He wanted to start over. He was only forty-four. He had lived a certain way all his life, but it was hurting his art. He wanted a sweeter romantic life. The resentment and the publicity had isolated him. Lee Krasner and Clem Greenberg liked him when he was down and out. I tried to break off with him. I told him I had this feeling we would probably die in a car wreck. But I couldn't do it. All these years, I've been blaming myself for what happened. I bought the myth that I was the seductress, that everything was my fault, that I killed Jackson Pollock. But he manipulated the separation [from Lee]."

I wonder if Ruth ever had any contact with Krasner, who has been dead since 1984. She sighs. "I tried to. I went up to her at a party back in the 1960s. I said, 'Jackson really cared about you.' She said, 'Thank you for telling me.' Then, over the years, she got really angry with me.

"I am the last one alive who really knew him," she says proudly as a war widow. "What is the destiny that I have, that I met him? I want someone to tell me."

She looks at me, half-imploringly, half-expectantly. She is still almost voodooishly youthful and attractive. "Maybe by dessert," I offer.

In 1957, a year after Pollock's death, Kligman became involved with perhaps the second most famous American painter of the twentieth century—the Dutch immigrant Willem de Kooning. Pollock and de Kooning were affectionate rivals, Pollock once telling de Kooning, "You *know* more, but I *feel* more."

De Kooning also apparently felt some affection for Ruth, having once chased Pollock and Kligman down the block outside the Cedar Bar, shouting, "Hey, Jackson, is that your new girl? Let me take a look." Of Pollock's relationship with Kligman, de Kooning said, "She must have cared for him a lot—kind of cared for me, too, later. She meant it but not like, you know, a great passion or anything like that. She was starting to paint, and she wasn't stupid about it, either . . . She could have become a painter, but nobody takes a person very seriously when they're just starting to paint, particularly if it's a woman."

Their relationship lasted four years. Like Kligman, de Kooning also hated middle-class life, what he called "the couples." "Bill and I would stay up all night talking about Rothko or technique," Kligman says. And every morning at breakfast, he read philosophy—Wittgenstein,

Kierkegaard. He reminded me a lot of Chaplin—very funny, witty, really intelligent.

"He always said I was the only woman who never bored him. He said I melted him. It was a beautiful love affair. He brought me tulips. Being involved with him was like getting a Ph.D. in art history. "Tell me more, tell me more." I'd say. He called me his sponge. He would always say. 'Compete with me.' He didn't want a woman to be a slave. He built me a painting wall. He'd look at my painting and say: 'I guess you don't get the point.' A couple of weeks later. I'd do another, and he'd say, 'Oh, you got the point.'"

Kligman has told me of her animus toward marriage (she was married once, from 1964 to 1971—to the Spanish painter Juan Carlos Sansegundo—and she didn't like it). But her relationship with de Kooning sounds ideal. "Why didn't you marry him?" I wonder. "It's complicated," is all she'll say, in a rare moment of reticence.

Once, when she was having supper with de Kooning at a restaurant in Manhattan called Angelina's, she got her first glimpse of Jasper Johns when he strode in with three other "slender, tall men." They all nodded greetings at de Kooning. "Who are they?" Kligman asked. "I'll tell you later," de Kooning said. "It's a small restaurant." They turned out to be Robert Rauschenberg, John Cage, Merce Cunningham, and Johns, who became Ruth's next art-world conquest.

"You've really done a survey course of the major American painters of the twentieth century," I say.

"I know," Ruth says, laughing. "But my motivation for these relationships was always misunderstood. It was for my desire for creativity. I was very lucky, and I knew it."

"Didn't you feel their presence would overwhelm your own art?" I ask. After all, perhaps there's not enough light at the easel when you're painting in the bulky shadows of genius, all those big foreheads.

"No," Ruth says. "Partly because of the age difference. They were more my mentors. But nobody ever told me what to do. People are always saying, 'What were those men like?' and I'll do something outrageous and say, 'That's what they were like.' Men are allowed to make a scene. Women are not. They call you crazy, difficult. But I've always chosen my own path.

"And the men I was with didn't want me to be otherwise. With Jasper," she says, "I would go out of my way to make him tough. He had a kind of sadness; I kept trying to bring him out of that. It was deep in his soul."

She tells me how she recently asked Johns, to whom she once proposed, what it was about her. He replied, laughingly, "Oh, Ruth, need you ask?"

"Sometimes I think they all wanted me because of Jackson—Warhol, Mapplethorpe, Brice Marden, Carl Andre, Robert Smithson, Terry Winters . . ." she says. "But it must have been something else. I have a lot of

Venus in me—my chart. I could be the oracle. The Muse. The Goddess. The embodiment of Venus. I imbue! I don't want to sound hubristic, but you know what I think it is: I'm very feminine but with a very masculine mind. Men adore it."

A few days later, the painter Brice Marden confirms that Ruth is not altogether off the mark when she talks of men wanting to know Pollock through her. "On her own, she's a strong and interesting person," he says. "But good heavens!" He laughs. "There are not many people kicking around these days who knew him. In a way, though, it's too bad, the whole Pollock thing. So distracting. It affects her whole life."

At times, quite unhappily. Her love life has provoked considerable (though often whispered) animosity, typified by one acquaintance's suggestion that Kligman's memoir might better have been entitled *Star Fuck*. In the view of some of Pollock's friends, Kligman has made a career (albeit not a very lucrative one) out of his death, as if she had engineered the crash for her own notoriety, as if her presence through Pollock's last days would confer upon her the apocalyptic glamour of a Gospel writer. The only possible author for the Last Book of Jackson—which, of course, she wrote.

In 1974, Kligman published *Love Affair*, a chronicle of her months with Pollock. The book is a passionate take indeed, though a queasy one—we know the ending, after all. It's also such an odd combination of overheated and prim that a Peter Pan collar could have served as the book's wrapper. ("He took me powerfully, with great confidence," she writes.) Are we talking about Fabio or Jackson Pollock? The narrative's tone is consistent with Kligman's assertion that "I was more about being adored than I was about sex." Despite his avidity for even marginalia about Pollock, Marden confesses that he's never been able to get past chapter two.

It helps to remember, however, that the affair died young, that it never had the chance to get fat and sloppy, to sit around the living room in its underwear and socks. Its premature demise makes Kligman and Pollock the Orpheus and Eurydice of the New York school. In the end, the book works best as a kind of *Lost Weekend* for abstract expressionists, an appalling glimpse through the studio skylights at the terror of an artist who fears he has lost the capacity for making art.

Love Affair drew a barbed response from Andy Warhol, a friend of Kligman's. His *Diary* shows Ruth asking Warhol to take her to meet Jack Nicholson, whom she hoped to interest in playing the part of Pollock in a movie of her book. "I said no," Warhol writes, snidely deadpan. "I wouldn't take her *anywhere* after reading her book. She actually killed Pollock, she was driving him so nuts." It seems more likely that Kligman was making Warhol insane; her book—and subsequent biographies—reveal that Pollock was already speeding down the backroads of self-destruction long before he met Ruth.

She became, in effect, the Yoko Ono of the art world, cultivated and reviled in almost equal measure. (And like Yoko, she even insisted on doing her own art.) "She was family," says a writer who traveled in her circle, "but she was the unwanted relative, because she was always causing trouble. But in a way, she was innocent, because she didn't know it." Her critics acted as if she had stolen Jackson Pollock from them. Others wanted to get closer to her because she had been close to Pollock, as if in some odd psychosexual equation, his genius might rub off on them.

"That whole scene [the abstract expressionists] had a puritanical reaction to Ruth," says the critic and curator Robert Pincus-Witten. "As if the legacy was going to be tainted because the god in question [Pollock] had a private life that was disapproved of . . . people really laid it on her."

ANECDOTES

ROBERT GOODNOUGH

1999

WHEN I wrote the article "Pollock Paints a Picture" for *ARTnews* magazine, Rudy Burckhardt, the photographer, and I stayed overnight at [Pol-
lock's] home on Long Island. When it was time to go to sleep, the Pollocks
found that they needed another cot to sleep on. They decided to ask the
neighbors next door if they could borrow a cot. Though it was not late the
neighbors were asleep, and ringing the bell woke them up. Jackson Pollock felt terrible; he was very sensitive. Waking them up really bothered
him. He said, "We must never do that again." Pollock was not a big talker,
but he was a very kind and thoughtful person.

Once when I was in Pollock's studio a visitor accidentally stepped on the
edge of a painting that he was working on. It was lying on the floor. The visitor was worried. Pollock said, "Please don't worry about it. I don't consider
my paintings to be precious." I heard a story that he once spilled a can of
beer on one of his paintings as he was working—so he left the beer stain
there as part of the picture.

One evening Jackson Pollock, Tony Smith, and I were walking in Greenwich Village. We stopped at a diner called, I believe, "The White Tower." We
sat at the counter, and Jackson ordered a steak. Jackson had large hands, and
when trying to cut the steak, the steak slipped to the floor. Jackson leaned over
and picked up the steak and said, "I'll show you how to eat a steak." With that,
he picked up the steak with his huge hands and proceeded to tear the steak
apart and put the pieces in his mouth, ignoring the knife and fork. When we
finished eating we walked out onto the street. It was a clear night and we
could see a mass of stars. Jackson looked up, pointed and said, "Look at that
stuff up there!" It was so much like his paintings. I never forgot that evening.

Jackson Pollock in the studio, 1950. Photographed by Rudy Burckhardt for Robert Goodnough's article, "Pollock Paints a Picture," *ARTnews*, May 1951.

A RECOLLECTION

BARNEY ROSSET

MAY, 2000

I thought Pollock was a great artist. To me, he was almost frightening, in the sense that he seemed extraordinarily quiet and tense. I felt an incipient violence in him, but the only violence I actually ever saw was against himself or an inanimate object. Of course, when he died in the car crash he had two others with him but I never saw him when he wasn't gentle — except one night when he got into a fight in the Cedar Bar. But with whom? Franz Kline and Bill de Kooning. I remember being at a table with the three of them. I was listening to them talk. Suddenly they were arguing. Pollock went to the men's room and I heard a crash. Afterwards, the three of them went out on the sidewalk and they were all happily saying goodnight. Even then Pollock didn't hurt anybody, just the bathroom door. Pollock was told by the owner not to come back — not forever, just a month, maybe, like a fine for a basketball player.

I remember big discussion between Joan Mitchell, my first wife, and de Kooning about different kinds of oil paints. Joan and Bill were very traditional in their likes and dislikes. Quality was uppermost. However, Pollock was using a commercial paint, Duco. The two of them thought that was an almost incredible idea, but amusing, and for Pollock, anything was possible, but it was not for them.

I first went out to East Hampton in 1950 with Joan, who like me, was a native Chicagoan. I thought it quite beautiful. Especially the ocean beaches, and about three years later, with my second wife, Loly, I bought Robert Motherwell's house in Georgica. We found ourselves in the midst of a wonderful social scene, very nurturing to artists, writers, and architects, but particularly artists. I've never experienced anything like it before or since. It was not quite the Cedar Bar, but it was as if the bar had suddenly added several new layers of personality.

Early on, Loly and I were invited to a party for Jackson at the house of someone we didn't know, Alfonso Ossorio. There was a big crowd that night at his estate, The Creeks. Ossorio, a formidable and iconoclastic artist himself, had an exquisite sensibility and a lot of money, and he helped other people financially, especially Pollock. The artists certainly weren't wallowing in money, but some of their friends were hardly poor. It was a highly unusual group with people like Pollock, Jeffrey Potter and his wife, Penny, Bill and Elaine de Kooning, Harold Rosenberg, Leo Castelli, Warren Brandt, Paul Brach and Mimi Shapiro, the architects Robert Rosenberg, Frederick Kiesler, Paul Lester Weiner and his wife Ingeborg, a very good painter herself—these people seemed to cover all the creative ground. Among those who later became my close friends were Berton Rouche and Joe and Milly Liss. All liked Jackson very much. There was a kind of extended family feeling that I didn't know could exist.

Still to me, Jackson was a little bit apart. I mean he wasn't somebody you could be exactly chummy with, as you could be with de Kooning. Actually, I felt much closer to his wife, Lee Krasner. We all thought of him as a great artist of the period, whether or not anybody knew what he was doing. Certainly Joan thought he was great—he and de Kooning and Kline; and of course, I saw painting through Joan's eyes.

I think it took the artists a long time to understand that they were becoming successful. I can only see this as being related to the Depression in some way. The older artists had never had money, didn't own things, like cars. Franz Kline had never had a car, but when he was living in the "Red House," in Bridgehampton, in the early fifties, he bought a car for $150, a huge Lincoln convertible. It looked to me like a steam locomotive. He and Pollock took it out on the road and hit more or less the first car coming toward them, head on. That night the artist Ludwig Sander, an ex-G. I., like me, came to my place and told me that Kline had to appear in court for demolishing the other car, which had about six people in it, uninjured, thank goodness. Franz said that the only thing he owned was his Lincoln, and he was afraid the judge would take it away from him, so I agreed to buy it. In court, the judge let Franz off with a warning. Even the law enforcement people in East Hampton looked kindly upon artists. So I gave Franz back the gorgeous car and he returned my $150 check. Jackson was a recipient of that same forgiveness more than once.

GREEN RIVER

BARBARA A. MacADAM

MAY, 2000

Forget the man. Forget the lifestyle. It's all cliché now. And the cultural, stylistic, mythical, and art historical routes to the essential Jackson Pollock tell too much. For me, the most revealing place to begin and end is at Pollock's gravesite—which is, perhaps, as it should be.

There, in East Hampton's Green River Cemetery, rests the gravestone—a big, irregular natural rock, untampered with but for a plaque with Pollock's signature and dates. By virtue of its shape, it looks far larger than it is, and it's certainly much bigger than those surrounding it. Decked out in greyish-green lichen and other of nature's various deposits, it boasts a texture, sparkle, and color, that bring the stone far closer than intention ever could to mimicking Pollock's paintings.

It comes off as expressive yet contained, grand yet simple, domineering yet nonchalant. It attracts attention through its air of false modesty. The stone presides from the cemetery's high point over the graves of Pollock's wife, Lee Krasner (her tombstone is a much, much smaller version of Pollock's), of critic Henry Geldzahler (the stone was chipped at to look natural—it doesn't), and avant-garde filmmaker Stan Vanderbeek (constructed of film reels), among the many other big and small guns. Discreetly, it wields its power over the whole cemetery, even the artistic luminaries up front, like Stuart Davis (his gravestone is a tall, polished black slab, like a pillar in a hotel lobby) and the wise and venerable critic, Harold Rosenberg (who rests among his family).

Without realizing it, visitors add to the conceptual nature of the object when they leave small stones on top of it as a gesture of respect. It's a fitting container for the abundance that filled his canvases—ultimately minimal in its controlled embrace of so much material and so many ideas. But in this instance Pollock couldn't flick his spatula from a distance to give order to the apparent chaos. Somehow nature seems to have understood.

I don't remember when I first encountered Pollock's work. He was the established avant-garde as I came of age—not at all shocking. In 1964 I bought a used copy of Frank O'Hara's concise and unpretentiously suggestive *Jackson Pollock* in Braziller's Great American Artists Series and mulled over the muddied reproductions. I vividly recall the Pollock-wannabes of the time, whose work decorated many Manhattan living rooms, coordinating with the furniture and rendering the homes instant period pieces. The imitators always looked dated. Pollock never did. Once, in a Thomas Jefferson–designed house outside Charlottesville, Virginia, I saw a painting by one of those Pollock descendants hanging in a modernish room, and it diminished the effect of the entire house.

So who cares about Pollock the bohemian, the self-indulgent, over-drinking womanizer? Pollock the artist remains in the category of those having the last word, like Richard Serra today. Abstract Expressionism can't go any farther than Pollock took it. For me, he'll always be modern—the young man who became an old master and remains as both. Nature, together with Pollock's admirers, offers a parallel, not only successfully translating his tombstone into sculpture but allowing it to evolve and remain a reflection of all times.

Robert Girard, *Jackson Pollock's Stone*, 1983. Silver print photograph, 16 x 20 inches. COURTESY OF ROBERT GIRARD.

CREATIVE
RESPONSES

Jackson Pollock

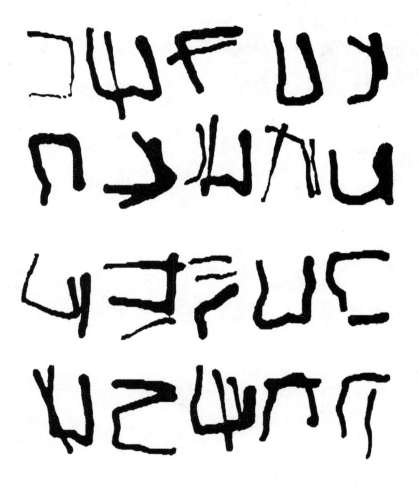

Path Soong, Painter

Morton Feldman's "GLASS SEQUENCE"

DANIEL STERN

MAY 2000

Morton Feldman and I had been close friends from Music and Art High School on. We both played in the Senior orchestra. I was a cellist and he played the bass—a big man playing a big instrument. He also played the piano, and with great delicacy. Our first encounter was during a rehearsal, when he put down his bass and took up the baton to conduct a piece he had written entitled "Dirge for Thomas Wolfe," a conventional piece not without its own beauty. And the title tells you how young we both were.

We both studied composition with Dante Fiorello, a relatively unknown composer; but later Morty went on to study with acknowledged major figures such as Wallingford Reiger and Stefan Wolpe. He never studied institutionally, but he learned what he needed from these teachers.

Morty became quite close with the Abstract-Expressionist painters. When Hans Namuth was to do a film on Jackson Pollock, Namuth and Paul Falkenberg asked him to write the score. He scored it for two cellos and asked me to play both parts.

It's a special piece, unlike the rest of his work. It was, as I interpreted it, intentional fragments that come together as a coherent whole, similar to the way Pollock's work is made. By this time Morty was definitely not interested in linear music; the very fragmentary nature of such a project was anti-linear. In most of his music, the motifs are quite hard to discern, but here the main motifs are quite prominent and are repeated as a sort of leitmotif. There are two of them. The one that opens the film is a series of high harmonics on the A-string, and the other is the pizzicato, or plucked, series. There's also a long, drawn-out tone—not a motif, exactly—that comes in several times. Interestingly, some of it is quite loud, whereas Morty's music became famous for its extraordinary softness, almost to the point of inaudibility.

In other words, Morty did not set out to write a piece that would stand on its own. The music was written very much in the spirit and the letter of the film. He really adapted the sounds to what was happening on the screen. It's an upside down, avant-garde version of the Hollywood composer working off the given visual material. There's no direct correlation, so it's not "movie music" in that sense, but it's very much a series of aesthetic moments, just as the film is a series of aesthetic gestures.

What Morty was looking for, and found, was an objective correlative for Pollock's act of painting. The main difference is that the disciplined nature of the repeated harmonic and pizzicato themes is a little more formal than you might imagine in terms of Pollock's work. But then again, I remember Pollock saying in the film's narration that he didn't just throw paint. He controlled it; he knew what he was doing.

I'm sure that Morty saw a rough cut of the film as he was writing the music, and at least once during the editing process we watched Pollock at work. He was staying in New York City at the town house of his friend, Alfonso Ossorio, in MacDougal Alley. We both went to see him there, and he was painting away. I don't recall if Morty took me along to familiarize me with the subject matter of the film, or if we were just hanging out together that day, as we did most days.

To tell the truth, I was no big fan of Abstract Expressionism. I was quite naïve and I thought it was all needlessly obscure. I remember sounding off about it at the Cedar Bar, and Morty saying, "What gives you the right to judge?" I had no right, just the chutzpah of youth. He'd known me since we were fifteen or so, and knew I was not very sophisticated about painting. But in spite of these differences we stayed very close. Once I went with him to the Museum of Modern Art, and he pointed out a painting by Balthus. "You want to talk about obscure," he said. "Why is that girl looking at the cat in that odd way? And why is the other girl lying on the floor with her skirt raised? That's much more obscure than Abstract Expressionism."

Morty was involved in the origin of "chance" or "aleatoric" music—picking notes at random, with a looser control than composers had traditionally exercised up until that time. But the so-called glass sequence (which actually accompanies Pollock as he paints on both glass and canvas) is definitely not aleatoric. It was composed, written down, and I played it exactly as it was written. Still, it's hard to put it into any specific category. It's certainly not tonal, not written in any key. It's in ⅜ time, but

Original score © 1995 Peter Namuth, courtesy the Estate of Hans Namuth.

there's no specified tempo. It could be played fast or slow; that was Morty's decision as we made the recording.

The actual recording was done at the studio of Peter Bartók, Béla Bartók's son. There were two separate scores, one for each cello part. I recorded one, then put on giant earphones and listened to it as I recorded

307

the second part. We did it in one session, and it took the better part of an afternoon. From a technical point of view, it was very hard to mix the harmonics with the pizzicatos and make them come out just right. Actually, I'll never know how much mixing was done on the console, and how much changing in the mix later on. But I think the final result captured the feeling of Pollock at work. When my grandson, who was eleven or twelve at the time, saw the film at the Museum of Modern Art, he said, perspicaciously, "the music kind of goes with the painting." And it does.

Everybody involved in the film was paid with a Pollock drawing. Morty got one, Namuth and Falkenburg each got one. But I never got mine. My life was then so chaotic—I was running here, playing there, working as a musician and already beginning to be a writer. I just never showed up to claim it.

All in all, it was an extraordinary moment for me in music, friendship, and my artistic education.

Jackson Pollock, Untitled, 1951. Ink on handmade paper, 13 x 16 1/4 inches. Gift of the artist to Hans Namuth, 1951. PHOTO: HANS NAMUTH © ESTATE OF HANS NAMUTH.

PATTI SMITH

MAY, 2000

Hail the surface of our speech
Hail the spirit whom we greet
Hail the dance in cryptic air
Hail the heart the holy hare
Stunned and flung by muscled wrist
A stellar mound for love to lift
Tarred, jeweled and crushed like frogs
To slide afresh the bright ravine
dripping fluid, silver green
Into a cup a swirling vat
A nature spawned to anchor need
The bounty hunter sips with ease
Landing upright on two feet
Bound in leather smeared to test
A privy jazz once motionless
A rage for worth the hunter stalks
Hail the surface that he waltzed
A spattered zone entombed in glass
Where blood and motion so infused
As a painter's righteous blues
Polarized as God's refuse
Silence rant by soles of shoes

"The New SOFT LOOK"

CECIL BEATON

1951

JACKSON POLLOCK'S ABSTRACTIONS

The dazzling and curious paintings of Jackson Pollock almost always cause an intensity of feelings. The puzzled call them idiotic; the admiring call him a genius. Among the latter are some of the most astute private collectors and museum directors in the country. Last summer Pollock paintings were shown at Milan, Amsterdam, and in the American section at the Venice Biennale along with the work of John Marin, Arshile Gorky, and Willem de Kooning. Spirited and brilliant, his canvases are often nailed to the floor of his studio on Long Island; there with brush, trowel, and sometimes sticks, with drippings from paint cans, thirty-nine-year-old Jackson Pollock encrusts his interwinding skeins of paint to give that extraordinary effect known as Pollock. (Photographed at the Betty Parsons Gallery.)

"The New Soft Look," 1951. CECIL BEATON.

310

CONNIE BECKLEY

Funny, how when I look at *Number 1*,
the words that come to mind
have to do with music.
Not the usual "wall of sound" kind of idea,
but rather words that have to do with playing together
all the melodies — in their individuality — that ever were.
But how strange,
I've never actually heard or even wanted to hear
something like that.
When Cage suggested such a thing,
I happily accepted it intellectually,
but in practice I just closed my ears.
With *Number 1* I hear through my eyes,
and leave the idea to fend for itself.

A STEP AWAY FROM THEM

FRANK O'HARA

1957

It's my lunch hour, so I go
for a walk among the hum-colored
cabs. First, down the sidewalk
where laborers feed their dirty
glistening torsos sandwiches
and Coca-Cola, with yellow helmets
on. They protect them from falling
bricks, I guess. Then onto the
avenue where skirts are flipping
above heels and blow up over
grates. The sun is hot, but the
cabs stir up the air. I look
at bargains in wristwatches. There
are cats playing in sawdust.
                                On
to Times Square, where the sign
blows smoke over my head, and higher
the waterfall pours lightly. A
Negro stands in a doorway with a
toothpick, languorously agitating.
A blonde chorus girl clicks: he
smiles and rubs his chin. Everything
suddenly honks: it is 12:40 of
a Thursday.

Neon in daylight is a
great pleasure, as Edwin Denby would
write, as are light bulbs in daylight.
I stop for a cheeseburger at JULIET'S
CORNER. Giulietta Masina, wife of
Federico Fellini, *è bell' attrice.*
And chocolate malted. A lady in
foxes on such a day puts her poodle
in a cab.
  There are several Puerto
Ricans on the avenue today, which
makes it beautiful and warm. First
Bunny died, then John Latouche,
then Jackson Pollock. But is the
earth as full as life was full, of them?
And one has eaten and one walks,
past the magazines with nudes
and the posters for BULLFIGHT and
the Manhattan Storage Warehouse,
which they'll soon tear down. I
used to think they had the Armory
Show there.
  A glass of papaya juice
and back to work. My heart is in my
pocket, it is Poems by Pierre Reverdy.

ODE TO JACKSON POLLOCK

MICHAEL McCLURE

1958

Hand swinging the loops of paint—splashes—drips—
Chic lavender, *duende* black, blue and red!

Jackson Pollock my sorrow is selfish. I won't meet
you here. I see your crossings of paint!
We are all lost in the cloud of our gestures—

—the smoke we make with our arms. I cry
to my beloved too. We are lost
in lovelessness. Our sorrows
before us. Copy them in air! We
make their postures with our stance.

They grow before us.
The lean black she-wolves on altars of color.
We search our remembrance for memories
of heroic anguish. We put down
our pain as singing testimony.
Gouges, corruptions, wrinkles, held loose

in the net of our feelings and hues—
we crash into their machinery making it
as we believe. I say

314

we. I—You. You saw the brightness
of pain. Ambition. We give in to the lie
of beauty in the step of creating.
Makes lies to live in. I mean you. Held
yourself in animal suffering.
You made your history. Of Pain.

Making it real for beauty, for ambition
and power. Invented totems from teacups
and cigarettes. Put it all down
in disbelief—waiting—forcing.
Each gesture painting.—Caught on
to the method of making each motion
your speech, your love, your rack

and found yourself. Heroic—huge—burning
with your feelings. Like making money

makes the body move. Calls you to action
swirling the paint and studying the feeling

caught up in the struggle and leading it.
For the beauty of animal action
and freedom of full reward.
To see it down—and praise—and admiration
to lead, to feel yourself above all others.

NO MATTER WHAT—IT'S THERE! NO ONE

can remove it. Done in full power.
Liberty and Jackson Pollock the creator.
The mind is given credit.

You strangled
the lean wolf beloved to yourself—
Guardians of the Secret
—and found yourself the secret
spread in clouds of color

burning yourself and falling like rain

315

transmuted into grace and glory, free
of innocence

containing all, pressing experience
through yourself onto the canvas.
Pollock I know you are there! Pollock
do you hear me? !! Spoke to himself
beloved. As I speak to myself
to Pollock into the air. And fall short
of the body of the beloved hovering
always before him. Her face
not a fact, memory or experience
but there in the air
destroying confidence.
The enormous figure of her mystery

always there in trappings of reason.

Worked at his sureness. Demanding
Her place beside him. Called

from the whirls of paint, asked for
a face and shoulders to stand naked
before him to make a star.

He pulling the torn parts of her body
together
to make a perfect figure — 1951.
Assembled the lovely shape of chaos.
Seeing it bare and hideous, new
to the old eye. Stark
black and white. The perfect figure
lying in it peering from it.
And he gave her what limbs and lovely face
he could
om the squares, angles, loops, splashes, broken shapes
he saw of all with bare eye and body.

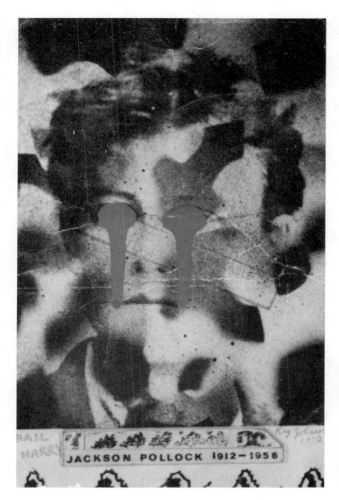

May Wilson's Rimbaud (Jackson Pollock 1912-1956), 1972. Ray Johnson.

"I'm the only painter in New York whose drips mean anything."
– Ray Johnson.

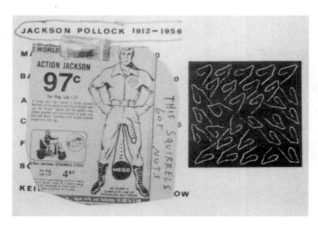

Action Jackson, 1973
Ray Johnson.

from PATERSON V

WILLIAM CARLOS WILLIAMS

—the virgin and the whore, which
most endures? the world
of the imagination most endures:

Pollock's blobs of paint squeezed out
with design!
pure from the tube. Nothing else
is real

WALK in the world
            (you can't see anything
from a car window, still less

"His spatter is masterful, but his dribbles lack conviction."

1961 Peter Arno

to William Thomas McKinley

SEVEN POLLOCK PAINTINGS

ROGER BOURLAND (1978)

Lavender Mist

Portion of the score, COURTESY OF ROGER BOURLAND.

On Jackson Pollock's INFLUENCE ON MY MUSIC

ROGER BOURLAND

APRIL 20, 2000

Fᴿᴼᴹ 1977 to 1983 I composed a number of works inspired by paintings. My favorite, and the one which has been played around the world, is *Seven Pollock Paintings*. It was influenced by a number of people. Composer Donald Martino composed his *Seven Pious Pieces* using the 12-tone technique to compose a tonal work, and was also instrumental in introducing me to new 7, 8, 9, 10, and 11 note modes, modes which I used in *7PP*. The dionysian energy of two of my other teachers, Les Thimmig (a saxophonist/composer who grew up with black jazz musicians in Chicago) and William Thomas McKinley (the wild and prolific composer on the faculty of New England Conservatory) infused their jazz-inspired music into my brain. However, it was also a time when I found myself more and more disillusioned by the avante-garde and atonal music. You can hear my flaunts with tonality in *7PP* which has actual major chords sounding: a very daring move at the time! So I decided that *7PP* would be my exorcism of modernist music and thereafter I would try to find out who I really was as a composer.

I modeled my tactics of composing the piece somewhat after Pollock. When he limited his colors, I used limited notes or modes. Using modes to compose all melodies provides a harmonic homogeneity, analogous to the way traditional classical and popular music use the major/minor scale.

I created large music paper (18" × 24"), each containing two large systems. And for each of the movements, my game plan was that I could *only* use two sheets of music paper for each movement. (The duration of the individual movements range ranges from one minute to around five minutes.

Five of them are titled after Pollock paintings; I invented titles for the other two.)

After this ground work, I began the input phase: I devoured every book, picture, slide, article, and story about Jackson Pollock that I could find. I became obsessed. I decided that I should experience what he did when he painted, and over a two month period, made fifty-some paintings using Pollock's techniques. I must admit that the experience of dancing around a canvas hurling, dripping, dropping paint, sometimes gently, sometimes violently, is a real rush. My heart pounded and I surprised myself with my unleashed demeanor. (Although I'm not an artist, I have dabbled over the years. Composer John Harbison thought that I'd be a wealthier man if I became an artist: alas, I did not heed his advice. I have recently taken up photography and have found myself gravitating to bizarre textures, which I trace back to Pollock.)

As I look at the more webbish paintings, I see a myriad of distinctive lines. Lines that imply melodic shapes. In music history, the wild lines and shapes of John Coltrane, Charlie Parker, and Eric Dolphy—to name a few—come closest to rhyming with Pollock's web of individual lines. This, in musical "interpretation," can best be served by choosing instruments that can play fast music. Hence the instrumentation: flute, clarinet, soprano saxophone, bass clarinet, tam tam (large gong), violin, viola, cello, and contrabass. In that I replace the oboe with the soprano sax, and instead of a bassoon, I use a bass clarinet, there is a definite resonance with jazz, or at the very least, an American sound quite different from the sound of a Mozart serenade.

The first (*Lavender Mist*) and third (*Eyes in the Heat*) movements of the set treat the kinship of line between Pollock's web paintings, and melodic counter point. In the first, I notate the rhythms very precisely, and in the third, the notes are to be played as fast as possible, with little breaths between the gestures, but not at all in sync with the rest of the ensemble. This was a little experiment on my part to explore the difference between a highly controlled and complicated reading of a painting, as opposed to what a more free treatment would be. In my mind, they ended up sounding quite similar.

The Wooden Horse is a piece which I musically "scanned," treating the vertical axis of the painting as pitch—low to high—and the horizontal axis as time. *Drawing 1950* was a very close melodic transcription of Pollock's spare and lyrical lines in this ink drawing. The white spaces between each of the black ink ejaculates is represented by long sustained chords. (An amusing note: the first chord is the chord of the ventilation system in the Boston Public Library, where I composed this movement. It was so imposing, I had to give in.)

For *Peacocks afraid of the color*, I invented a rather silly program: "In the beginning, peacocks were created in black and white. One day God looked down on them and decided to give them color. And when he did, they freaked out." The untitled ink drawing has a forest of black strokes and shapes that imply a forest of peacocks. Pollock then superimposes blobs of colored ink here and there on top of the web of spiky strokes. The drawing is then musically scanned from left to right. The black and white section sounds like hens pecking, and when the color blobs are encountered all hell breaks loose. People liked this one because it made them smile. My program helped give the movement a dramatic shape.

In *The Wooden Horse* and *The Deep*, I continually recycle a series of nine notes that pass from instrument to instrument. In *The Deep*, the composition is truly an emotional response to the painting and not a scan or something drawn from the shapes of line.

I titled the final movement *The Saint* (which is not Pollock's title) because the drawing that inspired it looks to me—in a Rorschach test vein—like a devout man praying with his hands clasped, in a beckoning upward pose. I saw this as an opportunity to tap into my preacher's kid mode and serve up an old Christian hymn, *How Great Thou Art* (which all of the critics referred to as a folk melody) that was played by the soprano saxophone. The harmonic progression of the piece is palindromic in its use of modes. Measures one and two use seven notes (A major), then the next two measures use eight, then the next two use nine, then ten, then eleven, then all twelve notes are evoking the chaotic webs. Symbolically it's a choir singing a hymn while outside the church murder, love, law, commerce, and the rest of reality are going on. The harmonic progression then goes backwards, and by the end of the piece we are back to "peace in the valley" and A major, and the piece ends on an A9th chord (again, very shocking and naughty in the new music world at that time!). The program for this movement has nothing to do with Pollock, but the drawing spawned a daydream that provided a scaffolding for the movement.

Pollock's work has tremendous energy, and very often huge statements are composed of individual lines, which musically, to me, evoke a kind of free jazz counterpoint. Traditional counterpoint where everyone plays precisely together seems too staid a solution. There is a very dark side of Pollock, as well as a playful side. These moods have analogues in music, and I feel I captured many of them in the piece.

It has seemed to me that one of the "diseases" of the twentieth century was that poets were only writing for other poets, painters painting for other painters, and composers forgetting their audiences and writing to impress each other. In the meantime, the audiences move on, complaining they don't understand the music, and find solace in *popular* music of all ilks, and music by dead composers.

In that *7PP* was an exorcism for me, I have not returned to this kind of musical language since that time. I received commissions from several groups in the late 1970s, half hoping they would get *7PP II*, but I was not interested in returning there yet.

WEST HOLLYWOOD, CA
APRIL 20, 2000

POEMS FOR JACKSON POLLOCK

FRANCIS V. O'CONNOR

1. Dining Out On Pollock
1978

*Written in a New Haven restaurant after a hard day editing
Jackson Pollock at the Yale University Press.*

The fish special: filet of pollock!
Overheard at the next table:
He: ". . . always threw it back . . ."
She: ". . . it's probably full of bones . . ."
They ordered lamb — a meek meat
easily fleeced, dressed, digested.

Pollock, if bitten, bit back.
He threw the symbol's surface back,
wanting to know why you *were*,
where *you* were, and *into* what —
and all that without *shit*.
Strength betrays the pose it needs. . . .

What is it with our gastronomes
that goat is not confidently consumed:
Goat steaks? Goat feet in aspic?
Burgers with melted goat cheese?
Goat bourguignon? Goat stomach,

Scotch-style: mutton-stuffed?

To lift a pollock's reaching spine
to another plate and pick about
lest sharpness lurk, lays bare a taste
for all the condiments of power.
Sliced from the bone, what sauce conceals
the latent horn within a stronger meat?

2. Sonnet for Jackson Pollock
1998

First published in "Two Methodologies for the Interpretation of Abstract Expressionism," Art Journal, *Fall 1988, p. 227.*

His brethren cozen a space to grope—
mess and measure the colored mud
till it tells. Given his rope,
he threw chance to the knowing flood.
You can read the ages of his eye
down to the weave. To enthrall
monsters is to testify—
to re-enact the primal brawl.
Unravel his skeins in space:
tease them out like DNA,
feature by feature's trace
down to the weave—where they stay
   birth's determining vote
   as spectra from young Joseph's coat.

3. Sonnet About Sets
1999

for Ed Harris

Set. n. Persons or things identified with a similar aim; theatrical scenery or a sound stage; readiness to respond to stimuli in a specific way.

The Armory Show of 1999!
All of Pollock's habitats, that fame

made filmable, planned out on a dim lot,
deftly reconstructed, antiqued, lit
to rake the familiar facts of a life's game,
betting iconographies of line
artfully intertwined—yet somehow fit
to simulate mother's old garrote.

He danced before the paintings, a charming quirk,
choreographing beats to fill each take
of himself as other—trying to refine
portrayal in a predetermined plot—
forgetting the lineage was itself an ache
to follow down to the weave's tight work.

Film set of Jackson Pollock's barn studio, ca. 1950, on the sound stage at the Bedford Armory, Brooklyn, May 1999. PHOTO HELEN A. HARRISON

TO J. P.
In Memoriam

ATRIS TUI

DATE UNKNOWN

Clumsy frailty from lavender
    lavender de tendresse
tendresse inevitable!
    to noonday children
        reappearing
            in
            forceful fusion.
   by April imprefections
     perfectly
         alive.

FRAGILE HANDS

      smearing
   into profound circle-in-squares
    of your autumns
various tuggings
     at the shoestrings
        of

WONDER.

O shimmering circle of utterance
    exhaust yourself
       on

                    grey-shrouded
                            insufficiency

            lines unalterable
                    stumbling past
                    YONDER
                    superworlds
                            worthy
                                of unending.

see!
                    chimneys with praising
                            echoing soundless
                    flames of
                            Heraclitean smoke

            Share the breath
                            atman presideth
                    with primeval meadows
                            of
            towering
                    strangeness.

                    vivid patterns of dancing light
                            revolve
                    in silent wonder
            traversing the Ominous.

            swirling eddy of emptiness
                    Yes!
            but Ah! gazing from lanterns
                            of ships crecsendoes
    the swirlings
                    vibrated, deafening the gaze
                            mocking the wilderness
                                of colour.

A PORTRAIT OF V. I. LENIN
in the Style of Jackson Pollock
(see color plate no. 8)

ART & LANGUAGE

1999

1.

A portrait of V. I. Lenin is now a thing much reduced in resonance. Lenin's was the indispensable icon of Soviet Socialist realist art. His stern and purposeful gaze is now rarely encountered. In 1979, people in the Soviet bloc and socialists in the West found it hard to avoid. While he remains an unavoidable reference point in the political history of the Twentieth century, his image is assailed (transformed) by revisions from (almost) all sides.

Images of Jackson Pollock and of Jackson Pollock's image-as-work have persisted under different circumstances. His is an image and an oeuvre which was both celebrated and put to use in the war which saw Lenin tarnished or effaced as international capital proclaimed its triumph. In the words of the song:

> Jackson Pollock was the artist of the Marshall Plan;
> He broke ice for artists when the Cold War began.

Lenin's image was conscripted to ratify Stalin's resistance to General Marshall's provisions for Europe.

Perhaps we can say—or might be expected to say—that Jackson Pollock—the superhero of a superseded modernism—carries with him the image of his vanquished political other as the second member of an ordered pair. We could also say that they are both more or less functional indices of a conflict (a field of contradiction) whose ideological and cultural fissures continue to be represented in the ruthlessly hidden contradictions of the present.

The *Portraits of V. I. Lenin in the Style of Jackson Pollock* were not originally intended to be exhibited as paintings at all. They were to be chopped up into A4 size pieces, color-xeroxed and reassembled both in the form of the portrait and, scrambled, as a large synthetic simulacrum of a Pollock. Indeed, a few of them were exhibited this way at the Van Abbemuseum, Eindhoven, in September 1980. The conditions of their original conception go naturally to mechanical reproduction. In short, the title came first. And its linguistic resonance supplied the pre-eminent motive for the project's realisation. One of the legacies of Conceptual Art was (and remains) the convention that painting had for long composed itself principally in the form of its image or reproduction. In the course of producing these reproducable simulacra a set of unforseen propositions supervened.

1) That some of them were preferable to, better than, etc., others. (The resonance of the title was no guarantee of technical—and consequently aesthetic—success.)

2) That various significant developments had occurred within and as a result of the production process which were remaindered by or invisible to the mechanical reproduction process (the various ramifications attendant on wrinkled paint, matte and shiny surfaces, silver paint, various impasto effects, etc.)

3) (Upon which (1) and (2) converge) that the power or the efficiency of the monstrous détente of Pollock and portrait was intimately connected to the capacity of the portraits to operate as paintings and not as images of paintings.

It was, as it were, necessary for these paintings to reproduce some significant aspect or modality of the aesthetic which Pollock's work exemplifies and by which it was (and is) sustained. And this directly—as a form of *oratio recta* and not *oratio obliqua*. Upon this impression (this phenomenological pay-off) depended the resonance of the monstrous détente of a "hidden" portrait of Lenin in the impossible armature of a Jackson Pollock. A portrait invested in an *image* of a Pollock readily reduces to something adjacent to an Escher-like trick—some sleight of graphic manipulation which distances the image from the aesthetic (and political etc.) implication of the Pollock itself. A portrait discovered in a more or less plausible Pollock represents a contradiction which might, for example, be a misreading or an hallucination (or etc.). With a reproduction or image, the hallucination might well be a property of the mechanically productive apparatus or a consequence of manipulative action by its operator distanced from the viewer.

Some writers have been much animated by the example of these paintings, imagining (or in any case assenting) that something aesthetic (conservative somehow) as a consequence of our entertaining the like of propositions (1)–(3). This idea is mistaken. It rests on a scrambling or confusion of the consequences of proposition (1), namely: that the title *Portrait of V. I. Lenin in the Style of Jackson Pollock* was no guarantee of artistic success, that some versions were better than others (this later observation is implied by the former as well as recording the facts of the situation), and 3), namely: that the monstrous détente which the title implies (or describes) would be better sustained if the viewer could imagine herself literally before a real-ish Pollock painting and not a reproduction. The question of preference for one version over another is likely to occur whether the works are seen as mechanically reproduced or not. In any case, there are bound to be technical (and other) questions whether a given version satisfies the import of the title or not, or is better or worse than another, or etc. The title was a *technical* prescription (a possible description) and not a label (a proper name) which could be accepted or satisfied by any old thing so long as it was dubbed that way. The matter of our reproducing a Pollock or various Pollocks in a first-order-ish way and not as photographic images was decided conceptually, i.e., in relation to the requirement that these works satisfy certain cultural and political conditions (necessary conditions of their being "aesthetic") which are encapsulated or signalled by the title.

It is a more or less ventriloqual by-product that, in order to make the whole thing "work" we had to try to make the paintings "work" as Pollock-ish paintings. Having already been cast (and we continue to be cast) between Scylla and Charybdis in the form of Adorno and Benjamin (or better or worse than them) we were not absolved of our an-aesthesia by this project. Indeed, the question of "the entry of the aesthetic" as some new and welcome indulgence or perversion is irrelevant to its intellectual and practical dynamic. The sense in which the work is or is not aesthetically driven won't be decided (and certainly not exhaustively analysed) by dramatic animadversions to the example of *Portraits of V. I. Lenin in the Style of Jackson Pollock*. If this project dramatized anything it was the realization that one's serviceable art theories (one's aesthetic(s)) are both self inflating and self-deflating—that they entail processes of self-transformation and that this often begins with illusion and deception. These are cultural and intellectual illusions: acting out of character.

It should be clear by now that these were polemical paintings. This polemical aspect is in no way inconsistent with the opportunities they offer for the "innocent" enjoyment of traditional pictorial illusions. To anyone familiar with the work of Pollock, the most noticeable aspect of these works is that they refer to his style. In fact, each painting in the series draws more or less directly on the appearance of some specific painting by Pollock. To those unfamiliar with Pollock's work however, the painting is likely to seem a meaningless or inscrutable mess — unless, that is, they successfully read the "ceremonial" icon of Lenin which the painting recomposes or reproduces or somehow contains.

2

The problems of analysis of the image commence with problems of description. These latter problems are relative to the competences of spectators. A set of four notional but conceivable spectators will give four different possible identities for the painting. The first spectator is not familiar with the style of Pollock and cannot see the picture of Lenin. For this spectator the painting is an arbitrary and virtually meaningless thing — or, at least, the painting's meaning is largely independent of its intentional character. The second spectator is familiar with the style of Pollock and cannot see the picture of Lenin. For this spectator the painting is a painting by Pollock, or it is a more or less competent, more or less interesting pastiche or fake, depending on the spectator's own competences as a connoisseur of Pollock's work, his or her disposition toward that work, and so on. The third spectator is not familiar with the style of Pollock but can see the picture of Lenin (and sees it *as* a picture of Lenin). For this spectator the painting is an ingenious or exotic or perverse portrait of Lenin. The fourth spectator is familiar with the style of Pollock and can see the picture of Lenin (and sees it *as* a picture of Lenin). For this spectator the painting is an intentionally paradoxical thing: a work which achieves an ironic stylistic détente between supposedly incompatible aesthetic and ideological worlds. It is not simply that the style of Jackson Pollock is supposed to eliminate the possibility of portraiture in general and of portraits of such as V I. Lenin is particular. More broadly, that estimation of iconic Realism which is associated with the state culture of socialism is generally seen as semantically and ideologically incompatible with those forms of priority which are accorded in Modernist culture to abstract art, to avant-gardism, to individuality and to spontaneity.

These different possible responses have the somewhat bloodless (or swatch-like) quality of philosophers' examples. They are easily animated and complicated in the mind, however, by considering how the various processes of "seeing," "seeing-as," and "seeing-in" might work in practice in front of the painting. Knowledge or ignorance of the painting's title is one obvious variable which will affect how it is seen and what it is seen as. Someone who saw the picture of a face in the painting might or might not recognize or see it as the face of Lenin. Someone who did not initially recognize the face of Lenin might still be persuaded to see the picture as a

333

Art & Language, *Picasso's Guernica in the Style of JacksonPollock,* 1980. Enamel on board, 140 1/2 x 305 inches. Museum van Hedendaagse Kunst, Ghent.

picture of him. More significantly, considerable flesh can be added to the bones of our imaginary spectators if it is allowed that different dispositions towards Pollock, or modern art, or V. I. Lenin, or the Russian Revolution are forms of *competence or incompetence* which will determine readings of such works of art as these. Thus a semantically competent reading of the portrait of Lenin will tend de facto to rule against the possibility of a semantically competent reading of the style of Pollock, and vice versa.

3

If the paintings are not simply representations of two opposed and independent systems, neither do they exemplify some ideal resolution between them. The rhetorical dilemma of Modernist culture defines the world from which these paintings emerge. But a dilemma is not such a condition as may be resolved dialectically or by thinking the solution to an equation. The culture of Modernism itself is not "overthrown" by the arguments of Realism, any more than it is transformed by the ironies of Conceptual Art or succeeded by the interests of Postmodernism. In the last instance each of these terms reduces to a form of redescription of an

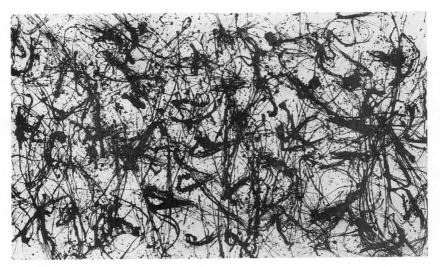

Jackson Pollock, *Number 32, 1950*. Enamel on canvas, 106 x 180 inches. Kunstsammlung Nordrhein-Westfalen, Düsseldorf. PHOTO: HANS NAMUTH © ESTATE OF HANS NAMUTH.

opposing face. In a world of dichotomies, the opposing face of the status quo is a mirror image. What is required for the resolution of dilemma is that the opposing terms be brought into collision so that the whole circumstance is changed. But the change involved is not then within the control of the individual agent. Action in the face of dilemma involves commitment to a more-or-less unpredictable outcome.

The representational materials of the Lenin–Pollock paintings are organized into an allegory of collision. The mythology of individual risk attached to Modernist painting is most compellingly associated with the style of Pollock, while the mythology of historical risk associated with class struggle is a component in the aura of Lenin. To paint the *Portrait of V. I. Lenin in the Style of Jackson Pollock* was to force these incommensurable mythologies into momentary synchronic coexistence upon a single surface.

4

One of the last works "in the style of Jackson Pollock" was *Picasso's Guernica in the Style of Jackson Pollock*. Here is a monstrous clash of two culturally and artistically asymptotic things. The politically charged icon which commemorates the Guernica atrocity is rendered in the style of that over which it exercised great influence: Jackson Pollock's *Number 32*. That is to say, *Guernica* is rendered in the style of that to which it is *genetically* connected.

LISTENING TO POLLOCK:
Scoring the Film *Jackson Pollock: Portrait*

ROGER TRÉFOUSSE

MAY 2000

WHEN the director Amanda Pope asked me to write the music for her PBS film, *Jackson Pollock: Portrait,* I was probably as nervous as Pollock had been when asked to create his huge mural for Peggy Guggeheim's front hallway. This would be a very different task from my work on other films. Normally, after looking at a film, I would write some music and then listen to how it related to the aims and dramatic vision of the director. After more discussion, and, usually, several more musical sketches, we'd reach a common ground between our ideas and I'd go to work on the score.

In this case, however, there was another presence, that of the artist himself. Most of the music for this film would accompany images of Pollock's painting, and I wanted to come up with a musical response to the painting before even looking at the film. I had a copy of the opulent catalogue from the Pollock show at the Beaubourg and began looking at it carefully.

Now I began to see a way to connect musically with the full range of Pollock's work. While I had no wish to mimic the canvases in any literal sense, I wanted to create a music for these paintings that would closely mirror their gesture and passion. I had seen the 1950 Hans Namuth film of Pollock painting, with its score by Pollock's contemporary, the composer Morton Feldman. Like Pollock, Feldman was a pioneer in the kind of abstract thinking that burst forth in the 1940s and 1950s in New York. Feldman's music has an astounding intensity of line, something it shares with Pollock, but I felt that the relation between the two artists stopped there. Feldman's music for the film, like all of his work, is spare, quiet, delicate in the extreme, while Pollock's work is dense, made from huge, sweeping gesture, and overlapping, conflicting thought.

Example 1: Autumn Rhythm (meas. 1-11)

(Opening Credits from the film *Jackson Pollock: Portrait*)

Roger Tréfousse

"Autmun Rhythm," measures 1-11 Roger Tréfousse.

I wrote a piece full of counterpoint and energy and sweep, with an underlying sense of conflict. Different themes and emotions come together in a whole, but never quite mesh, an underlying tension holding them together and at the same time struggling to break them apart. Listening to my rendition of the piece (on piano at this point), Amanda was unhappy with its effect. She felt that Pollock's work was still fairly inaccessible to a general audience, and wanted the music to stress the lyrical, gorgeous quality of his work.

This brought me up short. Weeks of studying and thinking about Pollock's art had me convinced that I had created a music that honestly reflected the paintings, and I wasn't sure that I could change my thinking so radically. But I wasn't only writing music about a Pollock painting. The task at hand was composing a score which also supported the director's ideas about the artist and his work.

The crucial piece of music was the opening credits, a montage of Pollock's all-over paintings. I had spent time on the east end of Long Island, where I now live, where Pollock painted these breakthrough canvases, and there was no question in my mind that that landscape, the light and the colors, were reflected in these paintings. Looking out over Accabonac creek, with the spring trees in bloom and the intense blue sky above them, it was certainly possible to see these canvases almost as a kind of abstract impressionism. For the opening credits, at least, the darker, more ambiguous aspect could be put aside.

Example 2: Portrait and a Dream (meas. 1-21)

(Black and White Paintings Montage from the film *Jackson Pollock: Portrait*)

Roger Tréfousse

"Portrait and a Dream," measures 1-21 Roger Tréfousse.

I kept the energy and dense counterpoint of my earlier effort, but added a clearer tonal center, and made the orchestration and the texture of the music glitter with a sense of light and color that the landscape, and the paintings, certainly possess. (see Example 1)

My original sketches came into the film as well, as accompaniment to the black and white paintings, Pollock's last important work before he began the downward spiral to the tragic end of his life in 1956. (see Example 2) These paintings still possess a strong, lyrical energy, but it is here where one most strongly feels the existential despair as well. The all-over paintings are much more optimistic, and deserved a music which reflected that life-affirming energy.

I later made a suite of my music from the film, which has become one of my most-performed works. Both the pieces I've discussed are incorporated in the suite, reflecting Pollock's energy and vision in all its shades of light and darkness.

from ARNESON and POLLOCK

ANDREA MILLER-KELLER

1992

IN an ongoing series begun in 1982, Robert Arneson has explored the complex and potent meanings of the life, the death, the art, and the myth of Jackson Pollock in numerous large-scale sculptures made of ceramic, bronze and wood, as well as paintings and drawings. Arneson has made more than sixty works based on Pollock and has brought an energy and concentration to this subject that mirrors the intensity of Pollock's own oeuvre.

Pollock's eager embrace of chance, combined with this highly developed control of the process, was an essential component of his famous drip technique of applying paint from a standing position to the canvas laid on the floor. Arneson has also welcomed chance and improvisation into his methodology. For instance, celebrating the fact that clay itself is an unpredictable medium, Arneson has said that he likes to "take the difficulties and exploit them. That's why . . . I prefer ceramics. Because there's always that *chance*. Potters always call the kiln the 'kiln god.' The element of chance takes over and you're no longer in control."

Arneson's profound admiration for Jackson Pollock informs his frequent return to the artist as a rich topic of inquiry. In Pollock, he has found the convergence of a broad range of significant issues. For Arneson, Pollock is a gifted genius of towering importance whose personality and life embodied the difficulty of being an artist. Alienated from conventional society, Pollock was alternately scorned and idealized. Proudly but painfully, he stood his ground as an outsider because he could not do otherwise. Often he was poised precariously on the edge of sanity. It is out of respect for Pollock that Arneson includes this turmoil in his portraits.

In the opinion of art critic Donald Kuspit, "Arneson's identification with Pollock recovers the sense of Pollock as victim, as disturbed, even deeply pathological—which is the only way to be authentic in the modern world. For Arneson, Pollock represents the socially rejected, isolated individual in American life . . . Pollock's life, like that of van Gogh, was in itself 'political'—both artists were, in Artaud's phrase, 'suicided by society'."

Jackson Pollock,
Cathedral, 1947. Oil
on canvas, 75 x 35
inches. Dallas
Museum of Fine Arts,
gift of Mr. And Mrs.
Bernard J. Reis. PHOTO:
OLIVER BAKER. © THE
POLLOCK-KRASNER
FOUNDATION, INC./ ARS.

Robert Arneson, *Cathedral Tower*, 1986. Cerqamic, 86 3/4 x 20 x 20 inches.
PHOTO: MICHELE MAIER. © ESTATE OF ROBERT ARNESON/ LICENSED BY VAGA, NEW YORK, NY.

Victor Raphael, *One Gesture of the Heart*, Polaroid photographs, 1986. COURTESY OF THE ARTIST.

ONE GESTURE OF THE HEART;
A Tribute to Jackson Pollock

VICTOR RAPHAEL

YEAR COMPLETED: 1986

My role in the creation of the work: Director, performer, co-producer
Production credits: Produced by: Ben Adams and Victor Raphael
Directed and performed by: Victor Raphael
Camera: Ben Adams
Editing: Theadore Levy
Production Assistance: Bruce Fier
Music by: The Red Onion Jazz Babies "Cake Walk Babies"
Poem by: Dylan Thomas "This Side of the Truth"
Jackson Pollock's last painting "Scent" courtesy of Marcia S. Weisman

Length of full work: Two minutes

Brief remarks: I was always facinated by Jackson Pollock's painting tec-
nique and the way he dealt with pictorial space. However, it was my strong
physical resemblance to the artist that led me to investigate the man
behind the artwork. This video is the culmination of several months of
research on Pollock, including three months at the Archives of American
Art going though the artist's own records and letters, with permission from
the artist's estate. As part of this research I visited Pollock's home and studio in Springs, Long Island. Playing Pollock gave me the opportunity to
"get inside his skin" and see things from his point of view. I wanted to separate the man from the myth. This two minute video is neither narrative
nor documentary but a tribute to the man and his struggles as an artist.

NEW LOOK AND NEWER LOOK:
The Commutation of Jackson Pollock
by Cecil Beaton and Mike Bidlo

RICHARD MARTIN

MARCH, 1988

"THE best way out," said Robert Frost, "is always through." A concept can be fulfilled in a simple expression of its idea and can be corroborated in that idea's reversible truth. The pertinence of Jackson Pollock's all-over paintings to the possibilities of fashion is proved once and is made evident once again.

The March 1951 issue of *Vogue* featured Cecil Beaton's photographs for an article on "The New Soft Look" in which models were posed wearing the new designs in front of the paintings shown at the Betty Parsons Gallery in November 1950.[1] There, the large Pollock paintings had assumed mural-like aspects as they seemed to cover every surface, even to the expediency of having at least one painting on its side in order to be accommodated with the space. Beaton realized the Pollock paintings in their expression of new American values and in their potential to provide a background for the clothing. That it may seem all but sacrilege to subordinate arguably the most important exhibition of its time to mere atmosphere for what proved to be quite inconsequential clothing is not to misprize Beaton's audacity but rather to recognize its authenticity. Later in lamenting in *The Glass of Fashion* (1954) that the glitter of fashion had vanished by the postwar years, Beaton conceived an alliance that could give sustained "glitter" to fashion. His choice was not, however, an abstract conception but one of particular stylistic imagination in realizing that the Pollock environment had the relation to the wall and the tradition of paint-

[1]See my " 'The New Soft Look': Jackson Pollock, Cecil Beaton, and American Fashion in 1951," *Dress*, 1981, pp. 1–8. (See color plate no. 6)

ing to the wall that permitted it to be as a mural to the designs presented in front of it, being as it were a kind of stage. Further, the inevitable recognition that was so difficult for others to see that the suppression of representation in the work of art was not a faculty of the work but an enterprise of the aesthetic, Beaton gave back an element of representation in allowing the work to be the two-dimensional environment for the tableau in fashion that he presents in front of the paintings. The splendidly brisk and lacy lines of the paintings, including *Autumn Rhythm*, become the ancillary animation of the soft flow of the dresses presented in the *Vogue* feature.

Beaton perceives the setting independent of the history of art. Perhaps the significant event of the history of art that this particular show represents is nothing other than coincidence to Beaton. If there is any conscious comprehension of the Pollock paintings, it is in the terms of an art director and stylist, not in reference to art history and art criticism. Why, then, does it happen as if still by coincidence that a stylist's selection is the same as history's elect moment? Surely there are profound relationships here, even if as much in synecdoche as Pollock's paintings are synecdochal ciphers and strategies for expression. Beaton knew of the parallels between art and fashion in his own training and the fashion-world affirmations of Vertes, Dali, and others. Yet, Pollock's work would not likely have stood in suite with frivolous masters of descriptive art and of fashion's finesse. The Pollock paintings clearly stood in 1950–51 outside of the matrix of fashion and yet were sufficiently convincing to Beaton to embrace them as fashion's cohort. Thus, Beaton understood the nature of the Pollock paintings to the extent that he realized what in an Ortega y Gasset meaning of dehumanization vis-à-vis nonrepresentational art could be addressed by the increment of fashion, clothing the nonhuman with form and giving form to dress as the abstraction intermediary between the figure and art. Similarly, Beaton also demonstrated that the properties of modernist painting readily affiliated with these Pollock paintings could be made to be the appropriate terms of a modern fashion as well. The soft tactility, the celebration of pattern in its complicated senses, and the ligature between textile sensibility and the painting permitted fashion and art to become one in Beaton's photographs. His synthesis is not entirely a happy one in the retrospect of history, so important are the Pollocks and so heavy is his own burden of history, but his concept is a sympathetic one.

Moreover, Beaton's postulation for Pollock is achieved in Mike Bidlo's 1982 Jackson Pollock wardrobe, including a dress for Gracie Mansion and a Pollock suit.[2] Whereas Beaton maintained the painting on the wall and placed the dress in its midst, Bidlo seizes the painting to be the clothes

---

[2]This essay is occasioned by Mike Bidlo's donation of *Pollock Suit* (1982) to the Edward C. Blum Design Laboratory, Fashion Institute of Technology in January 1982

Art dealer Gracie Mansion in a dress painted by Mike Bidlo. St. Marks Place, New York, October 1982. PHOTO: © GARY AZON.

with the aplomb of Scarlet O'Hara transmogrifying drapes into dress. Beaton's audacity had stopped at transformation and had remained only an act of juxtaposition or of imposition. Bidlo's act is more audacious and, in a significant way, more important. In transforming the painting to be the garment, Bidlo requires us to see the actual transformation that we would heretofore only be able to suppose. The all-over effect has become the painterly appearance of the dress in the same manner that Francesc Torres has made us see in *Field of Action* (1982) the character of Action painting as an aggressive paramilitary camouflage. In either case, we see the painterly convention anew on realizing its connection to a cover or concealment, and it can thereby no longer be solely associated with the "truth" of painting or modernism's authenticity but instead with the deceit and complexity of appearances.

To be sure, we would immediately assume that the form has been an inferior role in becoming an article of clothing. The painting is inevitably superior to fashion. Indeed, that Beaton leaves the Pollock exhibition unscathed and unchanged is testimony to painting's abiding power even as models and fashion pass across its screen. But Bidlo requires us to take a more challenging look at the painting as if its ideas could be taken out of painting and transferred to other, patently inferior, media. Are these attributes of painting, so manifest as Pollock's signature style, endemically the properties of painting as a high art if they can be readily lifted off the wall, or appropriated, to the enterprise of making clothes? The broad interval from Madison Avenue to Seventh Avenue would seem to be traversed, if not traduced, by the gesture.

The Wildean admonition that one should either be a work of art or wear a work of art may initially be dismissed as hyperbole and wit, but its lesson may be more than mere dandyism for the century that brings new definitions to art to consider taking the work of art off the walls and to clothe oneself not only in its concepts but in the painting itself. In this possibility, the painting is no longer merely the artificial horizon for the figure who stands before the painting, whether as model or actor on a stage with a backdrop designed as a flat surface by an artist. Indeed, there is a Pygmalionism for painting in allowing the painting to realize its role as surface, but also to touch the skin and to encase the observer. In this role, painting is not passive; it can be appropriated into an active role, seen, being seen, and incapable of being seen because it is ultimately a part of what we are as we see paintings. Bidlo neither denies nor denigrates, except in the most limited sense, the Pollock painting in his metamorphosis from art to apparel. Beaton had, after all, known by stylist's intuition that the conversion was possible and perhaps even necessary. Mike Bidlo gives action to ideas inherent in painting and gives a representational presence to art as it functions in the interstice between fashion and art. Bidlo's is a rarefied hybrid of ideas about art and fashion, sanctioned by the nature of the painting concerned and by the history of its imagery, but founded ultimately in the artist's consistent conviction that the art of the past continues to thrive in its reanimation and reexamination.[3]

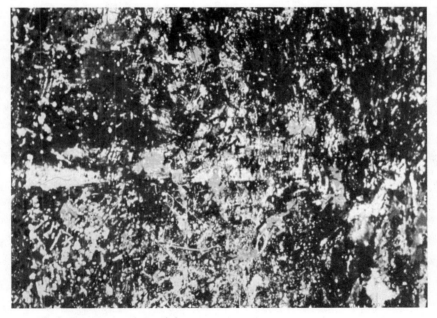

Not Pollock, 1994-95 Warren Neidich

3. I am as always, indebted to Harold Koda for suggestions and ideas about art and fashion that find their way into this essay.

"Jackson Pollock's Mother," Benno Friedman 1989. © THE PUSH PIN GROUP.

Holding a Crow With Alchemy,
1994-95 Warren Neidich. Installation
Photographs, Steffany Martz Gallery,
New York, July 1996.
COURTESY OF THE ARTIST.

"Lee and Jackson Pollock
and Krasner," 1996

Not Pollock
Installation,
1996

EXCERPTS FROM NUMBER ONE:
A Pollock Painting

ADAM SWARTZ, RICHARD SIMULCIK, JR., AND KEVIN DEL AGUILA

1997

First performed in NYC at Synchronicity Space, 1997
Produced by ONE theater group
Directed by Kevin Del Aguila
Written by Adam Swartz, Richard Simulcik, Jr., and Kevin Del Aguila
Set Design by Daniele Perna
Lighting Design by Andrew Billiau
The Stage Manager was Robert Shannon

THE CAST WAS AS FOLLOWS:

Jackson Pollock	Richard Simulcik Jr.
Lee Krasner	Sheila Murphy
Roy Pollock, Sande Pollock, Willem de Kooning,	
Hans Hofmann, Clement Greenberg	Adam Swartz
Stella Pollock, Peggy Guggenheim, Beatrice	Wendy Fencsak
Thomas Hart Benton, J. Krishnamurti, Piet Mondrian,	
Ben Heller, Man #1, Man #2	Kevin Del Aguila

1936, the Bowery, New York City, JACKSON is lying drunk on the street. The sounds of the city surround him—cars and sirens far off. JACKSON stares upward intently, studying something in the sky.

J. P.

You moon . . . you goddamned moon . . .

Enter SANFORD, JACKSON'S brother, with whom he shares an apartment at 46 East 8th Street.

SANDE

Shoulda fuckin' known.

J. P.

How ya doin' Sande?

SANDE

You know, I've been all over town looking for you? Shouldn't have wasted my time, shoulda come straight down here.

J. P.

Look at that moon, Sande, look at that moon . . . always following me . . . goddamned thing . . .

SANDE

Jackson, you all right?

J. P.

M'alright, Sande. Just fine.

SANDE

Yeah, you don't look so fine. Do you know where you are?

J. P.

What—now?

SANDE

Right now.

J. P.

I know where I am.

SANDE

Where's that?

Sheila Murphy as Lee; Richard Simulcik, Jr. as Jackson.

J. P.

I'm home, Sande.

SANDE

This ain't home. This is the Bowery.

J. P.

It's where I belong.

SANDE

Bullshit.

J. P.

It's the truth . . . not so bad, really, being a bum . . . they're free, aren't they? That's more than most people can say.

SANDE

Bullshit—you don't belong down here, now come on, I'm taking you home.

J. P.

Have a drink with me, Sande.

SANDE

No. No more drinking for you tonight. We're going home. I want to talk to you—

J. P.

No, no, no—can't go home yet. Gotta get me some fuckin' first. Need to get fucked.

SANDE

You know what you need to do? You need to tell me where you've been all night—that's what you need to do.

J. P.

I'm gonna fuck the world.

SANDE

Are you listening to me? I asked you a question.

J. P.

Doesn't matter . . .

SANDE

I'm gonna ask you one more time . . .

J. P.

I been everywhere!

SANDE

quietly

That include Gramercy Park?

Beat.

Or how about George's Tavern? Been by there, lately?

J. P.

Come on! Have a drink with me!

SANDE

Jackson, stop bullshitting me—this is important.

J. P.

Just leave me alone.

SANDE

Leave you alone? Leave you alone? I wish I could do just that. Because I am sick of chasing you around the city, taking care of you like some kind of a baby—

J. P.

Fuck you, Sande.

SANDE

What did you say to me?

L to R Sheila Murphy, Richard Simulcik, Jr., and Adam Swartz as Clement Greenberg.

J. P.

Get the fuck away from me—
>SANDE *rushes* JACKSON, *grabs him by the collar,*
>*punches him in the body, slaps him across his face.*

SANDE

You think you're tough now? Huh? Talking like a big man? Boy, I'll slap you up and down this fucking street! This is the third night this week alone I got to come down and get you out of the fucking gutter. You go off for days and nobody knows where you are or who the fuck you're with. You think I need this? I got a wife at home worried sick about me *and* you. I'm out here trying to help you out, you *selfish little shit,* and you don't even give a fuck! (*He throws* JACKSON *down one last time and releases him. Beat*) Meanwhile, I can't even have a drink at a bar—I got a couple of queers coming up and asking me where my little brother is—

J. P.

That don't matter . . .

355

SANDE

It does matter! I don't know where you've been or what you've been doing. All I know is that you drink yourself sick and disappear for days on end. I mean goddamnit, Jackson!—*Pause. JACKSON is silent, holding his face where SANDE slapped him.*

Look, it probably doesn't matter. I'm just—I want you to watch yourself. Watch what you're doing. Watch some of the characters you hang out with. Especially when you're all tight like now. I can't . . . I'm not always gonna be around to come and get you. Jesus, look around you. Why are you doing this? Why can't you just . . . I mean get yourself a girl and start settling down. I mean, what are you looking for?

J. P.

I don't know.

SANDE

Beat. SANDE takes the bottle, swigs.
I guess this is how you talk to the moon, huh?

J. P.

It's different here . . . Not like when we were kids. Remember? Out West?

SANDE

I remember. Long time ago.

J. P.

That moon was something . . . like you could reach out across the Grand Canyon and touch it.

SANDE

I remember.

J. P.

How many summers did we go out there, Sande? I don't even remember—

SANDE

Five, six summers, maybe.

J. P.

You know, when I used to look at the moon, then, I used to wonder if, out there, Dad was looking too. Like if we were looking at the same thing, it was almost like we were in the same place.
Pause. SANDE is silent.
You know he never wanted us around him, you know that don't you?

SANDE

Groans

Leave it alone, Jack.

J. P.

It's true—how come he always worked on different teams—never the same as us. All those summers and he never spent more than a couple of days with us . . . never.

SANDE

I don't give a shit, and neither should you. This is New York, and it doesn't have anything to do with that. He got his wish . . . worked himself to death. All those years of playing cowboy out in some desert . . . That was him. Not us. So just leave it be.

J. P.

He always thought I was bum. Maybe he was right.

SANDE

He was wrong.

J. P.

Sande . . . don't be mad at me, please.

SANDE

I'm not mad at you.

J. P.

I just don't know what to do. Can't draw. Can't paint. Can't do shit.

SANDE

That's bullshit, and you know it.

J. P.

I just . . . it hurts. I don't know what to do.

SANDE

You're gonna be fine, you hear me?

J. P.

Dad . . . was right. This is where I belong. In the Bowery with all the other bums.

SANDE

Listen to me . . . you don't belong here. You're better than this. I know you're having trouble, but you're gonna be all right, Jackson, I know you are. You're my brother, and I believe in you.

Blackout.
1942. JACKSON's 8th Street apartment/studio. LEE enters, tries to straighten up a bit. A knock on the door.

LEE

That's probably him—you okay? Don't be nervous, it'll be fine.
LEE opens the door and in steps HANS HOFMANN, an older man carrying himself proudly despite the fact that he is breathing heavily from the walk upstairs.

LEE

Hello! Thank you so much for coming, Hans. It really means a lot to me. Jackson? This is Hans Hofmann.
HOFMANN, slightly out of breath, shakes hands with JACKSON. He speaks with a heavy German accent.

HOFFMAN

Quite a walk up those stairs. What is that, five flights?

J. P

Warms you up in the winter time.

HOFMANN

I'm sure it does. Well then . . . (*he begins to take in the room, his expression slowly revealing a subtle horror, if not disgust.*) This—this is your *studio?* JACKSON *is silent.*

HOFMANN

mumbling to himself

Complete disorder, no cleanliness . . . how does one work in such conditions?

J. P

To LEE:

I thought he was here to look at paintings.

LEE

It's all right, don't worry—

HOFMANN

MY God!
(*Pause. LEE and JACKSON look over at HOFMANN, who slowly picks up a brush that has been fused a palette by dried paint. He holds it up, studying it with a look of horror, then turns towards JACKSON*). You know with this, you could kill a man!

LEE

Trying to interrupt.

Hans—

J. P

snapping to HOFMANN

That's the point, isn't it?

HOFMANN

Depends how you use it—

LEE

Hans, it's just a different environment than what you're used to. He's just starting out . . .

J. P

Interrupting

Are we gonna look at paintings or what?

HOFMANN

Drops the brush & palette, wipes his hands

Yah. The paintings.

JACKSON *solemnly pulls out his canvasses and lines them up.* HOFFMAN, *followed closely by* LEE, *begins to study each work,* JACKSON *fades back silent, watching nervously. Awkward pause.*

LEE

Very strong tension here . . . don't you think, Hans?

HOFMANN

Yah . . . this one here seems to have the beginnings of a good push-pull going . . . How long have you been painting abstractions?

J. P

Couple of years now.

HOFMANN

MmmHmm. Well. You've got some good basics. Your picture plane is generally flat—that's good. But many times the feeling of a certain color is overwhelming the balance of the surface tensions. Here, for example, you seem to have gotten carried away in a moment that ultimately disrupted the overall feel of the painting. Do you see what I mean? Right here? (*Pause, surveying*) Yah. A good beginning. Overall, though, it seems you work a bit too much from the heart. I suggest working more from nature.

J. P

You suggest working more from nature? I *am* nature.

HOFMANN

Oh? Is that right? So you have within you all the different elements—color, line, texture—that create the delicate balance of a landscape? You are a delicate balance of light and dark? You are a source of perfect equilibrium? Because if that is so, I do not see that occurring in your work.

360

J. P

I mean that I'm a man, and there are things inside of me much bigger and much more important than trees and sky.

HOFMANN

Don't confuse your emotions with technique, that will get you nowhere.

J. P.

I work from the inside, from what I feel.

HOFMANN

But whatever it is you're feeling, it seems to be making you miss the point of modern art.

LEE

Hans, surely an artist needs passion. That's all that Jackson's saying—

HOFMANN

Of course! Passion is vital! The passion to create something out of nothing. To touch a canvas that is blank and make the perfect picture—

J. P

Never mind modern art—what about the modern *age*—

HOFMANN

What about it?

J. P

They're making bombs that obliterate entire cities. The world right now, the future is so fucked up nobody knows what's going to happen. Things are not in balance—*we* are not in balance. That's where my art comes from.

HOFMANN

We're talking about painting. About the fundamental questions that face the modern painter. The world is on the brink of chaos. Fine. That doesn't change the challenge of standing in front of a blank canvas, having rejected the cheap illusions of the Renaissance painters. That doesn't change the fact that a painter still has to grapple, now, more so than ever before, with the limitations of his medium. He has to go even further than that and *embrace* those limitations. He must embrace the flatness of the canvass, the . . . how do you say . . . inert nature of colors, of paint. Do you understand? So you *feel*. You want to *express*. Good. Then shout! Dance! But if you want to *paint*, if you want to be a *painter*. Then pick up the mantle left for you from all the masters before. Deal with the problems that confront the modern painter everytime he steps before a blank sur-face. Your emotions will put a hole right in the middle of your work—they will swallow your paintings up. To paint a successful picture, you must learn to deal with the different tensions that exist within the plane. You must learn to strive for equilibrium. That's what exists in a Matisse, in a Picasso. That's what I teach.

J. P.

None of that matters if you don't paint from what counts. If you don't come from the the right place.

HOFMANN

The only place that exists is the surface of the picture. That's it. It's not metaphysics, or mysticism. It's painting.

J. P

I'm *talking* about painting! But I'm talking about a painting that's con-nected to something bigger. I'm talking about a man facing his emotions in a world that's gone completely insane.

HOFMANN

Still, it's the craft, the skill that's important. Otherwise you might as well be a caveman, or a cartoonist. *I'm* what's important. The artist. If that means I paint like a caveman. So be it. So long s it comes from me.

HOFMANN

That type of self-absorption is completely wrongheaded. You begin with emotions, with the passion to create. But you must end with a finished picture. And how will you know whether it's finished or not?

LEE

But sometimes you just *know*, don't you?

362

HOFMANN

Women's intuition aside—you know when a painting is done when it has arrived at a point of equilibrium. How can you know whether one emotion is better than another? You can't. But a painting is art. And art is a finished product. You work from inside and you will continually repeat yourself—you will never get out of your own emotional cycles. You will be forced to imitate yourself as your source runs dry.

JACKSON *is silent. The tension in the air is thick.*

LEE

But, Hans. He's got a good start, right? Maybe he could sit in—

J. P

Your theories don't interest me, Hofmann! Put up or shut up—Let's see your work. You see me, you've seen what I'm about. Now let's see *you.* Because right now I'm am fucking tired of all this bullshit.

HOFMANN

I don't have to show you anything. I've been painting since before you could walk. I've studied with Matisse—

J. P

Let's see 'em!

HOFMANN

—and you're just a young upstart whose feelings are hurt. Not one ounce of humility—

J. P.

Right now, let's go.

HOFMANN

You go to Paris, you learn from the masters, you see what art is about, *then* you come back and talk art with me—

J. P.

Let Paris come to *me.*

Pause. The two glare at each other.

I won't be drawn into this. You have flaws in your painting, Mr. Pollock. Either fix them or don't. You wanted an opinion on your work; I gave you one. Good day. Lee, I'll see you in class.
Exit HOFMANN.
Pause. LEE is looking at JACKSON.

J. P.

Like a young child, muttering to himself, pacing.

Yeah . . . good riddance . . . fucking teachers . . . can't teach art . . .

LEE recovers from what she just saw a few minutes ago and whirls on JACKSON.

LEE

You mind explaining what the hell that was all about?

J. P.

Don't bring any more teachers around here, you hear me? I don't need them.

LEE

You arrogant son of a bitch. I can't believe you just did that.

J. P

Me?

LEE

You!

J. P

What about *him?*

LEE

Oh come off it. Just stop it right now! That was Hans Hofmann. He doesn't just come to anyone's studio, you know—

J. P

—well he better not come around here anymore—

LEE

—And you acted like a fool! Like a little child! You can't take even the smallest criticism from someone who can help you out!

J. P.

I don't need any help.

LEE

Oh yes you do! I don't care how talented you are—if you don't start listening, you'll never be the painter you can be.

J. P

Bullshit.

LEE

It's no bullshit and you know it! I know what I'm talking about!

J. P

Bullshit—who else is there de Kooning? Gorky? I can beat them both.

LEE

There—what you just said. *That's* my point. You're groping for the wrong things, looking at the wrong people. You want to be the greatest painter of your generation? Then you had better set your sights on the right target! You want to be the best, you have to go *after* the best. And that's Picasso. Picasso, Jackson. But before you can beat him you have to learn what he's about. And Hans *knows* Picasso. Why else did you think I brought him here? But no, you couldn't listen, you won't see what he's trying to show you! And if you're too stubborn to see, then you'll spend of your life hearing all about how great de Kooning is, you can be sure of that!

J. P

I don't need any theories! I heard this a million times!

365

LEE

Theories? I'm not talking theory, I'm talking about the rules of the game, (*In a quick move. LEE grabs a brush and spins the nearest canvas towards JACKSON*). You are a painter (*she points towards the painting*), this is your medium. (*She points at all four sides*) Four sides, flat; here, here, here, and here—it's right in front of you!

    This time, LEE's brush actually touches the painting. Both go silent.

J. P

You want to work on the fucking thing?

LEE

Jackson, I'm sorry, I didn't mean—

J. P

You touch that painting, you're touching me.
Pause. A knocking on the door.

LEE

Come in.

    The door opens and HANS HOFMANN enters. He can sense the tension and is a bit sheepish at first.

HOFMANN

I uh, forgot my hat.

        JACKSON can take no more and exits.

HOFMANN

Interesting man, to say the least. Like an automobile, no? Lots of energy, you know? But along with that, a lot of noise and exhaustion.

LEE

What are you saying, Hans.

HOFMANN

    Shrugs

Big American automobile. All that power, one could be swept away. Lee, you are my best student. You are already one of the foremost avant-garde painters of this generation. If you stay with your work, you will make quite an important contribution to modern art. You will. But that man, no matter how interesting he may be—

LEE

That man is a genius, Hans.

HOFMANN

Pause.
You know, women painters are by nature much better than men. It's true. But then, when the woman marries, then she grows weaker while the man, he grows stronger. (*Pause. He smiles, fingers his hat.*) Well. The old man has got his hat back. And he has rested from that awful walk up those stairs—twice in one day, now. And he will leave. (*Beat*) Come to class tomorrow, Lee. Paint. And after, we will talk.

LEE

smiles back.
We'll see.

Exit HANS. Blackout.
1946 Springs, Long Island. Sounds of banging, punctuated by occasional grunts and curses. LEE is in the front room, on the telephone.

LEE

Hello? Hello. Yes—I'm looking for someone who can install indoor plumbing. Mmmhmmm . . . Well, is Jimmy there now? Mmm . . . I see . . .
    JACKSON emerges holding a small hammer. He crosses from one side to the other, comes back with a sledgehammer and exits out the other side. The banging grows louder.
Well does any one know where this Jimmy is? So no one else there knows anything at all about making appointments, is that what you're telling me . . .
    the banging stops

J. P

offstage
Oww! Jesus Christ Sonofabitch!
    the banging resumes even louder.

367

LEE

. . . Excuse me, hold on for one second: (*covers phone*) Jackson! What are you doing back there? I'm on the phone—Listen, I don't know how you handle your business, but—oh, he's there? Just walked in. Terrific.
(*Enter JACKSON again*)

LEE

These people are just unbelievable. Looks like we're going to have to wait on the plumbing.

J. P

What?

LEE

We're going to have to keep using that damn outhouse.

J. P

Fuck. You think Picasso shits outside?
starts to exit

LEE

You want to talk to them?

J. P

I'll fix it myself

exit, JACKSON.

LEE

calling after him
You will do nothing of—Oh, hi . . . you must be Jimmy. I'm Mrs. Pollock down on Fireplace Road . . . yes, the old Quinn place . . . yes, the city people. I am trying to get someone out here who can do indoor plumbing, and I was told by your—well whoever answered the phone told me that you are . . . (*LEE pauses, her eyes looking up towards the ceiling*) Oh my god. Jimmy, I'm going to call you back. (*She hangs up*). JACKSON! What the hell are you doing back there?

                          J. P

                         offstage

What?

                          LEE

Jackson you get out here this instant!
                enter JACKSON, holding the sledgehammer

                          J. P

What?

                          LEE

                    Points at the ceiling

Look.

                          J. P.

                    follows her pointing

What?

                          LEE

The ceiling.

                          J. P

The ceiling.

                          LEE

That ceiling of our new house is sagging.

                          J. P

                    squints, then shrugs

Maybe it's always been that way.

                          LEE

The hell it has, look at it! That can't be safe.

                          J. P.

Well, I'll be done tearing out the partitions tomorrow and then I'll see
about that ceiling—

Done doing what?

Tearing out those walls back there.

You will not tear out another wall before you call somebody to have a look at *that*. It looks like the whole second floor is about to cave in.
(*Pause. JACKSON looks again, as seeing for the first time.*)
Jackson, do you have any idea what you're doing, knocking out those walls?

What the hell, do I know—well—shit, yeah I know what I'm doing. Gonna get us a lot more space in this house—

Starts to laugh
Do you have any idea what you're doing to the *structure* of this house? Well, handyman? Do you?

Course I know what I'm doing—opening this house up, make the god-damned place *livable*—shit, if I wasn't a painter I could work re-doing houses—fixing things up—I'd show these locals, these Bonackers a little carpentry—I can do it good as they can, do it in "finest kind."
(*LEE continues to share doubtfully, swallowing a laugh*)
What, you don't believe me? I *can*, goddamit! I can! (*Beat. JACKSON stares up at the ceiling for a beat*)
But . . . maybe we just ought to give a call to someone, just in case. *He starts to laugh.* Well what the hell do you expect? Look who I got helping me, that clown from down the road?

Who?

Old George. You know, George Loper.

LEE

Well that's not nice, calling him a clown.

J. P.

What? No, that's what he is—he was a circus clown for some twenty years or so.

LEE

A retired clown, Jack?

J. P.

That's what I'm talking about—that kind of help and it's no wonder whole second floor's about to cave in! I mean Jesus Christ! You don't understand what I got to deal with!

LEE

laughs, puts her arms around JACKSON
All right, listen. I'll start on dinner, why don't you give a call for someone to come and look at that roof. You and the clown really did a number.

J. P.

Nods with a grunt. Pause.
Lee—things are all right out here, huh?

LEE

As long the roof doesn't drop in on us—Yes, things are all right.

J. P

It's just . . . nice. To have a home.

LEE

It is.
Sounds of birds, ocean. JACKSON sits on the ground, peaceful, gazing. Enter LEE, who sits silently next to him. Without looking, JACKSON lights two cigarettes and passes one to LEE. They sit silently. The lights indicate a passing of time—from dawn to dusk to night and then fading to black.

371

1950, Sounds of an art gallery opening. Loud voices, laughter, JACK-SON, ill at ease, stands off to one side. A man approaches him.

MAN

You're Jackson Pollock, right?

J. P.

Yes, I'm Jackson Pollock.

MAN

Congratulations. This show was . . . so you just drip the paint onto the canvas, that's your method, right?

J. P.

Yes.

MAN

Interesting. Let me ask you something, if you don't mind. What do you think of, when you're creating something like that?

J. P.

When it works, I'm not really thinking about anything except the painting.

MAN

How do you know if it works?

J. P.

You just know.

MAN

How do you know when you're done?

J. P.

How do you know when you're done making love?

MAN

Laughs for a beat.

It's fascinating, you've actually found a technique spontaneous enough to express your . . .

                            J. P.

My unconscious.

                            MAN

Your unconscious. Your inner world. (*Beat.*) You think your inner world is worth knowing?

                            J. P.

What?

                            MAN

I mean, this painting is an extension of you, right?

                            J. P.

Yes, it is.

                            MAN

Congratulations. You've just destroyed painting.

                            J. P.

What are you talking about?

                            MAN

Well, you've succeeded. You've broken down the barrier between the painter and the picture. And if I have to judge a painting by the artist, then the painting is irrelevant. That's why I wanted to talk to you. I figured I go right to the source. I mean, that's what all this is about, isn't it? Isn't it all just about you?

                            J. P.

No, it's about the work.

                            MAN

Work? To tell you the truth, it's so thoroughly abstract and introverted, well, it looks easy. Not a lot of work.
                    LEE enters, listens.

J. P.

What the fuck do you know about art, anyway?

MAN

Only what I read. In fact, I just read an interesting article. About this monkey they got and this monkey, they gave him a bunch of paints, let him go nuts on a canvas. I don't know what he was thinking while he was painting. How conscious he was of what he was doing . . . But, anyway, your stuff is definitely better than his. Much more evolved.

LEE

How dare you! How dare you talk to him like that? He's the greatest painter in the world!

MAN

Funny. He doesn't look like Picasso.

LEE

Who is this man? Get out of here!

MAN

Very nice meeting you.
MAN exits

LEE

Get the fuck out of here, this is a famous man you're talking to! Who the fuck does he think he is? Bullshit, pseudo-intellectual. (*Beat. LEE collects herself*) Jackson, Sidney is waiting, he's very interested in talking to you about the work . . .
JACKSON doesn't respond. Blackout.
1956. *In the darkness the sounds of a bar—heavy laughter, clinking of glasses. A door slams. When the lights come up Jackson is sitting downstage right, on the edge of the stage—i.e. on the curb in front of the Cedar Bar. Sounds of a bar filter in. A door slams and WILLEM DE KOONING enters, stumbling slightly, drunk. He sees Jack and moves towards him.*

DEKOONING

What's the matter with you, Jack, your fans are going to be disappointed.

J. P.

Came out to take a piss.

D. K.

Pushes a bottle towards Jack.
Well then, here. Replenish yourself (*Pause*). Taking a piss for over an hour. Your bladder is even bigger than your head.

J. P.

Look who's talking, Mr. famous painter. Willem de Kooning . . . the dutchman so good you'd think he was fucking French.

D. K.

Ah-ha, but I'm truly a nobody compared to the famous Pollock—

POLLOCK

Fuck off.

D. K.

What? It's true. I read all about you in *Life* magazine—the cowboy from the west, swirling what do you call it? Ropes, no, *lariats* of paint across a the great western range of canvas . . . or is it the canvas of the great western range? I can never remember the legend right. Which is it?

J. P.

Fucking *Life* magazine—worst thing to ever happen to me.

D. K.

Yah yah, you were suffering so much for that color photograph. You could tell, the way you were squinting into the camera, like James Dean or something—personally I thought you looked like some guy who pumped gas for a living . . .

375

J. P.

Gesturing back towards the bar

Everyone taking their shot at Pollock, everyone wanting a piece . . . fucking artists, fucking critics all of them, full of shit.

D. K.

Some of them.

J. P.

All of them! Oh yeah, forgot who I was talking to, the fucking darling of them all. Everybody loves de Kooning, don't say shit about that de Kooning bastard. French fucking painter. You hear me? French fucking painter.

D. K.

Yahyahyah — you're fucked up from the drinking . . .

J. P.

And you're fucked up over yourself — what the fuck was that last show about? Those paintings were a retreat and you know it! You betrayed it, Bill, you doing the figure again. You know you never got out of being a figure painter!

D. K.

And what the hell have you been doing lately?

J. P.

Fuck off, I know a decent painting when I see one, and those last ones of yours did not fucking work and you know it.

D. K.

Ah, and now listen to the critic himself, sounding like Greenberg with these statements about retreating, as if the artist *has* to do anything but what he *chooses* to do!

J. P.

Yeah, right. Choices for you — always a "re-examination" or some shit. People pulling their cocks out to your "re-examinations." Meanwhile, *I* do something different and its "Pollock has lost his shit" —

D. K.

Aww, bullshit—

J. P.

Go on, say it isn't true. Are you a painter, or a whore?

D. K.

Starts to exit.
Get the fuck out of here, I know who I am.

J. P.

Aww a lot of shit! Not in those last paintings you don't—not in those paintings! Goddamnit, de Kooning I'm talking about the paint, the work! You know what I see? Some famous painter, some rich painter believing his own shit—and other people's shit around him—

D. K.

Turns on JACKSON.
You shut the fuck up you drunken bastard!

J. P.

You think old Pollock is just some second rate poser. Well you're the fucking poser, de Kooning—all that shit you pull with the women and now look at you, got yourself a bastard child on the way, how 'bout that? Is that gonna make you a better painter? Make you more like Picasso, you Dutch fuck!

D. K.

Barely controlling his rage.
You're a bullshitter, you're a fucking bullshitter—

J. P.

I'm not the bullshitter, *you* are, you fucking whore—

D. K.

All you've got is your tough guy image; you don't even paint anymore, how long has it been? Two, three years? Can you even paint at all anymore? Or are you just washed up?

377

I'll tell you what I can do, I can knock the shit out of you is what I can do—

You're not going to knock the shit out of anyone!

I'll knock the shit out of you and those shit eating pictures of yours!

You're not going to knock the shit out of me, I'm going to knock the shit out of you!

Oh, you're going to knock the shit out of *me?*

I'm going to knock the shit out of *you!*
You sonofatitch! (*DEKOONING punches Jackson in the nose, hard, sending him down onto the ground. Pause.*)
Is that what you want? Tough guy, right? Tough guy Pollock. Well come on, then, get up! Get up and knock the shit out of me, if you've got it in you! Well do you?
   Jackson is sitting down, wiping his nose, silent.
COME ON POLLOCK!!

What . . . me, hit an artist?
  De Kooning is still raging, and the witty comeback only adds to his anger. He leaps for JACKSON, grabbing him by the collar, cocking back his fist. JACKSON doesn't move. They stand, locked for a beat.

You don't even fucking get it. So fucking smart and you don't even understand.
  The air is out of de Kooning, he lets JACKSON go.

J. P.

Everything comes so easy to you. You're the best painter in the whole country. You've got your technique, your academy training. You make the paint do what you want. The way you handle your brushes . . . it's all there. Not for me. I never held a brush that I didn't want to snap in half . . . Greatest goddamned painter around, that's what everyone says . . .

D. K.

You don't know a goddamned thing, Pollock. Because if you did, you'd know it has nothing to do with technique. Because the whole thing is hopeless anyway, and technique and training—they're just fucking illusions. Get that through your thick skull—what it takes, what it really takes . . . to *paint*. To get out of the formula, the goddamned formula of things. Christ, Pollock, I wipe my paintings down with a dirty rag, sand them down with bristles, scrape paint off and let it drop to the floor like dead skin, add more paint . . . splash turpentine across the it all . . . anything I can do to break out of the form—the prison, so that maybe, underneath it all, I'll find something, set something free. I paint a picture fifty times over looking for that something. So don't you tell me about struggle. Don't pretend you're the only one out here who can't find it.
Pause.

J. P.

De Kooning, you're the greatest goddamned painter in America.

D. K.

No no no no—*you're* the best painter in America.

J. P.

No way, you're the one they'll remember.

D. K.

Listen to me now, you baboon—you're the best painter this country has ever seen, and that's that!

J. P.

Hey, buy me another bottle of this stuff and I won't get up and whup you.

D. K.

I'm not buying anything, I'm broke.

J. P.

What—the best painter in America and you're broke?

D. K.

You got it.

J. P.

Well goddamn—maybe you ain't so good after all.

D. K.

Only God does the good stuff, Pollock. Only God.

POLLOCK

Aww fuck God! All that motherfucker did was a bunch of landscapes! All right, then, *I'll* buy *you* another bottle. Now come on, you old man. Gonna find me some fucking tonight, gonna get me some fuckin before I turn in! Gonna fuck the whole goddamned world—
(*JACKSON pauses before opening the door to the bar, looks down*)

D. K.

Are you all right, Pollock?

J. P.

I'm fine, de Kooning. Watch this:
                    (*he opens the door to the Cedar Bar, shouts in*)
Who's the greatest painter in the world?
                    From inside, the crowd responds:

CROWD

YOU ARE, JACKSON!! YOU ARE!!
    Pollock slaps de Kooning on the back, who laughs as they both exit,
    Blackout.

CREATING "NUMBER ONE: A Pollock Painting"

KEVIN DEL AGUILA

JUNE, 2000

ONE Theater Group came together as a circle of actors, writers, designers, and artists eager to create a play based on the life and art of Jackson Pollock. We were particularly inspired by the sincerity of Pollock's work and his genuine search for a deeper understanding of himself through art. The original idea was to make a performance art piece, evoking the emotional experience of a Pollock painting on stage, where the actors' gestures and movements would reflect those of the artist and the "motion" of the paintings.

I was brought in to direct the show, knowing virtually nothing about Pollock's life, work, or legacy. Originally his life was to serve merely as background, providing the skeleton of a plot, but the more we learned about Pollock the more we let such knowledge influence the shape the play was taking. So the portrait became more complex, and the questions it raised became too intricate for simple answers, or simple staging. As a result, the narrative content increased, but the story jumped through time and space in small, disjointed scenes. The structure seemed wild and random, but gained coherence as the play evolved—a theatrical attempt to mirror Pollock's work. And it didn't hurt that the actor playing Pollock bore a striking resemblance to the artist as a young man.

In any dramatization of a visual artist's life, the paramount obstacle is the art itself—not just the finished product but also the creative process. At the moment of artistic inspiration and while the work is in progress, there are rarely spectators. Theatrically, such moments are often too introspective and time consuming to sustain an audience's attention. With Pollock, however, both inspiration and creation could occur simultaneously—a

Publicity photograph of Richard Simulcik as Jackson Pollock. COURTESY OF ONE THEATER GROUP.

process that proved to be dramatic, emotional, and fascinating to witness. What we found was that, theatrically speaking, Pollock's brand of "drip painting" has the potential to express more about the character than dialogue. This became a pivotal device in our production: in an evening punctuated by alcoholic rages, urinating in a fireplace, and ultimately the reckless taking of human lives, such holy moments of pure artistic expression actually prevented the audience from dismissing Pollock as a worthless drunk. They also helped address the play's questions about the nature of art. Does it have value? Does it have limits? Can it transcend a life? How effective or impotent is artistic expression in America? None of these questions would have been raised effectively without this insight into the artist's creative side. Answers to the questions were another story. When you're dealing with Pollock, it seems, it always comes down to the degree of meaning you attribute to his dripped paint.

Two other obstacles, however, proved to be even more challenging, and I caution anyone dramatizing Pollock to be aware of them. The first problem was the paint itself. It gets everywhere, and there's no escape. We tried using water-based paint to make cleanup easier, but it did not drip well on the canvas. Every night, clumps of it would splat down like wet toilet paper. The paintings never really resembled Pollock's, and in fact looked so awful that we had to go back to the commercial enamels he used. That's when our play became a full treat for the senses. The fumes from the paint, coupled with plenty of cigarette smoke, wafted into the audience and caused more than one member to run out of the theater and vomit. Such a violent reaction, I have been assured, was in no way a critique of the play.

The other obstacle was Ruth Kligman. She heard about our play and became concerned about how she would be portrayed. I invited her to a performance, but the night she came New York was blanketed in snow and only two others showed up. So our audience was two people and Jackson Pollock's mistress. The evening got off to a grand start with Ms. Kligman screaming in the lobby, "I can't believe I have to watch a play written by people with graduate degrees — Jackson hated people with graduate degrees!" and, "How insulting to have to watch some actress I don't know playing out my life!" After she was assured that her character was treated with the utmost respect and that we were not making one red cent from the project, she took her seat and the fun began. I have to say that I never felt as much confusion or anxiety as I did during that performance. Actors would exit from the stage with their heads in their hands, muttering, "What the hell are we doing? We should stop the show. We're performing a show about Pollock for his mistress?" And during the play's final moments — the fatal car crash — I remember feeling chilled to my bones as I heard the description of the accident echoing through our sound system, knowing that the only survivor was sitting in the darkened theater, silently watching and listening.

By the end of the evening, however, Ms. Kligman was much calmer, and evidently relieved. Even the paint fumes hadn't gotten to her. We sat down with her and asked what she thought. Basically, she thought that what we'd written wasn't bad, although we couldn't write women, and the character of Ruth was nothing like her. She told us that her extremely long relationship with Jackson (which lasted about six months, apparently) was very intense, beautiful, and erotic. He would call her his angel, quote Dante's *Inferno* and refer to her as his Beatrice. She said that our "Ruth" character was too small a part to capture all that intensity and was, she felt, unnecessary to our play. She asked us to remove the character or we would be talking with her lawyers about it. In the end, we agreed with her that the "Ruth" we had written was nothing like her. Still, as she requested, we removed "Ruth" from our play and replaced her with a purely fictional character — a character affectionately named "Beatrice."

MEETING THE MASTER

A One-Act Play by B. H. FRIEDMAN

1996-1997

CHARACTERS:

Abby Friedman, 28
B. H. "Bob" Friedman, 28
Lee Krasner Pollock, 46
Jackson Pollock, 43

SCENE:

An elegant Manhattan apartment with contemporary furnishings. Downstage: two chairs and a small couch grouped around a coffee table on which there are ashtrays, a piece of sculpture, a few books and magazines, etc. Upstage: bookcase, built-in bar, another piece or two of sculpture. Pictures on one wall: Mondrian's Color Squares and a dripped Pollock. On another wall: a typical Miró. (Or simply use empty frames.) Almost entirely off-stage: entrance hall and kitchen, stage-right; bedroom and study, stage-left.

TIME:

Early spring 1955, evening.

AT RISE: ABBY and BOB, informally but conservatively dressed (she in cardigan and plaid skirt, with simple gold jewelry; he in open button-down shirt and slacks), are at coffee table skimming through magazines while drinking martinis.

B.H. Friedman and Jackson Pollock at Eddie Condon's jazz club, New York, 14 May 1956.
PHOTO: COURTESY OF B.H. FRIEDMAN.

BOB

Glancing at wristwatch

Maybe they're not coming.

ABBY

Of course they are. Relax. When Ben called he said they were running late.

BOB

How long does it take to stop for a beer?

ABBY

It's not Ben's stop. It's Pollock's. But you know Ben—super-executive— he'd call again if anything was wrong.

BOB

I probably made a mistake. Just because I wrote that article doesn't mean we'll be friends.

ABBY

Ben said how at home Pollock will feel here. With a work of his—
Pointing at Pollock painting
he'll see this is a sympathetic environment.

BOB

It *was*. Not any more. I canceled my squash game, so they could beat rush hour.
Glancing at watch again
It's almost seven. I could have played.
House phone rings
About time.
Gets up, walks quickly to kitchen, and answers phone
Yes. Send them up.

ABBY

Be nice.

BOB

Still standing
Me! He messed up the evening.

ABBY

Stop acting. You know you're dying to meet him.

BOB

And Mrs. Pollock.

ABBY

Poor Mrs. Pollock. She must have her hands full.

BOB

I'm sure. On top of everything else, she paints.

ABBY

Like him?

BOB

Don't know. She hasn't shown much. I've never seen anything.

Doorbell rings. ABBY gets up and goes to door with BOB. There, she turns on hall light, so LEE's and JACKSON's entrance is spotlighted. LEE is dressed in pullover, with Indian or other exotic beads, tweed skirt, sensible shoes; JACKSON, unshaved, in somewhat tight sport jacket and dress shirt open at collar, loosened wool-knit tie, slacks, loafers. Introductions and handshakes which follow are fast and informal, almost lost in blur of sound, after which ABBY turns off hall light and returns to living room with BOB, LEE, and JACKSON

LEE

Entering and extending hand to ABBY, then BOB

Lee.

ABBY

Abby.

BOB

Bob.

JACKSON

Following drunkenly

Jackson.

Waves hand at ABBY and BOB

What I need is a john.

BOB leads him to door, stage-left

LEE

To ABBY as BOB returns

Don't offer him anything hard. Ben was sorry he couldn't come up. His family's waiting for him.

BOB

That must have been a long beer.

LEE

Very. I don't remember how many stops we made. Four? Five?

You must need a drink.

Yes. But I'll wait and see what Jackson wants. Better if he eats.

I have something ready.
> *Goes to kitchen, as JACKSON emerges from bathroom*

> *Looking at Mondrian painting and assuming almost a fighter's stance as he seems to seize squares in it, one by one, between his hands, cupped like brackets*

Who in hell did that?

Mondrian. It's called *Color Squares*. Not typical. 1917. From between his plus–minus period and the later paintings.

Shit.

> *Disappointed*

Oh, Jackson.

> *To Jackson*

I thought you'd like it. Despite obvious differences in style, there are similarities—
> *Gestures, encompassing both paintings—*
> *the Mondrian and the Pollock nearby*

the rhythm; the sense of space, space extending beyond the canvas.

Shit. You sound like your article. What'd you call it?

BOB

"The New Baroque."

JACKSON

Yeah. More shit about space—endless space. Well, maybe it doesn't end. Maybe it goes on forever. But we'll have to wait a hell of a long time to find out, won't we? Meanwhile, how about a beer?—Bud? Schlitz?

ABBY returns with cheese and crackers, stuffed eggs, celery and dip, on tray and sets it on coffee table. As she and LEE see JACKSON become increasingly aggressive, they sit down and purposely begin their own mostly inaudible, conversation

BOB

Heineken is all.

JACKSON

Oh!. . . . Okay. . . . In the bottle.

BOB gets beer from bar. JACKSON studies the Mondrian until BOB hands him opened beer.
Shit. Why don't you have a Cavallon?

BOB

I prefer Mondrians *by* Mondrian.

JACKSON

Cavallon's a friend. A friend.

BOB

He's still not Mondrian.

JACKSON

Looking around at other paintings on the walls, while drinking beer and munching cheese.
Shit. You're looking for name art. Familiar art.

BOB

You know damn well, what's original becomes familiar. Isn't that what happened to Mondrian? And isn't it what's happening to you? Dozens of second-generation Pollocks?

JACKSON

Shit. Shit. Shit. There aren't any. My work stands alone. These kids don't come close.

LEE

Come off it, Jackson. You need some sleep.
                Turning to ABBY and speaking quietly
We go to bed early. Get up early for our trips to the city. But, with these stops on the way, even after a good night's sleep, he gets like this. Is there somewhere he can take a nap?

ABBY

Bob's study.
                        Points stage-left
There's a couch.

LEE

All he needs.
                    ABBY starts to lead the way
I'll go with him.

Leaving ABBY behind, holds JACKSON's arm and is leading him to study when he sees painting by Gorky on adjoining wall and stops in front of it, again assuming something like a fighter's stance but now tracing, almost caressing Gorky's shapes.

JACKSON

                    Muttering
That's better. Much better. Gorky—
                    Points at painting
I like him. Of course Picasso's the artist I love. *Love . . . and hate*. Because he's so fucking good. He and Miró. They're headlights. Headlights turned *up*. They're blinding. That's how good they are.

LEE tugs at his arm, continues to lead him to study.

BOB

To Abby after they exit
Well, he certainly feels at home here in our sympathetic environment. . . .
There's just so much *shit* I can take.

ABBY

Laughing
I was listening with one ear. You didn't take much. You were good with
him—cool. Lee said he likes you—and the piece you wrote—that he
wouldn't be putting you on, if he didn't. It's his way of establishing contact.

BOB

Contact!? More like distrust. The inarticulate Westerner's distrust of the
glib Easterner. And yet, despite his
Beat
limited vocabulary, there's no limit to his body language. I'm sure of one
thing—he likes Gorky. What did you and Lee talk about?

ABBY

The usual. Children. She said at first they couldn't afford them. Now she
can't have them. And then work, of course. You've heard that Jackson
hasn't painted in the past few years. I got the sense he sits in the barn—his
studio—waiting for something to happen, while Lee does the best she
can, working in a small extra bedroom. She wasn't complaining, but . . .
you know Ben was out this past weekend, wanting to buy one of Pollock's
big 1950-paintings, and never even looked at her work.

LEE

Returning
Well, now I could stand a drink. A real drink. A large Scotch on the rocks.
BOB nods, glances at ABBY, who also nods and gets drinks for all three of
them
Jackson went right to sleep. He'll be up in five or ten minutes. You'll see.
He gets like this when we come to New York—exhausted just anticipating
the city. Once a week, every week. Until August when the shrinks go on
vacation. Tomorrow we have our therapy sessions. Then the real battle
begins—to get him back out to Long Island. He's okay then, but until

391

then, when he's with his cronies at the Cedar Bar, it's not easy. I never know when he'll show up. One in the morning. Two. Three. Noon. Afternoon. Sometimes we stay an extra day. On balance, I wonder if the sessions are worth it. Jackson's not getting any work done. I'm not doing as much as I should. He keeps on drinking.

Beat

Have either of you been in therapy?

BOB

I was for a while. It centered mostly on my conflict between writing and the family building business. I like both—their different rewards, their different kinds of excitement. I was convinced that I could juggle the two, that there was no conflict. But the doctor didn't think I'd scratched the surface.

LEE

He wanted you to choose?

BOB

Laughing

To choose business. He seemed to think my wanting to write was sick—unrealistic, anyway. Of course he never came right out and said that.

LEE

They never do. What are you writing?

BOB

I'm working on a novel with one hand, some pieces on art with the other. There's no conflict there, either. I like writing fiction *and* non-fiction. One of the pieces is on Jackson—much longer than the one you saw. I want to do more on his life, relating it to his work. You know, his growing up in the West. Coming East to study with Benton. The drinking. The therapy. The way everything connects.

LEE

Smiling encouragingly but doubtfully

Good luck. But you'll have to ask Jackson. He doesn't like telling writers about his life.

To ABBY

And what about you?

                                    ABBY

I work for a medical journal.
                              Beat.
And help Bob edit his writing.

                                    LEE

That's familiar. For years I licked the stamps on every announcement of
Jackson's shows—But you were saying?

                                    ABBY

Unfortunately the world isn't as interested in what Bob writes as in what
he does in business.

                                    LEE

He's making it hard for himself—if not the world. With Jackson it's easy—
there's nothing but his painting.
                    Looks up as JACKSON enters
Well, look who's here.
                        To ABBY and BOB
I told you he wouldn't be long.
        JACKSON, *looking rumpled, enters carrying his unfinished beer.*
Are you okay?

                                  JACKSON

Hungry.

                                    LEE

He does this—a quick nap and he's a different person.

                                  JACKSON

Shit.

                                    LEE

                                Laughing
See?

393

ABBY

There's a steak house around the corner.

JACKSON

That sounds good. First let me finish this.
Holds up beer
What have you been up to?

LEE

Bob was saying he's writing another article on you. This one more about your life. And how it relates to your work.

JACKSON

To Bob
Shit, why would you want to do that? You know my work. You live with it. A man's work *is* his life; his life *is* his work. That's what bothers me—I'm not working anymore.

BOB

The way I see it, an artist's work can only be *part* of his life. Maybe it looks as big. Maybe it even looks bigger because it's stronger. And more lasting. *But—*

JACKSON

Shit, no! They're the same thing.
Locking together the fingers of his hands to show what he means
They're inseparable. What are you involved with, really involved with, that's *not* your life?

BOB

Of course business and writing are *parts* of my life. But they mean differ-ent things. One supports the other. I admire Wallace Stevens, Charles Ives—
(JACKSON looks puzzled, shrugs)
Artists who worked for insurance companies.

JACKSON

Shit. Why are you talking about other people's lives? Why—beyond looking at it on canvas—do you want to know more about mine? I'm asking about yours.

BOB

When I write I can do pretty much what I want—at least, what I'm able to do. In building I can't. The zoning laws, the cost of land—everything makes it nearly impossible to build beautiful buildings that are also profitable.

JACKSON

Get Tony Smith.

BOB

Who?

JACKSON

He's great architect. A student of Wright's. You should hear him recite Joyce. He knows whole hunks of *Finnegans Wake*.

BOB

I read the architecture magazines—don't recognize his name.

JACKSON

He won't let them reproduce his work. He did a studio for Fritz Bultman on the Cape. A house for Stamos at Greenport. One in an abandoned rock quarry outside New Haven for Dr. Olsen. I guess you know, Olsen bought one of my best paintings, *Blue Poles*. His house is built around it. Yes, Tony's a great architect. He's my friend.

LEE

Laughing
Maybe you've noticed—Jackson's loyal to his friends.

JACKSON

Shit, it's not such a long list. Still, we can't go through it tonight.
To BOB and ABBY
D'you know what you two should do? Come out for a weekend. Then we could talk.

To BOB

There's a writer about your age, Peter Matthiessen. Just published his first novel. You'd like him. And Jeffrey Potter. He does what you do—writing and construction.

To ABBY

And their wives, you'd like them too.

To BOB

And Alfonso.

BOB looks puzzled

Alfonso Ossorio. He'll interest you. He's just beginning to break away from his virtuoso draftsmanship.

Stops abruptly, then to LEE

What do you think, Lee? Shouldn't they come out?

LEE nods

And Bob? Should I talk to him? Tell him about the Old West?

LEE shrugs

Yeah, why not? Meanwhile, let's get something to eat.

Beat

Shit.

CURTAIN

POLLOCK DANCES

KARLA WOLFANGLE

MAY, 2000

Painting has been an inspiration for much of my choreography; I think of it as visual nourishment for my own creativity. For me, making a dance is a lot like making a painting, since both art forms fill space with movement, line, and balance.

Jackson Pollock once described his work as "energy and motion made visible," so it was not surprising to me that when I visited Pollock's paintings, I saw a dance. But I was also interested in his persona, and I wanted the choreography to be about more than the painting itself. I wanted to show a complex character, an artist filled with passion, conflict and, at the same time, transcendent creativity. It seemed to me that I could start from that point.

In the studio, Pollock rolls out his canvas on the floor and dreams about its coming to life. To make that imaginative process tangible, I dressed the dancer in layers of six-colored silk T-shirts and had him remove them one at a time and fling them onto the canvas. The discarded shirts represent the transition from dreaming about painting to actually doing it, but the colors fall almost at random and lie still on the canvas. As yet, they have no motion, no energy.

Five of the colors—silver, red, orange, yellow, and green—are embodied by five dancers. The artist and the colors move through space and over the canvas. Pollock performs much as he did in Hans Namuth's famous film, which shows him maneuvering like a dancer, streaming paint from the hardened brushes in his hand. He controls the colors, and their movements illustrate both their essential characters and their obedience to his directions.

The last color to emerge is black. It is Pollock's alter ego, a force he cannot control. Instead, it controls Pollock, taunts him, confuses him, and leaves him to destroy himself.

In the final section, the colors dance my impression of the drip paintings, which were a joy to draw my choreography from. As Pollock said, they have a life of their own, and this section celebrates that independence. Free of his biographical drama, their animated imagery—squiggles and splashes of movement interspersed with long loopy lines—was the perfect framework on which to hang my dance.

Choreographer Karla Wolfangle and Barrry Wizorek (Pollock) at work on "Pollock Dances," in the Pollock-Krasner Studio, 1992. Photos: Helen A. Harrison.

FUSED IN MIDAIR: A Work in Progress

PATRICK GRENIER

MAY 2000

*f*USED *in midair* is an homage to the symbiosis of Jackson Pollock and Lee Krasner. Many art historians and biographers have commented and speculated on their extraordinary and sometimes difficult relationship. This video attempts to communicate, through abstracted imagery, subtle impressions of these two major figures of the twentieth century. Information has been taken from books, interviews, and selected writings on Krasner and Pollock. By manipulating footage of the woods, sky, and roads surrounding their home in The Springs, East Hampton, the video aims to capture the artists' intensity and sensuality. Imagery is woven together to create a sense of energy flowing continuously through the landscape. The audio track includes ambient sounds gathered on the roads and in the woods of The Springs. After processing and manipulation, these sounds induce a feeling of eerie yearning.

The following excerpt from B. H. Friedman's 1972 biography, *Jackson Pollock: Energy Made Visible* (229), initially inspired the concept for this work:

> . . . there's an image—just that, not even a sentence—which an acquaintance reports Pollock used one night at the Cedar in much the same way he used his own locked hands or the spike on the living room floor to indicate the connection between seeming opposites. The image, profoundly impressed upon his mind, was something he had seen in the Gettysburg National Military Park—two musketballs, one Confederate, one Union, which had collided and fused in midair.

399

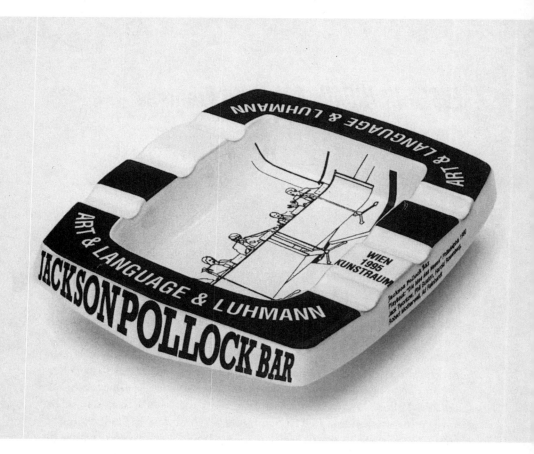

Jackson Pollock Bar ash tray, 1995 Klaus Merkel.

Helen A. Harrison

HELEN A. Harrison is an art historian, museum director, and journalist who specializes in modern American art. A native of New York City, she received her A.B. in art from Adelphi University and her M.A. in art history from Case Western Reserve University, where her research focused on the New Deal federal art patronage programs. After serving as Curator of the Parrish Art Museum in Southampton, New York, Director of the Public Art Preservation Committee in Manhattan, and Curator of Guild Hall Museum in East Hampton, New York, she became Director of the Pollock–Karsner House and Study Center, a National Historic Landmark and research collection in East Hampton that is administered by the State University of New York at Stony Brook. She has also been a Guest Curator at the Queens Museum of Art in Flushing, New York, has taught at the School of Visual Arts, and currently holds an adjunct faculty position in Stony Brook's Department of Art, Art History, and Art Criticism.

For more than twenty years, Mrs. Harrison has written art reviews and feature articles for the Long Island section of the *New York Times*. Her articles, essays, and reviews have appeared in numerous scholarly and popular publications, including *Journal of American Studies (U.K.)*, *Prospects*, the Archives of American Art *Journal*, *American Art*, *Provincetown Arts*, and *Winterthur Portfolio*. She is the author of many exhibition catalogues, chapters in several multi-author publications—most recently, *The American Art Book* (Phaidon, 1999)—and two books, *Dawn of a New Day: The New York World's Fair 1939/40* (New York University Press, 1980), and a monograph on the artist Larry Rivers (Harper & Row, 1984).

Mr. Harrison is a member of the Association International des Critiques d'Art (AICA), the Association of Historians of American Art, the American Studies Association, the National Historic Landmarks Stewards Association, and the regional advisory board of the Archives of American Art.

She lives with her husband, the painter Roy Nicholson, in Sag Harbor, New York.

402

Copyrights and Permissions

"An Interview by James T. Valliere: De Kooning on Pollock," *Partisan Review*, Vol. XXXIV, 4 (Fall 1967): 603–5. © Partisan Review. Reprinted by permission.

Arneson, Robert. *Cathedral Tower*, 1986. Glazed ceramic, 86¾ × 20 × 20 inches. © Estate of Robert Arneson/Licensed by VAGA, New York, NY.

Arno, Peter. "His spatter is masterful, but his dribbles lack conviction," *The New Yorker*, 23 September 1961. © Condé Nast Publications, Inc. Reprinted by permission.

Art & Language. *Portrait of V. I. Lenin in the Style of Jackson Pollock*, 1979. Oil and enamel on board mounted on canvas, 177 × 126 cm. Courtesy Galerie de Paris.

Art & Language. Statement, 1999. © Art & Language. Used by permission.

Beaton, Cecil. "The New Soft Look," photographs for *Vogue*, 1 March 1951, 158–61. One photograph in color, with caption. © *Vogue*, Condé Nast Publications, Inc. Reprinted by permission.

Benton, Thomas Hart, and Rita Benton. Joint letter to Jackson Pollock, 3 October 1938. Jackson Pollock Catalogue Raisonné Archives, Pollock-Krasner House and Study Center, East Hampton New York.

Berger, John. "The White Cell," *The New Statesman*, 22 November 1958, pp. 722–3. © The New Statesman. Reprinted by permission.

Blythe, Will. "The End of the Affair," *Mirabella*, October 1999, 139–45, 183. Reprinted by permission of the author.

Bourland, Roger. "Lavender Mist," musical score from *Seven Pollock Pieces*, 1978. © 1980 (Renewed) by Associated Music Publishers, Inc.

(BMI). International Copyright Secured. All Rights Reserved. Reprinted by permission.

Bourland, Roger. "Writing *Seven Pollock Pieces*," May 2000. Used by permission of the author.

Brach, Paul. Excerpts of a symposium, "Jackson Pollock: Portrait and a Dream," Guild Hall Museum, East Hampton, New York, 8 June 1986; revised May 2000. Based on an audiotape in the Oral History Collection, Pollock–Krasner House and Study Center, East Hampton, New York.

Brooks, James. Interview by James T. Valliere, November 1965. Pollock–Krasner Papers, Archives of American Art, Smithsonian Institution.

Busa, Christopher. " 'Being a Great Man is a Thesis Invented by Others': Peter Busa on Jackson Pollock," May 2000. Used by permission of the author.

Contract between Jackson Pollock and Peggy Guggenheim, 15 March 1946. National Archives and Records Administration, files of the U.S. District Court for the Southern District of New York.

de Laszlo, Violet Staub, M.D. Letter to the Examining Medical Officer, Selective Service System, 26 May 1941. Pollock–Krasner Papers, Archives of American Art, Smithsonian Institution.

Del Aguila, Kevin. Creating *Number One: A Pollock Painting*, June 2000. Used by Permission of the author.

Dedini, Eldon. "God! Your Jackson Pollock always puts me in a frenzy," *Playboy*, February 1995, p. 69. © 1995 by Playboy. Reproduced by Special Permission of *Playboy* magazine.

Feldman, Morton. "Glass Sequence," score for the film *Jackson Pollock*, by Hans Namuth and Paul Falkenberg, 1950–51. © Peter Namuth, 1995. Used by permission.

Feldman, Morton. "Jackson Pollock," Morton Feldman Papers, Music Library, State University of New York at Buffalo. First published in *Give My Regards to Eighth Street: Collected Writings of Morton Feldman*, edited by B. H. Friedman. Cambridge: Exact Change, 2000. Reprinted by permission of the editor.

Friedman, B. H. "Jackson Pollock," *Gutai #6* (Japan), 1 April 1957; corrected and revised February 2000. Used by permission of the author.

———. *Meeting the Master*, one-act play, read at the Pollock–Krasner House and Study Center, East Hampton, New York, 10 September 1996; revised July 1997. © B. H. Friedman. Used by permission of the author.

Friedman, Benno. "Jackson Pollock's Mother," photograph (published as a card by Palm Press), 1989. © The Pushpin Group, 1989. Reprinted by permission.

Glueck, Grace. Excerpts from "Scenes From a Marriage: Krasner and Pollock," *ARTnews*, December 1981, 57–61. © 1981 ARTnews LLC. Reprinted by permission.

Goodnough, Robert. Personal anecdotes sent to the Pollock–Krasner House and Study Center, East Hampton, New York, 1999. Used by permission of the author.

Greenberg, Clement. Interview by James T. Valliere, 20 March 1968. Pollock–Krasner Papers, Archives of American Art, Smithsonian Institution.

Grenier, Patrick. *"fused in midair*: A Work in Progress," artist's statement, May 2000. Used by permission of the author.

Guggenheim, Peggy. Excerpt of "Art of This Century," in *Out of this Century* (London: André Deutsch, 1980), 315–16. Reprinted by permission of André Deutsch, Ltd. / The Family of Peggy Guggenheim.

Harris, Edward. Foreword, April 2000. Used by permission of the author.

Hartigan, Grace. Excerpt of a statement in Milton Esterow, "The Second Time Around," *ARTnews* (Summer 1993) 152–3. © 1993 *ARTnews* LLC. Reprinted by permission.

Henderson, Joseph L., M.D Excerpts of an interview by Jeffrey Potter, 27 December 1982. Jeffrey Potter Oral History Collection, Pollock–Krasner House and Study Center, East Hampton, New York.

Hess, Thomas B. "Jackson Pollock 1912–56," *ARTnews*, September 1956, pp. 44–5, 57. © 1956 *ARTnews* LLC. Reprinted by permission.

Hunter, Sam. "Jackson Pollock," *Museum of Modern Art Bulletin* Vol. XXIV, No. 2, (1956–57) (catalogue of the Jackson Pollock memorial exhibition, 19 December 1956–3 February 1957):5–12. Reprinted by permission of the author.

"Jackson Pollock: An Artists' Symposium," *ARTnews*, April and May 1967. © 1967 *ARTnews* LLC. Reprinted by permission.

Jenkins, Paul. Excerpts of a symposium, "Jackson Pollock: Portrait and a Dream," Guild Hall Museum, East Hampton, New York, 8 June 1986; revised and amended May 2000. Based on an audiotape in the Oral History Collection, Pollock–Krasner House and Study Center, East Hampton, New York.

Jenkins, Paul. "The Arabesque and the Grid," unpublished essay, 1984. Used by permission of the author.

Johnson, Ray *May Wilson's Rimbaud*, 1972. Manipulated postcard with red enamel paint, 6 × 4 inches; *Action Jackson*, 1973, drawing and collage on paper, [size]. Collection of William S. Wilson.

Kadish, Reuben. Excerpt from an undated interview (ca. 1965) by James T. Valliere, 6–7. Pollock–Krasner Papers, Archives of American Art, Smithsonian Institution.

Kagan, Andrew. "Improvisations: Notes on Pollock and Jazz," *Arts*, March

1979, 96–9. Reprinted by permission of the author.

Kanemitsu, Matsumi. Excerpt of an interview by Marjorie Rogers, Oral History Program, University of California, Los Angeles, 14 January 1976. © The Regents of the University of California. Used by permission.

Karp, Ivan. "The Ecstasy and Tragedy of Jackson Pollock, Artist," *The Village Voice*, 26 (September 1956): 8, 12. © The Village Voice, Inc. Reprinted by permission.

Krasner, Lee. Excerpts of an interview with Emily Wasserman, 9 July 1968. Pollock–Krasner Papers, Archives of American Art, Smithsonian Institution.

Littlefield, W. H. Excerpt from a letter to Lee Krasner, 30 March 1967, 1–4. Pollock–Krasner Papers, Archives of American Art, Smithsonian Institution.

MacAdam, Barbara A. "Green River," May 2000. Used by permission of the author.

Mark, Grant. "Proteen" soy emulsion diet for treatment of Jackson Pollock's "biochemical imbalance" and alcoholism, 1951. Pollock–Krasner House and Study Center, East Hampton, New York.

Martin, Richard. "New Look and Newer Look: The Communication of Jackson Pollock by Cecil Beaton and Mike Bidlo," *Arts*, (March 1988): 20–21. Reprinted by permission of the Estate of Richard Martin.

McClure, Michael. "Ode to Jackson Pollock," from Huge Dreams by Michael McClure, © 1960, 1961, 1964, 1965, 1968, 1970 by Micheal McClure. Used by permission of Penguin, a division of Penguin Putnam Inc.

Merkel, Klaus. Jackson Pollock Bar ask tray, from a performance at Kunstraum, Vienna, 1995. Courtesy of Art & Language / Klaus Merkel Atelier, Freiburg, Germany

Miller, Daniel T. Interview by James T. Valliere, Fall 1965. Pollock–Krasner Papers, Archives of American Art, Smithsonian Institution.

———. Letter to Jackson Pollock, 9 November 1950. Pollock–Krasner Papers, Archives of American Art, Smithsonian Institution.

Miller–Keller, Andrea. Excerpts of "Arneson and Pollock," catalogue essay, Pollock–Krasner House and Study Center, East Hampton, New York, 1992. © The Wadsworth Atheneum, Hartford, Connecticut. Reprinted by permission.

Namuth, Hans. "Photographing Pollock," 17 November 1979, in *Pollock Painting: Photographs by Hans Namuth* (New York: Agrinde Publications Ltd., 1980), unpaginated. © Agrinde Publications. Reprinted by permission.

Neidich, Warren. *Not Pollock* and *Holding a Crow With Alchemy*, 1994–95. Manipulated photographs, various dimensions. Used by permission of the artist.

Neiman, LeRoy. Personal anecdote, March 2000. Used by permission of the author.

O'Connor, Francis V. "Jackson Pollock: Down to the Weave," Eleventh Annual Pollock–Krasner Lecture, John Drew Theater, East Hampton, New York, 16 August 1998. © Francis V. O'Connor. Used by permission of the author.

O'Connor, Francis V. Four poems: "Dining Out On Pollock," undated (1978); "Sonnet for Jackson Pollock," 1988; "Sonnet About Sets for Ed Harris," 1999. Compiled and revised March 2000. © Francis V. O'Connor. Used by permission of the author.

O'Hara, Frank. "A Step Away From Them," *Evergreen Review* Vol. I, no. 3, (1957): 60–1. © Evergreen Review. Reprinted by permission.

——. Excerpts of *Jackson Pollock* (New York: George Braziller, 1959), 12–3, 25–6, 34–5. © George Braziller, Inc. Reprinted by permission.

Ossorio, Alfonso. Essay for the catalogue of Jackson Pollock's solo exhibition, Betty Parsons Gallery, New York, 26 November–16 December 1951. Research library, Pollock–Krasner House and Study Center, East Hampton, New York. Reprinted by permission of the Ossorio Foundation, Southampton, New York.

Pollock, Jackson. Birth certificate, 1912. Pollock–Krasner Papers, Archives of American Art, Smithsonian Institution.

——. Letters to his brothers Charles and Frank, 22 October 1929; to his brother Charles, 31 January 1930; to his father LeRoy McCoy Pollock, 3 February [1933]. Jackson Pollock Catalogue Raisonné Archives, Pollock–Krasner House and Study Center, East Hampton, New York.

——. Fragmentary poem on a sheet of paper with a drawing, ca. 1942. The Pollock–Krasner Foundation, Inc./Joan T. Washburn Gallery, New York. Photograph: Jackson Pollock Catalogue Raisonné Archives, Pollock–Krasner House and Study Center, East Hampton, New York.

——. Letter to James Johnson Sweeny, undated [November 1943]. Jackson Pollock Catalogue Raisonné Archives, Pollock–Krasner House and Study Center, East Hampton, New York.

——. Selective Service (draft) card, 1945. Pollock–Krasner Papers, Archives of American Art, Smithsonian Institution.

——. Draft of a statement published in the magazine *possibilities I*, 1947. Jackson Pollock Catalogue Raisonné Archives, Pollock–Krasner House and Study Center, East Hampton New York.

——. Handwritten notes on his work, 1950. Pollock–Krasner Papers, Archives of American Art, Smithsonian Institution.

——. Interview by William Wright for broadcast on radio station WERI, Westerly, Rhode Island, 1950. Transcribed from an audiotape for the Jackson Pollock Catalogue Raisonné Archives, Pollock–Krasner House and Study Center, East Hampton, New York.

———. Passport, 1955. Pollock–Krasner Papers, Archives of American Art, Smithsonian Institution.

———. Car registration, 1956. Pollock–Krasner House and Study Center, East Hampton, New York. Gift of B. H. Friedman.

———. Death certificate, 1956. Pollock–Krasner House and Study Center, East Hampton, New York. Gift of B. H. Friedman.

———. Social Security card, undated. Pollock–Krasner Papers, Archives of American Art, Smithsonian Institution.

Pollock, Lee Krasner. Undated typescript on which the article, "Who Was Jackson Pollock?" (*Art in America*, May–June 1967) is based. Pollock–Krasner Papers, Archives of American Art, Smithsonian Institution.

Potter, Jeffrey. "Jackson Pollock and Relationships," *North Atlantic Review*, (1998) 17–24. Adapted from a lecture at the Pollock–Krasner House and Study Center, East Hampton, New York, 25 June 1989.

Potter, Jeffrey. Selected statements by Jackson Pollock, collected during their friendship, 1949–1956. Courtesy of Jeffrey Potter.

Raphael, Victor. Selections from *One Gesture of the Heart*, Polaroid photographs, still video images, and text, 1986. Used by permission of the artist.

Robertson, Bryan. Introduction to *Jackson Pollock* (London: Thames and Hudson, 1960), 17–19. Reprinted by permission.

Rockwell, Norman. "The Connoisseur," cover for *The Saturday Evening Post*, 26 September 1962. Reprinted by permission of the Norman Rockwell Family Trust © 1962 The Norman Rockwell Family Trust.

Rodman, Selden. "Jackson Pollock," in *Conversations with Artists* (New York: The Devin–Adair Co., 1957). 76–87. Reprinted by permission of the author.

Rosenberg, Harold. "The Art World: The Mythic Act," *The New Yorker*, 6 May 1967, 162–71. © Condé Nast Publications, Inc. Reprinted by permission.

Rosset, Barney. "A Recollection," May 2000. Used by permission of the author.

Roueché, Berton, in conversation with Enez Whipple, 6 April 1989. Excerpt of an audio taped interview in the archives of Guild Hall Museum, East Hampton, New York. Used by permission of Mrs. Berton Roueché.

Seiberling, Dorothy. "A shy and turbulent man who became a myth," *Life*, 9 November 1959, pp. 79–80. © Time Inc. Reprinted by permission.

Seixas, Frank A. "Jackson Pollock: An Appreciation," *The Art Gallery*, October 1963, pp. 11–13, 23. Reprinted by permission of The Hollycroft Foundation, Ivorytown, Connecticut.

Smith, Patti. "Hail the surface of our speech," May 2000. © Patti Smith. Reprinted by permission.

Smith, Tony and Paul Feeley. Interview by James T. Valliere, August 1965. Pollock–Krasner Papers, Archives of American Art, Smithsonian Institution.

Southgate, Patsy. "A Fragment," excerpts of an interview by Jeffrey Potter, 14 May 1980. Jeffrey Potter Oral History Collection, Pollock–Krasner House and Study Center, East Hampton, New York.

Star, East Hampton. "Toll of Ten Lives . . ." 19 August 1956, 1. Biographical archives, Pollock–Krasner House and Study Center, East Hampton, New York.

Stern, Daniel. "Morton Feldman's 'Glass Sequence'," May 2000. Used by permission of the author.

Swartz, Adam, Richard Simulcik, and Kevin Del Aguila. Selected scenes from *Number One: A Pollock Painting*, performed at Synchronicity Space, New York, N.Y. 6–8 April 1996 and 17 December 1996–4 January 1997. © ONE Theater Group. Used by permission of the authors.

Sweeny, James Johnson. Essay for the checklist of Jackson Pollock's first solo exhibition, *Art of This Century*, New York, 9–27 November 1943. Pollock–Krasner Papers, Archives of American Art, Smithsonian Institution.

"To J. P. / In Memoriam Artis Tui," undated poem. Pollock–Krasner Papers, Archives of American Art, Smithsonian Institution.

Tréfousse, Roger. Two segments of the score for "Jackson Pollock: Portrait," from the television series, *Strokes of Genius*, Cort Productions, 1982. Reproduced courtesy of the composer.

————. "Writing *Jackson Pollock: Portrait*," May 2000. Used by permission of the author.

Williams, William Carlos. Poem from *Paterson V*

Wilson, William S. "Jackson Pollock: Images to Think With," May 2000. Used by permission of the author.

Wolfangle, Karla. "Pollock Dances," choreographer's statement (May 2000) on her work, performed at the Merce Cunningham Studio, New York, N.Y., 21–23 May 1992. Used by permission of the author.